MACHINE LEARNING AND KNOWLEDGE ACQUISITION

Integrated approaches

Knowledge-Based Systems Book Series

Edited by

John Boose, Boeing Computer Services, Seattle, Washington, USA

Brian Gaines, Department of Computer Sciences, University of Calgary, Alberta, Canada

One of the most successful and engaging initiatives in Artificial Intelligence has been the development of knowledge-based systems (or expert systems) encoding human expertise in the computer and making it more widely available. Knowledge-based system developments are at the leading edge of the move from information processing to knowledge processing in Fifth Generation Computing.

The Knowledge-Based Systems Book Series publishes the work of leading international scientists addressing themselves to the spectrum of problems associated with the development of knowledge-based systems. The series will be an important source for researchers and advanced students working on knowledge-based systems as well as introducing those embarking on expert systems development to the state-of-the-art.

Titles in this series:

1. Knowledge Acquisition for Knowledge-Based Systems (*B. Gaines* and *J. Boose*, eds).
2. Knowledge Acquisition Tools for Expert Systems (*J. Boose* and *B. Gaines*, eds).
3. Machine Learning and Uncertain Reasoning (*B. Gaines* and *J. Boose*, eds).
4. The Foundations of Knowledge Acquisition (*J. Boose* and *B. Gaines*, eds).
5. Eliciting and Analyzing Expert Judgement: A Practical Guide (*M. Meyer* and *J. Booker*).
6. Intelligent Assistant Systems (*G. Boy*).
7. The AI Workbench BABYLON: An Open and Portable Development Environment for Expert Systems (*T. Christaller*, *F. di Primio*, *U. Schnepf* and *A. Voss*, eds).
8. Interactive Theory Revision: An Inductive Logic Programming Approach (*L. De Raedt*).
9. Critiquing Human Error: A Knowledge-Based Human-Computer Collaboration Approach (*B. G. Silverman*).
10. Knowledge Aided Design (*M. Green*, ed.).
11. KADS: A Principled Approach to Knowledge-Based System Development (*G. Schreiber*, *B. Wielinga* and *J. Breuker*, eds).
12. Knowledge Acquisition and Machine Learning: Theory, Methods and Applications (*K. Morik*, *S. Wrobel*, *J. U. Kietz* and *W. Emde*).
13. The Think Aloud Method: A Practical Guide to Modelling Cognitive Processes (*M. W. Van Someren*, *Y. F. Barnard* and *J. A. C. Sandberg*).
14. Machine Learning and Knowledge Acquisition: Integrated Approaches (*G. Tecuci* and *Y. Kodratoff*, eds).

MACHINE LEARNING AND KNOWLEDGE ACQUISITION

Integrated approaches

Edited by

Gheorghe Tecuci
Department of Computer Science, George Mason University, Fairfax, VA, USA

Yves Kodratoff
Laboratoire de Recherche en Informatique, University Paris-Sud, Orsay, France

ACADEMIC PRESS
Harcourt Brace & Company, Publishers
London San Diego New York Boston
Sydney Tokyo Toronto

ACADEMIC PRESS LIMITED
24/28 Oval Road
LONDON NW1 7DX

United States Edition published by
ACADEMIC PRESS INC.
San Diego CA 92101

This book is printed on acid-free paper

A catalogue record for this book is available from the British Library

ISBN 0–12–685120–4

Typeset by J&L Composition Ltd, Filey, North Yorkshire
Printed in Great Britain by WBC Book Manufacturers, Bridgend, Mid Glamorgan

Contents

Introduction

Gheorghe Tecuci and Yves Kodratoff

Knowledge acquisition and machine learning represent two different approaches to the process of acquiring and organizing the knowledge of a knowledge-based system. Knowledge acquisition research has focused on improving and partially automating the acquisition of knowledge from human experts by knowledge engineers. In contrast, machine learning research has focused on developing autonomous algorithms for acquiring knowledge from data and improving the organization of knowledge. Also, in knowledge acquisition, the acquired knowledge is directly verified by a human expert, while in machine learning the learned knowledge must be experimentally tested on independent data sets.

We distinguish three main phases in the process of building a knowledge base (KB): *systematic elicitation of expert knowledge*, *KB refinement*, and *KB reformulation* (Bareiss *et al.*, 1989; Tecuci, 1992).

During *systematic elicitation of expert knowledge*, the basic terminology and the conceptual structure of the KB is developed. The result of this elicitation is an initial incomplete and possibly partially incorrect KB that is refined and improved during the next phases of KB development. While systematic elicitation of expert knowledge is a main concern of knowledge acquisition research, it is largely ignored in machine learning research. Machine learning research has assumed that there already exists a representation language and background knowledge before any learning will take place. Some of the most successful methods for systematic elicitation of knowledge are knowledge acquisition methods of interviewing (Gammak, 1987; LaFrance, 1987), protocol analysis (Ericsson and Simon, 1984), elicitation of repertory grids (Shaw and Gaines, 1987; Boose and Bradshaw, 1988), domain modelling (Wielinga *et al.*, 1992), and guided elicitation for role-limiting problem-solving methods (Marcus, 1988).

In the *KB refinement* phase, the KB is extended and debugged. The result of the knowledge refinement phase should be a KB that is complete and correct enough to provide correct solutions to most problems to be solved by the system. Knowledge acquisition research has been oriented toward building refinement tools for an expert and a knowledge engineer. In general, the expert uses the problem-solving abilities of the KB to solve typical problems for which the solutions are already known to identify the need for additional knowledge (e.g. when the KB system cannot solve a problem), or errors in the KB (e.g. when the KB system proposes an incorrect solution to some problem). Many tools developed in mainstream knowledge acquisition research provide an inference engine, a representation formalism in which the KB could be encoded, and mechanisms for acquiring, verifying and revising knowledge expressed in that formalism. These tools trade power (i.e. the assistance given to the expert) against generality (i.e. their domain of applicability), covering a large spectrum. At the power end of the spectrum there are tools customized to a problem-solving method and a particular domain (Musen, 1989). At the generality end are the tools applicable to a wide range of tasks or domains (Davis, 1979). In between are tools that are method-specific and domain independent (Chandrasekaran, 1986; McDermott, 1988). A significant amount of work on KB refinement has been done in machine learning under the name of theory revision. Most often, the problem addressed is to revise the KB of a classification system to correctly classify a given set of positive and negative examples (Cohen, 1991; Mooney and Ourston, 1994; Towell and Shavlik, 1994). The machine learning methods of empirical induction from examples (Mitchell, 1978; Michalski, 1983), conceptual clustering (Fisher, 1987), learning by analogy (Prieditis, 1988), abductive learning (Josephson *et al.*, 1987), neural network learning (Rumelhart and McClelland, 1986), and genetic algorithm-based learning (Goldberg, 1989) could also be regarded as KB refinement methods. Of particular relevance are the multistrategy learning methods (Michalski and Tecuci, 1994) which combine several basic learning strategies to refine a KB.

During the *KB reformulation* phase, the KB is reorganized for improving the efficiency of problem solving. While this phase has been largely ignored in knowledge acquisition, it has been a main concern in machine learning. Representative examples of machine learning methods that address this problem are explanation-based learning methods for knowledge compilation or macro operator learning (Fikes *et al.*, 1972; DeJong and Mooney, 1986; Mitchell *et al.*, 1986; Minton, 1990), and for chunking (Laird *et al.*, 1986), as well as empirical inductive learning methods for the induction of optimal decision trees from examples (Quinlan, 1986).

As machine learning moves to more complex domains, and knowledge acquisition attempts to automate more of the acquisition process, the two fields increasingly find themselves investigating common issues with different approaches. Moreover, these approaches are complementary in the sense that many of the hard problems in machine learning are significantly easier in knowledge acquisition and vice versa.

Representative examples of hard problems in machine learning are the problem of new terms, the credit/blame assignment problem, and the definition of the learner's representation language, background knowledge, input examples, and bias. The difficulty of these problems can be alleviated by employing methods for systematic elicitation of knowledge, and by involving the expert in the learning loop.

Representative examples of hard problems in knowledge acquisition are the definition of general problem-solving knowledge that characterizes specific examples, the verification of KB consistency and reduction of any inconsistencies, as well as the reorganization of the KB to improve the problem-solving efficiency of the system. These are precisely the kinds of problems that have been successfully addressed by machine learning research.

An integrated machine learning and knowledge acquisition approach to the problem of building knowledge-based systems can take advantage of this complementariness, using machine learning techniques to automate the knowledge acquisition process and knowledge acquisition techniques to enhance the power of the learning methods. The increasing realization of this complementariness, as well as of the large potential of integrated approaches, has led to a growing interest in developing methods for integrating knowledge acquisition and machine learning (Tecuci, 1988; Marcus, 1989; Birnbaum and Collins, 1991; Buchanan and Wilkins, 1992; Tecuci *et al.*, 1993, 1994).

Some of the most representative approaches to the integration of machine learning and knowledge acquisition are:

- Learning apprentice systems. These are interactive knowledge-based assistants able to assimilate new knowledge by observing and analysing the problem-solving steps contributed by their expert users through their normal use of the systems. Examples of such systems are LEAP (Mitchell *et al.*, 1985), Disciple (Tecuci, 1988; Tecuci and Kodratoff, 1990), Odysseus (Wilkins, 1990), and CAP (Mitchell *et al.*, 1994).
- Example-guided KB revision systems. These are systems that improve a KB to become consistent with a given set of examples. Knowledge base revision may be explicitly controlled by the expert, as in the case of SEEK (Ginsberg *et al.*, 1988), or may be implicitly controlled by the expert, as in the case of PTR (Koppel *et al.*, Chapter 4 of this volume).
- Systems integrating elicitation of repertory grids with empirical inductive learning. Examples of such systems are AQUINAS (Boose and Bradshaw, 1988) and KSS0 (Gaines and Shaw, 1992) that elicit repertory grids from experts and then learn concepts and rules from these grids through conceptual clustering and empirical induction.
- Case-based reasoning systems. These are systems that integrate knowledge elicitation and refinement of cases with inductive generalization and automatic (re-)organization of cases. Examples of such systems are CABINS (Sycara and Miyashita, Chapter 9 of this volume), and CREEK (Aamodt, Chapter 8 of this volume). PROTOS (Porter *et al.*, 1990) is a case-based system that also integrates explanation-based learning.
- Interactive inductive logic programming systems. These are systems that integrate inductive logic programming with knowledge elicitation from experts as, for instance, CIGOL (Muggleton and Buntine, 1988), CLINT (De Raedt, 1993), and MOBAL (Morik *et al.*, 1993; Wrobel, Chapter 5 of this volume).
- Systems integrating systematic elicitation of knowledge with explanation-based learning. An example of such a system is COEX (Schmalhofer and

Tschaitschian, Chapter 6 of this volume) that helps in the elicitation of an initial KB which is then compiled for efficiency using explanation-based learning. Another example is LSPA that compiles the KB to provide several functionalities (Miller and Levi, Chapter 7 of this volume).

- KB development systems. These are systems that integrate learning, knowledge elicitation and experimentation to build a KB. Examples of such systems are DE-KART (Baudin *et al.*, Chapter 2 of this volume), Disciple-MTL (Tecuci, Chapter 1 of this volume), EXPECT (Gil and Paris, Chapter 3 of this volume), and PRODIGY (Carbonell *et al.*, 1989).

The integrated machine learning and knowledge acquisition systems have the potential for a wide range of applications. Some areas in which such systems have been applied are mechanical engineering production planning (Schmalhofer and Tschaitschian, chapter 6 of this volume), job shop scheduling (Carbonell *et al.*, 1989; Sycara and Miyashita, Chapter 9 of this volume), medical diagnosis (Ginsberg *et al.*, 1988; Porter *et al.*, 1990; Wilkins, 1990), mechanical diagnosis (Aamodt, Chapter 8 of this volume), telecommunication access control (Wrobel, Chapter 5 of this volume), programming language advising (Boose and Bradshaw, 1988), VLSI design (Mitchell *et al.*, 1985), manufacturing loudspeakers (Tecuci and Kodratoff, 1990), information retrieval (Baudin *et al.*, Chapter 2 of this volume), assisting pilots (Miller and Levi, Chapter 7 of this volume), and building personal assistants (Mitchell *et al.*, 1994).

This book presents, in a tutorial fashion, some of the most successful recent approaches to the integration of knowledge acquisition and machine learning for building knowledge-based systems, as well as their applications in complex domains. The following is a brief description of the chapters in this book.

The chapter by Tecuci presents a general approach to the process of building knowledge bases that integrates multistrategy learning, active experimentation and guided knowledge elicitation. This approach is illustrated in the domain of computer workstation allocation and configuration, and is characterized by three main features. First, it is based on a multistrategy learning method that dynamically integrates various types of inference that are employed by the single-strategy learning methods. Second, much of the knowledge needed is generated by the system itself. Therefore, most of the time, the human expert only needs to confirm or reject system-generated hypotheses. Third, the process of building the KB is efficient due to the ability of the multistrategy learner to generalize and reuse its reasoning process. The chapter shows how the expert and the learning system could allocate the tasks involved such that each is solving those for which they are best suited.

The chapter by Baudin, Kedar and Pell addresses the problem of acquiring and refining knowledge bases for knowledge-based retrieval systems. They present a knowledge acquisition and refinement tool that provides the user with increasing levels of assistance as the system acquires more knowledge (illustrated in the area of documentation for mechanical engineering design). While initially the knowledge is entered manually, as the system is used and acquires new knowledge, it starts providing assistance and suggestions, and gradually evolves toward a more automated acquisition system. The user initially provides the system with very general retrieval heuristics that are gradually refined by the system, based on successful and failed cases of their applications. The refinement of the heuristics is initially performed by the human expert who also defines new concepts needed for retrieval. As the conceptual language of the system is developed and the number of examples (either successful or failed) of heuristics application increases, the refinement of these heuristics is performed by utilizing an inductive learning method.

The chapter by Gil and Paris presents another approach to KB development that is based on a synergistic cooperation between a human expert and a learning system. The basic idea of their approach is that much of the domain knowledge needed by a system could be derived by analogy with knowledge it already possesses, or by analogy from knowledge of a different domain. Simple analogies can be made by the system and confirmed by the expert. In general, however, the expert guides the system through each step of the analogy: retrieval of the source of analogy, mapping from the source to the target, and adapting the solution to the target. On the other hand, the system takes care of properly representing and integrating the acquired knowledge into the existing knowledge structure, while the dialogue with the expert takes place at a conceptual level.

The chapter by Koppel, Segre and Feldman addresses the problem of revising the domain theory (i.e. the KB) of a classification expert system. Theory revision is a typical class of problems that shows the usefulness of a combined knowledge acquisition and machine learning approach to building knowledge-based systems. Generally, one would use knowledge acquisition techniques to elicit an initial domain theory which might be incomplete and partially incorrect. Then, this initial theory would be automatically revised by a machine learning system, to become consistent with a set of training examples. This chapter also shows an additional dimension of the complementarity of machine learning and knowledge acquisition with respect to this problem. The expert can provide a new type of knowledge in the form of bias to guide the theory revision process. This knowledge may take the form of numeric confidence in the components of the initial theory, preferred revision operations, or specific ways of revising a knowledge piece component, if the need arises. The chapter introduces an extended representation of clauses that allows the definition of these biases, and presents a theory revision method based on this representation.

The chapter by Wrobel shows how the existing, off-line, Inductive Logic Programming (ILP) algorithms can be used for knowledge acquisition, using a telecommunication access control problem for illustration. It describes the Balanced Cooperative Modelling paradigm, and illustrates it with the integrated knowledge acquisition and machine learning system Mobal. Mobal is an ILP toolbox consisting of several modules offering different knowledge acquisition services. It also features interfaces to the most popular and successful ILP algorithms that complement the internal tools. The chapter concludes with a discussion of the practical issues of using learning capabilities within larger application systems, and presents how Mobal's networked client/server concept supports embedded adaptivity and the integration of learning modules with conventional software components.

The chapter by Schmalhofer and Tschaitschian presents the cooperative knowledge evolution model of building a knowledge-based system, which includes all the three phases presented above: systematic elicitation of expert knowledge, KB refinement and KB reformulation. This methodology is based on several knowledge acquisition and machine learning tools integrated in their Case-Oriented Expert System Architecture (CECoS), an interactive conceptual clustering system that helps the expert to define a hierarchy of problem classes starting from specific descriptions of problems; SP-GEN, an autonomous explanation-based learning system that learns skeletal plans from plan instances; PABS, an interactive plan abstraction system that learns abstract plans from specific examples; and COKAM+, an interactive system that extracts knowledge from text. The cooperative knowledge evolution methodology is illustrated in two complex domains: production planning in mechanical engineering and clinical testing of new drugs.

The chapter by Miller and Levi presents an approach that integrates explanation-based generalization and knowledge reformulation into the knowledge acquisition process of developing a large knowledge-based pilot's associate system. This system consists of several independent subsystems, each using a different specialized representation of a common body of domain knowledge. Their approach is interesting in that it shows a novel way in which a traditional explanation-based learning method could be used in a complex system. Indeed, rather than "compiling for speed", explanation-based learning is "compiling for multiple functionality". The domain theory of the learning module is used as a common knowledge repository for the individual subsystems. This common knowledge is compiled and translated into the different representations of the subsystems. From a knowledge acquisition point of view, this approach reduces the problem of defining different knowledge bases for individual subsystems to one of maintaining a common knowledge repository and automatically generating different specialized knowledge bases.

The chapter by Aamodt presents a general modelling cycle for building and maintaining interactive knowledge-based consultants able to continuously learn from their own experience. Thus, the consultants do not need periodic updating from an expert which is very time-consuming. This chapter reviews the main approaches to case-based reasoning and shows that they provide a suitable basis for this general modelling cycle because of their natural integration of knowledge acquisition, problem solving and learning. This approach to knowledge-based systems development and maintenance is illustrated with the author's case-based reasoning system, CREEK, and its application to diagnosing car starting problems.

CREEK utilizes both case-specific and general domain knowledge, and continuously learns from its experience.

The chapter by Sycara and Miyashita presents an approach that integrates case-based learning with knowledge acquisition of user preferences to guide solution optimization in ill-structured domains. The approach, implemented in the CABINS system, is illustrated on job shop factory scheduling problems. The ill-structuredness of this domain and the presence of many potentially conflicting optimization objectives make schedule optimization difficult to formalize and costly to solve. In this domain, neither the system nor the human expert possess causal domain knowledge that can be used to guide schedule optimization. Extensive experiments described in this paper show that CABINS is capable of acquiring user optimization preferences and tradeoffs, can improve its own competence, is a flexible schedule optimization methodology that produces high quality schedules, and can adaptively revise a schedule in response to unexpected events during schedule execution.

The chapter by Kodratoff and Mignot describes several industrial applications of machine learning. Because in most of these applications one has to acquire the knowledge necessary to run the machine learning algorithms, one necessarily faces the problem of merging knowledge acquisition and machine learning techniques. This chapter presents five solutions that have been used by the authors of industrial applications, and analyses the implications of relying on compiled expert knowledge. It shows that a case-based approach is a good solution for the acquisition of this compiled expert knowledge, but not a miraculous one, since it raises also many new problems that must be solved before really efficient implementations are available.

This book addresses issues of interest to a large spectrum of readers from research, industry and academia. Researchers in knowledge acquisition will find methods of automating the knowledge acquisition process by using machine learning techniques. Researchers in machine learning will find ways of enhancing the power of learning methods through the employment of knowledge acquisition techniques. People in industry will find descriptions of successful practical applications of integrated knowledge acquisition and machine learning approaches, and may learn how to apply such approaches to their own projects of building advanced knowledge-based systems. The tutorial style of the chapters should facilitate understanding the basic approaches and their potential. Students will find an introduction to knowledge acquisition and machine learning, two closely related areas of artificial intelligence which are essential for building intelligent systems.

This book on integrating machine learning and knowledge acquisition has several ambitious goals. We hope that it will contribute to a better understanding of each research community by the other, will facilitate their collaboration, and will stimulate research toward the common goal of building complex knowledge-based systems for complex applications. We hope that it will show the power of integrated approaches and will contribute to their wider use in industrial and other applications. We also hope that it will contribute to artificial intelligence education by showing the relationships between two areas of artificial intelligence that have different approaches to solving the same problems, and by presenting ways of combining these approaches to take advantage of their complementariness.

Many individuals contributed to the preparation of this book. Our deep and heartfelt gratitude goes to all the contributors to this volume. They have made a special effort to write their chapters in a highly comprehensive and easy-to-read manner. We also thank the anonymous reviewers of the book proposal and the following reviewers of the individual chapters: Ray Bareiss, Andrew Black, Luc De Raedt, Rolando Fernandez, Brian Gaines, Jean-Gabriel Ganascia, Michael Hieb, Peggy Hwu, Ibrahim Imam, Steve Ku, Ray Mooney, Michael Pazzani, Smadar Kedar, Michael Schoelles, Mildred Shaw, Maarten van Someren, Lee Wagenhals, Kathryn Wright, Norman White. Their diligent and careful reviews were crucial for achieving the high quality of all the contributions. Special thanks to Smadar Kedar who contributed indirectly to this book by participating in the organization of the IJCAI–93 workshop *Machine Learning and Knowledge Acquisition: Common Issues, Contrasting Methods, and Integrated Approaches* and in the editing of the *Knowledge Acquisition Journal* issue on the integration of machine learning and knowledge acquisition.

In presenting this volume, we hope that it will stimulate interest in this novel and uniquely challenging area of integrated machine learning and knowledge acquisition.

References

Bareiss, E. R., Porter, B. W. and Murray, K. S. (1989). Supporting start-to-finish development of knowledge bases. *Machine Learning*, 3.

Birnbaum, L. A. and Collins, G. C. (editors) (1991). *Machine Learning: Proceedings of the Eighth International Workshop (ML91), Part I: Automated Knowledge Acquisition.* Morgan Kaufmann, San Mateo, CA.

Boose, J. H. and Bradshaw, J. M. (1988). Expertise transfer and complex problems: Using AQUINAS as a knowledge-acquisition workbench for knowledge-based systems In Boose, J. and Gaines, B. (editors), *Knowledge Acquisition Tools for Expert Systems.* Academic Press, London.

Buchanan, B. G. and Wilkins, D. C. (editors) (1992). *Readings in Knowledge Acquisition and Learning: Automating the Construction and Improvement of Expert Systems.* Morgan Kaufmann. San Mateo, CA.

Carbonell, J. G., Knoblock, C. A. and Minton, M. (1989). PRODIGY: an integrated architecture for planning and learning, *Research Report*, CMU-CS-89–189, School of Computer Science, Carnegie Mellon University, Pittsburgh, PA 15–213.

Chandrasekaran, B. (1986). Generic tasks in knowledge-based reasoning: high-level building blocks for expert systems design. *IEEE Expert*, 1: 23–29.

Cohen, W. (1991). The generality of overgenerality In L.A. Birnbaum and G.C. Collins (editors), *Machine Learning: Proceedings of the Eighth International Workshop*. Morgan Kaufmann, Chicago.

Davis, R. (1979). Interactive transfer of expertise: Acquisition of new inference rules. *Artificial Intelligence*, 12: 121–157.

DeJong, G. and Mooney, R. (1986). Explanation-based learning: An alternative view. *Machine Learning*, 1: 145–176.

De Raedt, L. (1993). *Interactive Theory Revision: An Inductive Logic Programming Approach*. Academic Press, San Diego, CA.

Ericsson, K. A. and Simon, H. A. (1984). *Protocol Analysis: Verbal Reports as Data*. MIT Press, Cambridge, MA.

Fikes, R. E., Hart, P. E. and Nilsson, N. J. (1972). Learning and executing generalized robot plans. *Artificial Intelligence*, 3: 251–288.

Fisher, D. H. (1987). Knowledge acquisition via incremental conceptual clustering. *Machine Learning*, 2: 139–172.

Gaines, B. R. and Shaw, M. L. G. (1992). Knowledge acquisition tools based on personal construct psychology. In *Knowledge Engineering Review*, special issue on automated knowledge acquisition tools.

Gammack, J. G. (1987). Different techniques and different aspects on declarative knowledge. In Alison L. Kidd (editor), *Knowledge Acquisition for Expert Systems: A Practical Handbook*. Plenum Press, New York.

Ginsberg, A., Weiss, S. M. and Politakis, P. (1988). Automatic knowledge base refinement for classification systems. *Artificial Intelligence*, 35: 197–226.

Goldberg, D. E. (1989). *Genetic Algorithms in Search, Optimization and Machine Learning*. Addison-Wesley, Reading, MA.

Josephson, J. R., Chandrasekaran, B., Smith, J. W. and Tanner, M. C. (1987). A Mechanism for forming composite explanatory hypotheses. *IEEE Trans. on Systems, Man and Cybernetics*, 17: 445–454.

LaFrance, M. (1987). The knowledge acquisition grid: a method for training knowledge engineers. *International Journal of Man–Machine Studies*, 27: 245–255.

Laird, J. E., Rosenbloom, P. S. and Newell, A. (1986). Chuncking in SOAR: the anatomy of a general learning mechanism. *Machine Learning*, 1: 11–46.

Marcus, S. (editor) (1988). *Automating Knowledge Acquisition for Expert Systems*. Kluwer, Boston, MA.

Marcus, S. (editor) (1989). *Machine Learning Journal*, special issue on Knowledge Acquisition. vol. 4, no. 3–4.

McDermott, J. (1988). Preliminary steps toward a taxonomy of problem solving methods, In S. Marcus (editor), *Automating Knowledge Acquisition for Expert Systems*. Kluwer, Boston, MA.

Michalski, R. S. (1983). A theory and methodology of inductive learning. In Michalski, R. S., Carbonell, J. G. and Mitchell, T. M. (editors), *Machine Learning: An Artificial Intelligence Approach* (Vol. 1). Tioga Publishing Co., Palo Alto, CA.

Michalski, R. S. and Tecuci, G. (1994). *Machine Learning: A Multistrategy Approach*, Vol. 4. Morgan Kaufmann, San Mateo, CA.

Minton, S. (1990). Quantitative results concerning the utility of explanation-based learning. *Artificial Intelligence*, 42: 363–392.

Mitchell, T. M. (1978). Version spaces: an approach to concept learning, *Doctoral Dissertation*. Stanford University.

Mitchell, T. M., Mahadevan, S. and Steinberg, L. I. (1985). LEAP: A Learning Apprentice System for VLSI Design, in *Proceedings of the International Joint Conference on Artificial Intelligence* (IJCAI-85), Morgan Kaufmann, Los Angeles, pp. 573–580.

Mitchell, T. M., Keller, T. and Kedar-Cabelli, S. (1986). Explanation-based generalization: a unifying view. *Machine Learning*, 1: 47–80.

Mitchell, T. M., Caruana, R., Freitag, D., McDermott, J. and Zabowski, D. (1994). Experience with a learning personal assistant. *Communications of the ACM*, 37: 81–91.

Mooney, R. J. and Ourston, D. (1994). A multistrategy approach to theory refinement. In Michalski, R. S. and Tecuci, G. (editors), *Machine Learning: A Multistrategy Approach*, Vol. 4. Morgan Kaufmann, San Mateo, CA.

Morik, K., Wrobel, S., Kietz, J. U. and Emde, W. (1993). *Knowledge Acquisition and Machine Learning*. Academic Press, London.

Muggleton, S. and Buntine, W. (1988). Machine invention of first order predicates by inverting resolution, *Proceedings of the Fifth International Conference on Machine Learning*, Ann Arbor, Michigan, pp. 339–352.

Musen, M. A. (1989). Automated support for building and extending expert models, *Machine Learning*, 4: 347–371.

Porter, B. W., Bareiss, R. and Holte, R. C. (1990). Concept learning and heuristic classification in weak-theory domains. In Shavlik, J. and Dietterich, T. (editors), *Readings in Machine Learning*. Morgan Kaufmann, San Mateo, CA.

Prieditis, A. E. (editor) (1988). *Analogica*. Kluwer, Boston, MA.

Quinlan, J. R. (1986). Induction of decision trees, *Machine Learning*, 1: 81–106.

Rumelhart, D. E. and McClelland, J. L. (editors) (1986). *Parallel Distributed Processing*. MIT Press, Cambridge, MA.

Shaw, M. L. G. and Gaines, B. R. (1987). An interactive knowledge elictation technique using personal construct technology. In Kidd, A. L. (editor), *Knowledge Acquisition for Expert Systems: A Practical Handbook*. Plenum Press, New York.

Tecuci, G. (1988). DISCIPLE: A theory, methodology, and system for learning expert knowledge, *Ph.D. Thesis*, University of Paris–South.

Tecuci, G. and Kodratoff, Y. (1990). Apprenticeship learning in imperfect theory domains, In Kodratoff, Y. and Michalski, R. S. (editors), *Machine Learning: An Artificial Intelligence Approach*, Vol. 3. Morgan Kaufmann, San Mateo, CA.

Tecuci, G. (1992). Automating knowledge acquisitions as extending, updating, and improving a knowledge base, *IEEE Trans. on Systems, Man and Cybernetics*, 22: 1444–1460.

Tecuci, G., Kedar, S. and Kodratoff, Y. (editors) (1993). *Proceedings of the IJCAI-93 Workshop on Machine Learning and Knowledge Acquisition: Common Issues, Contrasting Methods, and Integrated Approaches*, Chambery, France.

Tecuci, G. and Hieb, M. (1994). Consistency-driven knowledge elicitation: using a learning-oriented knowledge representation that supports knowledge elicitation in NeoDISCIPLE. *Knowledge Acquisition Journal*, 6: 23–46.

Tecuci, G., Kedar, S. and Kodratoff, Y. (editors) (1994). *Knowledge Acquisition*, vol. 6, no. 2, special issue on the integration of machine learning and knowledge acquisition.

Towell, G. G. and Shavlik, J. W. (1994). Refining symbolic knowledge using neural networks. In Michalski, R. S. and Tecuci, G. (editors), *Machine Learning: A Multistrategy Approach*, Vol. 4. Morgan Kaufmann, San Mateo, CA.

Wielinga, B. J., Schreiber, A. Th. and Breuker, J. A. (1992). KADS: a modeling approach to knowledge engineering. *Knowledge Acquisition*, 4: 5–53.

Wilkins, D. C. (1990). Knowledge base refinement as improving an incorrect and incomplete domain theory. In Kodratoff, Y. and Michalski, R. S. (editors), *Machine Learning: An Artificial Intelligence Approach*, vol. 3. Morgan Kaufmann, San Mateo, CA.

CHAPTER 1

Building knowledge bases through multistrategy learning and knowledge acquisition

Gheorghe Tecuci

Abstract

This chapter presents a new approach to the process of building a knowledge-based system which relies on a tutoring paradigm rather than traditional knowledge engineering. In this approach, an expert teaches the knowledge-based system in much the same way the expert would teach a human student, by providing specific examples of problems and solutions, explanations of these solutions, or supervising the system as it solves new problems. During such interactions, the system extends and corrects its knowledge base until the expert is satisfied with its performance. Three main features characterize this approach. First, it is based on a multistrategy learning method that dynamically integrates the elementary inferences that are employed by the single-strategy learning methods. Second, much of the knowledge needed by the system is generated by the system itself. Therefore, most of the time, the expert will need only to confirm or reject system-generated hypotheses. Third, the knowledge-base development process is efficient due to the ability of the multistrategy learner to reuse its reasoning process, as well as the employment of plausible version spaces for controlling the knowledge-base development process. This chapter illustrates a cooperation between a learning system and a human expert in which the learner performs most of the tasks and the expert helps it in solving the problems that are intrinsically difficult for a learner and relatively easy for an expert.

1.1. Introduction

Automating the process of building knowledge bases has long been the goal of both Knowledge Acquisition and Machine Learning. The focus of knowledge acquisition has been to improve and partially automate the acquisition of

Machine Learning and Knowledge Acquisition
ISBN 0-12-685120-4

knowledge from an expert by a knowledge engineer (Gaines and Boose, 1988; Buchanan and Wilkins, 1992). Knowledge Acquisition has had limited success, mostly because of the communication problems between the expert and the knowledge engineer, which require many iterations before converging to an acceptable knowledge base (KB). In contrast, Machine Learning has focused on mostly autonomus algorithms for acquiring knowledge from data and for knowledge compilation and organization (Shavlik and Dietterich, 1990). However, because of the complexity of this problem, the application of machine learning tends to be limited to simple domains. While knowledge acquisition research has generally avoided using machine learning techniques, relying on the knowledge engineer, machine learning research has generally avoided involving a human expert in the learning loop. We think that neither approach is sufficient, and that the automation of knowledge acquisition should be based on a direct interaction between a human expert and a learning system (Tecuci, 1992).

A human expert and a learning system have complementary strengths. Problems that are extremely difficult for one may be easy for the other. For instance, automated learning systems have traditionally had difficulty assigning credit or blame to individual decisions that lead to overall results, but this process is generally easy for a human expert. Also, the "new terms" problem in the field of machine learning (i.e., extending the representation language with new terms when existing terms cannot represent the concept to be learned), is very difficult for an autonomous learner, but could be quite easy for a human expert (Tecuci and Hieb, 1994). On the other hand, there are many problems that are much more difficult for a human expert than for a learning system as, for instance, the generation of general concepts or rules that account for specific examples, and the updating of the KB to consistently integrate new knowledge.

Over the last several years we have developed the learning apprentice systems Disciple (Tecuci, 1988; Tecuci and Kodratoff, 1990), NeoDisciple (Tecuci, 1992; Tecuci and Hieb, 1994), Captain (Tecuci *et al.*, 1994) and Disciple-Ops (Tecuci *et al.*, 1995) which use multistrategy learning, active experimentation and consistency-driven knowledge elicitation to acquire knowledge from a human expert. A significant feature of these systems is their ability to acquire complex knowledge from a human expert through a very simple and natural interaction. The expert will give the learning apprentice specific examples of problems and solutions, explanations of these solutions, or supervise the apprentice as it solves new problems. During such interactions, the apprentice learns general rules and concepts, continuously extending and improving its KB, until it becomes an expert system. Moreover, this process produces verified knowledge-based systems, because it is based on an expert interacting with, checking and correcting the way the systems solve problems. These systems have been applied to a variety of domains: loudspeaker manufacturing (Tecuci, 1988; Tecuci and Kodratoff, 1990), reactions in inorganic chemistry, high-level robot planning (Tecuci, 1991; Tecuci and Hieb, 1994), question-answering in geography (Tecuci, 1992) and, more recently, military command agents for distributed interactive simulation environments (Tecuci *et al.*, 1994) and operator agents for monitoring and repair (Tecuci *et al.*, 1995).

We have also developed a novel approach to machine learning, called *multistrategy task-adaptive learning by justification trees* (MTL-JT), which has a great potential for automating the process of building knowledge-based systems (Tecuci, 1993, 1994). MTL-JT is a type of learning which integrates dynamically different learning strategies (such as explanation-based learning, analogical learning, abductive learning, empirical inductive learning, etc.), depending upon the characteristics of the learning task to be performed. The basic idea of this approach is to regard learning as an inferential process for deriving new or better knowledge from prior knowledge and new input information. Taking this view, one can dynamically integrate the elementary inferences (such as deduction, analogy, abduction, generalization, specialization, abstraction, concretion, etc.) which are the building blocks of the single-strategy learning methods. This MTL method takes advantage of the complementary nature of different single-strategy learning methods and has more powerful learning capabilities.

Based on these results, we have started the development of a new methodology and tool, called Disciple-MTL, for building verified knowledge-based systems which also have the capability of continuously improving themselves during their normal use. A main goal of this research is to provide an expert with a powerful methodology and tool for building expert systems, significantly reducing or even eliminating the need of assistance from a knowledge engineer. The expert will develop the system by teaching it how to solve problems, in the same way he/she would teach a human apprentice. This chapter presents our current results in developing this methodology, by using an example of building a knowledge-based system for computer workstation allocation and configuration.

This paper is organized as follows. Section 1.2 presents the general Disciple-MTL methodology for building knowledge-based systems. Section 1.3 describes the application domain used to illustrate the methodology. Sections 1.4, 1.5 and 1.6 describe and illustrate three main phases of teaching the KB system how to solve problems. Finally, Section 1.7 summarizes the main results obtained and presents some of the future research directions.

1.2 General presentation of the Disciple-MTL methodology

The process of building a KB system consists of two stages:

- Building an initial KB for a general inference engine.
- Developing (i.e., extending and correcting) the KB until it satisfies required specifications.

In the first stage the expert, possibly assisted by a knowledge engineer, defines an initial KB (Gammack, 1987). There are two main goals of this stage:

- To allow the expert to introduce into the KB whatever knowledge pieces he or she may easily express.
- To provide the KB system with background knowledge which will support it in acquiring new knowledge from the expert.

During this stage the expert generates a list of typical concepts, organizes the concepts, and encodes a set of rules and various correlations between knowledge pieces expressed as determinations or dependencies (Davies and Russell, 1987; Collins and Michalski, 1989; Tecuci and Duff, 1994), which will permit the system to perform various types of plausible reasoning. This initial KB contains all the knowledge pieces which the expert may easily define, and is usually incomplete and partially incorrect.

In the second stage the KB is developed (i.e., extended and corrected), through training sessions with the expert (which no longer needs any support from a knowledge engineer), until it becomes complete and correct enough to meet the required specifications.

Figure 1.1 shows the Deductive Closure (DC) of the KB during the second stage of KB development. DC represents the set of problems that can be deductively solved by the system. The solutions of some of these problems may be wrong (because the KB is partially incorrect), while other problems may not be solvable at all (because the KB is incomplete). Figure 1.1 shows also the Plausible Closure (PC) of the KB during KB development. PC represents the set of problems that can be solved by using plausible inferences (Tecuci and Duff, 1994). Plausible inferences are made by using the rules from the KB not only deductively, but also abductively or analogically. They could also be made by using weaker correlations between knowledge pieces (determinations, dependencies, related facts, etc.). Employing plausible reasoning significantly increases the number of problems that could be solved by the system. In the same time, however, many of the solutions proposed by the system will be wrong. The goal

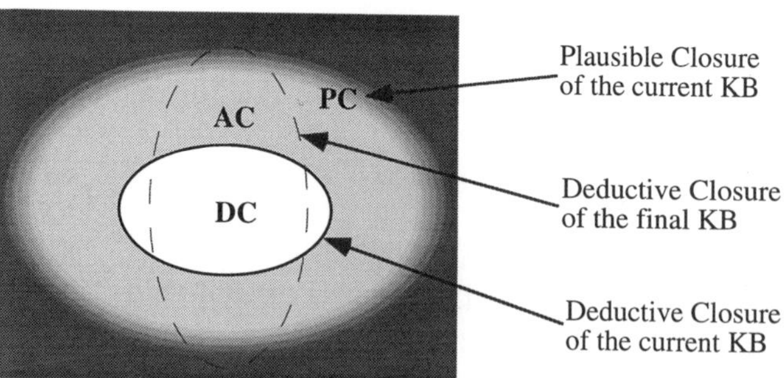

Figure 1.1 The relationship between DC, PC and AC during KB development

of KB development is to extend and correct the KB of the system until it meets the required specifications. The deductive closure of this final KB is called Acceptable Deductive Closure (AC).

As can be seen from Figure 1.1, the deductive closure during KB development (DC) is an approximate lower bound for AC (the deductive closure of the final KB) in the sense that most of DC is included in AC. Also, the plausible closure during KB development (PC) is an approximate upper bound for AC in the sense that most of AC is included in PC. The set AC is not known to the system. However, any set which includes most of DC and most of which is included in PC is a hypothesis for being the set of AC. We can therefore consider PC and DC as defining a *plausible version space* (Tecuci, 1992) which includes the sets that are candidates of being the set AC. With this interpretation, the problem of building the KB reduces to one of searching the set AC in the plausible version space defined by DC and PC. Because the goal is to develop the KB so that its deductive closure becomes AC, DC is used as the current hypothesis for AC, and PC is used as a guide for extending DC, so as to include more of PC $\cap$ AC, and for correcting DC, to remove from it more of DC–AC.

The main phases of the KB development process are schematically represented in Figure 1.2. They are:

- Inference-based multistrategy learning.
- Experimentation, verification and repair.
- Consistency-driven knowledge elicitation.

The system is trained by the expert with representative examples of problems and their correct solutions (Training input in Figure 1.2). Each training problem *P* lies generally inside the plausible closure PC and outside the deductive closure DC (see Figure 1.1). This input will initiate a KB development process in which the system will extend and correct its KB so as to correctly solve the problems from the class represented by *P*.

In the first phase, *Inference-based multistrategy learning*, the system performs a complex reasoning process building "*the most plausible and simple*" justification tree which shows that the training input indicated by the expert (consisting of a problem *P* and its expert-recommended solution *S*) is correct (Tecuci, 1993, 1994). The plausible justification tree is composed of both deductive implications and plausible implications (based on analogy, abduction, inductive prediction, etc.). Because this is the "most plausible and simple" justification tree which shows that *S* is a correct solution for *P*, the component implications and statements are hypothesized to be true, and are asserted into the KB (thus extending DC with a portion of PC).

In the second phase, *Experimentation, verification and repair* (see Figure 1.2), the system reuses the reasoning process performed in the previous phase in order to further extend, and also to correct, the KB so as to be able to solve the

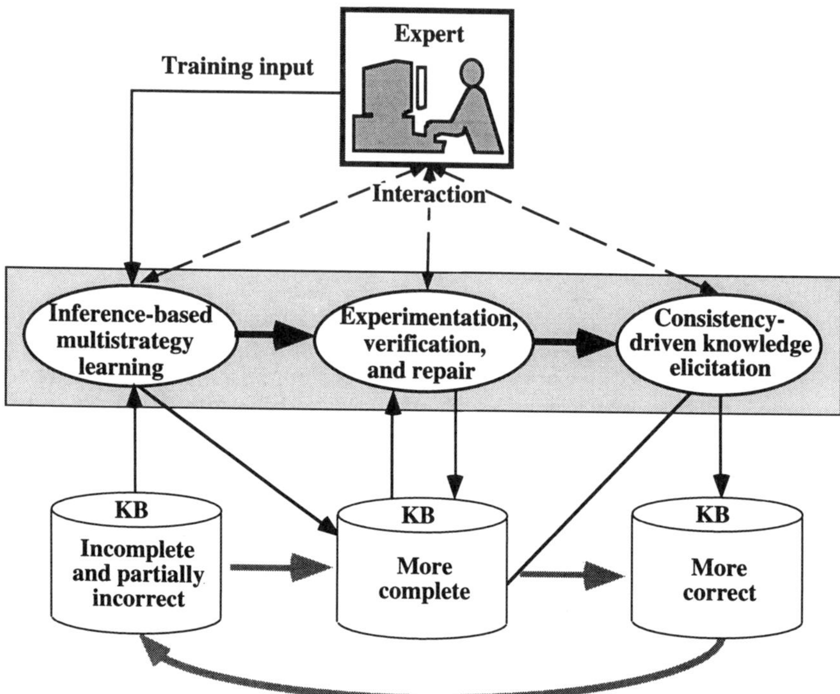

Figure 1.2 The main phases of the KB development process

problems from the class of which P is an example. The plausible justification tree corresponding to the problem P and its solution S is generalized by employing *various types of generalizations* (not only deductive but also empirical inductive, based on analogy, etc.). Instances of this generalized tree show how problems similar to P may receive solutions similar to S. The system will selectively generate such problems P_i and corresponding solutions S_i and will ask the expert to judge if they are correct or not. If the answer is "Yes", then the KB will be extended, causing DC to include P_i and its solution. If the answer is "No", then the wrong implications made by the system will have to be identified, with the expert's help, and the KB will be corrected accordingly. Due to the use of plausible version spaces and a *heuristic search* of these spaces, the system will usually ask a small number of questions.

Because the representation language of the system is incomplete, some of the general problem-solving rules learned during experimentation may be inconsistent (i.e. may cover known negative examples). In order to remove such inconsistencies, additional concepts are elicited from the expert, during the third stage called *Consistency-driven knowledge elicitation* (see Figure 1.2).

This KB development process will end when the system has been trained with examples of the main classes of problems it should be able to solve. This should allow the system to solve most of the problems from its area of expertise through deductive reasoning. However, it will also be able to solve an unanticipated problem through plausible reasoning, and to learn from this experience, in the same way it learned from the expert. Therefore, the systems developed using this approach will also have the capability of continuously improving themselves during their normal use.

The KB building process is characterized by a cooperation between the learning system and the human expert in which the learner performs most of the tasks and the expert helps it in solving the problems that are intrinsically difficult for a learner and relatively easy for the expert.

This approach produces *verified knowledge-based systems*, because it is based on verifying and correcting the way the system solves problems. Because this approach is not limited to a certain type of inference engine, one can also use it to build knowledge bases for existing expert system shells.

The rest of this chapter illustrates this methodology.

1.3 Exemplary application domain

We will use the domain of computer workstation allocation and configuration in order to illustrate our approach to building knowledge bases. The KB system to be built has to reason about which machines are suitable for which tasks and to allocate an appropriate machine for each task. Its inference engine is similar to a PROLOG interpreter except that it can perform both deductive and plausible reasoning.

In this example we will use the clausal form of logic. Therefore, instead of writing

"A & B → C", which is read "if A and B are true then C is true"

we will write the equivalent expression

"C :- A, B.", which is read "C is true if A and B are true"

The initial incomplete and partially incorrect KB defined by the expert contains information about various printers and workstations distributed throughout the workplace. A sample of this KB is presented in Figure 1.3. It contains different types of knowledge: facts, a hierarchy of object concepts, deductive rules, and a plausible determination rule.

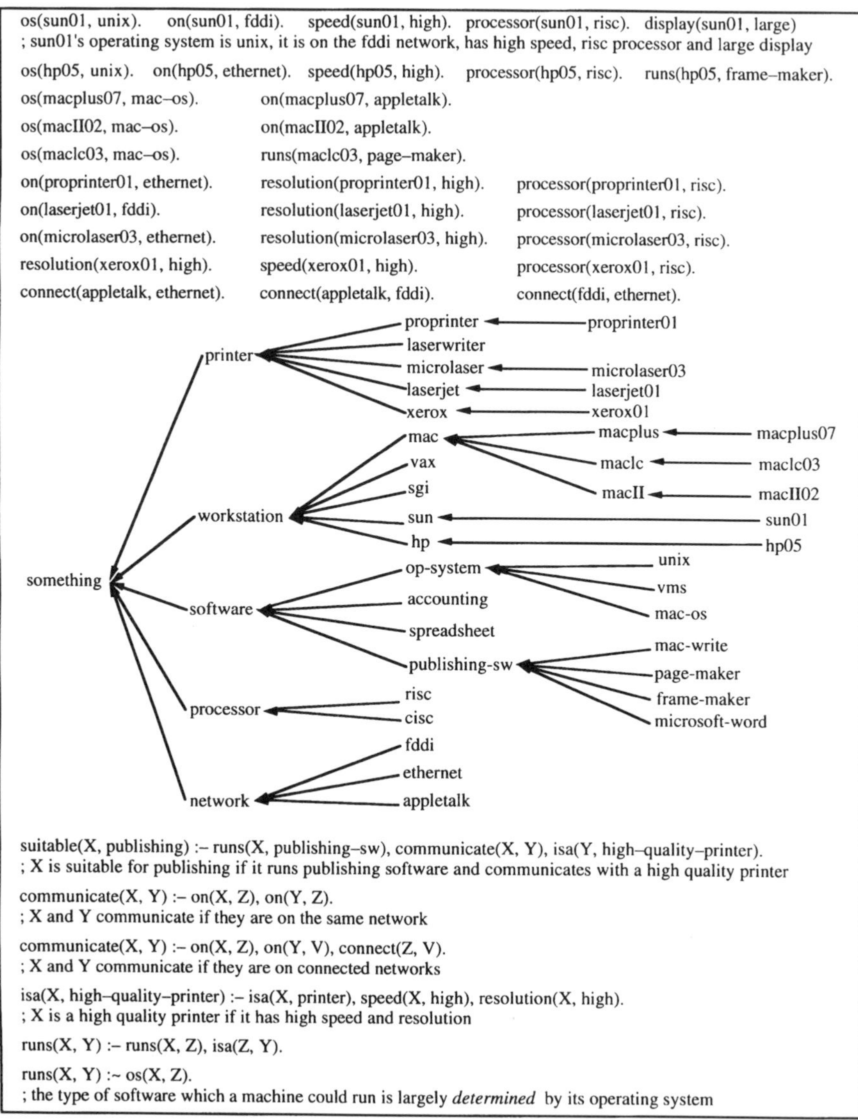

Figure 1.3 Part of the incomplete and partially incorrect KB for the domain of computer workstation allocation and configuration (the arrows represent "isa" relationships)

The individual facts express properties of the objects from the application domain, or relationships between these objects. For instance, "display(sun01, large)" states that the display of "sun01" is large, and "os(sun01, unix)" states that the operating system of "sun01" is "unix".

The hierarchy of concepts represents the generalization (or "isa") relationships between different object concepts. For instance, "microlaser03" is a "microlaser" which, in turn, is a "printer". These relationships will also be represented by using the notation "isa(microlaser03, microlaser)" and "isa(microlaser, printer)".

The top of the object hierarchy is "something", which represents the most general object concept from the application domain. It has the property that "isa(X, something)" is true for any X.

An example of a deductive rule is the following one:

```
suitable(X, publishing) :-
    runs(X, publishing-sw), communicate(X, Y), isa(Y, high-quality-printer).
```

It states that X is suitable for desktop publishing if it runs publishing software and communicates with a high-quality printer.

The KB in Figure 1.3 contains also the following plausible determination rule which states that the type of software run by a machine is plausibly determined by its operating system (":~" means plausible determination):

```
runs(X, Y) :~ os(X, Z).
```

After defining an initial KB like the one from Figure 1.3, the human expert may start training the system by providing typical examples of answers which the system should be able to give by itself. For instance, the expert may tell the system that "macII02" is suitable for publishing:

```
suitable(macII02, publishing)
```

This statement is representative of the type of answers which the KB system should be able to provide. This means that the final KB system should be able to give other answers of the form "suitable(X, Y)", where X is a workstation and Y is a task.

Starting from this input provided by the expert, the system will develop its KB so that the deductive closure DC of the KB will include other true statements of the form "suitable(X, Y)" and, at the same time, will no longer include false statements of the same form.

The next sections will illustrate this KB development process, following the phases indicated in Figure 1.2.

1.4 Inference-based multistrategy learning

1.4.1 Input understanding

1.4.1.1 Building the plausible justification tree

Let us suppose that the expert wants to teach the system which workstations are suitable for desktop publishing. To this purpose, it will give the system an example of such a workstation:

"suitable(macII02, publishing)"

First, the system tries to "understand" (i.e., to explain to itself) the input in terms of its current knowledge by building the plausible justification tree in Figure 1.4. The root of the tree is the input fact, the leaves are facts from the KB, and the intermediate nodes are intermediate facts generated during the "understanding" process. The branches connected to any given node link this node with facts, the conjunction of which *certainly* or *plausibly implies* the fact at the node, according to the learner's KB. The notion "plausibly implies" means that the target (parent node) can be inferred from the premises (children nodes) by some form of plausible reasoning, using the learner's KB. The branches together with the nodes they link represent individual inference steps which could be the result of different types of reasoning. This tree demonstrates that the input is a plausible consequence of the current knowledge of the system.

The method for building such a tree is a backward-chaining uniform-cost search in the space of all AND trees which have a depth of at most p, where p is parameter set by the expert. The cost of a partial AND tree is computed as a tuple (m, n), where m represents the number of the deductive implications in the tree, and n represents the number of the non-deductive implications (which, in the case of the current method, could be obtained by analogy, inductive prediction or abduction). The ordering relationship for the cost function is defined as follows:

$$(m1, n1) < (m2, n2) \text{ if and only if } n1 < n2 \text{ or } (n1 = n2 \text{ and } m1 < m2)$$

This cost function guarantees that the system will find the justification tree with the fewest number of non-deductive implications. In particular, it will find a deductive tree (if one exists) and the deductive tree with the fewest implications (if several exist).

The tree in Figure 1.4 is composed of four deductive implications, a determination-based analogical implication and an inductive prediction. It should be noticed that there is no predefined order in the performance of the different inference steps necessary to build a plausible justification tree (Tecuci, 1994). In general, this order depends of the relationship between the KB and the input.

Therefore, this method is an example of a dynamic and deep (i.e. at the level of individual inference steps) integration of single-strategy learning methods (each learning method corresponding to a specific type of inference).

The next sections present briefly the way the different implications in Figure 1.4 have been made.

1.4.1.2 *Deduction*

Four implications in Figure 1.4 are the results of deductions based on the deductive rules from the KB in Figure 1.3, as illustrated in the following.

It is known that

suitable(X, publishing)
:– runs(X, publishing–sw), communicate(X, Y), isa(Y, high–quality–printer).

and

runs(macII02, publishing–sw)
communicate(macII02, proprinter01).
isa(proprinter01, high–quality–printer).

Therefore one can conclude that

suitable(macII02, publishing).

1.4.1.3 *Analogy*

Analogical inference is the process of transferring knowledge from a known entity S to a similar but less known entity T. S is called the *source* of analogy since it is the entity that serves as a source of knowledge, and T is called the *target* of analogy since it is the entity that receives the knowledge (Winston, 1980; Carbonell, 1986; Gentner, 1990; Gil and Paris, 1995). The central intuition supporting this type of inference is that if two entities, S and T, are similar in some respects, then they could be similar in other respects as well. Therefore, if S has some feature, then one may infer by analogy that T has a similar feature.

A simple analogy is the one based on plausible determinations of the form

Q(X, Y) :~ P(X, Z)

which is read "Q is plausibly determined by P". This determination states that, for any source S and any target T, it is *probably true* that S and T are characterized by a same feature Q (i.e. Q(S, y_0) = true and Q(T, y_0) = true if

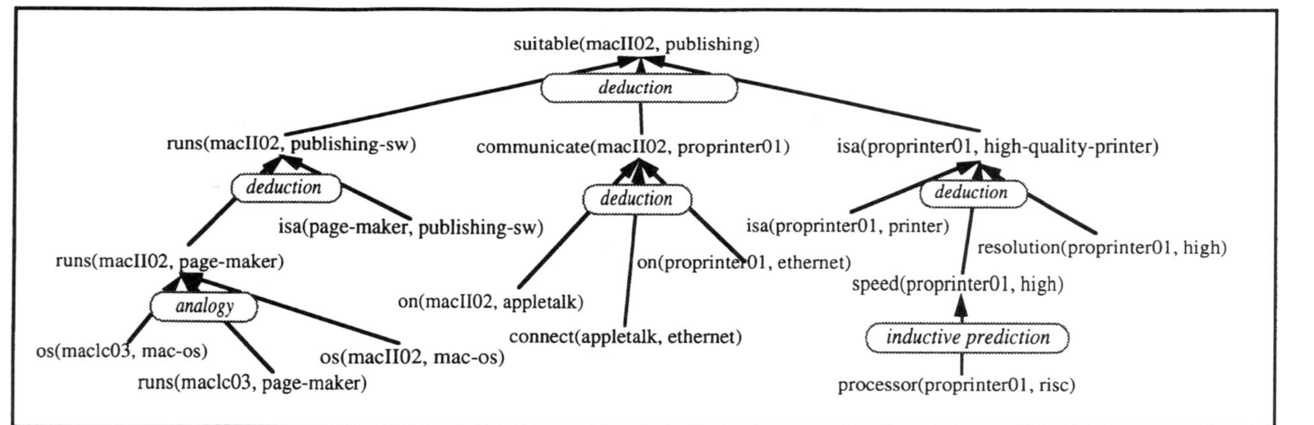

Figure 1.4 A plausible justification tree for "suitable(macII02, publishing)"

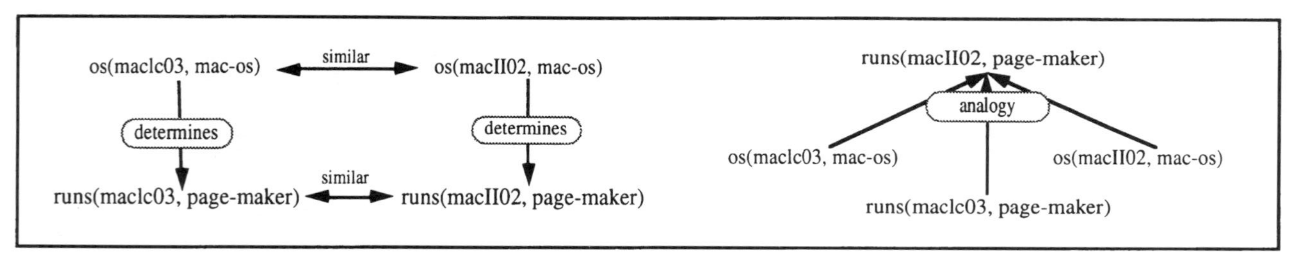

Figure 1.5 Inferring "runs(macII02, page-maker)" by analogy

they are characterized by the same feature P (i.e. P(S, z_0) = true and P(T, z_0) = true). Therefore, if Q(S, y_0) = true then one may infer by analogy that Q(T, y_0) = true.

We use the term "probably true" to express that the determination-based analogy we are considering is a weak inference method that does not guarantee the truth of the inferred knowledge. This is different from the determination rules introduced by Davies and Russell (1987) which guarantee the truth of the inferred knowledge.

The analogical implication in Figure 1.4 was made by using the plausible determination rule

runs(X, Y) :~ os(X, Z)

as indicated in Figure 1.5. According to this rule, the software which a machine can run is largely determined by its operating system. It is known that the operating system of "maclc03" is "mac–os", and that it runs "page-maker". Because the operating system of "macII02" is also "mac–os", one may infer by analogy that "macII02" could also run "page-maker".

One should notice that a plausible determination rule indicates only what kind of knowledge could be transferred from a source to a target (knowledge about the software which a machine could run, in the case of the considered determination), and in what conditions (the same operating system). It does not indicate, however, the exact relationship between the operating system (for instance, "mac–os") and the software ("page-maker"). The exact relationship is indicated by the source entity ("maclc03"). Therefore, a plausible determination rule alone (without a source entity), cannot be used in an inference process.

In general, our method of building plausible justification trees is intended to incorporate different forms of analogy, based on different kinds of similarities, such as similarities among causes, relations, and meta-relations (Tecuci, 1994).

1.4.1.4 Inductive prediction

Inductive prediction is the operation of finding an inductive generalization of a set of related facts and in applying this generalization to predict if a new fact is true.

To build the justification tree in Figure 1.4, the system needed to prove "speed(proprinter01, high)". Since there is no implication or determination rule which could be used to make this proof, the system has to analyse the facts from the KB in order to discover a rule which could predict if "speed(proprinter01, high)" is true. The main idea of this process is to look in the KB for other objects X which have high speed, and to take their descriptions as examples of the concept "speed(X, high)". Then, by generalizing these examples, one learns a rule which could be used to predict if

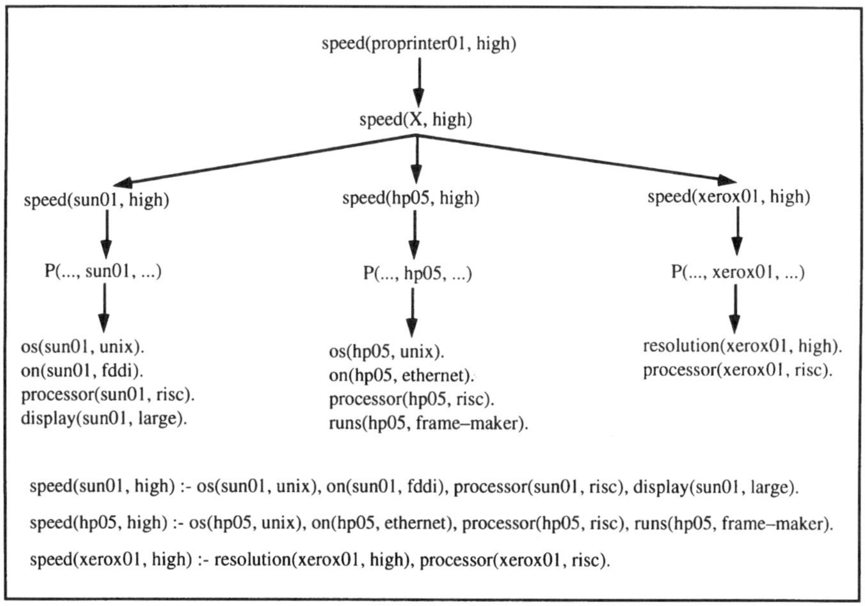

Figure 1.6 Hypothesizing examples of the concept "speed(X, high)"

"speed(proprinter01, high)" is true. This process is partially illustrated in Figure 1.6.

First, the fact "speed(proprinter01, high)" is generalized to "speed(X, high)". Then, instances of "speed(X, high)" are searched in the KB (see Figure 1.3). This identifies the objects with high speed. Next, the properties of these objects are determined. Then, the conjunction of the properties of each of these objects is hypothesized as accounting for the high speed of the corresponding object, and as representing an example of the "speed(X, high)" concept (see bottom of Figure 1.6). The hypothesized concept examples are inductively generalized to the rule

speed(X, high) :– processor(X, risc).; the speed of X is high if its processor is risc

which is applied deductively to infer "speed(proprinter01, high)".

It should also be noticed that the search for the properties of a given object in the KB is guided by schemas characterizing the general form of the rule to be learned, as described in Lee and Tecuci (1993).

1.4.2 Improvement of the KB

While there may be several justification trees for a given input, the attempt is to find the most simple and the most plausible one (Tecuci, 1993). This tree shows how a true statement *I* derives from other true statements from the KB. Based on Occam's razor (Blumer *et al.*, 1987), and on the general hypothesis used in abduction which states that the best explanation of a true statement is most likely to be true (Josephson, 1991), one could assume that all the inferences from the most simple and plausible justification tree are correct. With this assumption, the KB is extended by:

- Learning a new rule by empirical inductive generalization:

  speed(X, high) :– processor(X, risc).
  with the positive examples
  X = sun01. X = hp05. X = xerox01. X = proprinter01.

- Learning a new fact by analogy:

  runs(macII02, page-maker).

- Discovering positive examples of the determination rule, which is therefore reinforced:

  runs(X, Y) :~ os(X, Z).
  with the positive examples
  X = maclc03, Y = page-maker, Z = mac–os.
  X = macII02, Y = page-maker, Z = mac–os.

- Discovering positive examples of the four deductive rules used in building the plausible justification tree as, for instance:

  suitable(X, publishing) :–
  runs(X, publishing–sw), communicate(X, Y), isa(Y, high–quality–printer).
  with the positive example
  X = macII02, Y = proprinter01.

Therefore, the expert merely indicating a true statement allows the system to extend the KB by making several justified hypotheses. As a result of these extensions, the KB entails deductively "suitable(macII02, publishing)", while before this statement was only plausibly entailed.

During KB development, the rules are constantly updated so as to remain consistent with the accumulated examples. This is a type of incremental learning with full memory of past examples.

1.4.3 Reusing the reasoning process

As mentioned before, the input statement "suitable(macII02, publishing)" is representative for the kind of answers the final KB system should be able to generate. This means that the final KB system should be able to give other answers of the form "suitable(x, y)". It is therefore desirable to extend DC so as to include other such true statements, but also to correct DC so as no longer to include false statements of the same form.

Our method is based on the following general explanation-based approach to speed-up learning (Mitchell *et al.*, 1986; DeJong and Mooney, 1986). The system performs a complex reasoning process to solve some problem P. Then it determines a justified generalization of the reasoning process so as to speed up the process of solving similar problems P_i. When the system encounters such a similar problem, it will be able to find a solution just by instantiating this generalization.

The problem solved was the extension of the KB so as to deductively entail the statement "suitable(macII02, publishing)". This was achieved through a complex multitype inference process of building the plausible justification tree in Figure 1.4. This reasoning process is generalized by employing various types of generalization procedures (see Section 1.4.4), and then (during the experimentation phase) it is instantiated to various plausible justification trees which show how statements similar to "suitable(macII02, publishing)" are entailed by the KB. Each such plausible justification tree is then used to extend or correct the KB.

1.4.4 Multitype generalization

The plausible justification tree in Figure 1.4 is generalized by generalizing each implication and by globally unifying all these generalizations. The generalization of an implication depends on the type of inference made, as shown in Tecuci (1994). The system employs different types of generalizations (e.g. deductive generalizations, empirical inductive generalizations, generalizations based on different types of analogies, and, possibly, even generalizations based on abduction), as will be illustrated in the following sections.

1.4.4.1 Deductive generalization

A deductive implication is generalized to the deductive rule that generated it. This is a *deductive generalization*. For instance

```
suitable(macII02, publishing) :–
        runs(macII02, publishing–sw),
        communicate(macII02, proprinter01),
        isa(proprinter01, high–quality–printer).
```

is generalized to

```
suitable(X1, publishing) :–
        runs(X1, publishing–sw),
        communicate(X1, Y1),
        isa(Y1, high–quality–printer).
```

as shown in Figure 1.8. The other three deductive implications from the plausible justification tree in Figure 1.4 are replaced with their corresponding deductive rules, giving new names to the variables from these rules.

1.4.4.2 Generalization based on analogy

An analogical implication is generalized by considering the knowledge used to derive it. To illustrate this type of generalization let us consider again the analogical implication shown in Figure 1.4 and Figure 1.5. One could notice that the same kind of reasoning is valid for any machines Z3 and X3, as long as they have the same type of operating system T3, and Z3 runs the software U3. This general analogical reasoning process is illustrated in Figure 1.7. If one knows that "os(Z3, T3)", "os(X3, T3)", and "runs(Z3, U3)", then one may infer "runs(X3, U3)".

Consequently, one generalizes the analogical implication from Figure 1.4 to the general implication from the right side of Figure 1.7, as shown in Figure 1.8.

1.4.4.3 Empirical inductive generalization

An implication obtained through inductive prediction is generalized to the rule that produced it. Therefore, the predicted implication from Figure 1.4:

```
speed(proprinter01, high) :– processor(proprinter01, risc).
```

is generalized to

```
speed(Y6, high) :– processor(Y6, risc).
```

as shown in Figure 1.8.

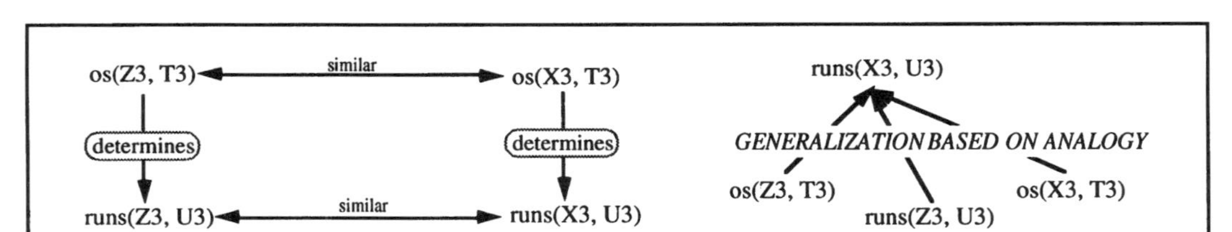

Figure 1.7 Generalization of the analogical reasoning illustrated in Figure 1.5

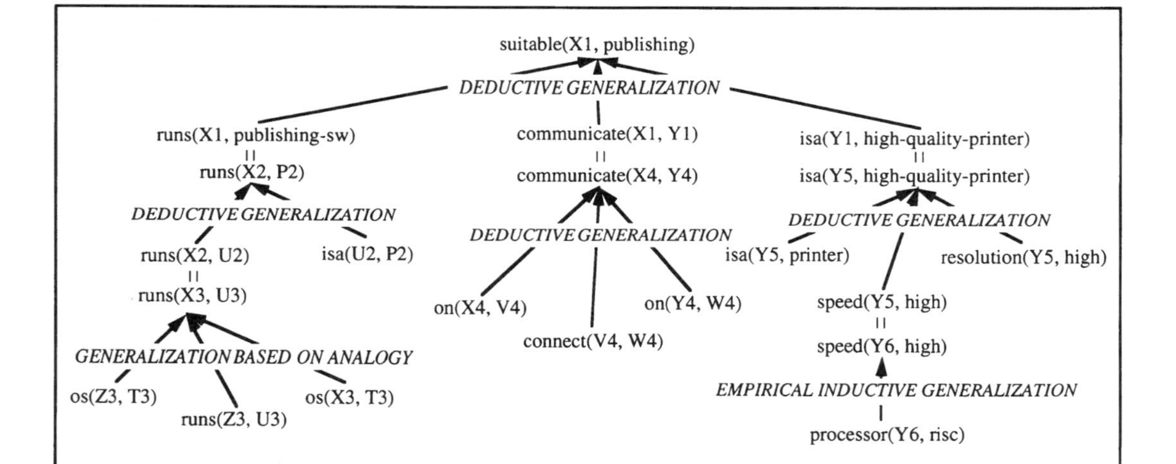

Figure 1.8 Explanation structure

1.4.4.4 Generalization of the plausible justification tree

The generalization of the implications from Figure 1.4 form the explanation structure from Figure 1.8. To transform this explanation structure into a general justification tree one has to determine the most general unification of the connection patterns, that is, one has to make identical the patterns connected by "||", as indicated in the following examples:

runs(X1, publishing–sw) X1 = X2, P2 = publishing–sw
||
runs(X2, P2)

runs(X2, U2) X2 = X3, U2 = U3
||
runs(X3, U3)

The most general unification is:

(X1 = X2 = X3 = X4, U2 = U3, Y1 = Y4 = Y5 = Y6, P2 = publishing–sw)

By applying this unification, and by renaming the variables so as to get rid of the numbers from their names, one obtains the general tree from Figure 1.9. This tree represents the most general plausible generalization of the justification tree from Figure 1.4.

1.4.5 An illustration of reusing a past reasoning process

The important feature of the general tree in Figure 1.9 is that it covers many of the plausible justification trees for statements of the form "suitable(X, publishing)". If, for instance, "sun01" is another computer for which the leaves of the plausible justification tree in Figure 1.9 are true, then the system will infer that "sun01" is also suitable for publishing, by simply instantiating the tree in Figure 1.9. The corresponding instance is the tree in Figure 1.10.

There are several things to notice when comparing the tree in Figure 1.4 with the tree in Figure 1.10:

- Although the structure of these trees and the corresponding predicates are identical (both being instances of the general tree in Figure 1.9), the arguments of the predicates are different and therefore the meaning of the trees is different.
- While the tree in Figure 1.4 was generated through a complex and time-consuming reasoning process, the generation of the tree in Figure 1.10 was a simple matching and instantiation process.
- Based on each of these trees the KB is improved in a similar way so as to

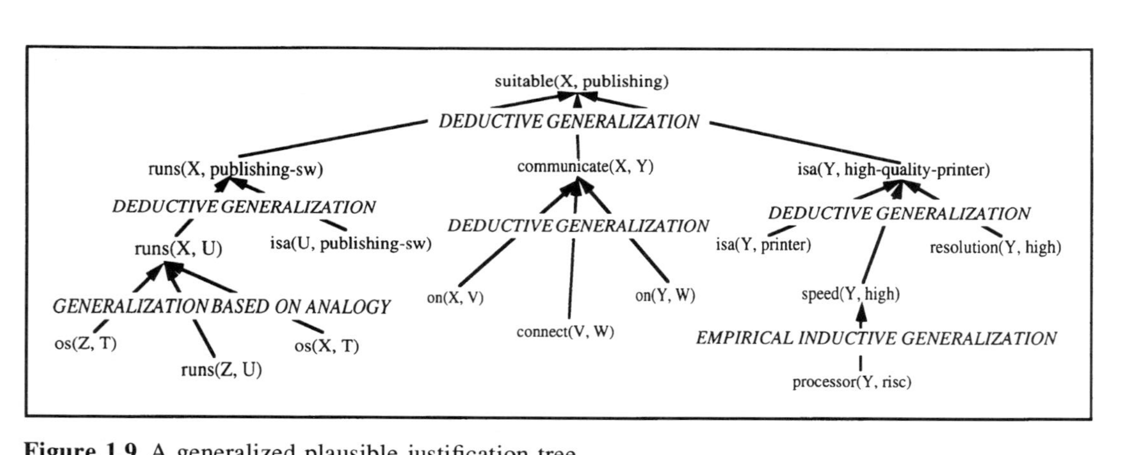

Figure 1.9 A generalized plausible justification tree

deductively entail the statement from the top of the tree (assuming that "suitable(sun01, publishing)" is also true).

As will be shown in Section 1.5.2, the expert confirmed that "suitable(sun01, publishing)" is true. Therefore, the KB is improved by:

- Discovering a new positive example of the empirically learned rule:

  speed(X, high) :– processor(X, risc).
  with the positive examples
  X = sun01. X = hp05. X = xerox01. X = proprinter01. X = microlaser03.

- Learning a new fact by analogy:

  runs(sun01, frame-maker).

- Discovering two new positive examples of the determination rule:

  runs(X, Y) :~ os(X, Z).
  With the positive examples
  X = maclc03, Y = page-maker, Z = mac–os.
  X = macII02, Y = page-maker, Z = mac–os.
  X = hp05, Y = frame-maker, Z = unix.
  X = sun01, Y = frame-maker, Z = unix.

- Discovering a new positive example of each of the four deductive rules used in building the plausible justification tree as, for instance:

  suitable(X, publishing) :–
  runs(X, publishing–sw),communicate(X, Y), isa(Y, high–quality–printer).
  with the positive examples
  X = macII02, Y = proprinter01.
  X = sun01, Y = microlaser03.

1.5 Experimentation, verification and repair

Building the plausible justification tree from Figure 1.4 and its generalization from Figure 1.9 was the first phase of the KB development process described in Figure 1.2. The next phase is one of experimentation, verification and repair. In this phase, the system will generate plausible justification trees like the one in Figure 1.10, by matching the leaves of the tree in Figure 1.9, with the facts from the KB. These trees show how statements of the form "suitable(X, publishing)"

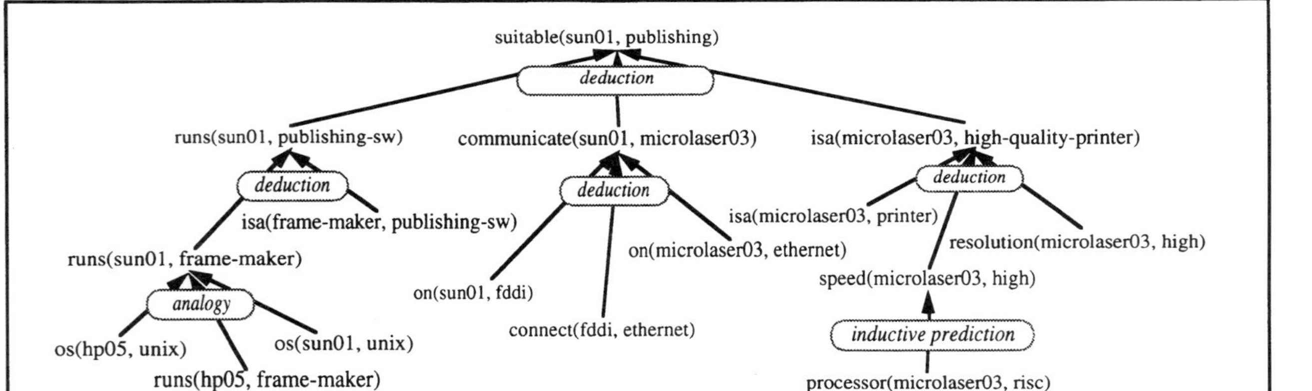

Figure 1.10 An instance of the plausible justification tree in Figure 1.9, justifying that sun01 is suitable for publishing

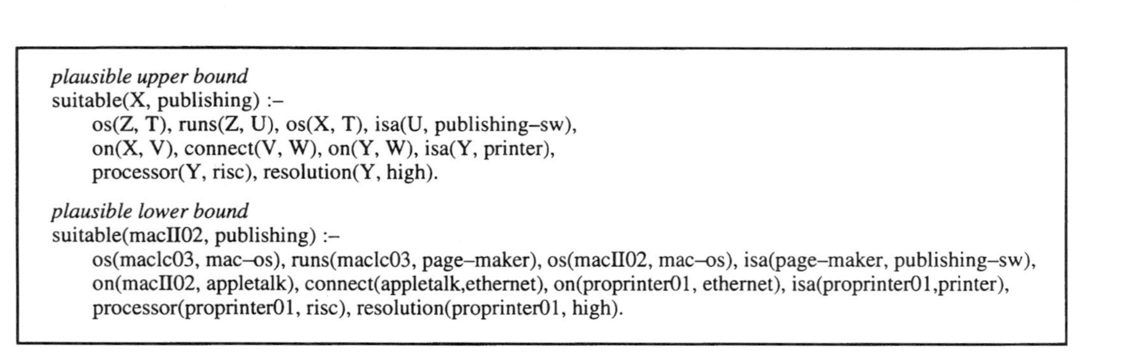

plausible upper bound
suitable(X, publishing) :–
os(Z, T), runs(Z, U), os(X, T), isa(U, publishing–sw),
on(X, V), connect(V, W), on(Y, W), isa(Y, printer),
processor(Y, risc), resolution(Y, high).

plausible lower bound
suitable(macII02, publishing) :–
os(maclc03, mac–os), runs(maclc03, page–maker), os(macII02, mac–os), isa(page–maker, publishing–sw),
on(macII02, appletalk), connect(appletalk,ethernet), on(proprinter01, ethernet), isa(proprinter01,printer),
processor(proprinter01, risc), resolution(proprinter01, high).

Figure 1.11 The plausible version space (PVS)

plausibly derive from the KB. Each such statement is shown to the expert who is asked if it is true or false. Then, the system (with the expert's help) will update the KB such that it will deductively entail the true statements and only them.

1.5.1 Control of the experimentation

The experimentation phase is controlled by a heuristic search in a plausible version space (PVS) which limits significantly the number of experiments needed to improve the KB (Tecuci, 1992). In the case of the considered example, the plausible version space is defined by the trees in Figure 1.4 and Figure 1.9, and is represented in Figure 1.11. The plausible upper bound of the PVS is a rule the left-hand side of which is the top of the general tree in Figure 9, and the right-hand side of which is the conjunction of the leaves of the same tree. The plausible lower bound of the PVS is a similar rule corresponding to the tree in Figure 4. We call these bounds plausible because they are only approximations of the real bounds (Tecuci, 1992). The plausible upper bound rule is supposed to be more general than the correct rule for inferring "suitable(X, publishing)", and the plausible lower bound rule is supposed to be less general than this rule.

The plausible version space in Figure 1.11 synthesizes some of the inferential capabilities of the system with respect to the statements of the form "suitable(X, publishing)". This version space corresponds to the version space in Figure 1.1, as indicated in Figure 1.12. The set of instances of the plausible upper bound corresponds to PC, the set of instances of the plausible lower bound corresponds to DC, and the set of instances of the correct rule corresponds to AC.

The plausible version space in Figure 1.11 is re-expressed in the equivalent, but more operational form from Figure 1.13. This new representation consists of a single rule the right-hand side of which (i.e. the condition) is a plausible version space. The left-hand side of the rule in Figure 13 together with the plausible upper bound of the right-hand side condition is the same with the plausible upper bound rule in Figure 1.11 (note that the statements of the form "isa(Q, something)" are

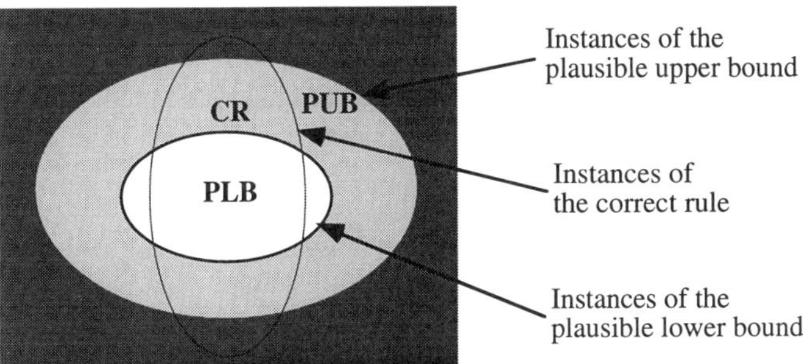

Figure 1.12 Plausible version space of a rule for inferring "suitable(X, publishing)"

```
suitable(X, publishing) :–

    plausible upper bound
      isa(T, something), isa(U, publishing–sw), isa(V, something), isa(W, something), isa(X, something),
      isa(Y, printer), isa(Z, something), os(Z, T), runs(Z, U), os(X, T), on(X, V), connect(V, W), on(Y, W),
      processor(Y, risc), resolution(Y, high).

    plausible lower bound
      isa(T, mac–os), isa(U, publishing–sw), isa(V, appletalk), isa(W, ethernet), isa(X, macII02),
      isa(Y, printer), isa(Z, maclc03), os(Z, T), runs(Z, U), os(X, T), on(X, V), connect(V, W), on(Y, W),
      processor(Y, risc), resolution(Y, high).

with the positive example
    T=mac–os, U=page–maker, V=appletalk, W=ethernet, X=macII02, Y=proprinter01, Z=maclc03.
```

Figure 1.13 Equivalent form of the plausible version space in Figure 1.11

```
suitable(sun01, publishing) :–
   isa(unix, something), isa(frame–maker, publishing-sw), isa(fddi, something), isa(ethernet, something),
   isa(sun01, something), isa(microlaser03, printer), isa(hp05, something), os(hp05, unix),
   runs(hp05, frame–maker), os(sun01, unix), on(sun01, fddi), connect(fddi, ethernet), on(microlaser03, ethernet),
   processor(microlaser03, risc), resolution(microlaser03, high).
```

Figure 1.14 An instance of the upper bound of the plausible version space in Figure 1.13

always true). The left-hand side of the rule in Figure 1.13, together with the plausible lower bound of the right-hand side condition and the instantiations of the variables of this condition indicated at the bottom of Figure 1.13, is the same as the plausible lower bound rule in Figure 1.11.

The version space in Figure 1.13 serves both for generating statements of the form "suitable(X, publishing)", and for determining the end of the experimentation phase. To generate such a statement, the system looks into the KB for an instance of the upper bound which is not an instance of the lower bound. Such an instance is the once from Figure 1.14.

Based on this instance, the system generates an instance of the general tree in Figure 1.9 which shows how "suitable(sun01, publishing)" is plausibly entailed by the KB. This is precisely the tree in Figure 1.10. The expert is asked if "suitable(sun01, publishing)" is true or false, and the KB is updated accordingly to the expert's answer, as shown in the following sections.

During experimentation, the lower bound of the plausible version space in Figure 1.13 is generalized so as to cover the generated statements accepted by the expert (the positive examples), and the upper bound (and, possibly, even the lower bound) is specialized so as to no longer cover the generated statements rejected by the expert (the negative examples). This process will end in one of the following situations:

- The bounds of the plausible version space become identical.
- The bounds are not identical, but the KB no longer contains any instance of the upper bound which is not an instance of the lower bound. Therefore, no new statement of the form "suitable(X, publishing)" can be generated.

1.5.2 The case of a true statement that is plausibly entailed by the KB

Because the expert accepted "suitable(sun01, publishing)" as a true statement, the KB and the plausible version space are updated as follows:

- The KB is extended so as to deductively entail "suitable(sun01, publishing)".
- The plausible lower bound of the PVS is conjunctively generalized to "cover" the leaves of the tree in Figure 1.10.

The extensions of the KB are similar to those made for the expert's initial input "suitable(macII02, publishing)", as shown in Section 1.4.5.

The plausible lower bound of the PVS is generalized as shown in Figure 1.15. For instance, "isa(T, mac–os)" and "isa(T, unix)" are generalized to "isa(T, op-system)", according to the generalization hierarchy in Figure 1.3.

suitable(X, publishing) :–

plausible upper bound

isa(T, something), isa(U, publishing–sw), isa(V, something), isa(W, something), isa(X, something), isa(Y, printer), isa(Z, something), os(Z, T), runs(Z, U), os(X, T), on(X, V), connect(V, W), on(Y, W), processor(Y, risc), resolution(Y, high).

plausible lower bound

isa(T, op–system), isa(U, publishing–sw), isa(V, network), isa(W, ethernet), isa(X, workstation), isa(Y, printer), isa(Z, workstation), os(Z, T), runs(Z, U), os(X, T), on(X, V), connect(V, W), on(Y, W), processor(Y, risc), resolution(Y, high).

with the positive example

T=mac–os, U=page–maker, V=appletalk, W=ethernet, X=macII02, Y=proprinter01, Z=maclc03.
T=unix, U=frame–maker, V=fddi, W=ethernet, X=sun01, Y=microlaser03, Z=hp05.

Figure 1.15 Updated plausible version space (PVS)

1.5.3 The case of a false statement that is plausibly entailed by the KB

Let us also consider the case of a system-generated statement which is rejected by the expert:

"suitable(macplus07, publishing)"

The corresponding plausible justification tree is shown in Figure 1.16. This tree was obtained by instantiating the general tree in Figure 1.9 with facts from the KB. It shows how a false statement is plausibly entailed by the KB. In such a case one has to detect the wrong implication(s) and to correct them, as well as to update the KB, the general justification tree in Figure 1.9, and the plausible version space in Figure 1.15 such that:

- The tree in Figure 1.16 is no longer a plausible justification tree.
- The KB does not entail deductively "suitable(macplus07, publishing)".
- The updated general justification tree no longer covers the tree in Figure 1.16.
- The plausible upper bound of the PVS no longer covers the leaves of the tree in Figure 1.16.

1.5.3.1 Identification of the wrong implication

Detecting the wrong implication from the plausible justification tree in Figure 1.16 is an intrinsically difficult problem for an autonomous learning system. One possible solution, which is presented in Tecuci (1993), is to blame the implication which is the least plausible, and the correction of which requires the smallest change in the KB. For a human expert, however, it should not be too difficult to identify the wrong implication and even to find the explanation of the failure, as shown in Tecuci (1992).

In the case of the tree in Figure 1.16, the wrong implication could be identified by the expert as being the deduction from the top of the tree. Although "macplus07" runs publishing software and communicates with a high-quality printer, it is not suitable for publishing because it does not have a large display.

1.5.3.2 Updating the KB, the plausible justification tree and the plausible version space

The rule which generated the wrong implication is specialized as indicated in Figure 1.17 (requiring X to have a large display). The predicate "display(X, Y)" could be defined by the expert, or could be suggested by the system as being a predicate which could distinguish the known positive examples of the rule from the discovered negative example. This process is described in Section 1.6.

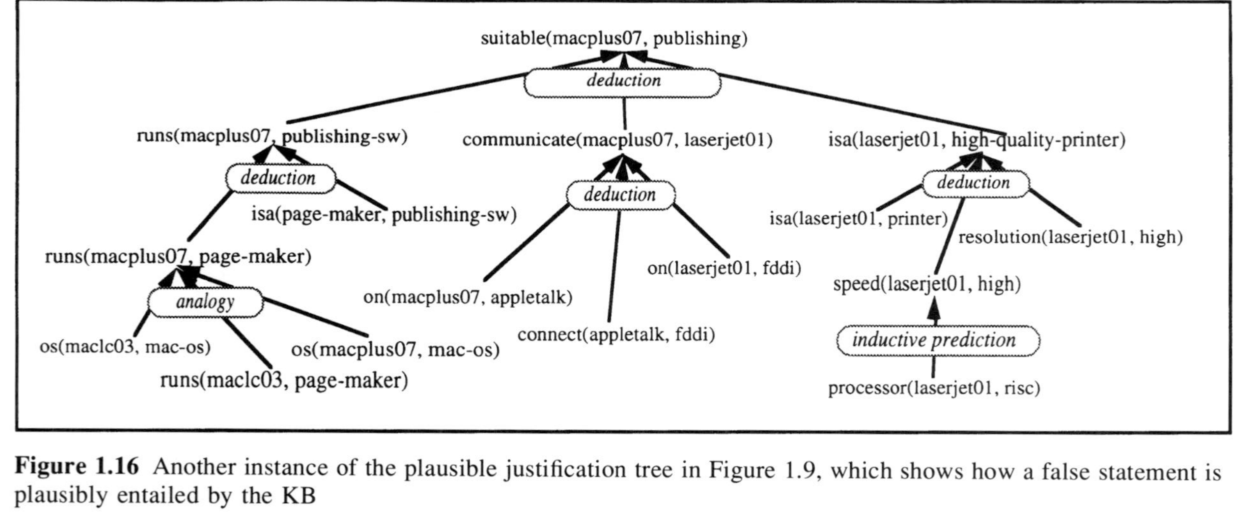

Figure 1.16 Another instance of the plausible justification tree in Figure 1.9, which shows how a false statement is plausibly entailed by the KB

Wrong implication:

suitable(macplus07, publishing) :–
  runs(macplus07, publishing–sw), communicate(macplus07, laserjet01), isa(laserjet01, high–quality–printer).

Rule which generated the wrong implication:

suitable(X, publishing) :–
  runs(X, publishing–sw), communicate(X, Y), isa(Y, high–quality–printer).
with the positive examples
  X=macII02, Y=proprinter01.   X=sun01, Y=microlaser03.

Updated rule:

suitable(X, publishing) :–
  runs(X, publishing–sw), <u>display(X, large),</u> communicate(X, Y), isa(Y, high–quality–printer).
with the positive examples
  X=macII02, Y=proprinter01.   X=sun01, Y=microlaser03.
with the negative example
  X=macplus07, Y=laserjet01.

Figure 1.17 Improving a rule based on a negative example

As a result of rule updating shown in Figure 1.17, the general plausible justification tree in Figure 1.9 is updated as shown in Figure 1.18, and the version space is updated as shown in Figure 1.19, by adding the predicate "display(X, large)".

Although the expert may easily identify the wrong implication, it is not as easy for him/her to identify the problem with a wrong implication. When the problem cannot be identified, the wrong implication is kept as a negative exception of the rule which generated it, as shown in Figure 1.20.

1.6 Consistency-driven knowledge elicitation

Because the KB is incomplete and partially incorrect, some of the learned knowledge pieces may be inconsistent (i.e. may cover negative examples), as illustrated in Figure 1.20. In order to remove such inconsistencies, additional knowledge pieces (which may represent new terms in the representation language of the system) are elicited from the expert, through several consistency-driven knowledge elicitation methods, as described in Tecuci and Hieb (1994). These methods are applied in the third phase of KB development, as shown in Figure 1.2. They will be briefly described with the help of the case of the inconsistent rule in Figure 1.20.

1.6.1 Consistency-driven property elicitation

A negative exception of a rule may be eliminated by identifying (or defining) a new object feature that discriminates between all the covered positive examples and the negative exception.

Let us consider, for instance, the rule in Figure 1.20 that has the covered positive examples represented by

(X = macII02, Y = proprinter01)
(X = sun01, Y = microlaser03)

and the negative exception represented by

(X = macplus07, Y = laserjet01)

To eliminate the negative exception of the rule, the system will look into the KB for a predicate which could characterize all the positive instances of X ("macII02" and "sun01"), without characterizing the negative exception of X ("macplus07"). If this search is not successful, the system will attempt to elicit such a property from the expert. Alternatively, the system may try to find or elicit

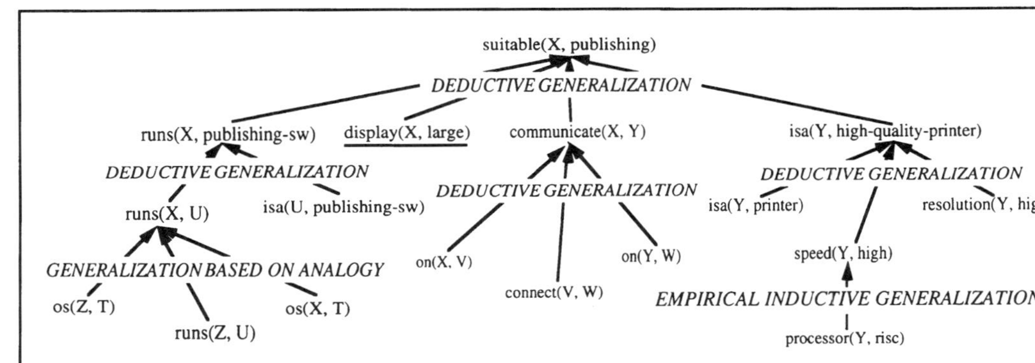

Figure 1.18 Updated general justification tree

suitable(X, publishing) :–

plausible upper bound
isa(T, something), isa(U, publishing–sw), isa(V, something), isa(W, something), isa(X, something), isa(Y, printer), isa(Z, something), os(Z, T), runs(Z, U), os(X, T), display(X, large), on(X, V), connect(V, W), on(Y, W), processor(Y, risc), resolution(Y, high).

plausible lower bound
isa(T, op–system), isa(U, publishing–sw), isa(V, network), isa(W, ethernet), isa(X, workstation), isa(Y, printer), isa(Z, workstation), os(Z, T), runs(Z, U), os(X, T), display(X, large), on(X, V), connect(V, W), on(Y, W), processor(Y, risc), resolution(Y, high).

with the positive examples
T=mac–os, U=page–maker, V=appletalk, W=ethernet, X=macII02, Y=proprinter01, Z=maclc03.
T=unix, U=frame–maker, V=fddi, W=ethernet, X=sun01, Y=microlaser03, Z=hp05.

with the negative example
T=mac–os, U=page–maker, V=appletalk, W=fddi, X=macplus07, Y=laserjet01, Z=maclc03.

Figure 1.19 Updated plausible version space

```
suitable(X, publishing) :–
    runs(X, publishing–sw), communicate(X, Y), isa(Y, high–quality–printer).
```

with the positive examples
X=macII02, Y=proprinter01.
X=sun01, Y=microlaser03.

with the negative exception
X=macplus07, Y=laserjet01.

Figure 1.20 A rule with a negative exception

a property of the positive instances of Y ("proprinter01", "microlaser03"), which is not a property of the negative exception of Y ("laserjet01").

More specifically:

- The system may look in the KB for a property of "macII02" that may be a property of "sun01" (i.e. the KB does not deductively imply that "sun01" does not have this property) without being a property of "macplus07".
- Or, it may look for a property of "sun01" that may be property of "macII02" without being a property of "macplus07".
- Or, it may look for a property of "proprinter01" that may be property of "microlaser03" without being a property of "laserjet01".
- Or, it may look for a property of "microlaser03" that may be property of "proprinter01" without being a property of "laserjet01".

An illustration of this property transfer dialogue is shown in Table 1.1. In this and the subsequent examples the expert's answers are shown in italics.

As a result of this dialogue, the system has found the property "display(X, large)" which discriminates between the covered positive examples of the rule in Figure 1.20 and its negative exception. By introducing the discriminating property into the rule's condition, the negative exception is no longer covered.

Another result of the above dialogue is that the descriptions of "macII02" and

Table 1.1 Sample of a dialogue for property transfer

I know that "display(sun01, large)".

Is it true that "display(macII02, large)" ? [Yes/No/Irrelevant] *Yes*

This means that "display(X, large)" is a property characterizing all the covered positive examples and may distinguish them from the negative exception.

Is it false that "display(macplus07, large)" ? *Yes*

Table 1.2 Sample of a dialogue for property elicitation

Consider the following groups of objects X: {macII02, sun01} Y: {macplus01} in the context of the following rule suitable(X, publishing) :– runs(X, publishing–sw), communicate(X, Y), isa(Y, high–quality–printer). Could you think of some property that discriminates the objects {macII02, sun01} from the object macplus01 [Yes/No]: *Yes* Describe this property for each object that it applies to: *display(macII02, large)* *display(sun01, large)* *display(macplus01, small)*

"macplus07" are refined by adding the transferred property. This is a case of consistency-driven property transfer from one concept ("sun01") to other concepts ("macII02" and "macplus07"). It is not unusual for an expert to define a property of an object, but then to fail to specify it when describing a related object. With the method presented above, the system may discover and repair such cases of incomplete knowledge.

It may also happen that the system cannot find a property to transfer. In such a case, it will try to elicit a new property by using a technique similar to the triad method employed in the elicitation of the repertory grids (Shaw and Gaines, 1987; Boose and Bradshaw, 1988). If the KB in Figure 1.3 does not contain the property "display(sun01, large)", the dialogue for eliciting a new property would be as shown in Table 1.2.

1.6.2 Consistency-driven relationship elicitation

A second method for removing the negative exception from the rule in Figure 1.20 is to look for a relationship between X and Y which could characterize all the positive instances of X and Y, without characterizing the negative exception. That is, the system will look for a relationship between "macII02" and "proprinter01" which could also hold between "sun01" and "microlaser03", without holding between "macplus07" and "laserjet01". Or, it could look for a relationship between "sun01" and "microlaser03" which could also hold between "macII02" and "proprinter01", without holding between "macplus07" and "laserjet01". Or it could try to elicit such a relationship from the expert.

1.6.3 Consistency-driven concept elicitation

The third method for removing the negative exception from the rule in Figure 1.20 is similar to the one described in Wrobel (1989). It consists of trying to elicit a new concept that covers all the positive instances of X ("macII02" and "sun01") without covering the negative exception of X ("macplus07"). Alternatively, one could try to elicit a concept that covers all the positive instances of Y ("proprinter01" and "microlaser03") without covering the negative exception of Y ("laserjet01").

1.7 Conclusions

We have presented a methodology for building KB systems for a general inference engine. This methodology, which integrates multistrategy learning, active experimentation, and guided knowledge elicitation, emerged from two related research directions:

- The knowledge acquisition methodology of Disciple (Tecuci, 1988; Tecuci and Kodratoff, 1990) and NeoDisciple (Tecuci, 1992; Tecuci and Hieb, 1994).
- The multistrategy task-adaptive learning method based on plausible justification trees MTL-JT (Tecuci, 1993, 1994).

On the one hand, it extends Disciple and NeoDisciple with respect to the knowledge representation used and the types of inference and generalization methods employed; on the other hand, it adapts and integrates the MTL-JT method into an interactive knowledge-acquisition scenario.

One important feature of the presented methodology is the use of plausible justification trees which dynamically integrate the elementary inferences employed by the single-strategy learning methods (such as deduction, analogy, abduction, generalization, specialization, abstraction and concreation), depending on the system's knowledge and the system's input. This allows the system to learn as much as possible from every input received from the human expert, generating by itself much of the knowledge needed to develop the KB. It is very similar in spirit to the knowledge acquisition methodology of Gil and Paris (1995) where much of the knowledge needed by the system is derived by analogy with the existing knowledge. This feature of our methodology provides it with a significant advantage over the traditional manual knowledge acquisition methods in which the expert provides all the needed knowledge to the system. It is also important to stress that the plausible justification tree itself represents a general framework for integrating a whole range of inference types (Tecuci, 1993). Therefore, theoretically, there is no limit with respect to the type or number of inferences employed in building such a tree.

Another important feature of the methodology is the employment of different types of generalizations. The current machine-learning research distinguishes only between deductive generalizations and inductive generalizations. Our research shows that one could make much finer distinctions by associating a specific generalization with each type of inference as, for instance, a generalization based on analogy. The generalization of an inference process synthesizes the assumptions supporting the inference and may therefore allow reusing that inference process in new situations. This feature is exploited by our methodology, which reuses the KB development processes, and is therefore very efficient.

The efficiency of the presented methodology is also due to the use of simple plausible version spaces and a human guided heuristic search of these spaces. The concept of plausible version space is both a generalization and an operationalization of the classical version space concept introduced by Mitchell (1978).

Finally, this methodology is based on a cooperation between a learning system and a human expert in which the learner performs most of the tasks and the expert helps it in solving the problems that are intrinsically difficult for a learner and relatively easy for an expert. In particular, the expert solves the blame assignment problem, as illustrated in Section 1.5.3, and the new terms problem, as illustrated in Section 1.6.

There are also several ways in which the presented methodology could be improved. First of all, the set of inferences involved is quite limited (deduction, determination-based analogy, inductive prediction, and abduction). New types of inference should be included, as well as more complex versions of the current ones. Consequently, new types of justified generalizations, corresponding to these new types of inference, should also be defined. Another issue is to determine a good measure for comparing the plausibility of different justification trees, so that the system only hypothesizes the most plausible knowledge.

The consistency-driven knowledge elicitation methods briefly presented in Section 1.6 could be extended so as, not only to add new concepts and relationships into the KB, but also to delete those that become unnecessary.

Another future research direction consists in developing a qualitative representation of the certainty of the knowledge pieces from the KB (e.g. some facts are characterized as true by the expert, while others are hypothesized as true by the system, some rules are initially defined by the expert, while others are learned by the system). In particular, one has to be able to estimate the confidence in the learned rules, to update the confidence of a rule when new examples or exceptions are discovered, as well as to maintain only a limited number of "representative" examples of a rule (during KB development) so as neither to overload the system, nor to lose important information.

Acknowledgements

David Duff contributed to the development of the application domain presented in this chapter.

References

Blumer, A., Ehrenfeucht, A., Haussler, D. and Warmuth, M. K. (1987). Occam's razor. *Information Processing Letters*, 24: 377–380.

Boose, J. H. and Bradshaw, J. M. (1988). Expertise transfer and complex problems: using AQUINAS as a knowledge-acquisition workbench for knowledge-based systems. In Boose, J. and Gaines, B. (editors), *Knowledge Acquisition Tools for Expert Systems*. Academic Press, London.

Buchanan, B. G. and Wilkins, D. C. (editors) (1992). *Readings in Knowledge Acquisition and Learning: Automating the Construction and Improvement of Expert Systems*. Morgan Kaufmann, San Mateo, CA.

Carbonell, J. G. (1986). Derivational analogy: a theory of reconstructive problem solving and expertise acquisition. In Michalski, R. S., Carbonell, J. G. and Mitchell T. M. (editors), *Machine Learning: An Artificial Intelligence Approach*, volume 2. Morgan Kaufmann, San Mateo, CA.

Collins, A. and Michalski, R. S. (1989). The logic of plausible reasoning: a core theory. *Cognitive Science*, 13: 1–49.

Davies, T. R. and Russell, S. J. (1987). A logical approach to reasoning by analogy, *Proc. IJCAI*, Milan, Italy. Morgan Kaufmann, San Mateo, CA.

DeJong, G. and Mooney R. (1986). Explanation-based learning: an alternative view. *Machine Learning*, 1: 145–176.

Gaines, B. R. and Boose, J. H. (editors) (1988). *Knowledge Acquisition for Knowledge Based Systems*. Academic Press, London.

Gammack, J. G. (1987). Different techniques and different aspects to declarative knowledge. In Alison L. Kidd (editor), *Knowledge Acquisition for Expert Systems: A Practical Handbook*. Plenum Press, New York.

Gentner, D. (1990). The mechanisms of analogical reasoning. In Shavlik, J. W. and Dietterich, T. G. (editors), *Readings in Machine Learning*. Morgan Kaufmann, San Mateo, CA.

Gil, Y. and Paris, C. (1995). Towards method-independent knowledge acquisition. In Tecuci, G. and Kodratoff, Y. (editors), *Machine Learning and Knowledge Acquisition: Integrated Approaches*. Academic Press, London.

Josephson, J. (1991). Abduction: conceptual analysis of a fundamental pattern of inference, *Research Report 91–JJ*, Laboratory for AI Research, Ohio State University.

Lee, O. and Tecuci, G. (1993). MTLS: an inference-based multistrategy learning system. In *Proc. InfoScience 93*, Korea, October 21–22.

Mitchell, T. M. (1978). Version spaces: an approach to concept learning, *Doctoral Dissertation*, Stanford University.

Mitchell, T. M., Keller, T. and Kedar-Cabelli, S. (1986). Explanation-based generalization: a unifying view. *Machine Learning*, 1: 47–80.

Quinlan, J. R. (1986). Induction of decision trees, *Machine Learning*, 1: 81–106.

Shavlik, J. and Dietterich, T. (editors) (1990). *Readings in Machine Learning*. Morgan Kaufmann, San Mateo, CA.

Shaw, M. L. G. and Gaines, B. R. (1987). An interactive knowledge elicitation technique using personal construct technology. In Kidd A. L. (editor), *Knowledge Acquisition for Expert Systems: A Practical Handbook*. Plenum Press, New York.

Tecuci, G. (1988). Disciple: a theory, methodology, and system for learning expert knowledge, *PhD. Thesis*, University of Paris–South.

Tecuci, G. (1991). A multistrategy learning approach to domain modeling and knowledge acquisition. In Kodratoff Y. (editor), *Machine Learning EWSL-91*. Springer-Verlag, New York.

Tecuci, G. (1992). Automating knowledge acquisition as extending, updating, and improving a knowledge base. *IEEE Trans. on Systems, Man and Cybernetics*, 22: 1444–1460.

Tecuci, G. (1993). Plausible justification trees: a framework for the deep and dynamic integration of learning strategies. *Machine Learning*, 11: 237–261.

Tecuci, G. (1994). An inference-based framework for multistrategy learning. In Michalski, R. S. and Tecuci G. (editors), *Machine Learning: A Multistrategy Approach*, vol. 4. Morgan Kaufmann, San Mateo, CA.

Tecuci, G. and Duff, D. (1994). A framework for knowledge base refinement through multistrategy learning and knowledge acquisition. *Knowledge Acquisition Journal*, 6: 137–162.

Tecuci, G. and Hieb, M. (1994). Consistency-driven knowledge elicitation: using a learning-oriented knowledge representation that supports knowledge elicitation in NeoDisciple. *Knowledge Acquisition Journal*, 6: 23–46.

Tecuci, G. and Kodratoff, Y. (1990). Apprenticeship learning in imperfect theory domains. In Kodratoff, Y. and Michalski, R. S. (editors), *Machine Learning: An Artificial Intelligence Approach*, Vol. 3. Morgan Kaufmann, San Mateo, CA.

Tecuci, G., Hieb, M. H. and Dybala, T. (1995). Building an adaptive agent to monitor and repair the electrical power system of an orbital satellite. In *Proceedings of the Goddard Conference on Space Applications of Artificial Intelligence and Emerging Information Technologies, NASA Goddard*, Greenbelt, Maryland, May.

Tecuci, G., Hieb, M. H., Hille, D. and Pullen, J. M. (1994). Building adaptive autonomous agents for adversarial domains. In *Proceedings of the AAAI Fall Symposium on Planning and Learning*, November, New Orleans.

Winston, P.H. (1980). Learning and reasoning by analogy. *Communications of the ACM*, Vol. 23.

Wrobel, S. (1989). Demand-driven concept formation. In Morik, K. (editor), *Knowledge Representation and Organization in Machine Learning*. Springer Verlag, New York.

CHAPTER 2

Increasing levels of assistance in refinement of knowledge-based retrieval systems

Catherine Baudin, Smadar Kedar and Barney Pell

Abstract

This chapter is concerned with the task of incrementally acquiring and refining the knowledge and algorithms of a knowledge-based system in order to improve its performance over time. In particular, we present the design of DE-KART, a tool whose goal is to provide increasing levels of assistance in acquiring and refining indexing and retrieval knowledge for a knowledge-based retrieval system. DE-KART starts with knowledge that has been entered manually, and increases its level of assistance in acquiring and refining that knowledge, both in terms of the increased level of *automation* in interacting with users, and in terms of the increased *generality* of the knowledge. DE-KART is at the intersection of machine learning and knowledge acquisition: it is a first step towards a system which moves along a continuum from interactive knowledge acquisition to increasingly automated machine learning as it acquires more knowledge and experience.

Keywords: Conceptual indexing, conceptual information retrieval, increasing levels of assistance, inductive learning, knowledge acquisition, knowledge-based retrieval, incremental indexing, incremental knowledge refinement.

2.1 Introduction and motivation

Knowledge-based conceptual retrieval systems assist users in retrieving information stored in a conceptual rather than literal form. These systems use models of a document's content to index the information, and use a reasoning component to search and retrieve information related to a user's query. Such systems need to interact with users at every stage of their life-cycle. First, system builders interact

Machine Learning and Knowledge Acquisition
ISBN 0-12-685120-4

with a bare-bones system in order to encode and debug the algorithms and heuristics which perform the retrieval task. Then, knowledge engineers encode and refine the domain knowledge. Finally, end-users interact with the system as it performs the retrieval task.

As in most realistic knowledge-based systems, the algorithms, heuristics and domain knowledge initially built into the system may be incomplete or incorrect. If the system operates incorrectly during system testing and operation (e.g. the wrong information is retrieved, or existing information is not found), the end-user may provide feedback on the failure. The knowledge engineer and system designer then need to diagnose the failure and refine the knowledge, heuristics or algorithms to improve the system's behaviour. Such a system refinement cycle never ceases – it is done incrementally over the life of a knowledge-based retrieval system.

In order to perform system refinement more precisely and efficiently, there is a need for tools that provide assistance throughout the life of the system. These tools should be able to monitor the performance of the task during operation; detect which portions of the knowledge are responsible for faulty behaviour; and assist the knowledge engineers and system builders in refining the knowledge and algorithms to improve performance over time.

In this chapter we present the design of such a knowledge acquisition and refinement tool, DE-KART (for DEDAL Knowledge Acquisition and Refinement Tool). It is designed to assist DEDAL (Baudin *et al.*, 1992a), a knowledge-based conceptual retrieval system currently applied to documents of mechanical engineering design. DE-KART is a tool at the intersection of machine learning and knowledge acquisition. Instead of performing acquisition and refinement at one endpoint of the spectrum or the other – that is, totally automated or totally interactive – DE-KART is a first step towards a system which moves along a continuum from interactive to increasingly automated, as the system acquires more knowledge and experience. We call this movement *increasing levels of assistance*. What the user does manually at one level, the system provides assistance and suggestions for at the next level of assistance, and performs some of the task more automatically at yet a higher level. A level of assistance is measured by the level of *generality* of the knowledge acquired, and by the level of *automation* provided by the system to acquire and refine the knowledge. The level of generality of the knowledge can range from project-specific knowledge to generic task knowledge, and the level of automation can range from totally manual to interactive to totally automated.

2.2 Acquisition and refinement of indexing knowledge: overview

The architecture of our system consists of two main components: the *performance system* DEDAL, and the *knowledge acquisition and refinement tool*, DE-KART.

Section 2.2.1 gives background on DEDAL, and Section 2.2.2 provides a sample of the user interaction with DEDAL and DE-KART. Section 2.2.3 presents the different types of indexing knowledge used by DEDAL to retrieve information. The rest of the chapter describes the knowledge acquisition and refinement task performed by DE-KART.

2.2.1 Background: document indexing and retrieval in DEDAL

DEDAL stores mechanical engineering design documents in the form of text, graphics and videotaped information such as meeting summaries, pages of a designer's notebook, technical reports, CAD drawings and videotaped conversations between designers. It uses a *conceptual* indexing and query language to describe the content and the form of design information. The query language is the same as the indexing language, and uses concepts from a *model* of the artifact being designed, and from a *task vocabulary* representing the classes of *topics* usually covered by design documents (Baya *et al.*, 1992; Baudin *et al.*, 1992a). A conceptual index can be seen as a structured entity consisting of two parts: the *body* of the index which represents the content of a piece of information, and the *reference* part that points to a region in a document. For instance: "The inner hub holds the steel friction disks and causes them to rotate" is part of a paragraph in page 20 of the record: report-333. It can be described by two indexing patterns:

<topic **function** subject **inner-hub** level-of-detail **configuration** medium **text** in-record **report-333** segment **20**>.

<topic **relation** subject **inner-hub** and **steel-friction-disks** level-of-detail **configuration** medium **text** in-record **report-333** segment **20**>.

The queries have the same structure as the body of an index and use the same vocabulary. A question such as: "How does the inner hub interact with the friction disks? " can be formulated in DEDAL's language as the query:

<get-information-about topic **relation** subject **inner-hub** and **steel-friction-disks** with preferred medium **equation**>.

For mechanical engineering design, the domain model includes aspects of the artifact structure, the requirements, the main design decisions and alternatives considered. The model (as illustrated in Figure 2.1) includes hierarchical relations such as *isa* and *part-of* that are used by DEDAL to match a query with a given index.

The retrieval module takes a query from the user as input, matches it to the set of conceptual indices and returns an ordered list of references related to the question. The retrieval proceeds in two steps: (1) **exact match**: find the indices that exactly match the query and return the associated list of references. If the exact match fails: (2) **heuristic match**: activate the *proximity retrieval heuristics*.

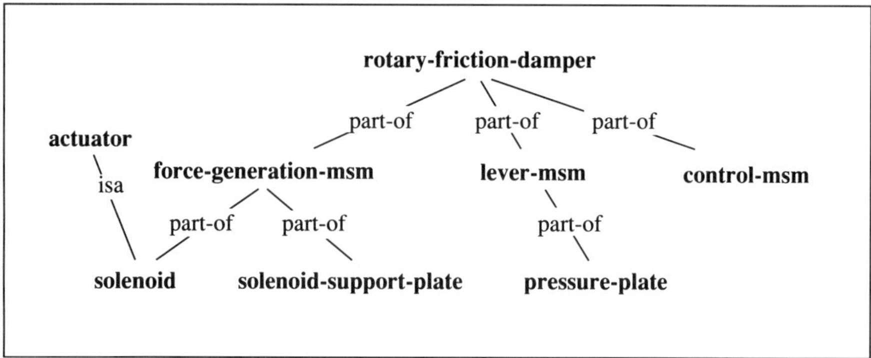

Figure 2.1 Part of the component hierarchy in the domain model

DEDAL currently uses 20 proximity retrieval heuristics to find related answers to a question. For instance, a heuristic may state that segments described by concepts like "*decision*" and "*alternative*" for a given part are likely to be located in nearby regions of the documentation. The retrieval procedure and the heuristics are described in Baudin *et al.* (1992b).

Each retrieval step returns a set of references ordered according to a set of priority criteria. The user selects a reference and goes to the corresponding segment of information.[1] If a user is not satisfied with the references retrieved he or she can request more information and force DEDAL to resume its search and retrieve another set of references.

2.2.2 A sample interaction with DEDAL and DE-KART

Initially both the domain knowledge and general retrieval heuristics are entered manually. Then, as the end-user queries the system to retrieve documents, he or she provides feedback to the system on the relevance of the documents retrieved. DE-KART, the knowledge acquisition component, monitors the different layers of knowledge involved in the retrieval. It assists the knowledge engineer in diagnosing and refining the knowledge, from the most specific document-dependent layer to the more general retrieval heuristics.

In this sample interaction, a mechanical engineering designer queries DEDAL to retrieve information about the "function of the solenoid", which is a sub-

[1] DEDAL communicates with a system with hypertext access to its text and graphic documents. Audio documents are accessible on a Sparc workstation. Video is not yet directly accessible, but indices to video clips are provided to the user who can then view the video on a separate device.

component of the "force generation mechanism" in the "rotary friction damper" (a kind of shock absorber), as illustrated in Figure 2.1.

DEDAL attempts to find an index matching the query. It cannot find an index that exactly matches the query, so it uses a proximity heuristic: "to find information about the *function* of a subcomponent, look for information about the *operation* of a mechanism that includes this component". Using this heuristic, the retrieval component assumes that the "function of the solenoid" might be documented in sections describing the "operation of the force generation mechanism". DEDAL presents the user with the retrieved information about the "operation of the force generation mechanism", and asks for feedback on whether or not the reference retrieved was relevant to the query.

If the user finds relevant information about the function of the solenoid, then the user's feedback is that the retrieved reference is *relevant*. Given a relevant reference, DE-KART automatically acquires a new index, associating the reference with the user's query (see Section 2.3).

After some time, the user may query the system to retrieve "the function of the lever mechanism", another subcomponent of the damper. Again, no direct index exists. DEDAL uses the same proximity heuristic once again, and retrieves a part of the document associated with the "operation of the damper", although this time the user cannot find information about the function of the level mechanism in that part of the document and provides feedback that this retrieval is *irrelevant*. No index is acquired.

After the system has been in operation for a while, some indices will fail to match a query more often than they succeed. DE-KART provides assistance to the knowledge engineer to re-prioritize, refine or even remove the offending indices. Similarly, after some time, some retrieval heuristics will prove to be more successful than others in retrieving relevant information in response to a query. Based on the monitoring information about the success and failure rates of the indices and the heuristics used to retrieve the information, DE-KART provides increasing levels of assistance to the knowledge engineer and the system builder to *detect* the parts of the knowledge that seem to fail, *diagnose* the causes of failure (incorrect index, unsuccessful heuristics, ill-formulated query), *refine* the offending knowledge, *validate* that the refinement in fact improves the retrieval performance over time, and continue to *incrementally refine* the knowledge until retrieval performance is satisfactory, according to some measure.

2.2.3 Types of indexing knowledge

As seen in Figure 2.2, knowledge in DEDAL exists at three levels of abstraction. At the top level are *task-dependent* retrieval heuristics. These heuristics are valid for the task of document retrieval in mechanical engineering. Below that are *domain-dependent* heuristics derived by applying task-dependent heuristics to particular user queries. These use terms defined within a specific domain

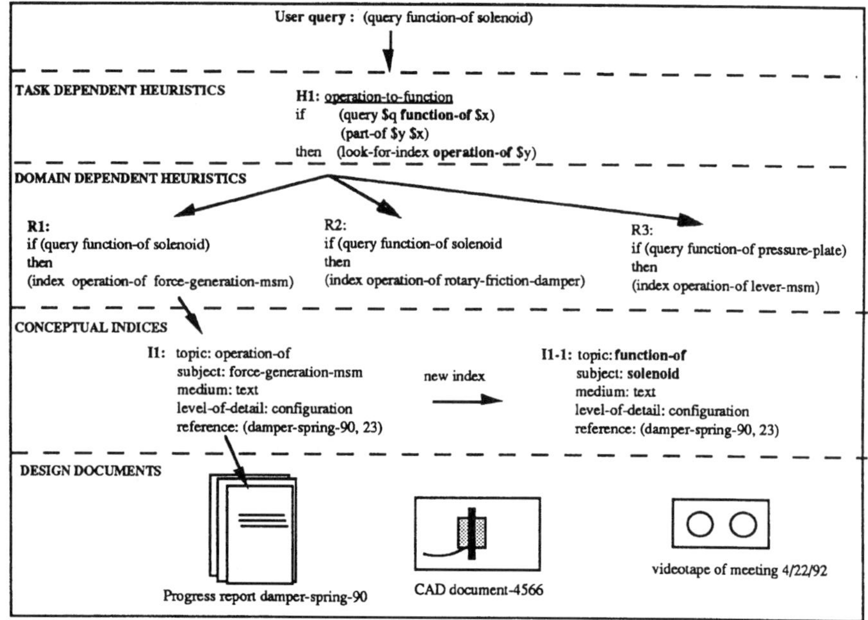

Figure 2.2 Three layers of indexing and retrieval knowledge in DEDAL

model, as seen in Figure 2.1. These domain-dependent heuristics match a user query with *document-dependent* conceptual indices. The following three sections show how these different levels of knowledge are acquired, used and refined.

2.3 Index acquisition and refinement

The conceptual indices are initially entered manually. The user poses queries, and the system uses its heuristic retrieval strategies to find a match between a query and a "related" index. After a successful retrieval, DE-KART updates the document descriptions by turning this query into a new index. This *query-based* index acquisition and refinement phase is described in more detail by Baudin *et al.* (1993). It is performed in six steps:

1. *Query formulation:* The end-user formulates a query using the conceptual language. For instance, "what is the function of the solenoid? " is translated as <topic **function** subject **solenoid**>.
2. *Information retrieval:* DEDAL searches for an index that exactly matches

the query. In this case, it does not find an exact match and applies a proximity heuristic to "guess" where the required information may be located. For instance, H1 (see Figure 2.2) states that any information describing the *operation* of a mechanism might also describe the *function* of its parts. Given that the solenoid is a subpart of the force-generation mechanism (Figure 2.1), it finds a more general index: "operation of the force-generation-msm".[2] In this case DEDAL found two pages describing the operation of the force generation mechanism, pointed to by indices I1 and I2 (only I1 is shown in the figure).

3. *Relevance feedback:* The user looks at the two references retrieved, finds that the reference pointed to by the index I1, page 23 in progress report damper-spring-90, describes the function of the solenoid, while the document associated with index I2, CAD document-4566, does not. The user rates the reference of I1 as *relevant* and the reference of I2 as *irrelevant*.
4. *Index generation:* Each time a reference is retrieved by the heuristic match and is rated relevant, DE-KART attaches the reference of the selected index to the query, turning the query into a new conceptual index. In this case DE-KART creates a new index I1-1 (see Figure 2.2). The system now knows that page 23 of progress report damper-spring-90 explicitly describes the function of the solenoid. Note that no new index was created for I2, as it was judged to be irrelevant. This process of index generation extends *relevance feedback* techniques (Salton and Buckley, 1990) to the acquisition of *conceptual* indices, and is described in more detail by Baudin *et al.* (1993).

   In addition, each time a heuristic is used to retrieve a reference, the system records the instance of the heuristic that was used. These *domain-dependent rules* are created by instantiating a generic heuristic with the arguments in the user query. In our example R1 is the domain-dependent rule used to retrieve the relevant reference pointed to by I1. It states that: "if a question is about the function of the solenoid, then look for indices about the operation of the force generation mechanism". In the figure, R2 and R3 are other instances of H1. This illustrates that domain-dependent rules are stored each time a heuristic is instantiated, whether or not their use led to relevant retrievals for the given query.
5. *Index monitoring:* After an index is created, the index and the heuristic used to create it are monitored for relevant and/or irrelevant retrievals. DE-KART increases a *success* or *failure* count each time a created index is matched exactly and judged to be relevant or irrelevant, respectively. The *success rate* of an index is computed as follows: success-rate = success-count/(success-count + failure-count). The procedure also keeps track of the relevance of each subject in an index (Baudin *et al.*, 1993).

[2] Force-generation-msm stands for force-generation-*mechanism*. In the rest of the chapter we will use the abbreviation *msm* for the word *mechanism*.

6 *Index refinement:* When the success rate of an index suggests that it should be repaired, DE-KART provides two types of assistance depending on the type of user who is interacting with the system. The first level of repair is attempted during the system's operation with the end-user asking queries of the system. Based on the low rate of the index, the system assigns it a low priority so as to prevent the retrieval component from selecting it during subsequent retrievals. This level of assistance to the end-user is performed automatically.

If the user is the knowledge engineer, the system engages him or her in a repair dialogue by first displaying the suspected indices along with the associated text, graphic or videotaped information. The system then enables the knowledge engineer to modify the parameters in the index, or to remove the index altogether. In this phase the system displays the rate of the index along with the rate of the subjects associated with the index.

2.4 Domain-dependent retrieval rules refinement

If the index was retrieved by a proximity retrieval heuristic, the system increases the success or failure count of both the domain-dependent retrieval rule (R1 in our example) and the generic heuristic used to generate the rule from the user query (H1 in our example).

When a particular instance of a retrieval heuristic seems to fail often, the system attempts two levels of repair. During the system's operation with the end-user the system lowers the priority of the domain-dependent rule, preventing it from being selected in subsequent retrievals. If the user is the knowledge engineer, the system displays the rule and enables the knowledge engineer to manually modify the rule by adding additional constraints to be matched with a given query. It then verifies that the previous indices that were created using this rule would still be generated.

For instance, in Figure 2.2, the rule R2 states that: "if the query is about the function of the solenoid, then retrieve information on the operation of the rotary friction damper". Given that R2 retrieved only irrelevant references, the knowledge engineer could attempt to specialize the rule by specifying, for example, that the query "function of solenoid" can only be matched with an index that points to information expressed in a *textual* medium. The rule then becomes:

R2′:
if (query function-of solenoid)
then (index operation-of rotary-friction-damper **medium text**)

A refinement at the level of domain-dependent rules is more general than a refinement of a specific index. For instance, the domain-dependent rule R2 can be reused for other documents in the same domain, whereas fixing an index is only a document-dependent repair.

2.5 Generic retrieval heuristics refinement

As a start, our goal is to decrease the number of irrelevant documents presented to a user (increasing precision) while maintaining the same number of relevant documents (preserving recall). With respect to this goal, we will consider that a heuristic *fails* if its failure count is high – that is, if it has retrieved many irrelevant references. At present, we do not consider recall failures, in which a heuristic fails to retrieve a relevant reference.

A set of proximity retrieval heuristics is first entered manually by the system builder. During system operation when DE-KART detects that a heuristic fails for specific queries, the conditions in the *if* part of the heuristic, the *applicability conditions*, need to be refined so as to restrict the irrelevant retrievals but preserve the successful ones and thus improve the *precision* of the retrieval (the percentage of relevant references retrieved over the total number of references retrieved for the user). Refinement of generic heuristics is performed by adapting an *inductive learning* technique. To review, inductive learning searches for a concept in some given generalization language which covers the *positive* instances of the concept, and none of its *negative* instances. In our case, the task of refining heuristics in DE-KART is to help the knowledge engineer find the concept which describes the applicable retrievals for a proximity heuristic. The positive and negative instances of the concept to be acquired are the instances of successful and failed retrievals of the heuristic. The induction task amounts to finding a concept to specialize the current applicability conditions of a heuristic, which is over-general, such that none of the failed retrievals would be generated, while all the successful ones would be.

Our approach differs from the classical automated approach to induction in that the system does not automatically perform the entire induction task, but provides the user with increasing levels of assistance in performing this induction interactively. We present here two levels of assistance. One, *interactive inductive refinement*, assists the knowledge engineer in discovering a concept which covers the positive and none of the negative examples by focusing attention on the positive and negative instances of a faulty heuristic (Figure 2.3) and by validating the refinement proposed by the user on previous and future retrievals. The second level of assistance, *autonomous inductive refinement*, performs induction using an off-the-shelf ID3 machine learning algorithm to automatically refine the applicability conditions for the faulty heuristics.

2.5.1 Interactive inductive refinement of heuristics

We first illustrate the interactive inductive refinement task for proximity heuristics. The interactive refinement task proceeds in four steps:

1. *Failure detection and diagnosis:* Both domain-dependent and generic task retrieval heuristics are monitored during the system's operation (see Section 2.3). When the failure rate of a heuristic exceeds some threshold, the heuristic refinement dialogue can be initiated. The typical user who interacts with the system during this dialogue is the knowledge engineer.

   The system presents the knowledge engineer with the suspect heuristic H1 (see Figure 2.3). It displays negative and positive instances of the heuristic H1. In our example, the instances of heuristic H1, R2 and R4 retrieved irrelevant references in response to the queries: "function of solenoid" and "function of pressure plate".
2. *Refinement:* The knowledge engineer interacts with the system in an attempt to find a concept which would cover all of the positive instances and none of the negative ones. The interaction with the system proceeds as follows:

   Concept selection: If the system has a base of pre-existing concepts, the knowledge engineer can select an appropriate concept, and apply it to the variables of the heuristic.

   Language extension: If no such concept exists, the knowledge engineer can extend the language and enter the definition of a new concept. In our example (see Figure 2.3), the knowledge engineer defines a concept that would prevent the generation of R2 and R4 while still enabling the generation of the successful retrievals R1 and R3. Looking at the instances of H1 he or she may notice that in both negative instances R2 and R4 the variable $Y was instantiated with the value "rotary-friction-damper" which is the top-level component of the whole device. The intuition for why retrievals failed in these instances is that documents that describe the operation of the top-level component are so general that the end-user could not find the description of a function of a subcomponent he or she was looking for, and deemed this retrieval "irrelevant". The knowledge engineer defines the new concept: (top-level-component $X) which is true if X is the top component of the part-of hierarchy (true in our example of the rotary friction damper).

   Heuristic repair: The system now assists the user in editing the applicability conditions of H1. In this example, the user restricts the variable $Y in H1, specifying that a query: <function of $X> can match an index <operation of $Y> only when $Y is *not* the top-level component in the part-of hierarchy.

   The modified heuristic H1′ is then:

H1: function-to-operation if (query **function-of** $X) and (part-of $Y $X) then (index **operation-of** $Y)	
Positive instances of H1	**Negative instances of H1**
R1: if (query function-of solenoid) then (index operation-of force-generation-msm)	R2: if (query function-of solenoid) then (index operation-of rotary-friction-damper)
R3: if (query function-of pressure-plate) then (index operation-of lever-msm)	R4: if (query function-of pressure-plate) then (index operation-of rotary-friction-damper)

Figure 2.3 Positive and negative instances of H1

Positive instances of H1	Negative instances of H1
R1: if (query function-of solenoid) then (index operation-of force-generation-msm)	R2: if (query function-of solenoid) then (index operation-of rotary-friction-damper)
R3: if (query function-of pressure-plate then (index operation-of lever-msm)	R4: if (query function-of pressure-plate then (index operation-of rotary-friction-damper)
R5: if (query function-of control-msm) then (index operation-of rotary-friction-damper)	

Figure 2.4 Positive and negative instances of domain rules

H1′: function-to-operation

if (query function-of $X)
(subpart $Y $X)
(not (top-level-component $Y))
then (index operation-of $Y)

The new concept "top-level-component" is added to the generalization vocabulary of the system and becomes usable to refine other heuristics.

3. *Validation:* The system checks that this new applicability condition prevents the generation of the negative instances of H1 while still enabling the generation of the positive instances. In our example (see Figure 2.3), any domain-dependent rule which instantiates $Y with the top-level component "rotary-friction-damper" would be prevented from being generated. The system then validates that the positive instances R1 and R3 would still be generated given this new restrictive applicability condition. The new heuristic H1′ is added to the retrieval knowledge. H1 however remains in the system to enable the retrieval component to fall back on it if the existing set of refined heuristics fail to retrieve relevant answers. DE-KART classifies the new heuristic as "tentative" until the system has enough experience to establish that no positive instances of H1 are prevented from being generated.
4. *Incremental refinement:* After some time, the user submits a new query about "function of the control mechanism". No index exactly matches the query and no heuristic (including H1′) succeeded in retrieving a reference. The system then falls back on H1 and generates the instantiated rule R5: "if the question is about the function of the control mechanism, then look for indices about the operation of the rotary friction damper". This rule retrieves a document based on the index: <operation of rotary-friction-damper>. In this case the retrieved document is rated as relevant by the user. The failure of H1′ to generate the positive instance R5 suggests that the concept (not (top-level-component $X)) is too restrictive, and H1 must be refined differently. DE-KART provides the knowledge engineer with a heuristic refinement dialogue and now focuses the attention of the user on R2, R4 and R5 (see Figure 2.4).

   At this point the knowledge engineer provides the concept, (parent $X $Y), which is true if Y is the immediate ancestor of X in the part-of hierarchy. This concept will cover all of the positive instances of H1 since in all of them the two components are close enough in the hierarchy (see Figure 2.1). The intuition is that the end-user was able to find information about the control mechanism where the operation of the "rotary-friction-damper" is described, whereas the "solenoid" component is too detailed a component to be documented at such a high level. The system assists the user in editing the applicability conditions of H1′ and generates a new heuristic H1″:

H1″: function-to-operation
if (query function-of $X)
(subpart $Y $X)
(parent $X $Y)
then (index operation-of $Y)

This time the new applicability condition of the heuristic prevents the generation of the negative instances of H1′ (R2, and R4) while enabling the positive instances (R1, R3 and R5) to be generated.

At this point DE-KART has refined the applicability conditions of heuristic H1, increasing the precision of future retrievals. The system also acquired two new concepts for the generalization hierarchy: (top-level-component $X) and (parent $X $Y).

Once enough concepts are entered in the generalization hierarchy and enough examples of successful and unsuccessful matches between queries and indices are recorded, DE-KART can provide a greater level of assistance to the system builder by autonomously selecting and adding restrictive applicability conditions for a faulty heuristic.

2.5.2 Autonomous inductive refinement of heuristics

At this level of assistance the system automatically suggests possible heuristic refinements to the system builder. This is accomplished using an inductive learning algorithm. In this section we provide a brief tutorial on inductive learning and then describe our application of induction for heuristic refinement.

2.5.2.1 Inductive learning: background

Induction works by extracting patterns, or regularities, in the training data which can then be used to predict properties of new examples. In the most common use of induction, called supervised learning, we are interested in predicting one property of an example, its membership in a class, based on features of the example. For example, it is possible to predict whether an animal is a mammal or reptile (the class) when told whether the animal has fur and is warm-blooded. The task of a supervised learning tool in this example would be to extract such decision rules from a database of animal descriptions in which each animal is pre-classified as mammal or reptile. Out of the set of all features describing different animals (such as furriness, lifespan, blood temperature, and so on), the algorithm uses the examples and decides for itself how to use those features to distinguish mammals from reptiles.

Inductive learning has been an active area of research, and off-the-shelf algorithms and tools are commercially available. These algorithms and tools vary along a number of important dimensions: how easy they are to implement, how easy they are to use, in what form the examples have to be described, how many examples are required to form good decision rules, how general those resulting rules are, how easily they can be used to classify new examples, and how well the algorithms perform when some examples are misclassified (partially incorrect data is called *noisy* data).

For our purposes, we chose an implementation of the ID3 inductive learning algorithm (Quinlan, 1986). We chose this algorithm for three reasons. For one, it classifies the kind of examples we have in our system (examples described by a set of discrete features and their values). Secondly, the algorithm is easy to use and readily available. Thirdly, the output of the algorithm is a set of compact rules which can be understood by a human (as opposed to, for instance, the opaque set of rules produced by neural networks that perform the same induction task).

Briefly, ID3 extracts regularities in features of examples, and creates decision rules in the form of a tree. Each node in the decision tree represents a test on one feature of an input example (for example, whether the animal has fur or not), and each possible value for the tested feature (for example, "has fur" or "no fur") leads to a distinct subtree. When the tree is used to classify an example, the tests are applied in turn to the example, starting with the test at the root of the tree, and following the branch which corresponds to the value of the tested feature (for example, if the animal to be classified does have fur, it would proceed down the "has fur" branch of the tree). When a leaf of the tree is reached (there are no more tests), the example is classified according to the class represented by that leaf. For instance, if an animal example proceeded down the "has fur" and "gives live birth" branches, it would then be classified as a "mammal".

The details of the ID3 decision-tree construction algorithm are as follows. ID3 takes as input a set of pre-classified examples. Each example consists of a fixed set of feature-value pairs (such as "blood temperature = warm, weight = 120 . . . "), and a final classification (e.g. mammal). If the examples are all of the same class (e.g. all mammals), the algorithm produces a leaf node labelled with that common class. Otherwise, the algorithm chooses the most discriminating feature which best separates the examples into different classes. For example, the feature "blood temperature" might take on one value ("warm") for most of the mammals in the example set, and another value ("cold") for most of the reptiles, so this would be a good discriminating feature. By contrast, the feature "body weight" might not be useful for distinguishing mammals from reptiles, as both classes of animal come in a variety of sizes. The algorithm then groups together all examples which have the same value for that feature. For instance, all examples with "blood temperature = warm" would form one group, and those with "blood temperature = cold" would form another. The ID3 algorithm is then called recursively to produce a subtree for each of these subgroups. A node is then created which corresponds to the tested feature ("blood temperature"), and for each possible value of this feature a link is created to the corresponding subtree (for instance, "blood temperature = cold" would be linked to the subtree constructed by calling the algorithm on the cold-blooded subgroup, as discussed above). This tree, consisting of the created node and the links to all the subtrees, is the output of the algorithm. It can then be used to efficiently classify new input examples.

2.5.2.2 *Inductive learning in DE-KART*

For our purposes, we apply ID3 to automatically suggest possible heuristic refinements to the system builder. Given a set of relevant and irrelevant instances of the retrieval heuristics, the algorithm produces a set of possible restrictions to the applicability conditions of those heuristics. In the language used to describe ID3 above, our features include "medium", "subject", and "retrieval-heuristic", and values for those features include "text", "solenoid", and "function-to-operation", respectively. The classes are "relevant retrieval" and "irrelevant retrieval". An example consists of a set of "feature = value" pairs (for example, "subject = solenoid, medium = video, topic = function, page = 22, retrieval-heuristic = function-to-operation") and a pre-classifed example is one in which an example is labelled as either an instance of a relevant or an irrelevant retrieval. A rule extracted from a decision tree in our case might read: "if a new example is one in which the query's subject is solenoid, the medium of the index is video, and the heuristic that generated the retrieval is function-to-operation, then predict that example to be an irrelevant retrieval".

The autonomous inductive refinement consists of the following steps:

1. *Failure detection and diagnosis:* This technique can take place after a preferably large and varied set of positive and negative examples of proximity heuristic retrievals have been collected. The system monitors the failure rates of the heuristics, and identifies those heuristics whose failure rate has passed some threshold.
2. *Example pre-processing:* The input to the induction algorithm is a set of positive and negative examples of a heuristic, each consisting of a set of features desribing the query, the matching index, and relations among the query and index. The examples are generated from successful and failed retrievals during system operation. To make possible the generation of domain-independent refinements, DE-KART adds some features to each example. These features represent different types of relations between the subjects in the query and the subjects in the matching index. For instance the feature "subjects-in-query-equal-subjects-in-index = yes" means that the subjects in the query are the same as the subjects in the matching index. In the same way, "subjects-query-is-part-of-subjects-index = yes" means that the subjects in the query are part-of some subjects in the matching index.

   Figure 2.5 shows a positive example for the heuristic H2 "operation-to-construction" which retrieves information about construction of a mechanism, in response to a query about the operation of that mechanism.

example 165 positive
retrieval-heuristic: operation-to-construction
query-topic = function-of
query- subjects= solenoid
index-topic = operation-of
index-subjects = force-generation-mechanism
index-medium = text
index-level-of-detail = conceptual
subjects-query-equal-subjects-index = yes
subjects-query-is-attributes = no
subjects-query-is-requirements = no
subjects-query-is-part-of-subjects-index = no
subjects-index-is-part-of-subjects-query = no
subjects-query-is-kind-of-subjects-index = no
subjects-index-is-kind-of-subjects-query = no
subjects-query-depends-on-subjects-index = no
subjects-query-influence-subjects-index = no
...

Figure 2.5 A positive example of query/index match

H2: Operation-to-construction
if (query operation-of $X)
then (index construction-of $X)

For this example, the query was about the "operation of the solenoid" <query-topic = operation-of, query-subject = solenoid> and the matching index was construction of solenoid <index-topic = construction-of, index-subject = solenoid>. This is a positive example, meaning that a piece of information describing the "construction of the solenoid", in a textual medium, and a conceptual level of detail, was relevant to the query: "operation of solenoid". The second part of this example (in bold) shows a set of relations between the subject(s) of the query and the subject(s) of the index, that are automatically added. For instance, in this example the subject of the query was the same as the subject of the index (subjects-query-equal-subjects-index = yes). In our initial tests, the parts of the example that are in italic are domain-dependent terms and were not fed to the induction algorithm.

3. *Refinement:* The system runs the ID3 induction algorithm on the faulty heuristics to characterize when they fail and when they succeed. The result is an *applicability tree*, a decision tree which describes the applicability conditions of the heuristic covering the positive examples seen so far, and none of the negative ones. Figure 2.6 shows an applicability tree for the proximity heuristic "operation-to-construction".

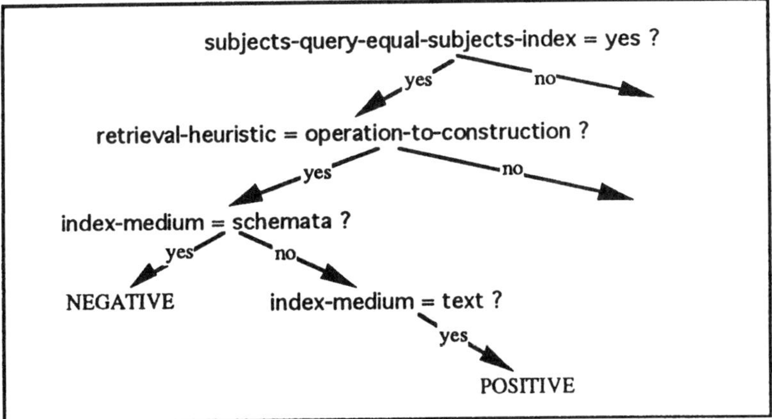

Figure 2.6 A portion of an applicability tree generated by the ID3 induction algorithm

The tree refines the applicability conditions for the heuristic in the following way: the initial applicability conditions state that any query about operation of a mechanism X can be matched with an index about construction of X (intuitively, the structure of an assembly reveals insights about its operation). The applicability tree refines this condition by specifying all of the conditions already in the heuristic, plus that any information about construction of X may be relevant to a query about operation of X *only if the medium of the document is text*, not if it is, say, a schemata. This refines the operation-to-construction heuristic H2 into H2′:

H2′ Operation-to-construction
if (query operation-of $X)
(index-medium text)
then (index construction-of $X)

4. *Validation and transfer:* The system validates that the applicability conditions of the heuristic, plus the applicability tree for it, do indeed prevent the generation of the negative instances of the heuristic while enabling the generation of the positive ones. It does so by classifying positive and negative examples from sessions with the user other than the session on which the training was done. In doing this, the system can compare its prediction of which examples should be negative and positive, with the user's classification of positive and negative examples.

An alternative to this automatic validation procedure is to rely on the knowledge of the knowledge engineer familiar with the domain to validate a refinement. The advantage is that this interactive validation can filter those refinements that are clearly incorrect, while enabling the system to experiment and validate interesting refinements with end-users.

For instance in the case of the heuristic "operation-to-construction", the refinement proposed by the system corresponds to the intuition that a piece of text describing how a mechanism is assembled is more likely to provide information about how the mechanism works (operates) than a photo or a schemata representing the mechanism. At this stage a system builder is likely to select this refinement and try it even though it could not yet be validated on a large sample of queries.

5. *Incremental refinement:* If the system discovers false negatives and false positives in its classification, it can now rerun the induction algorithm on the combined previous and current sessions. When the false positives and false negatives fall below some threshold, then the system can insert additional applicability conditions to provide a refined heuristic whose precision has been improved.

2.6 Discussion

We have presented the design of DE-KART, a knowledge acquisition and refinement tool that provides increasing levels of assistance in acquiring indexing and retrieval knowledge for a knowledge-based retrieval system. In the scenario presented, the knowledge of DEDAL is refined by: (1) increasing the *level of generality* of the knowledge repaired (from document-dependent indices, to domain-dependent rules, to task-dependent retrieval heuristics) as the system gains experience with different end-users and different queries, and (2) increasing the *level of automation* of the assistance provided to the knowledge engineer and to the system builder: from manual to semi-automated query-based indexing when repairing the conceptual indices; and from manual to automated with the knowledge engineer and the system builder when repairing the retrieval heuristics.

The system starts with a core of conceptual indices entered manually and refines this core of knowledge using the queries of the end-user and feedback about the relevance of the document retrieved in response to the query. This increases the level of automation of the index acquisition from manual to semi-automated when interacting with the end-user of the retrieval system. The level of generality remains at the document or project-specific level.

In the same way, the generic retrieval heuristics are first entered manually. This knowledge increases the recall of the system (Baudin *et al.*, 1993), but is over-general and occasionally leads to the retrieval of irrelevant references in response to a query. These failures provide the opportunities for refinement and repair. While the system is in operation with end-users, DE-KART tries to recover from failing retrieval heuristics by lowering their priority for retrieval. When the system starts interacting with the knowledge engineer it engages in a dialogue to refine the retrieval heuristics. During this refinement phase, the system increases the level of assistance provided to the knowledge engineer. If the system has no knowledge of concepts with which to repair a given heuristic, and few examples of its success and failure, it interacts with the knowledge engineer to refine the representation of the examples and to validate the proposed refinement on previous and future retrievals. When more knowledge of the relevant concepts used to fix heuristics is entered and enough examples of relevant and irrelevant retrievals are generated, the system can suggest a set of repairs by running an induction algorithm on these examples. Here again, the refinement proposed by the system can be first validated by the knowledge engineer before enabling end-users to experience the effects of the refinement.

In our current scenario, the role of the end-user is to provide feedback on the performance of the system during its operation, thus enabling examples of relevant and irrelevant retrievals to be generated. Because this relevance feed-back is performed by the end-users, the resulting data is noisy and must be further monitored by the system. For instance, a user might have misformulated a query and thus he or she will find a retrieval irrelevant although the proximity heuristic used was correct. Some of these false negatives can be filtered automatically by disregarding examples where the same question/index pair was judged relevant one time and irrelevant another time. However, it is still advisable to have the human expert review domain rules that seem to fail often. Moreover, the automated refinement based on this feedback should be designed to take such noise into account (Julian and Fenves, 1994).

Of course, an advantage of being able to gather examples during the system's operation is that: (a) it enables the system to experience a wide variety of situations that might be difficult to anticipate beforehand, (b) it provides some simple information retrieval enhancement in a non-obtrusive way by re-prioritiz-ing the rules and the indices during operation and (c) it can monitor its knowledge in the background and decide, for instance, when to increase its level of automation (Maes and Kozierok, 1993). This end-user-centred knowledge acqui-sition aspect is enabled by two factors. The first factor is that in an information retrieval task the end-user is able to *judge* the relevance of an answer provided by the system even though he or she might not be expert in the domain. This is not the case in most diagnostic tasks, in which only the domain expert is able to judge whether a diagnosis is relevant. The second factor is that, in an information retrieval task, there are generally no dire consequences in retrieving false posi-tives. This means that a system is still usable in early stages of development, before extensive refinement with an expert has taken place.

One phase of the heuristic repair in which the human plays a vital role is the *concept definition* phase where the knowledge engineer decides on new concepts to be added to the representation in order to discriminate positive and negative examples. From our experience with DEDAL, it seems that this concept definition phase is the activity that has the greatest impact on the performance of the system in the early stages of its development. At present, concept definition happens during the language extension part of the interactive refinement phase (see Section 2.5.1). This functionality still needs to be integrated into the automated refinement phase (Section 2.5.2), which could then be viewed as a form of *interactive induction* (Tecuci and Hieb, 1994; Buntine and Stirling, 1990; Shapiro, 1983; Muggleton, 1987).

2.7 Related work

Knowledge acquisition can be broadly classified into three stages: *elicitation*, *refinement* and *restructuring* (Bareiss *et al.*, 1989). DE-KART focuses on the refinement stage. Recently there has been work on integrating machine learning and knowledge acquisition techniques in the area of knowledge base refinement (see Tecuci and Duff, 1994, and the survey by Wilkins, 1991). Some of this work tries to automate the refinement process by combining knowledge acquisition with various machine learning techniques using: induction (Feldman *et al.*, 1994), explanation-based learning (Reinartz and Schmalhofer, 1994; Pazzani and Brunk, 1991), a combination of inductive and analytical techniques (Tecuci and Duff, 1994), or analogical reasoning (Gil and Paris, 1994).

Our work differs from most other efforts to integrate knowledge acquisition and machine learning in the area of knowledge base refinement in that it performs refinement at various levels of automation and generality. In this respect it is similar to recent work on procedure acquisition (Mathe and Kedar, 1992) which also provides increasing levels of assistance. DISCIPLE (Tecuci and Kodratoff, 1990) and NeoDISCIPLE (Tecuci, 1992) can be viewed as providing increasing levels of assistance, although the emphasis is on machine learning methods with rudimentary knowledge acquisition, whereas our emphasis is on knowledge acquisition, with some rudimentary machine learning. Given a taxonomy of interactive knowledge acquisition methods such as that proposed by Musen (1989), DE-KART cannot be placed at a fixed level of the taxonomy, but can be viewed instead as moving through various levels of the taxonomy as it increases its level of assistance, e.g. from a "task-level" tool for domain experts to a "method level" tool geared toward knowledge engineers.

One interesting aspect of our work is that DE-KART acquires knowledge both from the novice end-user during the system's operation, and from the domain expert or knowledge engineer in a separate refinement phase. The presence of these distinct contexts for knowledge acquisition places DE-KART midway between systems which learn primarily from the end-user, and can provide immediate but shallow knowledge refinement during performance (such as Maes and Kozierok, 1993; Clouse and Utgoff, 1992) and knowledge acquisition tools that can perform deep knowledge restructuring but do so primarily through interaction with the domain expert or the knowledge engineer.

2.8 Future work and conclusion

We need to conduct more experiments to evaluate our knowledge acquisition and refinement approach for indexing and retrieval knowledge. So far, we have acquired and collected examples from the queries asked by two mechanical designers while they were accessing information in the context of the "rotary friction damper" problem in the mechanical engineering design domain. During the first year of the system's operation we acquired new concepts to discriminate between positive and negative examples. We then applied the induction algorithm on 300 examples of successful and unsuccessful matches. The refinements proposed by the induction algorithm were reviewed by the knowledge engineer, who decided which ones should be incorporated into the system. Among the proposed refinements, the ones that involved additional conditions on the medium and level of detail of the retrieved information usually appealed to the human's intuition even though the system builder and the knowledge engineer could not always give an opinion on the quality of the proposed refinement. This manual selection phase is necessary in the first stages of the life of the system where its experience with different users and different domains is still limited. However, we need to conduct more experiments to confirm the human intuition and measure the impact of the acquisition on the *precision* and *recall* of future retrievals.

To evaluate the generality of the acquired knowledge we are experimenting not only with different classes of users but with different domains. In particular, we are now running the system to retrieve text, graphics and video records for the design of an innovative bioreactor, a device that will enable NASA life scientists to study microbial growth.

While our acquisition and refinement methods are not dependent on the specifics of the mechanical engineering domain, they currently address only some of the issues in supporting acquisition and refinement in knowledge-based retrieval systems. Currently, DE-KART can refine a heuristic by constraining the variables in the applicability conditions of the heuristic. However, some refinements involve the addition of new variables. We also need to provide assistance when heuristics are too specific, in order to enhance the system's recall. This will involve fixing the domain model representing the device being designed as well as the retrieval heuristics. Finally, this methodology assumes that acquisition and refinement are ongoing tasks performed during the life of the system, and that time is available to interact with the system to correct the knowledge base.

Currently, DE-KART is not integrated with the induction algorithm, and the refinements proposed by the system must be manually integrated in DEDAL to enable the system to monitor the repair. We also need to provide more guidance in the dialogue with the user to select the different levels of assistance.

In conclusion, this chapter has presented a tool which acquires knowledge through interaction both with possibly naive end-users, during performance of a task, and with domain experts and knowledge engineers, in an incremental but off-line refinement phase. These dual contexts enable the system to continually improve its performance throughout its lifetime, to acquire knowledge at several levels of generality, and to increase its level of automation as its base of knowledge and experience accumulate. So far, this functionality has been implemented within the context of a knowledge-based information retrieval task, in which the end-user, while not an expert, is still able to provide feedback on the performance of the system. An important area for future work is to identify the class of problems for which this dual-context approach to continuous knowledge acquisition is applicable.

Acknowledgements

Thanks to Vinod Baya, Ade Mabogunje and Jody Gevins Underwood who helped us evaluate the results of our experiments and for fruitful discussions about question-based indexing. Thanks to Larry Leifer and to the other members of the GCDK group for their feedback and support on this project, and to Wray Buntine, Tom Hinrichs, and members of NASA Ames and the Institute for the Learning Sciences for useful interactions and comments on earlier drafts.

References

Bareiss, R., Porter, B. W. and Murray, K. S. (1989). Supporting start-to-finish development of knowledge bases. *Machine Learning*, 4: 259–283.

Baudin, C., Gevins, J., Bava, V. and Mabogunje, A. (1992a). DEDAL: using domain concepts to index engineering design information. *Proceedings of the Meeting of the Cognitive Science Society*, Bloomington, Indiana.

Baudin, C., Gevins, J. and Baya, V. (1992b). Using device models to facilitate the retrieval of multimedia design information. In *Proceedings of IJCAI 93, Chambéry, France*, volume 2.

Baudin, C., Kedar, S., Gevins, J. and Baya, V. (1993). Question-based acquisition of conceptual indices for multimedia design documentation. *Proceedings of the Eleventh National Conference on Artificial Intelligence*, Washington, D.C.

Baya, V., Gevins, J., Baudin, C., Mabogunje, A. and Leifer L. (1992). An experimental study of design information reuse. *Proceedings of the 4th International Conference on Design Theory and Methodology*, ASME, Scottsdale, Arizona, pp. 141–147.

Buntine, W. and Stirling, D. (1990). Interactive induction. In Hayes, J. Michie, D. and Tyugo, E. (editors), *Machine Intelligence 12, Analysis and Synthesis of Knowledge*, pp. 121–137. Oxford University Press, New York.

Clouse, J. and Utgoff, P. A. (1992). Teaching method for reinforcement learning. In Sleeman, D. and Edwards, P. (editors), *Proceedings of the 9th International Workshop on Machine Learning*, pp. 92–101. Morgan Kaufmann, San Mateo, CA.

Feldman, R., Koppel, M. and Segre, A. (1994). Biased revision of approximate domain theories. *Knowledge Acquisition Journal* 6.

Gil, Y. and Paris, C. (1994). Toward method-independent knowledge acquisition. *Knowledge Acquisition Journal* 6.

Julian, B. and Fenves, S. (1994). Guiding induction with expert knowledge. *Knowledge Acquisition Journal* 6.

Maes, P. and Kozierok, R. (1993). Learning interface agents. In *Proceedings of the Eleventh National Conference on Artificial Intelligence*, Washington, D.C.

Mathe, N. and Kedar, S. (1992). Increasingly automated procedure acquisition in dynamic systems. In *Proceedings of the 7th Banff Knowledge Acquisition for Knowledge-Based Systems Workshop*, Vol. 2, Banff, Canada.

Muggleton, S. (1987). Structuring knowledge by asking questions. In Bratko, I. and Lavrac, N. (editors), *Progress in Machine Learning*, pp. 218–229. Sigma Press, Wilmslow, England.

Musen, M. A. (1989). Conceptual models of interactive knowledge acquisition tools. *Knowledge Acquisition Journal*, 1, 73–88.

Pazzani, M. J. and Brunk, C. A. (1991). Detecting and correcting errors in rule-based expert systems: an integration of empirical and explanation-based learning. *Knowledge Acquisition Journal* 3: 157–173.

Quinlan, J. R. (1986). Induction of decision trees. *Machine Learning*, 1: 81–106.

Reinartz, T. and Schmalhofer, F. (1994). An integration of knowledge acquisition techniques and EBL for a complex application. *Knowledge Acquisition Journal* 6.

Salton, G. and Buckley, C. (1990). Improving retrieval performance by relevance feedback. *J. of ASIS* 41, 288–297.

Shapiro, A. D. (1983). The role of structured induction in expert systems. *PhD thesis*, University of Edinburgh.

Tecuci, G. (1992). Automating knowledge acquisition as extending, updating and improving a knowledge base. *IEEE Transactions on Systems, Man, and Cybernetics* 22: No. 6, 1444–1460.

Tecuci, G. and Duff, D. (1994). A framework for knowledge base refinement through multistrategy learning and knowledge acquisition. *Knowledge Acquisition Journal* 6: 137–162.

Tecuci, G. and Hieb, M. (1994). Consistency-driven knowledge elicitation: using a learning-oriented knowledge representation that supports knowledge elicitation in NeoDISCIPLE. *Knowledge Acquisition Journal* 6: 23–46.

Tecuci, G. and Kodratoff, Y. (1990). Apprenticeship learning in imperfect domain theories. In Kodratoff, Y. and Michalski, R. S. (editors), *Machine Learning: An Artificial Intelligence Approach*, vol. III. Morgan Kaufmann, San Mateo, CA.

Wilkins, D. C. (1991). A framework for integration of machine learning and knowledge acquisition techniques. In *Proceedings of the 6th Banff Knowledge Acquisition for Knowledge-Based Systems Workshop*, Vol. 2, Banff, Canada, October 6–11.

CHAPTER 3

Towards method-independent knowledge acquisition

Yolanda Gil and Cécile Paris

Abstract

Rapid prototyping and tool reusability have pushed knowledge acquisition research to investigate method-specific knowledge acquisition tools appropriate for predetermined problem-solving methods. We believe that method-dependent knowledge acquisition is not the only approach. The aim of our research is to develop powerful yet versatile machine learning mechanisms that can be incorporated into general-purpose but practical knowledge acquisition tools. This chapter shows through examples the practical advantages of this approach. In particular, we illustrate how existing knowledge can be used to facilitate knowledge acquisition through analogy mechanisms within a domain and across domains. Our sample knowledge acquisition dialogues with a domain expert illustrate which parts of the process are addressed by the human and which parts are automated by the tool, in a synergistic co-operation for knowledge-base extension and refinement. The chapter also describes briefly the EXPECT problem-solving architecture that facilitates this approach to knowledge acquisition.

Keywords: Knowledge acquisition, knowledge-base refinement, learning by analogy, explanation.

3.1 Introduction

The science of artificial intelligence started with and continues to build on general principles. Newell and Simon's pioneering work on understanding human problem solving shows us that the same mechanisms come to play when trying to find solutions to problems that may seem very different (Newell and Simon, 1972). GPS implemented this principle and demonstrated that, given domain-specific knowledge, a general-purpose reasoning engine can be used to solve problems in that specific domain, and that the same engine can be used for different problem-solving applications. Decades later, a constellation of expert

Machine Learning and Knowledge Acquisition
ISBN 0–12–685120–4

systems was possible thanks to the expert system shell version of GPS (e.g. Buchanan and Shortliffe, 1984). Inference is understood, said common AI wisdom, the hard part is getting the knowledge right. General-purpose inference mechanisms, general-purpose representation mechanisms (a similar argument can be shown with Minsky's frames for the field of knowledge representation) gave AI, like any other science, the beauty of building on principles. Researchers turned then to the next issue in the automated reasoning agenda: machine learning and the acquisition of knowledge. The work ranges from learning heuristic knowledge (Minton, 1988; Knoblock, 1993) to acquiring factual knowledge (Gil, 1992), and shows us that complete automation of the learning or acquisition task in domains of technical expertise is far from reach. Semi-automated general-purpose knowledge acquisition (KA) tools (Davis, 1980) are not enough to achieve efficient prototyping. Generality does not provide the tool with much basis to support the knowledge engineering process.

At the same time, we witnessed the surge of special-purpose mechanisms to support real-world applications. General-purpose tools seemed incapable of performing well in applications such as manufacturing or robot path planning (Lozano-Perez, 1987; Chang and Wysk, 1985). The new common AI wisdom reflects that general-purpose is good, but may not be enough as we currently understand it. The field of knowledge acquisition has rightly taken this lesson. General-purpose KA tools are augmented with application-independent method-specific inference structures (Chandrasekaran, 1986; McDermott, 1988). For example, SALT (Marcus and McDermott, 1989) provides support for propose-and-revise tasks. PROTEGE (Musen, 1989) helps in acquiring knowledge in temporal skeletal planning applications. Although the resulting tools have less generality, they allow the semi-automated production of fast prototypes in novel domains once the appropriate inference mechanism is manually determined. The inference mechanisms provide expectations about the role of each piece of knowledge that are powerful guidance in the knowledge acquisition process.

However, this approach to building KA tools has limitations that arise from the need of more flexibility than they provide in adapting them to an application (Musen, 1992). The problem-solving structure of an application cannot always be defined in domain-independent terms. Furthermore, these method-specific inference mechanisms may not address some of the particulars of an application simply because they were designed with generality in mind. Another problem with the method-specific KA tools is that they raise the non-trivial issue of determining a library of possible methods (Chandrasekaran, 1986; McDermott, 1988). The work involves handcrafting this library of methods making sure to provide both wide coverage of tasks and well-understood characterizations of the inference capabilities of each method.

To address these limitations, some researchers (Klinker *et al.*, 1991; Puerta *et al.*, 1992) are developing libraries of problem-solving methods that handle finer-grained inference structures than the ones above. These approaches provide much more flexibility in building a knowledge-based system but two major issues remain. One is the task of building method libraries. Another issue is the accessibility of KA tools to domain experts. The users of these tools still need to be knowledge engineers (Kitto, 1988).

The goal of the EXPECT project is to provide an environment for the development of knowledge-based systems that aids in the acquisition, maintenance, and documentation of the knowledge about a task. Our KA tool is independent of the inference structure or problem-solving method of the task. This chapter concentrates on EXPECT as a tool for knowledge refinement and describes our work on how to correct and extend an existing knowledge base. Our tool uses machine learning techniques to support knowledge refinement independently of the inference structure of the task. Our KA work focuses on the integration of machine learning methods in KA tools that can automatically (or semi-automatically) come up with generalized versions of methods that express domain-specific inference structures and support their reuse in new domains and new situations through analogy. This chapter shows our first results in this direction and illustrates through examples the practical advantages of this approach. In particular, we show how EXPECT currently uses the same general-purpose mechanism (analogy) to support knowledge refinement within a domain and across domains. The system and the user work in synergy: unlike other machine learning approaches, our system does not attempt to deduce all the information needed to form an analogy by itself. Rather, it relies on input from the user to guide its analogical learning. On the other hand, the user does not need to know a lot about the knowledge base or enter all the new necessary knowledge explicitly, but can rely on the tool to guide the knowledge acquisition process.

The issue of accessibility to domain experts has been central in the design of our architecture (Neches *et al.*, 1985; Swartout *et al.*, 1991; Swartout and Smoliar, 1987). The explicit representation of factual and problem-solving knowledge and the ability to produce flexible explanations in an interactive dialogue provide the basis for building a KA tool that communicates with an expert much in the way a colleague in their field of expertise would. Our work in this area is not the main focus of this chapter, and it is discussed elsewhere (Paris and Gil, 1993; Moore and Paris, 1993).

The examples throughout the chapter are from a logistics transportation application that evaluates proposed routings, taking into account restrictions on objects transported, destination points, and vehicles used. Users are specialists in sea transportation planning. EXPECT is given knowledge about ships, seaports, packages, berths, etc. as well as plans for transporting objects. Users are interested in estimating how long it takes to transport some number of objects from one location to another with the resources available.

The chapter runs as follows. We first describe briefly our problem-solving architecture and our knowledge representation language. Then we illustrate how EXPECT makes use of analogy to facilitate KA within a domain and across domains. Later, we describe our plans for future work through an example scenario that uses the same analogy techniques augmented with generalization to facilitate KA in a different domain. Our scenarios illustrate the user's involvement during knowledge acquisition, as well as which parts of the process are automated by the tool.

3.2 The EXPECT architecture

EXPECT builds upon previous work on the Explainable Expert System (EES) framework (Neches *et al.*, 1985; Swartout *et al.*, 1991; Swartout and Smoliar, 1987), which allows for the construction of expert systems that can provide good natural language explanations of their behaviour (Moore and Paris, 1993; Swartout and Moore, 1993; Moore, 1989; Moore and Swartout, 1989, 1991). EXPECT's architecture is shown in Figure 3.1. In EXPECT, different kinds of knowledge are specified in distinct knowledge bases in a high-level specification

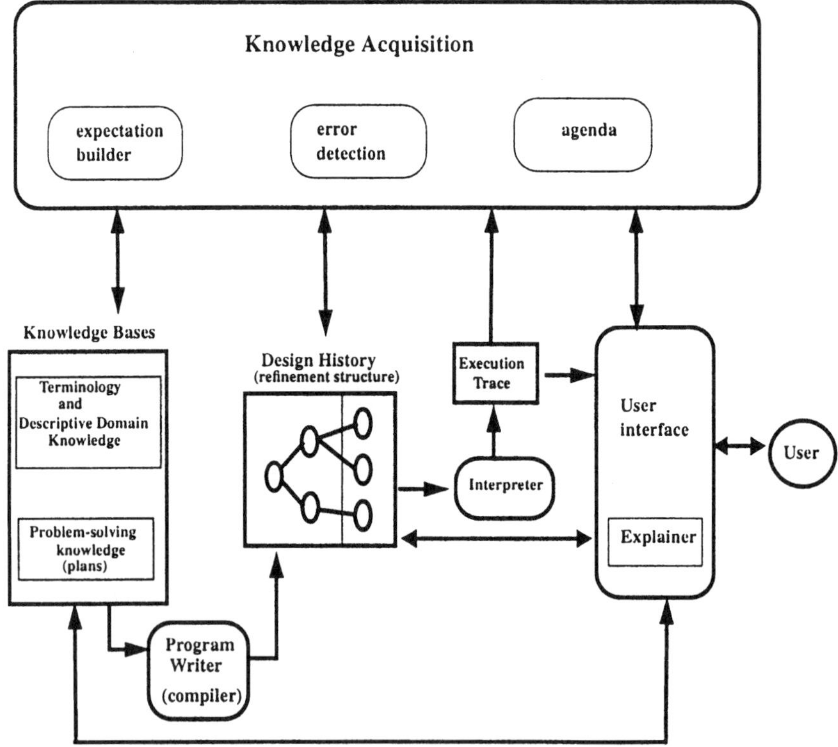

Figure 3.1 A schematic representation of EXPECT. The design history and the knowledge base components are used to form expectations for knowledge acquisition

```
(defconcept seaport
    :is (:and port
              (:some r-ships ship)
              (:some r-berths berth)
              (:some r-piers number)
              (:some r-covered-storage-area number)))
```

Figure 3.2 Definition of a seaport in the domain model

language. The specific actions that are to be executed by the system to solve a specific problem are *derived* from these knowledge bases by the system, and a record of the derivation is stored to provide the rationale for these actions. The knowledge acquisition tool uses this rationale and the knowledge bases themselves to form expectations to support the interaction with the user (Gil, 1994). A natural language generation module produces justifications and explanations of the system's behaviour to the user.

The knowledge bases capture what the system knows about the domain and how to solve problems in that domain. They comprise:

- A domain-descriptive knowledge base (or *domain model*), which stores definitions and facts in the task domain. The domain model is written in LOOM (MacGregor, 1988, 1991), a knowledge representation formalism of the KL-ONE family. LOOM uses a descriptive logic representation language, and includes a classifier for inference.
- A problem-solving knowledge base, which contains an organized collection of plans. A plan in EXPECT is an abstract and generic description of how a goal can be achieved, instead of a sequence of operators (Fikes and Nilsson, 1971). The plan language allows for an explicit representation of *intent* (what is to be done to achieve a goal) and supports a wide range of control structures to combine subgoals (e.g. conditionals, variable assignments, iteration).

As an example, consider Figures 3.2 and 3.3, which contain samples of these knowledge bases for the logistics transportation domain. In that application, the domain model includes descriptions of `ports`, `seaports`, and `airports`. The representation of a `seaport` is shown in Figure 3.2: a `seaport` is a type of `port`, and it has attributes such as the ships available at the seaport, its piers, its berths, and the available storage areas.[1]

Figure 3.3 shows two very simple plans of the problem-solving knowledge

[1] We use the prefix "r-" to indicate names of relations.

```
(define-plan FIND-IF-SHIP-FITS-IN-SEAPORT
   :capability (determine-whether-fits-in (OBJ (?s is (inst-of ship)))
                                           (IN (?p is (inst-of seaport))))
   :result-type boolean
   :method (less-than (r-ship-length ?s)
                      (compute-max-vessel-length-in-seaport ?p)))


(define-plan COMPUTE-MAX-VESSEL-LENGTH-IN-SEAPORT
   :capability (compute-max-vessel-length-in-seaport
                                    (OBJ (?s is (inst-of seaport))))
   :result-type number
   :method (let ((?berth-types (r-berth-type (r-berth-availability ?s))))
             (max (r-berth-length ?berth-types))))
```

Figure 3.3 Two plans from the transportation domain

base. The capability describes the goals that the plan can achieve, the method represents the body of the plan, and the result type indicates what is returned by the method. The first plan can be used to determine whether a specific type of ship is supported by (or "fits in") a given seaport. This is done by testing whether the length of the ship is less than the maximum vessel length allowed in that particular seaport. The second plan finds the maximum ship length a seaport supports based on the length of its berths.

Given a high-level goal, a *Program Writer* integrates these structured knowledge bases by refinement and reformulation from that goal (Neches *et al.*, 1985; Swartout *et al.*, 1991) to produce a system that will be capable of solving specific instances of that goal. The goal is matched against the problem-solving knowledge base. The method of the plan found causes additional subgoals to be posted, and the process is iterated. EXPECT's matcher unifies goals and plans according to the semantic representation of the goal's arguments. For example, a goal to find the distance between two cities matches a plan to find the distance between two locations, since cities are locations. Type constraints are also propagated through the method of plans. The Program Writer also reformulates goals when no plan is found to match them.

The Program Writer records all its steps and decisions in an annotated *design history*. For example, Figure 3.4 shows the most relevant parts of the design history for the general goal to transport a set of objects to a location using a set of ships. The design history reflects both the goal/subgoal expansion as well as some goal reformulations. For example, the subgoal `determine-whether-fits-`

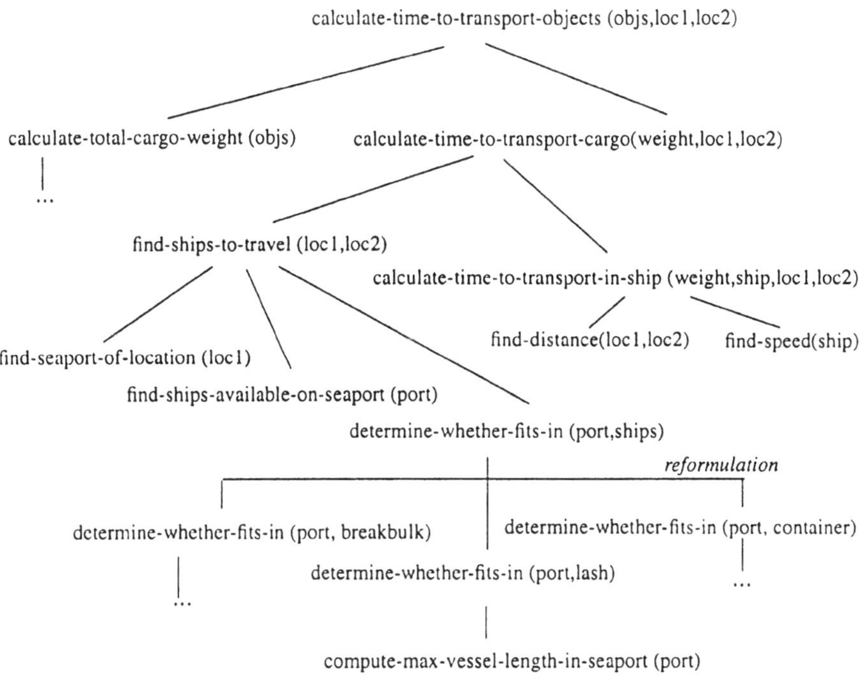

Figure 3.4 Relevant portions of the design history produced by the problem solver

`in` was reformulated into three goals, one for each type of ship that the system knows of, as indicated in the domain model.

The design history tells the system whether a definition is used and where, what it is used for, and how. The system understands that the type of a ship will require taking a different path in the tree, because there are different procedures to determine if a ship fits in a seaport depending on what type of ship it is. The same can be said about each plan: the design history records whether they are used and where, for what goals, and with what arguments. In essence, it represents the *functionality of the knowledge that the domain model contains*. It thus allows the system to reason about *how* knowledge will be used. This is crucial as one cannot indiscriminately add new knowledge into a system but rather needs to understand how that knowledge will be used. Otherwise, there is a danger that the knowledge added will be useless or incomplete to achieve the task for which the system is designed. The design history also provides an important piece of information: what knowledge is not used for problem solving. The system is aware of what plans are not being matched with any goals and which

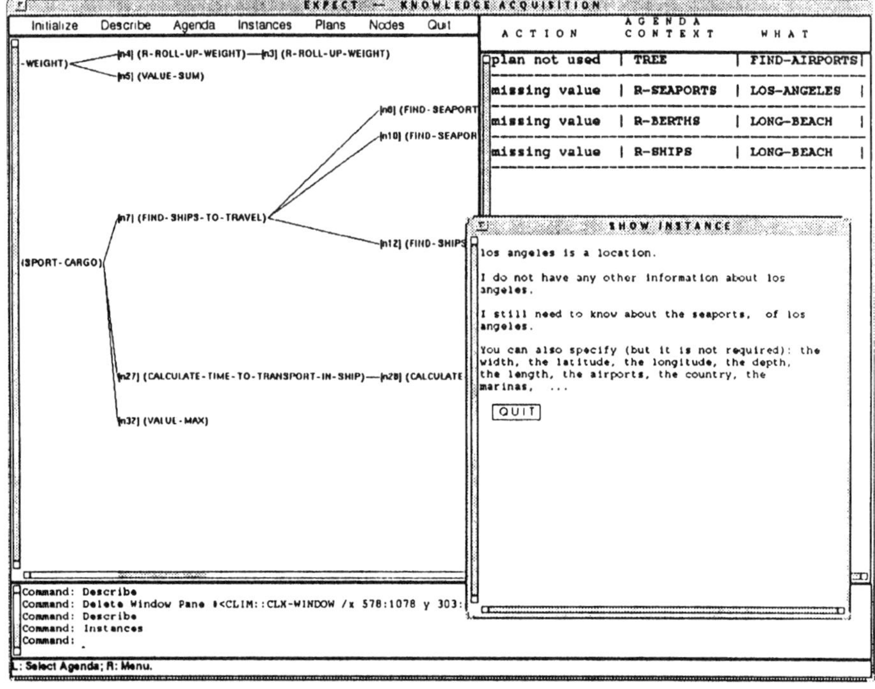

Figure 3.5 EXPECT's user interface

parts of the domain model are not currently relevant for the task. These are signs that the user needs to correct the system's current knowledge to make all of it useful for the task at hand. The scenarios in the next sections illustrate in more detail how these features of the architecture support knowledge acquisition.

Figure 3.5 shows EXPECT's user interface. The user can examine the current contents of knowledge bases by pulling menus and choosing to display the concept hierarchy or the design history. When the user clicks on a concept, the system provides a description of what is currently known about it. The user can also examine instances. When the user clicks on a node in the design history, the system describes in detail both what goal is accomplished in a node and how (a reformulation, a grammar construct, a plan). The user can also look up plans from the problem-solving knowledge base. In short, the interface allows the user to inspect the knowledge currently available to the system, which is the first step toward detecting errors that can be corrected through knowledge acquisition.

When the user detects a knowledge fault through this inspection process, the interface offers several possibilities to change the contents of the knowledge bases, and at different levels of detail. The user can change existing information about instances or add new instances (e.g. new locations, new seaports). The user can also change any plan by manipulating its components (adding, removing, or substituting substeps), or add new plans either created by the user or created by the system by analogy with existing plans. Finally, the user can change portions of the design history by manipulating its nodes. Adding or removing a step in a node causes the plan in that node to be changed, as well as any plans that appear in the subtree originating at that node. If any new subgoals cannot be matched with existing plans, the system creates new plans by analogy with the plans in the original subtree. The next section shows an example of this behaviour.

3.3 Transfer of problem-solving knowledge within a domain

Figure 3.6 shows a scenario in which existing problem-solving knowledge is corrected. The user is presented with menus (instead of being allowed to type in free English), but we paraphrase here the user's intervention in English for clarity and indicate this with italics. EXPECT generates language descriptions of plans of the type shown in this figure and carries out the modifications to its knowledge base as indicated by the user.

In this scenario, the system is given the problem of transporting a unit to the seaport of Cabra (line [1]). The system solves the problem and reaches the conclusion that it takes 3 days (line [2]). The user is surprised that it could be done so fast in such a small seaport and asks why (line [3]). The system explains its conclusion by retracing its reasoning (line [4]). Notice that, at this point, only a summary of the whole reasoning is included in the explanation, thus providing a high-level justification for the conclusion. The user can, however, "zoom-in" on a particular part of the problem solving by asking further questions. This is illustrated in lines [5–6].

The justifications provided by the system allow the user to detect a potential error: the user disagrees with some of the information given by the system and provides conflicting information (line [7]). Given this new information, EXPECT now reasons about the design history to localize the problem, and a dialogue to debug the system is initiated.

First, EXPECT finds the exact place in the design history that led to the conclusion questioned by the user and explains that part of the reasoning (line [8]). This allows the user to detect the problem more precisely. In this case, the user realizes that the plan to determine whether a ship fits in a port is incorrect (or incomplete). The user thus provides the additional information, namely that the draft of a ship must also be taken into consideration (line [9]) at a particular node of the design history. The system asks the user how to check the draft, and whether the analogy with checking the length is appropriate. This is possible

U: *How long does it take to transport that unit to Cabra with the ships available?* [1]

S: 3 days [2]

U: *Why?* [3]

S: To transport unit X to a location, first I calculated that the total weight of the cargo is 300,000 tons, then I determined that I could use 3 container ships and 10 breakbulk, and distributed the cargo among the ships. [4]

U: *Why breakbulk ships?* [5]

S: I used the Cabra seaport, and determined that breakbulk ships fit in the Cabra seaport. [6]

U: *This is wrong. Cabra is too small for breakbulk ships.* [7]

S: I concluded that breakbulk ships fit in the Cabra seaport. To do this, I checked that the ship length is less than the maximum vessel length in that seaport. Is this right? (Yes; No; Yes with constraints) [8]

U: *Yes, with constraints: you have to check both the length and the draft.* [9]

S: I know how to check the length. Do I check the draft in a similar way? (Yes; No; Yes with constraints) [10]

U: *Yes* [11]

S: What corresponds to (1) the ship length (2) less than (3) the maximum vessel length in that seaport? [12]

U: *(1) ship draft (2) less than (3) maximum vessel draft in the seaport* [13]

S: Ok. So to determine what ship types fit in a seaport, I determine if the ship length is less than the maximum vessel length in that seaport, and then I determine if the ship draft is less than the maximum vessel draft allowed in the seaport. Both have to be true in order for a ship type to fit in a seaport. Correct? (Yes or No) [14]

U: *Yes* [15]

[...]

S: Re-solving the problem with the updated method for determining what ship types fit in a seaport. It takes 10 days to transport the unit to Cabra. [16]

⋮

Figure 3.6 Example scenario: modifying existing plans

because the system already has a plan to check the length, and it can use it to form an expectation for how to check the draft (line [10]). Upon positive reaction (line [11]), EXPECT prepares the elements that can be the source of the analogy, and prompts the user for their correspondents (line [12]). After the user's response (line [13]), EXPECT summarizes to the user the change made to the knowledge base (line [14]). Notice that since the results of both checks are boolean, the system also has a suggestion about how to combine them. The plan is now corrected. After the problem has been fixed, EXPECT re-works the original goal (line [16]). Notice that since the system did not find a plan to compute the maximum vessel depth on a seaport, it created a new plan by analogy with the plan that achieves the goal of computing the maximum vessel length. The acquisition of this new plan is done autonomously by the system, based on the user's suggested changes on how the problem was solved. This is possible because the design history reflects the fact that this plan is used in the part of the reasoning that the user wants to modify. If the new plan had any inconsistencies, EXPECT would notify the user. This can be caused by incompleteness in the mapping that the user gives the system to do the analogy. It is important to realize that had the system found an existing plan to solve the new goal, it would have used this plan to expand the new subtree. EXPECT is acquiring new plans for its problem-solving knowledge base, effectively learning at the knowledge level (Newell, 1982).

Figure 3.7 shows a different scenario where new plans are added to the knowledge base by the user. Much like in the previous scenario, the user communicates to the system the analogy of ships and ports with aircrafts and hangars: what to retrieve (line [2]), what the correspondences are (line [4]), and

---

S: ... [1]

U: *To service a type of aircraft, first check if it fits in a hangar. Similar to how a ship fits in a seaport.* [2]

S: To determine what ship types fit in a seaport, I determine if the ship length is less than the maximum vessel length in that seaport, and then I determine if the ship draft is less than the maximum vessel draft allowed in the seaport. Both have to be true in order for a ship type to fit in a seaport. We want to describe a way to determine if a type of aircraft fits in a hangar. What corresponds to (1) the ship length (2) less than (3) the maximum vessel length in that seaport (4) the ship draft (5) less than (6) the maximum vessel draft allowed in the seaport (7) both have to be true? [3]

U: *(1) aircraft length (2) less than (3) hangar length (4) aircraft height (5) less than (6) hangar height (7) both have to be true.* [4]

S: Ok. So in order to check if a type of aircraft fits in the hangar, I determine if the aircraft length is less than the hangar length, and then I determine if the aircraft height is less than the hangar height. Both have to be true in order for an aircraft type to fit in the hangar. [Yes; No; Yes with constraints] [5]

U: *Yes, with constraints: you have to check length, height, and width.* [6]

S: Ok. I know the length, width, and height of hangars. I know the length and height of an aircraft. What is the width of an aircraft? [7]

U: *Wing span?* [8]

S: I understand. I know how to check the length and the height. Do I check the width in a similar way? (Yes; No; Yes with constraints) [9]

U: *Yes* [10]

S: Ok. So in order to check if a type of aircraft fits in a hangar ... [11]

Figure 3.7 Example scenario: adding new plans

what the exceptions are (lines [6–10]). The system takes charge of the rest, including updating the corresponding parts of the different knowledge sources.

3.4 Transfer of problem-solving knowledge across domains

The analogies in the above scenarios involve plans within the same domain, but exactly the same mechanism applies if the new plans are in a different domain. For example, the user can suggest the similarities with checking if a package fits in a truck, or if any physical object fits in another. Because the analogy is not worked out automatically and the user is in charge of guiding the KA tool through all the stages (retrieval, mapping and adaptation), the analogy can be as far-fetched as the user finds suitable. For example, one can imagine using the plan to check if a ship fits in a port to check if an event happens during another one by checking if the corresponding time intervals fit within one another. Thus, the same general mechanism can be used throughout any stage of knowledge acquisition and throughout any application domain at hand. Notice that this requires that knowledge acquisition does not happen in a vacuum, and by that we mean that the system should have access to as many knowledge bases in different domains as possible. Some efforts in very large knowledge bases already aim in this direction (Neches *et al.*, 1991; Lenat and Guha, 1989). This is much as humans communicate and learn things from each other: by first establishing backgrounds and then using constructs that the other person is accustomed to. For example, doctors may not teach new things to biologists in the same way that they would explain them to engineers, since they would have common ground concepts with the former to build upon. Having knowledge bases shared by different knowledge-based systems will some day provide this common ground for our knowledge acquisition tools.

3.5 Next step: generalization of problem-solving methods

Of course, acquiring knowledge by analogy has its limits. For example, a user who is entering knowledge in a medical domain may not know in detail what problem-solving knowledge is involved in our transportation domain. This is also common in humans: the more we know about the other person's areas of knowledge, the easier it is to explain things to them. Again, we can turn to machine learning techniques for an answer. This section describes our plans for future work regarding the use of generalization and induction techniques to extend the current analogical reasoning in EXPECT.

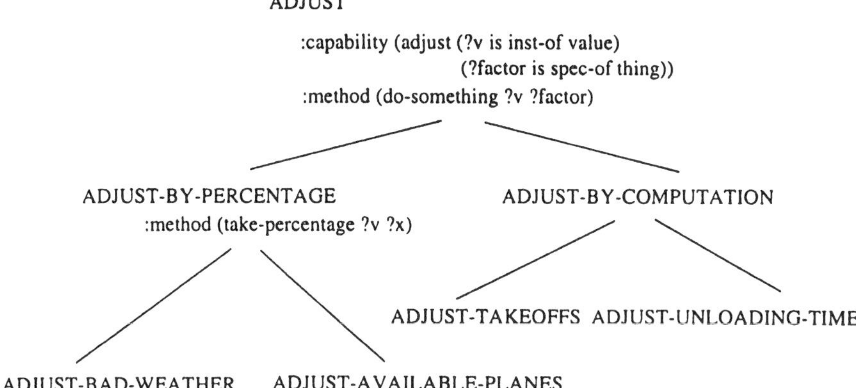

Figure 3.8 A hierarchy of plans for adjusting values

Let us consider an example from our transportation domain. There is a plan to calculate the throughput (takeoffs per day) that an airport can handle. To do that, the given throughput is adjusted by a percentage factor determined by the presence of bad weather, and by how many docks are available for unloading.[2] There is also a different plan to calculate how many planes are available for a transportation problem. To do so, the amount of planes assigned for the task is adjusted by a percentage factor that takes into account the rate at which each type of plane tends to break down and how much time it takes to repair it. Induction techniques, and, in particular, generalization from examples, could be extended and applied in these cases to provide the system with the concept of a plan to do adjustments of values, as shown in Figure 3.8. The following example illustrates how these generalized plans could be used to cooperate with an expert during KA.

In summary, this scenario illustrates how EXPECT could use plan generalization and analogical reasoning to guide knowledge acquisition. The knowledge about adjustments in the transportation domain is used to acquire adjustments for drug therapy. We used two very different domains to illustrate the potential of this approach, but the impact should be greater when the nature of the domains is not so diverse.

Suppose that a medical expert is using EXPECT for administering drugs, in particular to advice with digitalis therapy (Swartout, 1983). The default dose of a drug has to be reduced if the patient has certain conditions (called sensitivities to the drug). To treat a patient with digitalis, the normal dose (1 μg/kg) needs to be adjusted by a factor of 0.8 if the patient has a high level of serum calcium and by

[2] If there are not enough unloading docks the planes would be idle wating for a dock to become available.

U: *Add a new sensitivity for digitalis: high serum calcium. [...]* [1]

S: Ok. What method should I use to adjust the dose for high serum calcium sensitivity [Take percentage; Do computation; Other]? [2]

U: *Take percentage* [3]

S: Ok. Which percentage? [4]

U: *0.8* [5]

S: Ok. Now I need to know how to combine the results of the adjustments. Choose one of [MIN;MAX;ADD;MULTIPLY;Other]. [6]

U: *Why?* [7]

S: We are adjusting digitalis dose. To do an adjustment, I need to know: (1) value to be adjusted, (2) factors, (3) methods to adjust the value, and (4) how to combine the results. In this case, (1) digitalis dose (2) drug sensitivities (3) take percentage 0.8 for high serum calcium, take percentage 0.7 for low serum potassium. Now I need to know (4) how to combine the results. [8]

U: *How to combine the results?* [9]

S: For example, when I compute the takeoffs per day in an airport, I adjust the default value of takeoffs for the airport according to weather conditions and to available unloading docks. To do an adjustment, I need to know: (1) value to be adjusted, (2) factors, (3) methods to adjust the value, and (4) how to combine the results. In this case, (1) takeoffs per day (2) weather, unloading docks (3) take percentage, compute docks throughput (4) take minimum value. In the digitalis dose adjustment, I need to know how to combine the results of the adjustments. Choose one of [MIN;MAX;ADD;MULTIPLY;Other]. [10]

U: *multiply* [11]

S: Ok. High serum calcium is now a new sensitivity for digitalis. [12]

Figure 3.9 Hypothetical scenario: adding new plans in a different domain

a factor of 0.7 when serum potassium is low. If both sensitivities are present, the default dose is adjusted by the product of both factors (0.8×0.7).

Suppose now that the system knows only about one sensitivity (low serum potassium), as well as how to adjust the dose of digitalis if the patient has this condition. Figure 3.9 shows a scenario where the user wants to add a new sensitivity: high serum calcium. The user enters whatever information he or she is aware that the system needs about drug sensitivities in line [1]. EXPECT updates the domain model accordingly. Now EXPECT examines the problem-solving knowledge to determine what sensitivities are used for. This causes the question in line [2] of how to adjust the dose for this new sensitivity.

The system knows to acquire an adjustment for this sensitivity based on how sensitivities are used for problem solving. Because a general plan for doing adjustments is available, the system knows that when more than one adjustment is present it needs a method to recombine the results (line [6]). The system could justify the reason for the questions to the user (lines [7–8]), as well as to produce examples that undo the generalization and facilitate a ground analogy to the user in terms of airport takeoffs (line [10]).

This example illustrates how, through plan generalization, the system could further support analogies across domains. The generalization hierarchy would provide the grounds for transferring knowledge across different domains through its abstraction from domain-specific knowledge. The type of language that we use in EXPECT's plans combined with the LOOM knowledge representation system would facilitate this, but in addition we plan to research on general-purpose machine learning methods to induce these generalized plans automatically or semi-automatically. In the latter case, a knowledge engineer would be involved, but we believe this is a much lighter burden than other current KA environments would impose. Either way, these machine learning methods could prove more useful for automating KA than a general KA tool for a particular generic method.

3.6 Related work

NEODISCIPLE (Tecuci, 1992) integrates several machine learning techniques in a knowledge acquisition tool. NEODISCIPLE takes a user-given answer to a problem and applies explanation-based learning to build a plausible proof tree, abduction to complete the proof, and several other learning techniques to generalize the proof. Its predecessor, DISCIPLE (Tecuci and Kodratoff, 1990), built an analogy with an existing proof when the system lacked domain knowledge to build the proof for a new input. Our approach automates different parts of the analogical process. The user suggests the source of the analogies, the mapping, and any necessary adaptations. The tool provides the *supporting environment* by navigating through the system's reasoning and carrying out the user's corrections through analogical reasoning. EXPECT provides a framework for analogical reasoning where the tool takes responsibility for suggesting corrections and for making the adequate changes in the knowledge base.

Other work on analogy uses the derivational traces of the problem solver to guide the system in solving a new problem (Veloso, 1992; Carbonell, 1986). EXPECT uses the design history as a source of analogies as well, and its problem solver will find plans to match any new goals that arise as a result of the mapping. However, the crucial difference is that EXPECT will create new problem-solving knowledge when no plan is found to achieve a goal. A new rule is created in our first scenario to compute the maximum depth of a berth, without which the system could not have solved the problem. In other words, EXPECT is learning at the knowledge level (Newell, 1982).

The Spark/Burn/FireFighter framework (Klinker *et al.*, 1991) treats knowledge acquisition as a programming effort, and aims to provide a set of *mechanisms* as basic blocks for building knowledge-based systems. The goal is to design such mechanisms to be both *usable* (understandable by domain experts) and *reusable* (applicable to several tasks and domains). The PROTEGE-II system (Puerta *et al.*, 1992) is also based on reusable mechanisms as building blocks for knowledge acquisition, and addresses usability by integrating domain-dependent knowledge in the process of putting these mechanisms together. EXPECT shares both goals, and the aim is to achieve them without explicitly building such mechanisms. If at all, these mechanisms would be a by-product of the tool's interaction with the user and its learning capabilities. Problem-solving knowledge in EXPECT is usable because it is accessible to domain experts through explanations. Knowledge is reused when the user proposes analogies with new situations, as well as through any generalizations over existing cases.

Another general-purpose knowledge acquisition approach is that proposed by KADS (Wielinga *et al.*, 1992), a methodology for building knowledge based systems, which, unlike EXPECT, emphasizes the initial building of a system (as opposed to its refinement). KADS views knowledge acquisition as a modelling activity and proposes a number of models that a knowledge engineer needs to build. Each model emphasizes a specific aspect of the system to construct and contains part of the knowledge needed. KADS also separates the domain model from the control knowledge, which is in turn divided into the inference model, the task model, and the strategic knowledge. These last three models together indicate how knowledge from the domain model is to be used in problem solving, and could thus theoretically be also used to guide refinement of a knowledge-based system once an initial prototype has been built. This is not currently done, however. KAD's current aim is to help the knowledge engineer faced with the task of building a new knowledge-based system by providing an explicit set of building blocks (or models) that the knowledge engineer should be concerned about, thus using a divide-and-conquer approach to the initial knowledge acquisition task. Our aim in EXPECT is a complementary one: it is to aid in refining and debugging a knowledge-based system automatically once a prototype scenario exists. Because EXPECT derives code from the specification automatically (i.e., the domain model and the plans), changes done at the specification level are automatically reflected in the executable code. In contrast, until executable systems are automatically derived from the models designed with the KADS methodology, guidance from the models would only apply to refining the models themselves. The changes would then need to be reflected in the code by hand.

3.7 Conclusion

We have shown our approach to building KA tools to achieve knowledge reuse based on general-purpose machine learning methods. In particular, we showed how a learning-by-analogy mechanism can be incorporated in a knowledge acquisition tool to facilitate the knowledge acquisition process. In our system, the current content of the knowledge base is used to create expectations dynamically for what knowledge is to be acquired. These expectations are based on the functionality of each piece of knowledge in the overall system, and on analogies derived from the current knowledge base. Importantly, the system and the user work in synergy: unlike other machine learning approaches, our system does not attempt to deduce all the information needed to form the analogy by itself. Rather, it relies on input from the user to guide its analogical learning. On the other hand, the user does not need to know a lot about the knowledge base or to enter all the new necessary information explicitly, but can rely on the tool to guide the process. We showed how this approach can be employed to acquire information both within a domain and across domains.

We also outlined how other general learning mechanisms (such as generalization and induction techniques) might be incorporated into our system. We hope to support with this work our claim that powerful, versatile and yet practical knowledge acquisition tools can be built by coupling general machine learning mechanisms with more traditional knowledge acquisition techniques.

Acknowledgements

We would like to thank Kevin Knight, Bing Leng, Vibhu Mittal and Bill Swartout for their feedback during the writing of this paper. We would also like to thank the anonymous reviewers for their helpful comments on earlier drafts of this paper, and especially the editors of this book, Gheorghe Tecuci, and Yves Kodratoff for their detailed and valuable feedback. This work was possible thanks to the efforts of current and previous members of the EXPECT group, in particular Pedro Gonzalez, Bing Leng, Vibhu Mittal, Ramesh Patil, Bill Swartout and Marcelo Tallis. Finally, we would also like to thank Sheila Coyazo for her prompt support on the keyboard.

We gratefully acknowledge the support of the Advanced Research Projects Agency under contract no. DABT63–91-C-0025. The view and conclusions obtained in this document are those of the authors and should not be interpreted as representing the official policies, either expressed, or implied, of ARPA or the US Government.

References

Buchanan, B. G. and Shortliffe, E. H. (1984). *Rule-Based Expert Systems: The MYCIN Experiments of the Stanford Heuristic Programming Project.* Addison-Wesley, Reading, MA.

Carbonell, J. G. (1986). Derivational analogy: a theory of reconstructive problem solving and expertise acquisition. In *Machine Learning, An Artificial Intelligence Approach, Volume II*. Morgan Kaufmann, San Mateo, CA.

Chandrasekaran, B. (1986). Generic tasks in knowledge-based reasoning: high-level building blocks for expert system design. *IEEE Expert*, 1(3): 23–30.

Chang, T. C. and Wysk, R. A. (1985). *An Introduction to Automated Process Planning Systems*. Prentice-Hall, Englewood Cliffs, NJ.

Davis, R. (1980). *Knowledge-based Systems in Artificial Intelligence*. McGraw-Hill, New York.

Fikes, R. E. and Nilsson, N. J. (1971). STRIPS: a new approach to the application of theorem proving to problem solving. *Artificial Intelligence* 2(3–4): 189–208.

Gil, Y. (1992). Acquiring Domain Knowledge for Planning by Experimentation. *PhD thesis*, Carnegie Mellon University, School of Computer Science, Pittsburgh, PA.

Gil, Y. (1994). Knowledge refinement in a reflective architecture. In *Proceedings of the Twelfth National Conference on Artificial Intelligence*, Seattle, WA, 1994.

Kitto, C. M. (1988). Progress in automated acquisition tools: How close are we to replacing the knowledge engineer? In *Proceedings of the Third Knowledge-Acquisition for Knowledge-Based Systems Workshop*, Banff, Alberta, Canada.

Klinker, G., Bhola, C., Dallemagne, G., Marques, D. and McDermott, J. (1991). Usable and reusable programming constructs. *Knowledge Acquisition*, 3(2): 117–135.

Knoblock, C. A. (1993). *Generating Abstraction Heirarchies: An Automated Approach to Reducing Search in Planning*. Kluwer, Norwell, MA.

Lenat, D. B. and Guha, R. V. (1989). *Building Large Knowledge-Based Systems*. Addison-Wesley, Reading, MA.

Lozano-Perez, T. (1987). A simple motion-planning algorithm for general robot manipulators. *IEEE Journal on Robotics and Automation*, 3(3): 224–238.

MacGregor, R. (1988). A deductive pattern matcher. In *Proceedings of the 1988 Conference on Artificial Intelligence*, St Paul, MN.

MacGregor, R. (1991). The evolving technology of classification-based knowledge representation systems. In Sowa, J. (editor), *Principles of Semantic Networks: Explorations in the Representation of Knowledge*. Morgan Kaufmann, San Mateo, CA.

Marcus, S. and McDermott, J. (1989). SALT: A knowledge acquisition language for propose-and-revise systems, *Artificial Intelligence*, 39(1): 1–37.

McDermott, J. (1988). Preliminary steps towards a taxonomy of problem-solving methods. In Marcus, S. (editor), *Automating Knowledge Acquisition for Knowledge-Based Systems*. Kluwer, Boston, MA.

Minton, S. (1988). *Learning Search Control Knowledge: An Explanation-based Approach*. Kluwer, Boston, MA.

Moore, J. D. (1989). A Reactive Approach to Explanation in Expert and Advice-Giving Systems, *PhD thesis*, University of California, Los Angeles.

Moore, J. D. and Paris, C. L. (1993). Planning text for advisory dialogues: capturing intentional and rhetorical information. *Computational Linguistics*, 19(4): 651–694.

Moore, J. D. and Swartout, W. R. (1989). A reactive approach to explanation. In *Proceedings of the Eleventh International Joint Conference on Artificial Intelligence*, Detroit, MI, pp. 1504–1510.

Moore, J. D. and Swartout, W. R. (1991). A reactive approach to explanation: taking the user's feedback into account. In *Natural Language Generation in Artificial Intelligence and Computational Linguistics*, pp. 3–48. Kluwer, Boston, MA.

Musen, M. A. (1989). Automated support for building and extending expert models. *Machine Learning*, 4(3/4): 347–375.

Musen, M. A. (1992). Overcoming the limitations of role-limiting methods. *Knowledge Acquisition*. 4(2): 165–170.

Neches, R., Fikes, R., Finin, T., Gruber, T., Patil, R. and Swartout W. R. (1991). Enabling technology for knowledge sharing. *AI Magazine*, 12(3): 36–56.

Neches, R., Swartout, W. R. and Moore, J. D. (1985). Enhanced maintenance and explanation of expert systems through explicit models of their development. *IEEE Transactions on Software Engineering*, SE-11(11): 1337–1351.

Newell, A. (1982). The knowledge level. *Artificial Intelligence*, 18(1): 87–127.

Newell, A. and Simon, H. A. (1972). *Human Problem Solving*. Prentice-Hall, New Jersey.

Paris, C. L. and Gil, Y. (1993). EXPECT: Intelligent support for knowledge-based system development. In *Proceedings of the Seventh European Knowledge Acquisition for Knowledge-Based Systems Workshop*, Toulouse, France. Also published in Aussenac, N., Boy, G., Linster, M., Ganascia, J.-G. and Kodratoff, Y. (editors), *Knowledge Acquisition for Knowledge-Based Systems*, Springer Verlag, New York, NY, 1993. ISI Technical Report # RR-93–339.

Puerta, A. R., Egar, J. W., Tu, S. W. and Musen, M. A. (1992). A multiple-method knowledge-acquisition shell for the automatic generation of knowledge-acquisition tools. *Knowledge Acquisition*, 4(2): 171–196.

Swartout, W. R. (1983). XPLAIN: A system for creating and explaining expert consulting systems. *Artificial Intelligence*, 21(3): 285–325.

Swartout, W. R. and Moore, J. D. (1993). Explanation in second generation expert systems. In David, J. M., Krivine, J. P. and Simmons, R. (editors), *Second Generation Expert Systems*, pp. 543–585. Springer Verlag, New York, NY.

Swartout, W. R., Paris, C. L. and Moore, J. D. (1991). Design for explainable expert systems. *IEEE Expert*, 6(3): 58–64.

Swartout, W. R. and Smoliar, S. W. (1987). On making expert systems more like experts. *Expert Systems*, 4(3): 196–207.

Tecuci, G. (1992). Automating knowledge acquisition as extending, updating, and improving a knowledge base. *IEEE Transactions on Systems, Man, and Cybernetics*, 22(6): 1444–1460.

Tecuci, G. and Kodratoff, Y. (1990). Apprenticeship learning in imperfect domain theories. In *Machine Learning: An Artificial Intelligence Approach*, volume 3. Morgan Kaufmann, San Mateo, CA.

Veloso, M. M. (1992). Learning by Analogical Reasoning in General Problem

Solving, *PhD thesis*, Carnegie Mellon University, School of Computer Science, Pittsburgh, PA.

Wielinga, B. J., Schreiber, A. Th. and Breuker, A. (1992). KADS: a modelling approach to knowledge acquisition. *Knowledge Acquisition*, 4(1): 5–54.

CHAPTER 4

An integrated framework for knowledge representation and theory revision

Moshe Koppel, Alberto Maria Segre and Ronen Feldman

Abstract

In this chapter, we present an integrated framework for knowledge representation and theory revision. This framework supports the evolution of correct knowledge bases using approximately-correct, expert-provided knowledge as a point of departure. Support is provided not only for representing the expert's domain knowledge, but also for representing additional information that can be used to help guide the theory revision process.

4.1 Introduction

It is by now generally recognized that for many domains, correct knowledge bases, or *domain theories*, need to evolve from approximately-correct, expert-provided knowledge using some automatic, example-driven, refinement scheme (Kodratoff, 1994). In order for this combination to be exploited most effectively, it is essential that both the initial acquisition and representation of the expert-provided knowledge and the refinement method be part of a single, integrated framework. In particular, the initial representation must capture all knowledge possessed by the expert which is potentially useful at the refinement stage; the refinement algorithm must, in turn, be designed so that it both exploits all the knowledge captured by the initial representation and does not interfere with the domain expert's ability to interpret the resulting domain theory.

In this chapter we will discuss one such integrated framework. The results presented here are based upon those reported previously in Koppel *et al.* (1994).

Machine Learning and Knowledge Acquisition
ISBN 0-12-685120-4

4.2 Knowledge representation and theory revision

We take as our starting point a concept definition consisting of a set of clausal rules of the form

$$h \leftarrow b_1 \wedge \ldots \wedge b_k$$

where h, the *clause head*, is a proposition and $b_1 \wedge \ldots \wedge b_k$, the *clause body* or the *antecedents*, are each positive or negative literals.[1] Each h and b_i is called an *element* of the domain theory. An h that does not appear in the body of any other clause is called a *top-level proposition*, or, more simply, a *root* of the domain theory. Similarly, a b_i that does not appear as the head of any other clause is called an *observable proposition*.

For example, consider the following simple propositional domain theory Γ loosely based on the example from Koppel *et al.* (1994):

buy-stock ← *increased-demand* ∧ ¬*product-liability*
product-liability ← *popular-product* ∧ *unsafe-packaging*
increased-demand ← *popular-product* ∧ *states-available>10*
increased-demand ← *new-market* ∧ *superior-flavor*
states-available>10 ← *states-available=11*
states-available>10 ← *states-available*=12
. . .
states-available>10 ← *states-available=50.*

The theory is meant to describe when an investor should buy stock in a soft drink company; it has therefore a single root *buy-stock*. Observable propositions that appear in the theory are *popular-product*, *unsafe-packaging*, *new-market*, and *superior-flavor*, while the literal *states-available>10* is defined explicitly in terms of the observable propositions *{states-available=1, . . . , states-available=50}*.

Informally, the theory states that one should buy stock if demand for the product is expected to increase and the company is not expected to face product liability lawsuits. In this theory, product liability lawsuits may result if the product is popular (and therefore may present an attractive target for sabotage) and if the packaging is not tamper-proof. Increased product demand results if the product is popular and enjoys a large market share, or if there are new market opportunities and the product boasts a superior flavor.

Typically, theories like Γ are provided by a domain expert who is keenly aware of the fact that he or she may have included unnecessary clauses or antecedents or may have left out needed clauses or antecedents. The fact that the theory is not perfect is discovered when the output of the theory violates the underlying phenomena the theory was intended to model. Suppose, for example, that we do not buy stock when the heavily advertised product, already available in eight

Table 4.1 Examples

Example	*Observables*	*Outcome*
E_1	{*unsafe-packaging, new-market, heavily-advertised, states-available=8*}	*buy-stock = true*
E_2	{*popular-product, states-available=12, superior-flavor*}	*buy-stock = false*
E_3	{*popular-product, states-available=16, ecologically-correct*}	*buy-stock = false*
E_4	{*unsafe-packaging, states-available=12*}	*buy-stock = false*
E_5	{*popular-product, states-available=11, celebrity-endorsement, nutritious*}	*buy-stock = true*
E_6	{*new-market, celebrity-endorsement, states-available=6, heavily-advertised*}	*buy-stock = true*

states, hits a new market without tamper-proof packaging. Later, we find that, contrary to the domain theory's predictions, the stock posts a significant gain. Such divergence – technically a *misclassified example* – indicates that the theory is flawed and needs to be corrected.

Somewhat more precisely, let an *example* be a truth assignment to a set of observable propositions along with the expected output of the theory. For example, consider six classified examples (Table 4.1) adapted from Koppel *et al.* (1994), where the first example corresponds to the scenario just described.

According to the theory Γ given above, *buy-stock* is true – that is, derivable from the given truth assignments to the observable propositions using the theory Γ and some valid inference procedure – for examples E_2, E_3, and E_5. Thus examples E_1, E_2, E_3 and E_6 violate expectations in the sense that the output of the existing theory Γ does not agree with the given expected output. It is the job of the automatic refinement system to produce a corrected domain theory that agrees with whatever phenomena it was meant to model.

Clearly, there may exist many more than one such corrected theory; a revision system should produce the theory that is close, in some meaningful way, to that originally intended by the domain expert. Precisely which consistent corrected theory is produced is a function of the revision system's internal *bias*.

In order to appreciate the meaning of bias in theory revision, note that any method for finding correct theories can be seen as a search through some hypothesis space of theories. Bias is the use of available information to guide this search and/or to prune the hypothesis space by giving preference to certain classes of theories. The object of this chapter is the specification and application of useful, expert-provided, revision bias; in particular, we focus on including in, or alongside, the theory all such useful biases. The biases are typically of one of the following three varieties:

- *Relative confidence levels:* The expert may indicate that if one of several elements of a theory must be repaired, then some particular one is to be preferred as the subject of the repair, essentially establishing a priori that a particular element's correctness is less certain.
- *Under-constrained clauses:* The expert indicates that some clause may be too easily satisfied. The expert may further indicate that – if this is indeed the case – that clause should be deleted altogether. Alternatively, the expert may specify that antecedents of a particular type should be added to the body of the clause to make it less permissive.
- *Over-specific antecedents:* The expert indicates that some antecedent in a clause may be too constraining. The expert may further indicate that the antecedent should be deleted altogether, replaced by less constraining literals of a particular type or, alternatively, essentially redefined in terms of other antecedents of a particular type.

As the original domain theory is constructed, the expert should be free to specify any additional knowledge of this type so that this knowledge can later be used to guide the theory revision process.

4.3 Representing explicit bias

We will show how the various types of additional information outlined above can be represented in the form of annotations to the basic theory. In our framework, the additional information is encoded in two explicit values assigned to each element of the theory. The first value, the *location bias*, indicates the desirability of retaining that element "as is", while the second value, the *repair bias*, indicates the preferred type of repair that is to be made to a given element if that element is indeed selected for repair.

4.3.1 Location bias

Each domain theory element, e, is assigned a value, $p(e)$, called its *weight*, in the range [0, 1]. This weight can be thought of as representing the expert's confidence that that element does not require repair: thus, the assignment $p(e) = 1$ means that e should certainly not be repaired; the assignment $p(e) = 0$ means that e certainly should be repaired.[2] In addition, a *root weight* is assigned to each top-level proposition, although such elements are not technically among the antecedents of any clause, indicating the expert's confidence that clauses do not need to be added directly to the definition of that proposition.

In general, we can think of $p(e)$ as the probability that e need not be repaired. Formally, the semantics of the probability are based on an underlying assignment of a priori probabilities to each possible theory that that theory represents the correct concept definition. Then $p(e)$ is the sum of the probabilities of all the theories which can be obtained from the initial one without repairing e.

Initially, these weights could be assigned to reflect standard, default, application-independent biases concerning the desirability of repairing particular elements. Such application-independent biases are typically based on syntactic criteria. The expert then can override these weight assignments by assigning weights which reflect his or her confidence in various clauses and antecedents in the theory. For example, the expert may assign $p(e) = 1$ to clauses and antecedents which constitute definitions or which are established beyond doubt, and may assign appropriately low values to $p(e)$ where it is known that information is missing concerning e. For example, if the clause

springtime ← *april*

is part of the theory (indicating that the observable *april* is sufficient reason to conclude that it is *springtime*), it is unlikely the expert would want the system to consider changing such a "definition". Here, the expert would assign unit weight to this clause and each of its antecedents, preventing any change to the definition. An alternative example is present in the sample theory Γ, where it is unlikely that the expert would want the system to delete the clause

states-available>10 ← *states-available=11*.

If one of several domain theory elements can be repaired so as to bring the theory into accord with given examples, the optimal element to repair is the one for which $p(e)$ is lowest (or, in other words, for which $1 - p(e)$ is highest). More generally, a set, S, of clauses and antecedents constitutes an *optimal set of culprits* precisely to the extent that

$$\prod_{e \in S} (1 - p(e))$$

is maximal.

4.3.2 Repair bias

As we have just seen, location bias can be quite useful in formalizing precisely what we mean by the "best" set of culprits, that is, elements suitable for repair.

But that is just one half of the problem; once the culprits are found, some reasonable operation must be carried out to repair the identified element. Thus in addition to the location bias, each clause C is also assigned one of the following repair biases:

DELETE C
ADD an antecedent to C using only the propositions $\{L_1, \ldots, L_K\}$

That is, we either delete an overly-generous clause or else we merely weaken it by adding antecedents to its body. Similarly, each antecedent A is assigned one of the following repair types:

DELETE A
ADD a clause to the definition of A using only the propositions $\{L_1, \ldots, L_K\}$
REPLACE A using only the propositions $\{L_1, \ldots, L_K\}$

Here, we either delete an overly-restrictive antecedent, weaken it by adding alternative means of proving the antecedent, or replace it by a more general version.

The assignment of a repair type to a domain theory element means that if that element is chosen for repair, then only the indicated repair may be done. Note that if a root weight is paired with a REPLACE repair type, then theory revision reduces to traditional concept learning; thus, root weights are normally paired with the ADD repair type, indicating that additional clauses defining the concept of interest may be needed.

Initially, each observable antecedent is assigned the default repair type REPLACE with no restriction placed on the proposition with which it can be replaced. All other components are assigned the repair type ADD with no restriction placed on the propositions which can be added to it. The expert can then override these assignments by indicating, for example, that certain antecedents or clauses should either be left alone or deleted (but not added to) or that if antecedents are added to some clause they must be of a certain type and so forth. We shall see below, in an example, how typical expert-provided information is captured by this format.

Several points regarding the restriction to certain propositions in ADD and REPLACE must be clarified. First, the restriction to $\{L_1, \ldots, L_K\}$ does *not* mean that the new antecedent is limited to one of the propositions L_i. It means, rather, that the new antecedent is some semantically-empty new literal from outside the language which is then defined by a set of clauses all of whose antecedents are chosen from among $\{L_1, \ldots, L_K\}$.

Second, while the restriction to DELETE is intended to absolutely preclude the possibility of ADD or REPLACE, the converse is not true. Even when ADD or REPLACE is indicated, the possibility of deleting can be left open by including the always-false proposition F or the always-true proposition T among the

Table 4.2 Sample domain theory Γ with explicit bias

Clause	*Domain theory*	*Location bias*	*Repair bias*
C_1	*buy-stock* ←	.99	ADD*{any}*
	increased-demand ∧	1.0	
	¬product-liability	.95	DELETE
C_2	*product-liability* ←	.9	ADD*{pending-suit}*
	popular-product ∧	.8	DELATE
	unsafe-packaging	.99	REPLACE*{unsafe-display}*
C_3	*increased-demand* ←	.9	ADD*{celebrity-endorsement, superior-flavor, ecologically-correct}*
	popular-product ∧	.8	DELETE
	states-available>10	.8	REPLACE*{states-available>X*, $0 \leq X \leq 9$*}*
C_4	*increased-demand* ←	.9	ADD*{any, F}*
	new-market ∧	.8	REPLACE*{growing-market}*
	superior-flavor	.8	DELETE

allowable propositions. Adding F as an antecedent to a clause is equivalent to deleting it; adding the clause $e \leftarrow T$ is equivalent to deleting the antecedent e. (Whether or not F (or T) is actually invoked to achieve the effect of deleting, even though ADD or REPLACE is indicated, depends on the algorithm used in executing ADD or REPLACE; typically, an element will be deleted if it plays no constructive role in the classification of any known example and will be added to or replaced otherwise.)

4.3.3 Example

An example should help make these concepts clear. Consider once again our sample theory Γ with the expert-provided explicit bias shown in Table 4.2. The numbers following each domain theory element in Table 4.2 are the original weight assignments obtained from the expert, while the repair biases are given on the far right. The lone root *buy-stock* is assigned a root weight of .999 and a repair bias of ADD*{any}* (not shown).

The weights reflect, for example, that the expert is relatively more confident of the effect of *increased-demand* on forecasted sales (and therefore on *buy-stock*) than of the negative effect of *product-liability*. The unit weight assigned to *increased-demand* in the first clause precludes any change to this domain theory element, while the .95 weight assigned to *¬product-liability* (also in the first clause) leaves open some chance of repair. Also, the root weight value of .999

assigned to *buy-stock* reflects the expert's confidence that *buy-stock* will not require additional clauses.

Let us consider clause C_3 more carefully. The expert has indicated that if the clause proves to be too generous then a new antecedent should be added, and that antecedent must be defined in terms of the propositions *celebrity-endorsement*, *superior-flavor*, and *ecologically-correct*. Moreover, if the clause proves to be too strict, its two existing antecedents are equally likely candidates for repair. If *popular-product* is to be repaired then it can only be deleted. On the other hand, if *states-available>10* is to be repaired, then only the threshold 10 can be changed; the expert is certain that some threshold is needed but is unsure what that threshold should be.

Ignoring location bias and repair bias for the moment, there are at least four simple ways to revise this theory so that all six examples are handled correctly.

1. First, one might delete the antecedent *superior-flavor* from clause C_4 and add *celebrity-endorsement* as a new antecedent in clause C_3.
2. Alternatively, one might delete the antecedent *superior-flavor* from clause C_4 and add *nutritious* as a new antecedent in clause C_3.
3. Another solution is to add a new clause *increased-demand* ← *heavily-advertised* and add *nutritious* as a new antecedent in clause C_3.
4. Finally, one might delete clause C_1 altogether, replacing it with two new clauses *buy-stock* ← *nutritious* and *buy-stock* ← *states-available<10* (this last solution essentially corresponds to abandoning the original theory and providing a new one).

The bias provided by the expert precludes, however, the third solution altogether since the unit weight assigned to the antecedent *increased-demand* in clause C_1 means that this antecedent cannot be weakened by deletion or the adding of clauses to its definition. Moreover, since the fourth solution entails the deletion of clause C_1 (whose weight is .99) and the addition of a clause to the root (whose weight is .999) the "desirability" of this revision is very low ($[1 - .99] \times [1 - .999] = .00001$). It is much more economical to use one of the first two revisions, each of which entails deleting *superior-flavor* from clause C_4 (.8) and adding an antecedent to clause C_3 (.9), since $[1 - .9] \times [1 - .8] = .02 >> .00001$. Finally, note that the second revision is precluded by the expert since *nutritious* is not among the propositions which can be used to "tighten" clause C_3. Thus according to the bias provided by the expert the first of the above revisions is the optimal one.

4.4 The revision method

Thus far we have defined what we mean by an optimal revision but we have not shown how to find one. We will see, however, that the representation of bias suggested above is ideally suited to a broad and proven-effective class of methods for finding optimal revisions. The central idea of these methods is that given examples can be used to update the initial bias. More specifically, the weights associated with domain theory elements can be incrementally adjusted up/down in accordance with the positive/negative role they play in the correct classification of the given examples. This idea forms the basis of *probabilistic theory revision* (PTR) (Koppel *et al.*, 1994), RAPTURE (Mahoney and Mooney, 1993) and TopGen (Opitz and Shavlik, 1993) (it should be noted, though, that in the latter two cases the semantics of the weights are different from that presented here).

The adjusted weights are then used to identify culprit clauses and antecedents for repair. For each such culprit we search for an addition/replacement which preserves its positive role in classifying examples while undoing its negative role (Koppel *et al.*, 1994; Ourston and Mooney, 1994). The repair type bias can be invoked at this stage to restrict the search space of possible revisions.

In this section, we briefly review the PTR method, and show how it can be extended to take advantage of repair bias. Imagine that we have interviewed a domain-expert and obtained a biased approximately-correct theory such as the one just described. Now we wish to revise the theory on the basis of examples which may expose inaccuracies in the theory. We will do so using two interacting modules. The first module is used to locate flawed elements in the theory by adjusting the location bias in accordance with the information implicit in the examples provided. Once a domain theory element is selected for repair by the first module, the second module determines what repair to apply so as to optimally improve the performance of the theory within the constraints determined by the repair bias.

4.4.1 Misclassified examples

Before we can describe the revision method, we first specify more precisely what constitutes a misclassified example. Recall that an example is a truth assignment to a collection of observable propositions along with an expected outcome. To determine whether or not an example is misclassified, we require a logically sound inference procedure that can determine a truth assignment for the domain theory roots: for reasons that will become clearer in the next section, we present here one such procedure.

Let Γ be some possibly-flawed theory for a top-level proposition r. Formally, an *example*, E, is a truth assignment to the observable propositions of Γ along with the intended truth value of r. For any such example we can compute whether r is true according to Γ.

For each observable proposition P, define

$$u(E, P) = \begin{cases} 0 & \textit{if } P \textit{ is false in } E \\ 1 & \textit{if } P \textit{ is true in } E \end{cases}$$

For each clause C with antecedents $l_1, \ldots, l_n$, let

$$u(E,C) = \prod_{i=1}^{n} u(E, l_i).$$

For each non-observable proposition P which is the head of the clauses $C_1, \ldots, C_m$, let

$$u(E,P) = 1 - \prod_{i=1}^{m} (1 - u(E, C_i)).$$

For each negated proposition $\neg P$, let

$$u(E, \neg P) = 1 - u(E, P).$$

These formulas are simply arithmetic forms of the Boolean functions $\wedge$, $\vee$ and $\neg$, respectively. Thus E is a *positive example* of r if and only if $u(E, r) = 1$.

We can restate this a bit more elegantly if we first define the *children* of a clause or literal in a theory as follows: (i) $Ch(C)$ for some clause C are the antecedents of C, (ii) $Ch(P)$ for some proposition P are the clauses of which P is the head, and (iii) the only child of a negated proposition $\neg P$ is P. Then for an observable proposition P, let

$$u_0(E, P) = \begin{cases} 0 & \text{if } P \text{ is false in } E \\ 1 & \text{if } P \text{ is true in } E. \end{cases}$$

For any other clause or literal e, let

$$u_0(E, e) = \begin{cases} 0 & \text{if } Ch(e) = \varnothing \\ 1 - \prod_{s \in Ch(e)} u_0(E, s) & \text{otherwise.} \end{cases}$$

For any clause C, $u_0(E, C) = 1 - u(E, C)$, but otherwise $u_0(E, e) = u(E, e)$. Thus in particular, $u_0(E, r) = 1$ if and only if $u(E, r) = 1$. This formula corresponds to a reformulation of the usual AND/OR form of a theory in terms of NAND relation.

Now suppose that for some example E, $u(E, r) = u_0(E, r) = 1$, i.e. E is alleged by the theory to be a positive example of r, but we are told that E is in fact a negative example of r. Such an example is said to be *misclassified* by the theory; likewise, if $u(E, r) = u_0(E, r) = 0$ but we are told that E is a positive example of r.

4.4.2 Locating flawed elements

We will use the information implicit in the correctly and incorrectly classified examples to adjust the weights associated with each domain theory element. Recall that for an element e, the weight $p(e)$ can be thought of as the probability that e does not require repair. It is therefore perfectly natural to compute the *conditional probability* that e does not require repair when given an example and its actual classification. This conditional probability becomes the new weight assigned to e. Should it be below a prespecified revision threshold σ, then this fact alone is taken as sufficient evidence that the given element e does, in fact, require repair.

Fortunately, there is an extremely efficient method for computing the conditional probability under certain independence assumptions, and for approximating it in the absence of those assumptions. We do so in two stages. In the first stage we compute the probability that E is a positive example of r according to the current assignments $p(e)$. In the second we use this newly-obtained value to compute for each domain theory element e the conditional probability that e need not be repaired given the correct classification of E. This conditional probability becomes a new value of $p(e)$.

The first stage is performed via a generalization of the function u_0 considered above. For every observable proposition P let

$$u_p(E, P) = \begin{cases} 1 - p(P) & \textit{if } P \textit{ is false in } E \\ 1 & \textit{if } P \textit{ is true in } E \end{cases}$$

For any other clause or literal e, let

$$u_p(E, e) = \begin{cases} 1 - p(e) & \textit{if } Ch(e) = \varnothing \\ 1 - p(e) \prod\limits_{s \in Ch(e)} u_p(E, s) & \textit{otherwise} \end{cases}$$

The additional term $p(e)$ in the product reflects the probability indicated by the location bias that a clause might be blocked or an antecedent circumvented in some way which does not appear in the current theory. Thus, $u_p(E, r)$ reflects the probability that the actual theory is such that r is provable for the example E.

In the second stage of the updating algorithm, we propagate the difference between each computed root value $u_p(E, r)$ (which lies somewhere between 0 and 1) and its target value (the actual classification for the example, which is either 0 or 1) back down through the domain theory in a process similar to neural network back-propagation. As we proceed, we compute updated values of $p(e)$ for each domain theory element using an intermediate value $\upsilon(E, e)$ as follows. Let $\varepsilon > 0$ be some very small constant[4] and let

$$\upsilon(E, r) = \begin{cases} \varepsilon & \textit{if } r \textit{ is meant to be false for } E \\ 1 - \varepsilon & \textit{if } r \textit{ is meant to be true for } E. \end{cases}$$

Now we proceed recursively down through the domain theory, computing $\upsilon(E, e)$ for each element. In each case we compute $\upsilon(E, e)$ on the basis of $u_p(E, e)$, that is, on the basis of how much of the proof (or refutation) of E flows through the element e. The precise formula is

$$\upsilon(E, e) = 1 - (1 - u_p(E, e)) \times \frac{\upsilon(E, f(e))}{u_p(E, f(e))}$$

where $f(e)$ is that parent of e for which

$$\left| 1 - \frac{\max[\upsilon(E, f(e)), u_p(E, f(e))]}{\min[\upsilon(E, f(e)), u_p(E, f(e))]} \right|$$

is greatest. Finally, we compute $p_{new}(e)$, the new value of $p(e)$, using the current value of $p(e)$ and the values of $\upsilon(E, e)$ and $u_p(E, e)$ just computed:

$$p_{new}(e) = 1 - (1 - p(e)) \times \frac{\upsilon(E, e)}{u_p(E, e)}.$$

If $p_{new}(e) < \sigma$, then this is an indication that domain theory element e is in need of repair. The use of this procedure is more formally justified in Koppel *et al.* (1994).

4.4.3 Multiple examples

Given this procedure for updating the location bias on the basis of a single example, we must now consider what to do when presented with more than one example. Of course, this will be the typical situation in most applications: rarely, if ever, will a theory be revised on the basis of a single example.

There are several options for compounding the effects of multiple examples. One might, for example, choose to process all of the examples in parallel and use average resulting values for $p(e)$. An alternative approach, that in fact used by PTR, is to process the examples one at a time in some random order, so that their composite effect might be approximated by the incremental updating of $p(e)$. Of course, processing the examples one at a time abandons any pretense that the algorithm is Bayesian and is more in the spirit of connectionist learning algorithms in which it is assumed that the sequential processing of examples in random order, as if they were actually independent, approximates the collective effect of the examples.

If at any stage during the processing of examples the weight of some element drops below the prespecified threshold, then that element is chosen for repair.

4.4.4 Repairing flawed elements

Once an element (a *culprit*) has been chosen for repair we must decide which repair to make. If a clause has dropped below the revision threshold then this is an indication that it is too generous and must be tightened. This can be achieved in one of two ways: the clause can be deleted altogether or an antecedent can be added to its body. If an antecedent has dropped below the revision threshold then this is an indication that it is too strict and must be loosened. This can be achieved in one of three ways: the antecedent can be deleted altogether, a new clause can be added to the definition of the antecedent, or the antecedent can be replaced by a more easily-satisfied antecedent.

Bear in mind that any such culprit element is on the one hand *obstructive* for some set of examples O (for which it facilitates undesired proofs or prevents desired ones), and on the other hand *needed* for another set of examples N (for which it facilitates desired proofs or prevents undesired ones). Note that $N \cup O$ may not comprise the entire set of examples, as many of the examples may not involve the culprit at all. We call $N \cup O$ the set of *relevant* examples; we show elsewhere (Koppel *et al.*, 1994) how the same bottom-up updating mechanism used for the computation of u in Section 4.4.2 can also be used to quickly and efficiently filter irrelevant examples from the exemplar set, leaving only the relevant examples.

Ideally we wish to repair the culprit such that it will then correctly handle those examples in the set O while at the same time continuing to handle the examples in N correctly. This is achieved by adding to the culprit some new element which is defined in terms of some Boolean combination of primitive propositions which distinguishes between N and O (i.e. is true for all the examples in N and false for all the examples in O). Typically, many such combinations can be found (especially if N and O are small sets) and there are many syntactic (i.e. domain independent) techniques for finding them. For example, the implementation of PTR presented in Koppel *et al.* (1994) uses ID3 (Quinlan, 1986). But precisely because these methods are purely syntactic, they often select distinguishing features of the example sets which are inappropriate in the context of the culprit element under repair.

It is precisely at this point that repair bias is critical. Repair bias might completely circumvent the process of distinguishing N from O by indicating that the culprit should be deleted forthwith. More subtly, though, the repair bias might pare down the search for distinguishing features to those primitive propositions which are appropriate to the culprit under repair. Standard inductive techniques like ID3 can then be employed using the restricted set of propositions indicated by the bias.

Note that the use of repair bias not only nudges the system towards the appropriate repair type, but can also significantly affect both the cost and effectiveness of a repair by restricting the inductive learning component's selection of attributes. Such restrictions can have very real effects on the size of the search space explored by an inductive learning system, and can also result in more appropriate additions or replacements to the theory.

4.5 Effects of bias

An example should make the whole process clear. In this section, we illustrate the performance of the modified version of PTR just introduced on two identical domain theories with different biases using a single collection of examples. The first theory is the theory introduced earlier, while the second theory is identical modulo slightly different location and repair biases. Recall that we have been given six examples (see Table 4.1), where examples E_1, E_2, E_3 and E_6 are misclassified. For this illustration, we use an arbitrarily chosen revision threshold of $\sigma = .12$.

4.5.1 Illustration 1

Let us consider what happens as we update the location bias assigned to each element in the domain theory by processing the examples in some random order (for the sake of expository simplicity, we use the "random" ordering $\{E_1, E_2, E_3, E_4, E_5, E_6\}$).

We begin by processing the misclassified positive example E_1, which, while decreasing the weights of the elements which prevent possible proofs, does not cause any of the weights to drop below the prespecified revision threshold. Processing the misclassified negative example E_2, however, does cause the weight associated with clause C_3 to drop below the threshold, indicating that clause C_3 is overly generous and in need of repair.

The repair bias given for clause C_3 indicates that the clause is to be repaired via the addition of appropriate antecedents selected from the set *{celebrity-endorsement, superior-flavor, ecologically-correct}*. Note that this set constitutes an ordered, restricted set from which these additional antecedents will be selected, presumably by some inductive learning component such as ID3. Note also that the inductive learning component is not simply invoked on the sum total of the known examples, but rather on the more restricted set $N \cup O = \{E_5\} \cup \{E_2, E_3\}$ which is efficiently determined. More precisely, we need to find some property (expressible in terms of the propositions *celebrity-endorsement, superior-flavor, ecologically-correct*) which holds for the correctly classified positive example E_5 (for which clause C_3 is and should be satisfied) but does not hold for the negative examples E_2 and E_3 (for which clause C_3 is but should not be satisfied). Since *celebrity-endorsement* is such a property, the result is the addition of a new antecedent *celebrity-endorsement* to clause C_3. Note that the antecedent *nutritious* would have also fixed this problem, but it was not selected because, unlike *celebrity-endorsement*, it was not explicitly listed in the repair bias and was therefore unavailable to the inductive learning component.

We now return to the processing of the misclassified examples in random order, processing examples E_3, E_4 and E_5 without further need for revision. When we encounter the misclassified positive example E_6, however, antecedent *superior-flavor* in clause C_4 drops below the revision threshold, indicating that this antecedent is responsible for preventing a proof. This particular antecedent's explicit DELETE repair bias results in its removal. At this point, every known example is properly classified and PTR terminates, with the resulting revised theory:

buy-stock ← *increased-demand* ∧ ¬*product-liability*
product-liability ← *popular-product* ∧ *unsafe-packaging*
increased-demand ← *popular-product* ∧ *states-available>10* ∧
  celebrity-endorsement
increased-demand ← *new-market*
states-available>10 ← *states-available=11*
states-available>10 ← *states-available=12*
 . . .
states-available>10 ← *states-available=50*.

Note that PTR, in this case, returns precisely that revision which we had previously informally determined to be optimal from among the four revisions considered (in fact, it is optimal among all revisions). It should be noted, however, that PTR does not always return the optimal revision.

4.5.2 Illustration 2

Let us now consider the same theory Γ but with different initial biases and see how this affects the performance of PTR (see Table 4.3). The alternative bias of Table 4.3 differs from the bias shown in Table 4.2 in three places. First, the location bias for *increased-demand* in clause C_1 is down from 1.0 to .7; the repair bias for this antecedent has also been changed to ADD*{popular-product, heavily-advertised}*. This reflects this expert's belief that it is very possible that a clause is missing in the definition of *increased-demand*, a possibility explicitly excluded by the previous expert. Second, the location bias for *superior-flavor* in clause C_4 has increased from .8 to .99; this reflects this particular expert's belief that it is unlikely that *superior-flavor* should be deleted from clause C_4, while the previous expert considered it a reasonable possibility. Finally, the repair bias for clause C_3 has also been changed, with *nutritious* added at the head of the list.

Table 4.3 Alternative sample domain theory Γ with explicit bias

Clause	*Domain theory*	*Location bias*	*Repair bias*
C_1	*buy-stock* ←	.99	ADD{*any*}
	increased-demand ∧	.7	ADD{*popular-product, heavily-advertised*}
	¬*product-liability*	.95	DELETE
C_2	*product-liability* ←	.9	ADD{*pending-suit*}
	popular-product ∧	.8	DELETE
	unsafe-packaging	.99	REPLACE{*unsafe-display*}
C_3	*increased-demand* ←	.9	ADD{*nutritious, celebrity-endorsement, superior-flavor, ecologically-correct*}
	popular-product ∧	.8	DELETE
	states-available>10	.8	REPLACE{*states-available>X, 0 ≤ X ≤ 9*}
C_4	*increased-demand* ←	.9	ADD{*any, F*}
	new-market ∧	.8	REPLACE{*growing-market*}
	superior-flavor	.99	DELETE

Recall that in principle there are at least four simple ways to revise this theory so that all six examples are handled correctly. Thanks to the different bias in this version of the theory, however, the relative quality of these solutions has changed dramatically with respect to the version of the theory given in Table 4.2. Here, the first two candidate repairs (deleting antecedent *superior-flavor* from C_4 while adding either *celebrity-endorsement* or *nutritious* to the antecedents of C_3) are much less desirable than they were previously given the relatively high weight (.99) initially assigned to *superior-flavor*, while the third candidate repair (adding *nutritious* to the antecedents of C_3 and incorporating the new clause *increased-demand* ← *heavily-advertised*) is now preferred given the lower weight assigned to *increased-demand.* The fourth candidate repair has very low priority also for this version of the theory.

Now let us apply PTR, processing the examples in the same presumably random order as in the previous case. Immediately after processing example E_1, the weight of antecedent *increased-demand* in clause C_1 drops below the revision threshold. This implies that the antecedent is overly restrictive, preventing a desirable proof of *buy-stock* for this example. The invocation of ID3 on the restricted set of examples $N \cup O = \{ E_4\} \cup \{E_1, E_6\}$ yields the addition of a new clause, *increased-demand* ← *heavily-advertised*, thereby "loosening" the overly-restrictive definition of *increased-demand* (note that the clause *increased-demand*

$\leftarrow$ *new-market* would discriminate perfectly but is excluded from consideration by the given repair bias).

We next run E_2, adjusting weights but not resulting in any additional repairs. When example E_3 is processed, however, the weight associated with clause C_3 drops below the revision threshold σ and C_3 is selected for repair. ID3 is once again invoked on the restricted set of examples $N \cup O = \{E_5\} \cup \{E_2, E_3, E_4\}$, resulting in the addition of the new antecedent *nutritious* to clause C_3 (note that *celebrity-endorsement* would also work as well, but that *nutritious* is preferred since it appears first in the list of allowed propositions). At this point all examples are correctly classified and PTR terminates, resulting in the revised theory:

buy-stock $\leftarrow$ *increased-demand* $\wedge$ $\neg$*product-liability*
product-liability $\leftarrow$ *popular-product* $\wedge$ *unsafe-packaging*
increased-demand $\leftarrow$ *popular-product* $\wedge$ *states-available>10* $\wedge$ *nutritious*
increased-demand $\leftarrow$ *new-market* $\wedge$ *superior-flavor*
increased-demand $\leftarrow$ *heavily-advertised*
states-available>10 $\leftarrow$ *states-available=11*
states-available>10 $\leftarrow$ *states-available=12*
. . .
states-available>10 $\leftarrow$ *states-available=50*.

Note how this revised theory reflects this particular expert's belief that it is preferable to "soften" the *increased-demand* condition by adding a clause to its definition than by deleting the antecedent *superior-flavor* from clause C_4. Moreover, it is preferable to "tighten" clause C_3 by adding the antecedent *nutritious* than by adding the antecedent *celebrity-endorsement*.

4.6 Conclusion

The kind of information typically available from experts along with tentative or imperfect domain theories falls into two main categories: (i) bias regarding which elements of the theory require repair and (ii) bias regarding the type of repair an element is likely to require. Conveniently, theory revision subdivides very naturally into two subtasks which reflect precisely those two types of bias: (i) finding those elements which require repair and (ii) repairing them. Several important theory-revision methods employ this division including EITHER (Ourston and Mooney, 1994), PTR (Koppel *et al.*, 1994) and TOPGEN (Opitz and Shavlik, 1993).

It is therefore only natural to integrate the representation of the expert-provided bias and the theory revision method in a fashion which allows maximal exploitation of the available information. We have shown here how this can be done with the PTR system. We have shown elsewhere (Feldman *et al.*, 1994;

Koppel *et al.*, 1994) that the PTR system is in fact effective on real-world domains including the PROMOTER theory (Murphy and Aha, 1992) intended to recognize certain sequences in DNA nucleotides, the classic soybean theory (Michalski and Chilausky, 1980) used to classify a number of common soybean diseases, and the "illegal board" CHESS theory (Pazzani and Kibler, 1992). In particular, we have used some of these domains to illustrate how the judicious choice of bias can significantly increase both the accuracy and efficiency of theory revision methods such as PTR (Feldman *et al.*, 1994).

The smooth integration of knowledge representation with theory revision lies at the heart of several important features of our approach to theory revision. In particular:

1. By assigning location bias, we implicitly define what constitutes an "optimal" revision, thereby clearly defining the objective of a theory revision algorithm.
2. By incrementally updating the location bias on the basis of known examples, we can efficiently identify the flawed domain theory elements.
3. Repair bias facilitates the efficient determination of appropriate repairs, and provides a convenient representational framework for exploiting additional knowledge about the semantics of the domain.

Finally, we note that a remaining important issue at the interface of knowledge acquisition and machine learning within the framework considered here is the dynamic introduction of bias during the revision process. In particular, we might consider a case in which various biases are available (say, for example, from multiple experts) and the revision process is used to dynamically assess the utility of the respective biases at various stages of the revision process.

Acknowledgements

The authors wish to thank Hillel Walters of Bar-Ilan University for his contributions to the content of this paper. Support for this research was provided in part by the Office of Naval Research through grant N00014–90–J–1542 (AMS) and by the Advanced Research Project Agency through Rome Laboratory Contract Number F30602–93–C–0018 via Odyssey Research Associates, Incorporated (AMS).

Notes

1. The central points we wish to make in this chapter are equally interesting for propositional and first-order theories; for the sake of expository clarity, we will discuss propositional theories only.

2. In the case of a clause, "repair" means either outright deletion or the addition of antecedents, and, in the case of antecedents, "repair" means either outright deletion, replacement, or the addition of clauses to its definition.
3. For the sake of expository simplicity, the 39 clauses which, taken together, define the literal "states-available > 10" are not shown in Table 4.2. Since we can safely assume that the elements of these clauses are all assigned unit weight by the expert, they are not subject to revision and can be excluded from the discussion that follows without loss of generality.
4. Strictly speaking, for the computation of conditional probabilities, we need to use "$\varepsilon = 0$". However, as noted in Koppel *et al.* 1994, in order to ensure convergence of the algorithm in all cases, we choose "$\varepsilon > 0$".

References

Feldman, R., Koppel, M. and Segre, A. M. (1994). Extending the role of bias in probabilistic theory revision. *Knowledge Acquisition*, 6(2): 197–214.

Kodratoff, Y. (1994). Induction and the organization of knowledge. In Michalski R. S. and Tecuci G. (editors), *Machine Learning: A Multistrategy Approach*, volume 4, pp. 85–106. Morgan Kaufmann, San Mateo, CA.

Koppel, M., Feldman, R. and Segre, A. M. (1994). Bias-driven revision of logical domain theories. *Journal of Artificial Intelligence Research*, 1: 159–208.

Mahoney, J. and Mooney, R. (1993). Combining connectionist and symbolic learning to refine certainty-factor rule-bases. *Connection Science*, 5: 339–364.

Michalski, R. S. and Chilausky, R. L. (1980). Learning by being told and learning from examples: an experimental comparison of the two methods of knowledge acquisition in the context of developing an expert system for soybean disease diagnosis. *Policy Analysis and Information Systems*, 4(2): 125–160.

Murphy, P. M. and Aha, D. W. (1992). *UCI Repository of Machine Learning Databases [Machine-readable data repository]*. Department of Information and Computer Science, University of California at Irvine, Irvine, CA.

Opitz, D. W. and Shavlik, J. W. (1993). Heuristically expanding knowledge-based neural networks. *Proceedings of the Thirteenth International Joint Conference on Artificial Intelligence*, 1360–1365.

Ourston, D. and Mooney, R. J. (1994). Theory refinement combining analytical and empirical methods. *Artificial Intelligence*, 66(2): 273–310.

Pazzani, M. and Kibler, D. (1992). The utility of knowledge in inductive learning. *Machine Learning*, 9(1): 57–94.

Quinlan, J. R. (1986). Induction of decision trees. *Machine Learning*, 1(1): 81–106.

CHAPTER 5

From balanced cooperative modelling to embedded adaptivity: using inductive logic programming techniques for knowledge acquisition

Stefan Wrobel

Abstract

Inductive Logic Programming (ILP), the subfield of machine learning concerned with inductive methods based on first-order representations, has become a very active and rapidly developing field that offers a host of powerful and efficient algorithms. In this chapter, we examine how ILP learning techniques can be used to effectively support the knowledge acquisition process and the construction of intelligent knowledge-based application systems. Starting from the well-known notion of balanced cooperative modelling, we show how ILP techniques can assist the user within this style of knowledge acquisition. Proceeding towards the usage phase of a knowledge-based system, we develop the concept of embedded adaptivity, referring to learning services integrated into or coupled with a larger application system. We illustrate the basic ideas in the context of the knowledge-based systems workbench MOBAL and its ILP modules.

5.1 Introduction

One of the most fundamental characteristics of a learning system is the representation formalism in which input examples and learning results are expressed. While many learning systems are based on *attribute-value* formalisms equivalent in expressiveness to *propositional logic* (e.g. the decision-tree family first made popular by Quinlan (1983) and Breiman *et al.* (1984)), it has become clear that for

Machine Learning and Knowledge Acquisition
ISBN 0-12-685120-4

many applications, it is necessary to be able to represent not only attributes of objects, but also information about the internal structure and components of objects and about logical and temporal relations between objects. Such knowledge is best represented in *relational* or *object-oriented* formalisms, the expressiveness of which is equivalent to (subsets of) *first-order logic*.

Even though algorithms based on first-order representations have always been a topic in machine learning, for a long time it seemed that the unfavourable computational properties of first-order logic would exclude any practical and efficient use of such techniques. Correspondingly, only relatively few systems were developed, and they did not meet with great practical success. In recent years, however, this situation has changed fundamentally due to significant theoretical and practical advances in controlling the complexity of learning in logic. Today, the field of *Inductive Logic Programming* (Muggleton, 1991), as it is now commonly called to emphasize the close connection to logic programming, is one of the most active and rapidly developing subfields of machine learning, and offers a host of powerful and efficient algorithms for induction in (clausal) first-order logic.

In the rest of this chapter, we will examine how these powerful new first-order learning techniques can be used to effectively support the knowledge acquisition process and the construction of intelligent knowledge-based application systems. We begin with an informal introduction to the ILP field and the additional power of first-order techniques using a telecommunications access control problem for illustration (Section 5.2). We then discuss how ILP algorithms can be used for interactive knowledge acquisition based on Morik's (Morik, 1993) Balanced Cooperative Modelling paradigm (Section 5.3). As a concrete example of this paradigm, the integrated knowledge acquisition and machine learning system MOBAL is presented, including its major modules and the services they offer for knowledge acquisition (Section 5.4). Within the balanced cooperative modelling paradigm, MOBAL has been extended into an "ILP toolbox" and now features interfaces to the most popular and successful ILP algorithms which complement the internal tools. After discussing the toolbox concept (Section 5.5), we turn to the practical issues of using learning capabilities within larger application systems, and present how Mobal's networked client/server concept supports embedded adaptivity and the integration of learning modules with conventional software components (Section 5.6). The chapter ends with a discussion of related approaches (Section 5.7) and conclusions (Section 5.8).

5.2 Inductive Logic Programming

5.2.1 The goals of ILP

Even though, at first sight, the term "Inductive Logic Programming" might seem to indicate that the goal of the field is the inductive synthesis of logic programs in a narrow sense, the field actually addresses learning issues in first-order representations more broadly. The major goals of ILP can informally be stated as follows:

- To develop algorithms that are capable of using examples and background knowledge expressed in a first-order formalism to induce general first-order rules or concepts "describing" or "explaining" the examples.
- To examine the computational and theoretical properties of the algorithms or the ILP learning problem as such.

The classical motivation for the choice of first-order logic or variants thereof as a representation or description formalism is certainly that first-order logic offers a powerful, uniform and elegant way to describe and formalize even relatively complex domains. As stated in the introduction, this theoretical motivation is more and more augmented by a very practical one: in many applications where learning could be of value, it is inconvenient, difficult or even impossible to express the learning examples, the necessary background knowledge, or the concepts to be learned in propositional logic.

5.2.2 A sample application

As an example, consider a learning problem from the domain of telecommunications originally described in Sommer *et al.* (1994). In this domain, the goal was to replace an existing, manually created access control database with a set of verifiable access control rules in a declarative language. The database stated, for each employee, which switching systems this employee was allowed to access, but did not include the reasons why this was the case. The access rules, on the other hand, were to use the available background knowledge about the network and the employees, their affiliations and qualifications to decide about access rights in a general and explicit fashion.

In this application, the manually created access rights database can be represented by a set of first-order facts that are used as *positive examples* of the target concept `may_operate`:[1]

```
may_operate(bode,pabx_17).
may_operate(meyer,pabx_15).
```

Here, and for the rest of the chapter, we follow the convention from logic programming and Prolog (see, for example, Lloyd, 1987) and use lowercase names for predicates, functions, and constants, whereas variable symbols always begin with an uppercase letter.

[1] The example is a simplified variant of the representation used in Sommer *et al.* (1994).

Further facts about unauthorized access are used as *negative examples* of the target concept:

```
not(may_operate(bode,pabx_15)).
not(may_operate(meyer,pabx_17)).
not(may_operate(miller,pabx_15)).
```

To be able to learn from these examples, it is also necessary to represent the available *background knowledge* about the domain. Usually, this is done in the form of first-order facts and rules (clauses):

```
operator(bode).
operates(telplus,pabx_17).

engineer(meyer).
operates(talkline,pabx_17).

accountant(miller).
operator(X) → technical(X).
engineer(X) → technical(X).

works_for(bode,comtel).
subsidiary(comtel,
  telplus).
works_for(meyer,nettalk).
subsidiary(nettalk,
  talkline).
works_for(miller,nettalk)
```

where the intended meanings of predicates are as follows:

`operator(P)`: person `P` is an operator
`works_for(P,C)`: person `P` works for company `C`
`operates(C,S)`: company `C` operates system `S`
`subsidiary(C1,C2)`: company `C1` is a subsidiary of company `C2`
`engineer(P)`: person `P` is an engineer
`accountant(P)`: person `P` is an accountant
`technical(P)`: person `P` belongs to technical personnel

From the above set of facts and rules, an ILP learning system can learn the rule:

```
works_for(P,C1) & operates(C2,S) & subsidiary(C1,C2)
& technical(P) → may_operates(P,S).
```

stating that all technical personnel in a subsidiary company may operate all systems managed by the parent company. In a top-down ILP learning system such as FOIL (Quinlan, 1990), such rules are learned by taking a rule with empty premise list and then specializing it progressively by adding premises based on their suitability for covering positive examples and excluding negative examples.

This example problem shows why first-order representations are necessary in applications. In a propositional representation (such as the attribute-value representation used by most propositional learning systems), it is impossible to directly express the necessary relationship between `P`, `C1`, `C2` and `S`. Knowing what the target rule is, one might object that in principle we could define a special attribute `related` that would be true of an example iff the employee and the system mentioned in the example are related as required by the above rule. The fact that this particular relationship is important is exactly what we want to learn, however, so this is not a fair objection. Only a learning system capable of working with a first-order representation can actually *discover* the importance of this relationship. The same is true for applications involving *structural* or *time-oriented* data.

5.2.3 The ILP learning problem

The telecommunications access control problem described above illustrates the central learning task of ILP, inductive learning of concept descriptions from examples with the goal of predicting classifications of future examples. This problem is usually formalized in ILP as follows (Muggleton and De Raedt, 1994; Kietz and Dzeroski, 1994).

Given:

- positive examples E^+ (expressed in an example language L_E)
- negative examples E^- (expressed in an example language L_E)
- background knowledge B (expressed in a background knowledge language L_B) such that B is consistent with E^+ and E^- ($B \cup E^+ \cup E^- \not\models \Box$),

find:

- a learning hypothesis H (expressed in a hypothesis language L_H) such that H together with B derives the positive examples ($H \cup B \models E^+$), and does not derive any of the negative examples, i.e. is consistent with E^- ($H \cup B \cup E^- \not\models \Box$).

In other words, the learning hypothesis H must be such that together with B it correctly predicts (derives) the positive examples, and does not predict any negative examples as true. The representation languages involved are implicitly assumed to be subsets of first-order logic, as in the example above, where we have used function-free first-order Horn clauses for examples, background knowledge, and learning result. A large array of systems is now available for solving learning problems cast in the above framework, including, for example, FOIL (Quinlan, 1990), GOLEM (Muggleton and Feng, 1990), RDT (Kietz and Wrobel, 1992), CLINT (De Raedt and Bruynooghe, 1992), ITOU (Rouveirol, 1992), LINUS (Lavrac and Džeroski, 1993), and several others (see, for example, Muggleton and De Raedt (1994) or Lavrač and Džeroski (1993) for overviews).

While the above definition is general enough to cover many possible uses of

ILP techniques (e.g. program synthesis from examples), the field has had its most prominent successes in applications where the primary goal was data analysis, i.e. inductive acquisition of predictive rules from a given database of examples. Published examples of such applications include:

- Drug design (King *et al.*, 1992)
- Protein secondary structure prediction (Muggleton *et al.*, 1992)
- Integrated circuit floorplanning (Herrmann *et al.*, 1994)
- Technical diagnosis (Bergadano *et al.*, 1990; Feng, 1992)
- Medical diagnosis (Morik *et al.*, 1993a; Lavrač *et al.*, 1993)
- Air-traffic control (Kodratoff and Vrain, 1993)
- Finite element mesh design (Dolsak and Muggleton, 1992)
- Telecommunications (Sommer *et al.*, 1994)
- Robotics (Morik and Rieger, 1993).

This impressive list of applications clearly demonstrates that in the sense of data analysis, the use of ILP techniques for knowledge acquisition has already been very successful. In many of these applications, however, we find that a non-interactive ILP tool was used to analyse a given set of examples. Following the problem specification above, these tools take a set of examples, background knowledge and additional bias specifications as input, process the examples non-interactively, and output the learning result ("compiler-like"). If the learning result is not satisfactory, the user edits the input files using his or her favourite text editor, and runs the ILP learning algorithm again. A significant part of the knowledge acquisition problem is thus left to the user without direct support from the learning system. How can ILP learning techniques be used to cooperate more effectively with the user?

5.3 Balanced cooperative modelling

In her work on the nature of knowledge acquisition processes, Katharina Morik (Morik, 1989, 1991a) has introduced the notion of knowledge acquisition as a cyclical *sloppy modelling* process: starting from an initial domain model that out of necessity is incomplete, inconsistent or incorrect ("sloppy"), the user makes additions or revisions in order to improve the model, observes and evaluates the effects of these changes, makes further modifications, etc., until the overall quality of the model is judged satisfactory. This iterative process of knowledge acquisition occurs independently of the kind of system support that is available. In the batch learning scenario described above, the user prepares an initial "model" of the application domain that consists of examples and background knowledge. This model is then completed by the learning system with induced rules. The user manually inspects these rules, manually makes changes to the model (examples and background knowledge) and repeats the process.

This style of interaction with a learning system corresponds to the first of three cooperation styles that are distinguished in Morik (1993):

- *One-shot learning* As described above, the (ILP) learning system is used in a compiler-like fashion to induce rules from background knowledge and examples.
- *Interactive learning* In this form of cooperation, the learning system controls the acquisition process by asking questions to the user. CLINT or MIS are ILP systems of this type.
- *Balanced interaction* Both user and system can contribute to the evolving domain model in a mixed-initiative fashion; the system supports not only addition, but also inspection, revision and restructuring of the model.

As argued in Morik (1993), the balanced style of interaction (also referred to as *balanced cooperative modelling*) has a number of advantages compared to the other two in supporting knowledge acquisition by learning. In contrast to purely query-driven learning systems ("interactive learning"), the user controls the acquisition process and can work on whatever part of the model he or she sees fit. In contrast to batch learning systems, however, the system still provides feedback interactively, complements the user's inputs, and points to problems (e.g. inconsistencies) in the emerging model. As in query-driven learning systems, and unlike one-shot learning, all information need not be present right away. Unlike in query-driven systems, however, the user can provide whatever information is available at whatever moment. Most importantly, perhaps, the user can revise the emerging model at any point, and does not have to go through a query process again; nonetheless, the revision step is supported by the system, which is not the case in batch learning systems.

If ILP techniques are to be used in a system that supports a balanced interaction style, they must possess a number of properties not captured by the core problem definition given above: for balanced cooperative modelling, systems must provide immediate feedback and inspection capabilities, they must maintain integrity and consistency, and, most important, they must be "revisable" (Wrobel, 1988). This means that in addition to induction of first-order theories from examples, other tasks such as revision must also be addressed by learning modules capable of working with first-order representations. Moreover, since the learning system no longer consists of a single module, the different modules must be properly integrated, resulting in a *multistrategy* learning system (Michalski and Tecuci, 1994).

5.4 MOBAL

As an example of an ILP system that integrates algorithms for different tasks (e.g. induction and revision) as well as different algorithms for the same task (induction), we will now describe the knowledge acquisition and learning system MOBAL (Morik *et al.*, 1993b) developed by the Machine Learning group at GMD over the past years. In this section, we will only briefly present the core ideas, while in Sections 5.5 and 5.6 we will describe in detail novel additions to the system that are specifically geared towards the use of different ILP techniques in knowledge acquisition (Section 5.5) and towards supporting the embedding of MOBAL's learning capabilities into larger application systems (Section 5.6).

5.4.1 MOBAL's architecture and knowledge representation

MOBAL is a multistrategy learning system that is organized as a collection of cooperating learning modules organized around a knowledge representation subsystem (Figure 5.1). The knowledge representation subsystem, the inference engine IM-2 (Emde, 1989, 1991; Morik *et al.*, 1993b), is responsible for manipulating the entries that make up a domain model or knowledge base (see below), for making inferences with these entries, and for offering reason maintenance services so that inferences are automatically retracted when they become invalid.

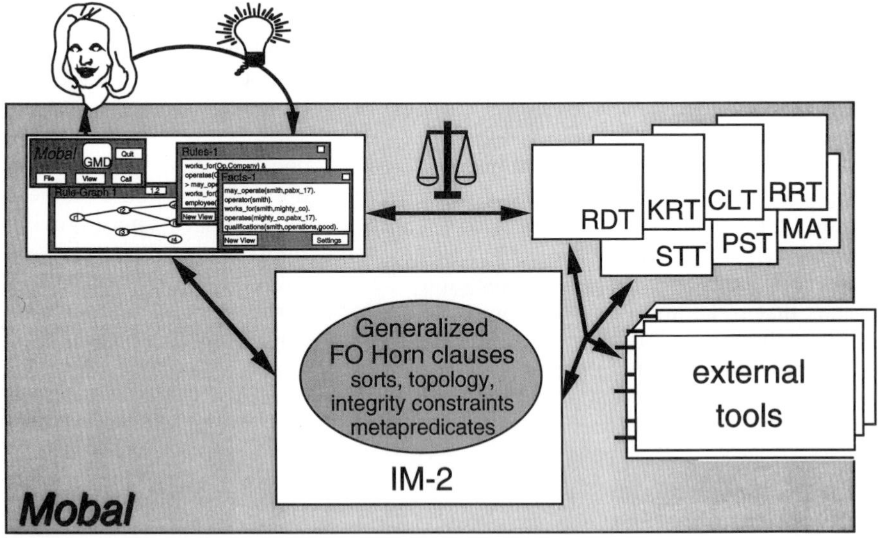

Figure 5.1 MOBAL's system architecture

In Section 5.2.2 above, we have already given examples of the core elements of MOBAL's first-order knowledge representation, namely facts and rules.

A *fact* is simply a predicate symbol with an appropriate number of constants as arguments, as in

```
may_operate(bode,pabx_17).
```

Facts are thus required to be ground (contain no variables), and function symbols other than constants generally are not used in MOBAL's representation (function-free). In contrast to many other ILP systems which use the standard two-valued Prolog semantics with negation as failure, MOBAL employs a four-valued paraconsistent semantics (Morik *et al.*, 1993b) that allows negation and contradictions to be explicitly represented with truth values `true`, `false` (indicated by `not`), `both` (contradictory) and `unknown` (usually not listed in the knowledge base). Examples of false and contradictory facts are

```
not(may_operate(meyer,pabx_17)).
both(may_operate(bode,pabx_15)).
```

If desired, it is possible (but not required) in MOBAL to declare the argument sorts of predicates:

```
may_operate/2: < employee >, < system >.
```

declares `may_operate` as a binary relation taking employees and systems as arguments. MOBAL's sort taxonomy tool STT can use this information to create a *sort lattice*, but will also automatically generate such declarations when they are missing (see Section 5.4.2 below). Additional information about predicates can be expressed in the domain *topology*. A topology consists of named groups of predicates that can be linked to each other. For example,

```
'Access Rights' - [may_operate,may_access] ←
['Employees','Situation Info','Company Info',
'Operations','System Info']
```

defines `'Access Rights'` as a topology node consisting of the predicates `may_operate` and `may_access` the computation of which is intended to depend on the predicates contained in the nodes `'Employees'`, `'Situation Info'`, `'Company Info'`, `'Operations'`, and `'System Info'`. Figure 5.2 graphically represents this simple two-level topology named `system`.

A *rule* is a clause that consists of a number of premise literals and a single conclusion literal, as in

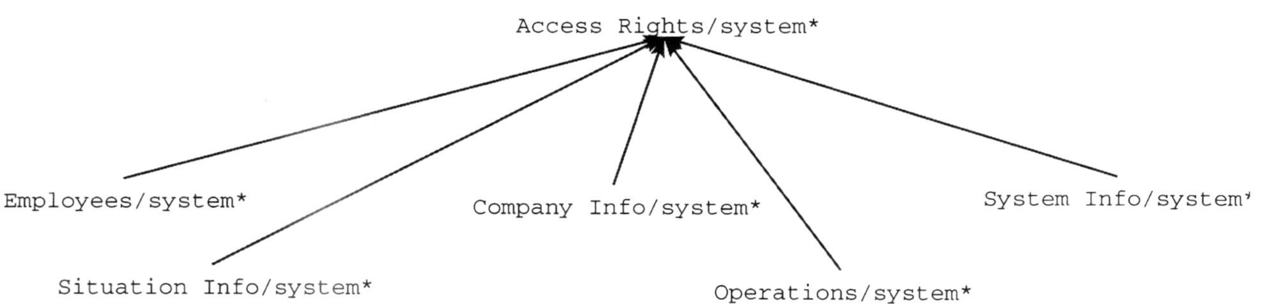

Figure 5.2 Example of a predicate topology

```
works_for(P,C1) & operates(C2,S) & subsidiary(C1,C2)
& technical(P) → may_operate(P,S).
```

As in Prolog, variables are written uppercase in rules and are assumed to be universally quantified. Just as facts, the premises or conclusion of a rule can have any of the four possible truth values. MOBAL's representation thus closely corresponds to generalized Horn programs (Blair and Subrahmanian, 1989). Additional predefined predicates can be used to perform arithmetics (e.g. add) or to draw inferences based on the current state of the knowledge base (e.g. \+ to denote currently unprovable facts) (Emde, 1989; Morik *et al.*, 1993b).

Whereas rules are used by the inference engine for forward and backwards inferences, *integrity constraints* are not used for inferences, but are simply checked on the current knowledge base. They can therefore take a more general form than rules, and can be used to state disjunctive or negative information that cannot be expressed using rules:

```
operator(X) & manager(X) ⇝.
```

states that no one can be both manager and operator, and

```
employee(X) ⇝ operator(X); manager(X).
```

states that every employee must be either operator or manager.

In addition to facts and rules themselves, MOBAL also offers higher-order constructs called (meta-)metapredicates, (meta-)metafacts and (meta-)metarules that can be used to declaratively state properties of (meta-)predicates and inferential relationships between (meta-)rules. For example, given the meta-predicate

```
inclusive_1(P,Q): P(X) → Q(X).
```

we can use the metafact

```
inclusive_1(operator,employee).
```

to state that all operators are employees. Internally, this metafact is translated into the rule

```
operator(X) → employee(X).
```

The transitivity of inclusive_1 can be expressed with a metarule:

```
inclusive_1(P,Q) & inclusive_1(Q,R) → inclusive_1(P,R).
```

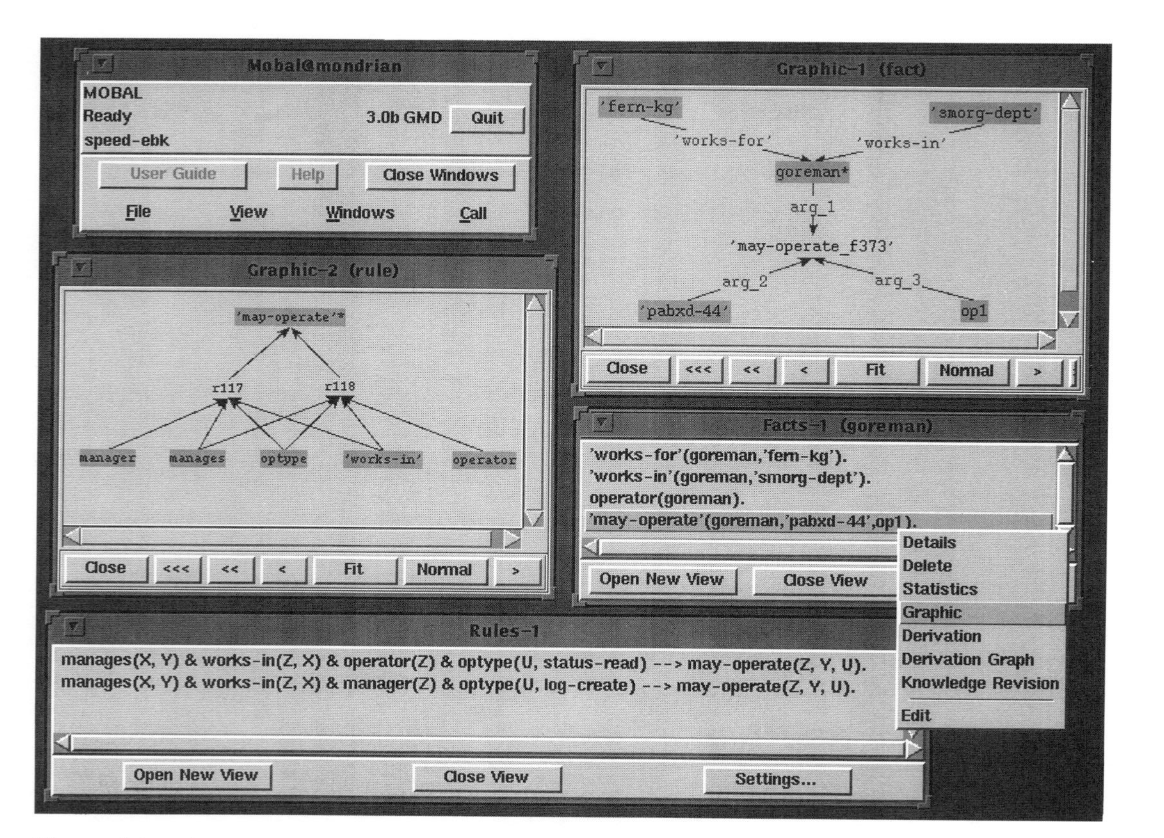

Figure 5.3 MOBAL's graphical knowledge acquisition environment

For all these representational items, MOBAL's graphical knowledge acquisition environment can be used to view textual and graphical presentations (see Figure 5.3), and to make additions, modifications or deletions. The inference engine is responsible for making forwards and backwards inferences with the knowledge base, and thus provides feedback about the operational properties of the emerging model. MOBAL's learning tools, finally, provide additional services and cooperate with the user to complete and improve the emerging domain model.

5.4.2 Services offered by MOBAL's learning tools

The central principle of the balanced cooperative modelling paradigm is the idea of *balanced* cooperation, i.e. for every kind of knowledge source that can be entered by the user, there should be system components that are capable of working on this kind of knowledge, and, if possible, capable of automatically generating and revising this kind of knowledge (see Morik, 1993). Clearly there will always be a qualitative difference between knowledge input by the user and knowledge generated automatically, since only the user has access to the external world to validate the model, while the machine must rely on user inputs alone. The role of the system is to make implicit knowledge explicit, to perform tasks that are tedious or too time-consuming to do manually, whereas the user uses the machine's results as feedback about necessary changes to the domain model.

In MOBAL, almost all knowledge sources can be filled and revised both manually and automatically. At the basic level of *facts*, the inference engine IM-2 (Emde, 1989) is capable of using rules to infer additional facts from the user's inputs. Whenever the user changes the set of input facts, the set of derived facts is automatically changed by removing inferences that are no longer true or adding those that have become valid (reason maintenance).

For information about predicates and their argument sorts, two modules are available to construct both *sort lattice* and *predicate topology*. The *sort taxonomy tool* STT (Kietz, 1988) records the actual usage of terms at the different argument positions of a predicate in input facts, and dynamically constructs and permanently updates a lattice of so-called *argument sorts*. Wherever necessary, predicate declarations are added automatically, and wherever declarations have been entered manually, their corresponding sorts are inserted in the proper place in the lattice (Figure 5.4). For the automatic construction of a topology, the *predicate structuring tool* PST (Klingspor, 1991) analyses the set of rules input by the user, builds a call graph among them, and employs several graph abstraction operations to build a topology which the user can then refine further.

For the automatic acquisition of rules themselves, the *rule discovery tool* RDT (Kietz and Wrobel, 1992) can be used which performs a classical ILP learning task (akin to the non-monotonic/descriptive ILP setting of Helft (1989) and De Raedt and Lavrač (1993)). Given a knowledge base which contains facts about a specified target predicate and additional facts and rules as background

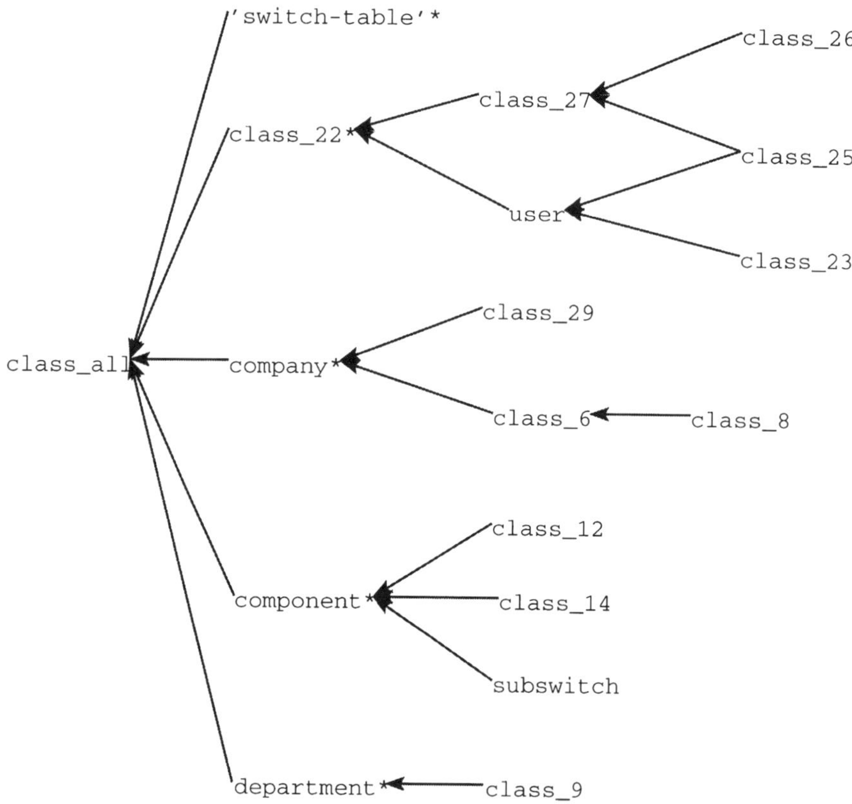

Figure 5.4 Example of a sort lattice

knowledge, RDT finds all most general rules which use the target predicate as conclusion and are true for the given examples (meet a user-specified acceptance criterion). To constrain the search, metapredicates are given as *rule schemata*, and RDT will search only for instantiations of the given rule schemata. Using RDT as a subroutine, the *concept learning tool* CLT (Wrobel, 1994a, b) can search for all rules about a target predicate (premise or conclusion), and is capable of evaluating the quality of the resulting set of rules with respect to its suitability as a concept definition.

Two additional modules are available for aiding the user in making changes to the existing rules. The *knowledge revision tool* KRT (Wrobel, 1993, 1994a) is used whenever the knowledge base produces incorrect inferences, and is capable of computing a well-defined set of minimal revisions of rules or facts that would fix the problem (using a minimal base revision operator based on exception sets).

KRT also offers a two-tiered heuristic confidence model which is used to propose a preferred revision among the possible minimal ones. The *ruleset restructuring tool* RRT (Sommer, 1994b), on the other hand, is used whenever a knowledge base, even though correct, is non-optimal in terms of performance or understandability. RRT offers a number of operations for restructuring such rule bases, including a rule base stratification operator.

The acquisition of metaknowledge, finally, is supported both by the *model acquisition tool* MAT (Thieme, 1989) and the learning algorithm INCY (Sommer, 1993). When given a rule as input, MAT is capable of automatically abstracting a metapredicate definition from it. INCY, on the other hand, proposes new metapredicates specifically as rule schemata for learning: in a bottom-up learning pass, potential rules built according to a heuristic criterion are tested against the knowledge base, and the promising ones are entered as metapredicates and rule schemata for RDT. For integrity constraints, work to extend RDT into an *integrity constraint discovery tool* ICDT has been carried out (Englert, 1995).

5.5 MOBAL as an ILP toolbox

In the preceding section, we have described how the balanced cooperative modelling paradigm is implemented in MOBAL by combining different learning modules for *different* tasks into an integrated multistrategy learning system. Traditionally, the orthogonal direction, namely integrating different learning algorithms that can be substituted for each other for performing the *same* task, has also been of interest in machine learning. Given that the ILP field now offers a large number of first-order rule induction algorithms, each with different design choices and different strengths and weaknesses, this question is also of particular relevance for using ILP in knowledge acquisition. If different tools could be used effortlessly on the same data, it would be possible to use for each problem the tool that is perfectly suited, or to compare different ones to see which one is best. How can such integration be achieved?

To answer this question, we can draw on the experiences made in the Machine Learning Toolbox (MLT) ESPRIT project in the past years (Kodratoff *et al.*, 1992). In MLT, the goal was to integrate several different learning systems – some for the same tasks, some for different tasks – into an easily usable toolbox for applications. Two architectural extremes were considered for integration (Ludwig, 1989; Morik, 1991b): tight vs. loose coupling.

5.5.1 Tight vs. loose coupling in MLT

In a *tight coupling* approach, all tools of the toolbox would be using the same knowledge representation subsystem for storage and inferences. In this architecture, there would have been no effort in order to use different tools on the same data. Common access to shared data would even have offered the possibility of inter-tool cooperation during one learning run. The tight coupling scenario corresponds to the kind of integration that today's multistrategy learning systems try to achieve. MOBAL's learning tools, for example, are coupled tightly, using a common inference engine and cooperating to solve subproblems for each other. These advantages, however, also place heavy requirements on the design of the learning tools and the common knowledge representation system. Realistically, these requirements can be met only for learning modules developed within one or a small number of development teams, and for algorithms that use reasonably similar representations. Otherwise, independent development of each individual component is severely hindered. Furthermore, if representations are too dissimilar, serious performance losses are to be expected by relying on a common representation system.

In the MLT project, these arguments lead to the choice of a *loose coupling* architecture, where each learning tool continues to exist as an individual program, and where learning results are communicated through a transfer language understood by all participating tools. Each tool can thus be individually developed with whatever programming language and internal representation is appropriate, but is required to be able to read in and generate the transfer language. The transfer language must encompass all the representational elements needed by all tools, but since it is not used for processing or inference, this is not a performance problem. In MLT, a transfer language called CKRL (Common Knowledge Representation Language) (Morik *et al.*, 1991) was developed, and translators written for all participating tools.

Interestingly, the process of writing translators for CKRL proved more demanding than expected by many participants. Due to the wide range of tools and data that were represented, it turned out to be difficult to ensure that all tools would assign the same semantics to all constructs. Even more, since, usually, a single tool is only able to use a subset of the information of a CKRL input file, the unused parts of the input file need to be stored so they can be re-added when the tool has finished learning and creates its output file for the next tool. To implement this, quite sophisticated two-stage translators with internal CKRL databases had to be developed (Kietz, 1991).

5.5.2 Coupling ILP systems

Returning to the issue of integrating different ILP systems, we see that in many respects, the situation in the field is similar to the situation in MLT. The different systems that are available are all developed in different research groups, in different programming languages. If a tight coupling approach were to be chosen, all or at least some of these algorithms would need to be reimplemented in a common framework. Even if sufficient manpower for this were available, this still would mean that, in the integrated system, there would be a certain time lag in releases of the component systems. Furthermore, very likely it would not be feasible for one group to produce versions as efficient and optimized as the original systems. Tightly coupled approaches are thus useful only for special goals, such as for teaching purposes (as for example in the MILES system, see Section 5.7).

This leaves us with a loose coupling approach as the only viable alternative to integrating existing systems without rewriting them. Within such an approach, we can take advantage of the fact that, in ILP, the representations used by the different learning system vary, but they are all subsets of first-order clausal logic. For expressing examples, background knowledge and learning results, we thus do not need a separate transfer language. All that needs to be done to couple different learning tools is to adapt the surface syntax of their inputs to each other. Care must of course be taken to take into account any additional assumptions that a learning tool makes about the semantics about its input or output data. Additional complexity is added by the fact that different tools use different parametrizations and different bias languages, i.e. additional knowledge not expressible in the language of first-order clauses.

5.5.3 MOBAL's external tool concept

Based on the above arguments, in MOBAL we have chosen a loose coupling approach towards integrating different ILP algorithms into the system, implemented through the notion of "external tools" (Emde *et al.*, 1993). An external tool in MOBAL is a learning system developed outside of MOBAL, but interfaced to the system using special interface modules. As soon as such an interface module is available, the external tool can be "loaded" into MOBAL, and, after this, can be used in the same fashion that the internal module RDT was used before. "Loading" an external tool simply means that the interface to this tool is made known to MOBAL, a tool description acknowledging the authors of the external tool is shown to the user, and appropriate menu entries are created in MOBAL's user interface. When an external tool is to be run, the interface routines produce input files in the appropriate format, run the external tool with the right parameters, read its output file and enter the resulting rules into MOBAL's inference engine.

Special care has been taken in the external tool concept to support the different parametrizations and additional knowledge (e.g. bias descriptions) needed by the different external tools. In the external tool interface module, tool parameters and additional knowledge sources can be declared along with their appropriate syntax. After this, it is possible to enter, inspect and change these parameters and other entries from MOBAL's user interface, and the external tool can rely on MOBAL to maintain these knowledge sources if this is desired. This kind of integration thus offers a twofold advantage. On the one hand, it is now possible to use a wider variety of tools from the same system in a uniform fashion. On the other hand, algorithm developers, if they so choose, can concentrate on the algorithm itself and need not worry about creating editing, browsing, and graphic environments for them.

At present, we have developed interface files for the following external ILP algorithms in cooperation with their authors whose support is gratefully acknowledged:

- **FOIL**
  FOIL by Ross Quinlan and colleagues (Quinlan, 1990) is an efficient top-down ILP learning algorithm based on heuristic search control. FOIL was the first system to be interfaced to MOBAL according to the external tool concept; currently, version 6 of the system (Cameron-Jones and Quinlan, 1993) can be used. FOIL's special treatment of negative examples and the closed-world assumption is taken care of in the interface module.
- **MFOIL**
  MFOIL by Saso Dzeroski (Dzeroski and Bratko, 1992) is a variant of FOIL with a stochastic search control criterion; it is integrated in a fashion very similar to FOIL.
- **GOLEM**
  GOLEM by Stephen Muggleton and Cao Feng (Muggleton and Feng, 1990) is a very efficient bottom-up LGG learning algorithm based on the idea of *ij*-determinacy which ensures polynomial search complexity.
- **GRDT**
  GRDT, or grammar-based RDT, by Volker Klingspor (Klingspor, 1993) is a variant of RDT that uses antecedent description grammars to specify search bias instead of rule schemata. The GRDT external tool interface is designed so that grammar rules for GRDT can be entered and manipulated through MOBAL's user interface.

In addition to these learning tools from external groups, we are also using the external tool concept to integrate newly developed algorithms of our own. COLA (Emde, 1994) is an ILP learning system that learns from very few examples, employing the first-order clustering system KBG (Bisson, 1992) as a subroutine. The INCY algorithm (Sommer, 1993) mentioned in Section 5.4, and its successor LINK (Sommer, 1994a), are also integrated as external tools.

5.6 Embedded adaptivity

From the point of view of using ILP techniques for knowledge acquisition, the toolbox concept can be a significant advantage, since it is now easily possible to try out and compare different ILP systems on the same problem. There is another, sometimes overlooked, perspective on integration, however, which can be as important for the success of learning in an application: namely the question of how the learning results are ultimately integrated into the deployed application software.

In the past, two approaches have been taken in many applications because they do not require special provisions in the design of the learning system. In the first approach, learning results are simply used as background knowledge in the development of the application system. In other words, learning is used to gain an improved understanding of the problem domain, and rules output by learning are then hard-wired into the application system by programming it accordingly. The second approach is possible whenever the application problem is a relatively isolated task that can be solved almost exclusively with a knowledge-based system: the learning rules are incorporated into the knowledge base of a shell that is then used to solve the application problem.

Experience shows, however, that in most applications, neither of these approaches is quite what is desired. The first approach wastes a lot of the potential of learning, since as soon as learning is finished and the results are programmed into the application, they are as hard to change as any conventional program. This is avoided in the second approach, but very few applications can be solved using a knowledge-based system alone. It is much more typical to assume that machine learning (and, in fact, AI techniques) are used to solve a rather small subproblem within an existing, conventional application software system. The goal in these cases is to use machine learning as an "added-value" module which *embeds* adaptive properties into a system that previously was not adaptive.

In MOBAL, we are supporting two possible approaches towards such *embedded adaptivity*. The first is a traditional software engineering approach. Due to the modular software architecture of MOBAL, it is possible to integrate one or more of its modules into an application system where it would realize adaptive capabilities. This approach requires modules written in different programming languages and with different goals to be integrated, however, so it is suitable only for cases in which complex and very deep integration is aimed at.

In other applications, we can imagine that the application software needs only very limited "services" from the learning system. This suggests that for integration in these cases, we can benefit from using a client/server oriented conceptualization, where the learning system is a "server" offering knowledge-based inference and learning services, and the application system is the "client" requesting these services. In the new release of MOBAL (3.0), we have therefore chosen to base the interaction between MOBAL's system core and its user interface on a network-based client/server protocol. MOBAL's user interface (built with Tcl/Tk) is now a client that requests information from MOBAL's core through a TCP network stream protocol (proprietary at present, but open towards integration with standards such as KQML (Finin *et al.*, 1993)).

In the short term, this separation of system core and interface offers performance benefits when operating MOBAL across a network; interface and system core can be on different machines. In the long run, the client/server protocol offers an attractive possibility for building custom interfaces and for using MOBAL as a knowledge or learning "server" to which the application would send requests across the network and would receive answers back. As a concrete example, consider the telecommunication security application described in Section 5.2.2. The decision about access rights is only a small part of a telecommunications network management system, but it can transparently be handled by MOBAL if a client/server protocol is used. Whenever information about access rights is required, they are simply requested across the network.

This kind of client/server integration thus offers application developers a chance to incorporate learning capabilities into their systems without the need to have access to or to understand the internal code of the learning system. All that is required is an understanding of the communication protocol understood by the learning system, and the ability to write to and read from TCP streams. Application and learning systems can therefore be developed in different programming languages, on different platforms, and can even run on different computers when they are used to improve performance. Since the required communication bandwith is small, even remote access from small systems is possible.

5.7 Related work

To complement our discussion of the use of ILP techniques in knowledge acquisition, in this section we will look at some other integrated systems besides MOBAL.

5.7.1 WHY

The system WHY (Saitta *et al.*, 1993; Baroglio *et al.*, 1994) is a multistrategy learning system based on a first-order representation specialized for classification problems.[2] A knowledge base consists of facts and rules. Facts can have the truth values true, assumed true, assumed false, and false. The set of rules of the knowledge base is partioned into three subsets: the first set of clauses are said to belong to the *causal model*, the second set of clauses are said to belong to the *phenomenological theory* and the third set of clauses are said to belong to the *heuristic classification knowledge base*. While not different in form, the three sets of clauses are used differently in reasoning (see below). An important subset of predicates are the causal node predicates (naming system states). The conclusion of a causal model rule is a causal node predicate.

Deduction with clauses can be performed both forward and backward in WHY. To allow better control of reasoning, different subsets of premises are identified in

[2] We have mapped back the terminology used in WHY to standard ILP terms. The user presentation and implementation in WHY is different.

the body of each causal model clause: causal node predicates, groups of premises regarded as "context" premises, and groups of premises regarded as "constraint" premises. In deduction (for classification), constraint premises and causal node premises must be proved true while context premises can be assumed. In *abduction*, the conclusion and the constraint premises of a rule must be provable, the context and causal node premises are then assumed. A special nullary predicate Ω may be included in the body of a clause to denote that the body is still incomplete. During deductive and abductive reasoning, Ω is always assumed true, but inferences made with it are recorded as plausible only. Control knowledge for *induction*, which is performed in a style similar to ML-SMART (Bergadano *et al.*, 1991), can be provided by special dependency rules that identify a set of predicates upon which another predicate is known to depend. This is very similar to the possibilities offered by MOBAL's topology.

The underlying scenario for using ILP techniques in WHY for knowledge acquisition is very similar to the ideas of the balanced cooperative modelling paradigm. An expert is assumed to first input a knowledge base consisting of causal and phenomenological rules, and facts description examples and background knowledge. WHY completes the initial knowledge base by forward deduction on the phenomenological rules and by backward abduction on causal model rules, trying to create derivations for all examples. The system then creates an initial set of rules: for each example, a variabilized rule is created using all constraint and context literals occurring on its derivation path. The set of rules created in this way usually is not complete and may not be consistent (since assumptions were made that might not be true). In these cases, theory revision is attempted. Rules can be removed or specialized, or induction can be used to replace remaining Ωs in rules, both under the interactive control of the expert or autonomously. Just as in balanced cooperative modelling, the initial model can be incomplete, and the system helps in extending and refining it.

In sum, like MOBAL, WHY tightly integrates the performance element with the rest of the learning system. In both systems, the expert can at any time use the existing knowledge base for classification. Both systems are multistrategy learning systems and integrate induction and interactive revision components. Unlike MOBAL, WHY specifically addresses the needs of classification by allowing abduction and imposing additional structure on the knowledge base that controls reasoning. MOBAL, on the other hand, has a more powerful base language and offers additional functionality with integrity constraints, sort lattice, topology creation and concept formation. It is also more versatile as a toolbox, since multiple learning algorithms can be used to work on a given problem.

5.7.2 APT

The APT system (Nédellec and Causse, 1992), a successor of DISCIPLE (Tecuci and Kodratoff, 1990), is also an integrated multistrategy learning tool based on a first-order representation especially designed for decomposition planning problems. A knowledge base in APT consists of a generalization hierarchy of predicates and a set of first-order decomposition rules. While the premises of a decomposition rule are as in standard clauses, its conclusion can consist of facts to be added, facts to be deleted, or of a decomposition of the problem to be solved into subproblems. When APT is solving a problem, the premises of rules are matched against the problem state, and if successful, the rule is applied leading to a changed knowledge base and new subproblems. Rules in APT are thus more like control rules or production rules than inference rules or implications. The inference mechanism of APT is interactive: before each rule application, the user is asked if the application is correct.

Whenever the user rejects a proposed rule application, theory revision is triggered. Since the faulty rule is clear, the revision process can be relatively simple and focused (compared to the more general problem of, for example, KRT): if the rule was erroneously proposed because another, preferable rule is missing, the user is asked to input this new rule. APT then generalizes the new rule so it becomes applicable in more cases. To this end, the user's rule is first completed by adding potentially relevant facts from the current state as additional premises, letting the user add additional premises and decide which ones to keep. APT then generalizes each premise along the generalization hierarchy. After each step, new so-called "discriminant" examples are generated for the generalized rule and presented to the user for approval to prevent overgeneralization. If the faulty rule should not apply at all, APT proposes specializations to the user, generated by two main operators (Nédellec, 1992): the first operator introduces a new predicate to replace an overly general concept definition based on separating predicates in negative and positive examples. The second operator more classically adds new premises to the definition, taken from the generalization hierarchy, or obtained interactively. The user can provide additional negative examples to guide the system, and can also change the background knowledge.

Compared to MOBAL and WHY, APT's knowledge representation and execution, while based on a first-order representation, is considerably further away from "standard" ILP. Its use of ILP techniques for multistrategy learning is at a different level of granularity. Whereas MOBAL offers a set of modules that are used under the control of the user, APT combines individual generalization and specialization operators to use at appropriate times. Its underlying philosophy differs from balanced cooperative modelling, in that the dialogue is much more system-driven than user-driven. At each inference step, the user can be queried by the system, and the user is shown examples to judge. This allows, for example, more focuses and simpler revision, but also constrains and burdens the user more than in MOBAL.

5.7.3 MILES

Whereas WHY and APT are similar to MOBAL in that they integrate logical learning methods for different tasks (multistrategy), the system MILES (Stahl and Tausend, 1993) is similar to MOBAL in offering several different methods and operators for the core ILP task of rule induction from examples, along with operations for editing and executing a knowledge base. A knowledge base in MILES consists of a set of first-order horn clauses (facts and rules) plus information about the argument types of predicates. The user can manipulate the knowledge base by adding or deleting rules, and by entering or deleting examples. Knowledge bases can be saved and reloaded, inspected in various ways using a graphical interface, and executed using an interactive deepening theorem prover.

MILES offers a large set of atomic learning operators. *Generalization* operators generalize a single clause or a set of clauses. Here, three least general generalization (lgg) operators are offered for θ-subsumption (Plotkin, 1970), and two for generalized subsumption (Buntine, 1988) and relative least general generalization (Plotkin, 1971) with respect to background knowledge. Also included are the operators of inverse resolution (Muggleton and Buntine, 1988; Rouveirol and Puget, 1990; Wirth, 1989). *Specialization* operators include a refinement operator in the style of MIS (Shapiro, 1983), and a simple predicate invention operator (Kijsirikul *et al.*, 1992). *Reformulation* operators transform the knowledge base to facilitate learning; they include clause reduction and flattening (Rouveirol and Puget, 1990). Similarly, *preprocessing* operators are used to generate additional information from the examples that can then be exploited during learning, such as argument types or general clause heads (Stahl *et al.*, 1993). Finally, *evaluations* of size, completeness, consistency and accuracy are possible with appropriate operators.

All of these operators can be employed within a generic parametrized learning algorithm with predicate invention capabilities by specifying in which places of this algorithm which operators are to be used. Alternatively, other control regimes can be realized by the user. In this fashion, it is possible to turn MILES into different ILP learning algorithms with different capabilities to experiment with, to learn about, or to compare them. In contrast to MOBAL, where the different ILP learning algorithms are incorporated *in toto* as external tools (essentially treated as black boxes), the operators of MILES are atomic ILP operations that can be configured through a generic control mechanism. As discussed above, this most likely results in some loss of efficiency when compared to the original tools, but it allows for easy creation of and experimentation with variants of algorithms.

5.8 Conclusions

In this chapter, we have discussed the issues involved in using ILP learning algorithms for the purposes of knowledge acquisition. Based on the preceding discussion, it should have become clear that besides the classical ILP learning task, batch learning from examples, integrated approaches to the use of ILP techniques in knowledge acquisition are possible. Following the balanced cooperative modelling paradigm of Morik (Morik, 1993), the knowledge acquisition and machine learning system MOBAL exemplifies the two possible directions of this integration. On the one hand, ILP techniques for different tasks have been tightly coupled to effectively assist the user in the modelling cycle (multistrategy learning). On the other hand, MOBAL has been extended into an ILP toolbox that offers interfaces to multiple different ILP algorithms for learning from examples.

For the future, the challenge for applications of ILP and machine learning will be to demonstrate that besides providing assistance during the creation of a knowledge base, these techniques are also useful for realizing adaptive capabilities in larger software systems. We have introduced the term "embedded adaptivity" to emphasize the supporting role that learning techniques will play as a small part of a larger deployed application system. In this chapter, we have hinted at how, in MOBAL, embedded adaptivity can be supported both through a modular software structure and, more conveniently, through a client/server architecture. In the future, applications will have to be developed that practically demonstrate the potential of this concept.

Acknowledgements

This chapter builds on the many contributions that have been and are being made by the different developers of MOBAL whom I want to thank: The Machine Learning group at GMD presently consists of Werner Emde, Jörg-Uwe Kietz, Edgar Sommer, Stefan Wrobel and students Roman Englert and Marcus Lübbe who jointly develop the MOBAL system. Significant contributions were made by Volker Klingspor and Katharina Morik (now University of Dortmund). MOBAL is a successor of the BLIP system developd at TU Berlin by Werner Emde, Katharina Morik, Sabine Thieme and Stefan Wrobel (all names in alphabetical order).

GMD grants a cost-free licence to use MOBAL for academic non-commercial purposes. The latest release of MOBAL can always be FTP'ed from the ML Archive at GMD (server ftp.gmd.de, directory/gmd/mlt/Mobal). The X-Windows interface of the current release (3.0) was developed using Tcl/Tk with the help of Sven Delmas (TU Berlin).

The work described in this article was partially supported by the CEC's ESPRIT program under contract no. 6020 ("Inductive Logic Programming").

The development of the external tool concept would not have been possible without the cooperation of the authors of the various tools inside and outside of the ILP project. Previous development of MOBAL was partially supported by ESPRIT contract no. 2154 ("Machine Learning Toolbox").

References

Baroglio, C., Botta, M. and Saitta, L. (1994). WHY: a system that learns using causal models and examples. In Michalski R. and Tecuci G. (editors), *Machine Learning – An Artificial Intelligence Approach, volume IV*, pp. 319–347. Morgan Kaufman, San Mateo, CA.

Bergadano, F., Giordana, A. and Saitta, L. (1991). *Machine Learning: An Integrated Framework and its Applications.* Ellis Horwood, Chichester, UK.

Bergadano, F., Giordana, A. Saitta, L., De Marchi, D. and Brancadori, F. (1990). Integrated learning in a real domain. In *Proc. Seventh Intern. Conf. on Machine Learning*, pp. 322–329. Morgan Kaufman, San Mateo, CA.

Bisson, G. (1992). Conceptual clustering in a first order logic representation. In *Proc. European Conference on Artificial Intelligence (ECAI–92).*

Blair, H. A. and Subrahmanian, V. S. (1989). Paraconsistent logic programming. *Theoretical Computer Science*, 68: 135–154.

Breiman, L., Friedman, J., Olshen, R. and Stone, C. (1984). *Classification and Regression Trees.* Wadsworth, Belmont.

Buntine, W. (1988). Generalized subsumption and its applications to induction and redundancy. *Artificial Intelligence*, 36: 149–176.

Cameron-Jones, R. and Quinlan, R. (1993). Avoiding pitfalls when learning recursive theories. In *Proc. 13th International Joint Conference on Artificial Intelligence*, pp. 1050–1055. Morgan Kaufman, San Mateo, CA.

De Raedt, L. and Bruynooghe, M. (1992). Interactive concept-learning and constructive induction by analogy. *Machine Learning*, 8(2): 107–150.

De Raedt, L. and Lavrač, N. (1993). The many faces of inductive logic programming. In Komorowski, J. and Ras, Z. (editors), *Proc. 7th Int. Symposium on Methodologies for Intelligent Systems*, Lecture Notes in Artificial Intelligence, vol. 689, pp. 435–449. Springer Verlag, Berlin, New York.

Dolsak, B. and Muggleton, S. (1992). The application of Inductive Logic Programming to finite element mesh design. In Muggleton, S. (editor), *Inductive Logic Programming*. Academic Press, London.

Dzeroski, S. and Bratko I. (1992). Handling noise in inductive logic programming. Technical Report TM–1182, ICOT, Tokyo, Japan. *Proc. Second International Workshop on Inductive Logic Programming.*

Emde, W. (1989). An inference engine for representing multiple theories. In Morik, K. (editor), *Knowledge Representation and Organization in Machine Learning*, pp. 148–176. Springer Verlag, Berlin, New York.

Emde, W. (1991). Modellbildung, Wissensrevision und Wissenrepräsentation im Maschinellen Lernen, *Dissertation*. Informatik-Fachberichte 281. Springer Verlag, Berlin, New York.

Emde, W. (1994). Inductive learning of characteristic concept descriptions from small sets of classified examples. In Bergadano, F. and De Raedt, L. (editors), *Machine Learning: ECML–94, European Conference on Machine Learning, Catania, Italy, April 1994, Proceedings*, pp. 103–121. Springer-Verlag, Berlin, New York. Also as *Arbeitspapiere der GMD* No. 821.

Emde, W., Kietz, J., Morik, K., Sommer, E. and Wrobel, S. (1993) *MOBAL 2.0 User Guide. Arbeitspapiere der GMD*. GMD, St Augustin. To appear.

Englert, R. (1995). Repräsentation, prüfen und lernen von integritätsbedingungen im MOBAL-system. *Arbeitspapiere der GMD*. GMD, Sankt Augustin, Germany.

Feng, C. (1992). Inducing temporal fault diagnostic rules from a qualitative model. In Muggleton, S. (editor), *Inductive Logic Programming*, chapter 24. Academic Press, London, New York.

Finin, T., Fritzson, R. and McKay, D. (1993). KQML: an information and knowledge exchange protocol (extended abstract). In Fuchi, K. and Yokoi, T. (editors), *Proc. 1993 Int. Conference on Building and Sharing of Very Large-Scale Knowledge Bases*. Tokyo, Japan.

Helft, N. (1989). Induction as nonmonotonic inference. In *Proceedings of the 1st International Conference on Knowledge Representation and Reasoning*, pp. 149–156. Morgan Kaufman, San Mateo, CA.

Herrmann, J., Ackermann, R., Peters, J. and Reipa, D. (1994). A multistrategy learning system and its integration into an interactive floorplanning tool. In *Machine Learning: ECML–94 (Proc. Seventh European Conference on Machine Learning)*, Lecture Notes in Artificial Intelligence, pp. 138–153. Springer Verlag, Berlin, New York.

Kietz, J.-U. (1988). Incremental and reversible acquisition of taxonomies. *Proceedings of EKAW-88*, pp. 24.1–24.11. Also as KIT-Report 66, Technical University Berlin.

Kietz, J.-U. (1991). Mobal's CKRL interface. Technical report, GMD, Sankt Augustin.

Kietz J.-U. and Dzeroski, S. (1994). Inductive logic programming and learnability. *SIGART Bulletin*, 5(1): 22–32.

Kietz, J.-U. and Wrobel, S. (1992). Controlling the complexity of learning in logic through syntactic and task-oriented models. In Muggleton, S. (editor), *Inductive Logic Programming*, chapter 16, pp. 335–359. Academic Press, London. Presented at the *Int. Workshop on Inductive Logic Programming, 1991*. Also available as *Arbeitspapiere der GMD* No. 503.

Kijsirikul, B., Numao, M. and Shimura, M. (1992). Discrimination-based constructive induction of logic programs. In *AAAI-92 Proc. Tenth Natl. Conference on Artif. Intelligence*, pp. 1 44–49. AAAI Press/The MIT Press, Menlo Park, Cambridge, London.

King, R., Muggleton, S., Lewis, R. and Sternberg, M. (1992). Drug design by machine learning: the use of inductive logic programming to model the structure-activity relationships of trimethoprim analogues binding to dihydrofolate reductase. *Proceedings of the National Academy of Sciences*, 89(23).

Klingspor, V. (1991). *MLT deliverable 4.3.2/G: MOBAL's predicate structuring tool*. GMD, St. Augustin.

Klingspor, V. (1993). Grdt: Enhancing model-based learning for its application in robot navigation. LS-8 Report 5, Universität Dortmund, FB Informatik, Germany.

Kodratoff, Y., Sleeman, D., Uszynski, M., Causse, K. and Craw, S. (1992). Building a machine learning toolbox. In Le Pape, B. and Steels, L. (editors), *Enhancing the Knowledge Engineering Process – Contributions from ESPRIT*. Elsevier, Oxford.

Kodratoff, Y. and Vrain, C. (1993). Acquiring first-order knowledge about air-traffic control. *Knowledge Acquisition*, 5: 1–36.

Lavrač, N. and Džeroski, S. (1993). *Inductive Logic Programming: Techniques and Applications*. Ellis Horwood, Chichester.

Lavrač, N., Džeroski, S., Pirnat, V. and Krivzman, V. (1993). The use of background knowledge in learning medical diagnostic rules. *Applied Artificial Intelligence*, 7: 273–293.

Lloyd, J. (1987). *Foundations of Logic Programming*, 2nd edition. Springer Verlag, Berlin, New York.

Ludwig A. (1989) Specification of the Overall Architecture of the MLT. Deliverable 1.1.1, Machine Learning Toolbox ESPRIT Project P2154.

Michalski, R.S. and Tecuci, G., editors (1994). *Machine Learning – a Multistrategy Approach*, volume IV of *Machine Learning*. Morgan Kaufman, San Mateo, CA.

Morik, K. (1989). Sloppy modelling. In Morik, K. (editor), *Knowledge Representation and Organization in Machine Learning*, pp. 107–134. Springer Verlag, Berlin, New York.

Morik, K. (1991a). Underlying assumptions of knowledge acquisition and machine learning. *Knowledge Acquisition Journal*, 3(2): 137–156.

Morik, K. (1991b). Modelling with a toolbox of systems. Arbeitspapiere der GMD 527, GMD.

Morik, K. (1993). Balanced cooperative modelling. *Machine Learning*, 10(1): 217–235. Revised version of the paper presented at: *Proc. First Int. Workshop on Multistrategy Learning (MSL-91)*, Michalski, R. S. and Tecuci, G., George Mason Univ., pp. 65–80, 1991.

Morik, K., Causse, K. and Boswell, R. (1991). A common knowledge representation integrating learning tools. In Michalski, R. S. and Tecuci. G. (editors), *Proc. First Int. Workshop on Multistrategy Learning (MSL-91)*, pp. 81–96, George Mason Univ.

Morik, K., Potamias, G., Moustakis, V. and Charissis, G. (1993a). Knowledgeable learning using MOBAL – a case study on a medical domain. In Kodratoff, Y. and Langley. P. (editors), *Proceedings of the Applications Workshop at ECML-93, Vienna*.

Morik, K. and Rieger, A. (1993). Learning action-oriented perceptual features for robot navigation. In Giordana, A. (editor), *Proc. ECML–93 Workshop on Learning Robots*, pp. 13–26, Vienna. Also as Univ. Dortmund technical report no. 3.

Morik, K., Wrobel, S., Kietz, J.-U. and Emde, W. (1993b). *Knowledge Acquisition and Machine Learning: Theory, Methods and Applications.* Academic Press, London, New York.

Muggleton, S. (1991). Inductive logic programming. *New Generation Computing*, 8(4): 295–318.

Muggleton, S. and Buntine, W. (1988). Machine invention of first-order predicates by inverting resolution. In *Proc. Fifth Intern. Conf. on Machine Learning*, Morgan Kaufman, San Mateo, CA.

Muggleton, S. and De Raedt, L. (1994). Inductive logic programming: Theory and methods. *Journal of Logic Programming*, 19/20: 629–679.

Muggleton, S. and Feng, C. (1990). Efficient induction of logic programs. In *Proc. First Conf. on Algorithmic Learning Theory*, Ohmsha Publishers, Tokyo.

Muggleton, S., King, R. and Sternberg, M. (1992). Protein secondary structure prediction using logic-based machine learning. *Protein Engineering*, 5(7): 647–657.

Nédellec, C. (1992). How to specialize by theory refinement. In Neumann, Bernd, (editor), *Proc. European Conference on Artificial Intelligence (ECAI–92)*, pp. 474–478. John Wiley & Sons.

Nédellec, C. and Causse, K. (1992). Knowledge refinement using knowledge acquisition and machine learning methods. In *Current Developments in Knowledge Acquisition – EKAW '92*, pp. 171–190. Springer Verlag, Berlin, Heidelberg, New York.

Plotkin, G. D. (1970). A note on inductive generalization. In Meltzer, B. and Michie, D. editors, *Machine Intelligence 5*, chapter 8, pp. 153–163. Edinburgh Univ. Press, Edinburgh.

Plotkin, G. D. (1971). A further note on inductive generalization. In Meltzer, B. and Michie, D. editors, *Machine Intelligence 6*, chapter 8, pp. 101–124. Edinburgh Univ. Press, Edinburgh.

Quinlan, J. R. (1983). Learning efficient classification procedures and their application to chess end games. In Michalski, R., Carbonell, J. and Mitchell, T. editors, *Machine Learning – An Artificial Intelligence Approach*, pp. 463–482. Tioga, Palo Alto, CA.

Quinlan, J. R. (1990). Learning logical definitions from relations. *Machine Learning*, 5(3): 239–266.

Rouveirol, C. (1992). Extensions of inversion of resolution applied to theory completion. In Muggleton, S. (editor), *Inductive Logic Programming*, chapter 3, pp. 63–92. Academic Press, London, New York.

Rouveirol C. and Puget, J. F. (1990). Beyond inversion of resolution. In Porter, B. and Mooney, R. (editors), *Proc. Seventh Intern. Conf. on Machine Learning*, pp. 122–130, Morgan Kaufmann, Palo Alto, CA.

Saitta, L., Botta, M. and Neri, F. (1993). Multistrategy learning and theory revision. *Machine Learning*, 11(2/3): 153–172.

Shapiro, E. Y. (1983). *Algorithmic Program Debugging.* ACM Distinguished Doctoral Dissertations. The MIT Press, Cambridge, Mass.

Sommer, E. (1993). Cooperation of data-driven and model-based induction methods for relational learning. In Michalski, R. and Tecuci, G. (editors), *Second Interna-*

tional Workshop on Multistrategy Learning, pp. 180–187, Harpers Ferry, West Virginia, USA.

Sommer, E. (1994a). Learning relations without closing the world. In Bergadano, F. and De Raedt, L. (editors), *Machine Learning: ECML–94, European Conference on Machine Learning, Catania, Italy, April 1994, Proceedings*, pp. 419–422, Springer-Verlag, Berlin.

Sommer, E. (1994b). Rulebase stratification: an approach to theory restructuring. In Wrobel, S. (editor), *Proc. Fourth International Workshop on Inductive Logic Programming*, 53754 Sankt Augustin, Germany. GMD. GMD-Studien Nr. 237. Order from teuber @ gmd.de.

Sommer, E., Morik, K., Andre, J.-M. and Uszynski, M. (1994). What online machine learning can do for knowledge acquisition – a case study. *Knowledge Acquisition* (to appear). Also appeared as GMD Report No. 757.

Stahl, I. and Tausend, B. (1993). MILES, a modular inductive logic programming experimentation system. ILP-Project Deliverable STU 1.2, Universität Stuttgart, Fachbereich Informatik, Stuttgart, Germany.

Stahl, I., Tausend, B. and Wirth, R. (1993). Two methods for improving inductive logic programming systems. In *Proc. Sixth European Conference on Machine Learning (ECML-93)*, Lecture Notes in Computer Science, pp. 41–55. Springer Verlag, Berlin, New York.

Tecuci, G. and Kodratoff, Y. (1990). Apprenticeship learning in imperfect domain theories. In Kodratoff, Y. and Michalski, R. (editors), *Machine Learning: an Artificial Intelligence Approach, Volume 3*, pp. 514–551. Morgan Kaufmann, San Mateo, CA.

Thieme, S. (1989). The acquisition of model knowledge for a model-driven machine learning approach. In Morik, K. (editor), *Knowledge Representation and Organization in Machine Learning*, pp. 177–191. Springer Verlag, Berlin, New York.

Wirth, R. (1989). Completing logic programs by inverse resolution. In Morik, K. (editor), *Proc. Fourth European Working Session on Learning (EWSL)*, pp. 239–250. Pitman, London; Morgan Kaufmann, San Mateo, CA.

Wrobel, S. (1988). Design goals for sloppy modelling systems. *Intern. Journal of Man–Machine Studies*, 29: 461–477. Also appeared in Boose, J. and Gaines. B. (editors) (1990). *The Foundations of Knowledge Acquisition*, volume 4. Academic Press, London.

Wrobel, S. (1993). On the proper definition of minimality in specialization and theory revision. In *Proc. Sixth European Conference on Machine Learning (ECML-93)*, pp. 65–82. Also as Arbeitspapiere der GMD No. 730.

Wrobel, S. (1994a). *Concept Formation and Knowledge Revision*. Kluwer, Dordrecht, Netherlands.

Wrobel, S. (1994b). Concept formation during interactive theory revision. *Machine Learning*, 14: 169–191.

CHAPTER 6

Cooperative knowledge evolution for complex domains

Franz Schmalhofer and Bidjan Tschaitschian

Abstract

This chapter describes how machine learning and knowledge acquisition techniques can be combined and how knowledge-based systems can be employed in complex domains like mechanical engineering, material science, laboratory medicine and clinical studies in the pharmaceutical industry. Based upon our previous research, cooperative knowledge evolution is proposed as a means for coping with complex and ever-changing application fields and a set of coordinated interactive and machine learning tools are advocated for continuously evolving a knowledge based system.

6.1 Introduction

Machine learning (ML) research and the development of knowledge-based systems (KBS) have a separate but in many respects similar history. In both areas, significant progress was first achieved in quite restricted application domains. When it was subsequently attempted to apply these solutions to industrial problems, multi-faceted problems were accounted in both areas.

In ML the basic successes of research in inductive learning or explanation-based learning were achieved in micro-worlds, such as the blocks world, sorting tasks, or chess end-game problems. First-generation KBS like MYCIN were similarly restricted to relatively narrow domains (like diagnosis and therapy of a few infectional diseases). The scope of possible applications of ML has been subsequently extended by apprenticeship and multistrategy learning. The second generation of KBS also tried to extend the areas of applications by developing appropriate shells, knowledge engineering frameworks, knowledge acquisition (KA) tools, and model-based methodologies for the development of KBS.

Thus, in both areas, more or less restricted micro-worlds functioned as the drosophila of artificial intelligence (AI), where the basic successes were achieved

Machine Learning and Knowledge Acquisition
ISBN 0-12-685120-4

and demonstrated. The transfer of these solutions to the real world is, however, by no means guaranteed by the current theoretical and experimental results in the micro-world. Buchanan (1989, p. 5), for example, reported that, "except for simple classification systems, expert systems do not employ a learning component to construct parts of their knowledge bases from libraries of previously solved cases".

Similar to the human genome project, extensive application-oriented research was (and still is) needed in AI to utilize the fundamental results for applications in the complex real world. Within the last five years we have performed ML and KBS research for production planning in mechanical engineering, as well as documentation, decision-support and explanation in medicine. In this paper we describe cooperative knowledge evolution as a framework for ML and KA in complex real-world domains that emerged from this application-oriented AI research. For brevity, we also refer to the combination of machine learning and knowledge acquisition simply as learning.

Cooperative knowledge evolution is based on apprenticeship learning emphasizing the cooperation of system and user on the one hand and supporting knowledge sharing and reuse in model-based KBS development on the other hand. Thus, through cooperative knowledge evolution, techniques from ML and KBS are unified. In Section 6.2, we first summarize the characteristics of complex real worlds, show that no single micro-world technique can satisfy all of the respective requirements and describe cooperative knowledge evolution as a possible solution to knowledge-base development and learning in such domains. In order to show how the approach can be applied to different areas, we will give examples from different application domains. Using the example of production planning in mechanical engineering, Section 6.3 will discuss the initial construction phase of a KBS (which is termed seeding; see Fischer *et al.*, 1994). The cooperative use and the evolution of such a knowledge base will be shown with respect to a second application domain, clinical testing of new drugs, before reorganization of a KBS is discussed in more general terms.

6.2 Cooperative knowledge evolution via the integration of KA and ML methods

Characteristic for real world domains are higher order complexities of the problems, continuous innovations and documentation, as well as incomplete and conflicting knowledge in the application area. No single technique and no straightforward combination of micro-world techniques can fulfil all demands of such complex real-world domains. However, if techniques are appropriately chosen and unified they can provide a solution in cooperation with the user (Schmalhofer *et al.*, 1995). Complexity can be reduced by introducing appropriate abstractions (Knoblock, 1990). In order to construct knowledge bases which rely upon the actual practice in a field and which would also reflect the continuous innovations, the available documents (e.g. previously solved cases or textual descriptions) and their updates should be used as foundation. Machine learning techniques like conceptual clustering (e.g. Lebowitz, 1987) and explanation-based learning (Ellman, 1989) may be applied to these documents, so that abstract schemata are constructed from concrete cases by reversed engineering. Although the existing domain knowledge is often incomplete and conflicting, a useful system may be formed when the knowledge base construction is guided and supplemented by a human expert as suggested by the apprenticeship learning paradigm (Tecuci and Kodratoff, 1990). Consequently, a close cooperation between user and system is postulated, so that the various AI techniques will not be employed autonomously, but to support human users in the whole life cycle of a knowledge-based system.

In the life cycle of a KBS, at least three phases can be distinguished, which Fischer *et al.* (1994) have termed seeding, growth, and reseeding:

1. *Seeding:* Initial construction of the KBS (initial knowledge acquisition).

   In the seeding phase, conceptual clustering, learning by being told and explanation-based generalization/abstraction are employed in interactive learning tools. Knowledge engineers and particularly domain experts are involved in the initial construction of the KBS.
2. *Growth:* Use and update of the KBS (application and adaptive maintenance).

   In the growth phase, intelligent information retrieval and application-oriented inference services are employed in a highly interactive working environment for problem solving and learning. The system is applied as a discussion and learning partner, where the user as well as the system jointly perform tasks and learn from it. When the system is used by several users it can serve as a communication medium. The KBS tries to give crucial hints to the solution of the actual problem providing the right information at the right time. Furthermore, it is a comfortable information source, keeps track of the user's work, and listens to the user in the sense that it provides a user- and situation-specific selection of information from heterogeneous information sources. The system–user tandem thus shares tasks in a dynamically and rapidly changing world. Thereby system and user perform those subtasks which correspond to their competences, rather than competing in performing the same tasks. The application of the system and adaptive maintenance proceed hand in hand and is supported by a documentation component. The updating of the KBS during this phase is performed by the user rather than a knowledge engineer.
3. *Reseeding:* Generational changes of the KBS (corrective and perfective maintenance).

   In the reseeding phase, the cycle of seeding and growth is repeated by reapplying and possibly adapting the various knowledge acquisition tools considering the updates which have been done during the use in the growth

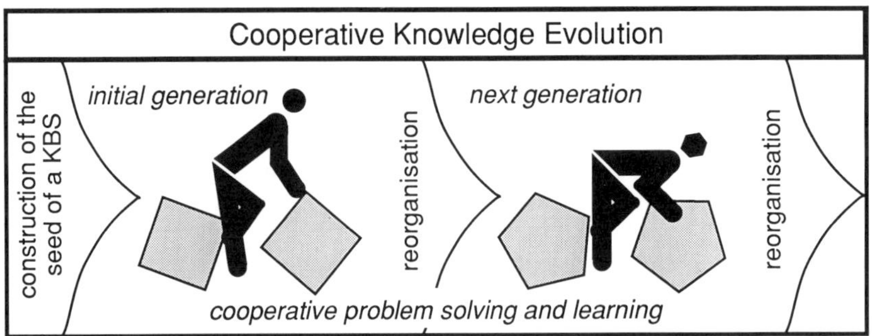

Figure 6.1 Cooperative knowledge evolution as a symbiotic tandem of user and system. Over time user and system adjust to each other, as well as to the specific task environment

phase. In the reseeding phase, assistance from knowledge engineers is required in addition to domain experts.

Figure 6.1 shows the process of cooperative knowledge evolution by a metaphor. In the seeding phase, a gadget (piece of equipment) is constructed, which will assist for performing various tasks. For example, an initial system may be developed with model-based knowledge-engineering techniques. With this piece of equipment a user can already reach his or her goals significantly faster than without it. The user exploits the gadget for achieving a better adjustment to the environment, so that the goals can be achieved more efficiently.

The cooperation of user and system furthermore yield that they adjust themselves more to each other and this adjustment also yields an additional adjustment to the (task) environment. After reseeding, the conceptualizations of a user and the categories represented in a system will thus be more similar. Within the proposed metaphor, the thoughts of the user become more formal and the categorizations of the system, which were originally very rigid, become more flexible and well rounded.

In the next section, we will describe the seeding of a KBS by a model-based engineering methodology. The growth phase will then be described for a domain, where KBS are best understood as communication media between different users.

6.3 The seed of a knowledge-based system

6.3.1 The case-oriented expert system architecture (COEX)

Although the fields of machine learning and knowledge acquisition share the common goal of developing operational knowledge-based systems, there is no learning architecture where the specific advantages of automatic machine learning methods, model-based knowledge acquisition techniques, knowledge elicitation from human experts and terminological representation languages have been combined. Significant advances in combining human expertise with machine learning methods have already been achieved with apprenticeship learning systems.

To construct a seed of a KBS we have configured and coordinated ML and KA tools according to model-based knowledge engineering methods (Breuker and Wielinga, 1989). Furthermore, domain experts and knowledge elicitation techniques (Boose and Gaines, 1989) are employed to cooperatively acquire the knowledge that is used as guidance in the apprenticeship learning paradigm. The knowledge is acquired on different levels ranging from informal to formal knowledge. The formalization of informal knowledge is facilitated by performing a stepwise formalization (see Schmalhofer, Kühn, and Schmidt, 1991, Figure 4; Schmalhofer *et al.*, 1992; Shipman and McCall, 1994). Corresponding knowledge items on different formalization levels are linked as nodes in a hypertext. This hypertext provides a comfortable means for various users, like knowledge engineers or domain experts, to access the knowledge base. The resulting seed of the KBS can be seen as the initial generation of a KBS which is subsequently updated through adaptive maintenance during use. From time to time a generational change of the KBS is carried out in the reseeding phase via corrective and perfective maintenance assisted by knowledge engineers and domain experts.

By pursuing such a unified approach for the domain of production planning in mechanical engineering, we obtained the Case-Oriented EXpert system or COEX architecture (Schmalhofer and Thoben, 1992), which is built upon the model of skeletal plan refinement (Friedland and Iwasaki, 1985; Kühn and Schmalhofer, 1992; Aitken *et al.*, 1993). According to this model, planning problems are solved by classifying a new problem into the abstract problem class that is most specific for the given problem. The associated procedure schema is then selected and refined to a concrete plan (see Figure 6.2).

The COEX architecture describes which and how machine learning tools as well as knowledge elicitation and knowledge representation techniques are combined, so that the seed of a knowledge-based system is obtained. The upper section of Figure 6.2 shows the learning architecture. Under the guidance of human experts the Case-Experience Combination System (CECoS; Reinartz and Schmalhofer, 1994) forms abstract problem classes from cases. An abstract terminology and description language is obtained as a by-product. The Plan ABStraction procedure (PABS; Schmalhofer and Tschaitschian, 1993) uses this terminology. For each problem class obtained with CECoS it abstracts a procedure schema from the cases that are subsumed by this problem class definition. The Skeletal Plan GENeration procedure (SP-GEN; Bergmann, 1992a), on the other hand, only constructs generalizations from the concrete cases which belong to terminal problem classes of the CECoS hierarchy. The Case-Oriented Knowledge Acquisition Method from text (COKAM+; Schmidt, 1992) is used for

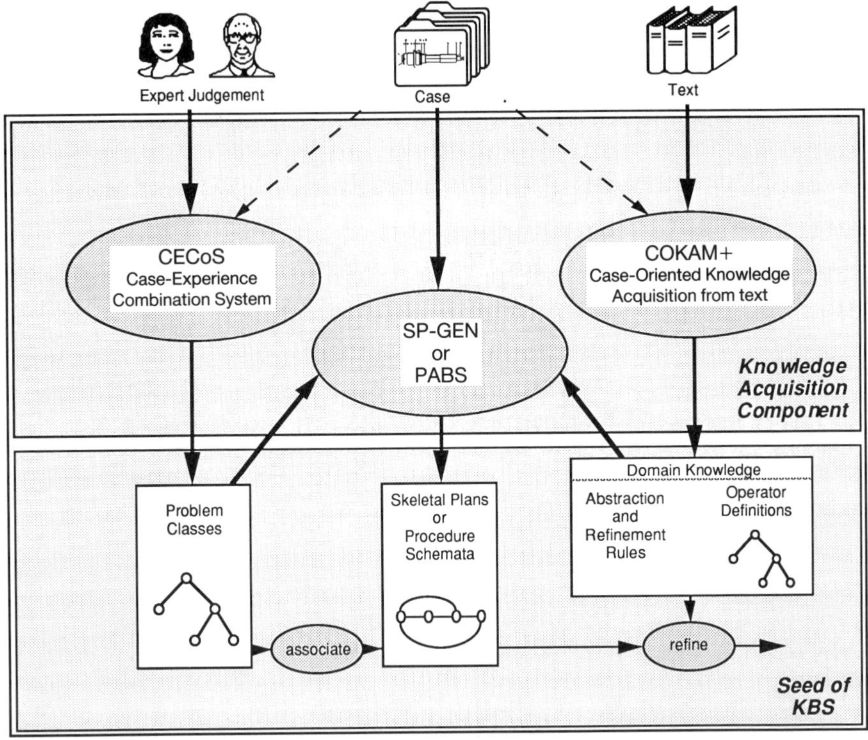

Figure 6.2 The COEX architecture: an integrated learning method (knowledge acquisition and machine learning) and the coordinated tools CECoS, SP-GEN, PABS and COKAM+ are applied to form the initial KBS (adapted from Schmalhofer and Thoben, 1992)

eliciting supplementary domain knowledge (e.g. abstraction/refinement rules) from relevant documents like texts or technical descriptions.

Because of the need for reducing complexity, in real-world domains the employed learning techniques should form true abstractions of problem descriptions and plans rather than only generalizations. The knowledge acquisition and machine learning tools CECoS and PABS provide a unified approach to conceptual clustering and explanation-based learning by constructing abstract problem classes and associated procedure schemata from concrete cases and related background knowledge within the framework of apprenticeship learning. Rather than surprising the human with unexpected learning results, CECoS and PABS were thus developed to empower the user to form abstract problem class definitions and associated procedure schemata from concrete cases.

The abstractions are formed by construction–integration processes. In the construction phases various abstract descriptions and terms are attached to the concrete problem description or case. In the integration phases, a coherent and consistent abstract characterization of the concrete case is formed by analysing the global context based on the constructed abstractions. Thereby, irrelevant and inconsistent abstract descriptions are deleted.

6.3.2 Interactive conceptual clustering with CECoS

In CECoS, the concept formation is initially guided by numerical judgements of the similarity between different domain objects that are provided by a human expert. These judgements are used to construct a hierarchy of problem and operator classes with a hierarchical cluster analysis. It is assumed that each class can be described as an abstract concept. The user supplies all those natural language descriptions which characterize the different classes. These descriptions are stored in a hypertext structure and then formalized step by step. Via different templates, which yield semiformal representations, the natural language descriptions are transformed into formal representations. The formal concepts of the different classes are finally verified against the hierarchical class structure. The abstract terms used for the class descriptions also provide the seed for the abstract description language which is used for forming abstractions with PABS. Rather than presupposing the terms of the abstract description language, CECoS thus constructs a seed for such a language during the course of its application. In this respect, CECoS is quite different from conceptual clustering systems like COBWEB (Fisher, 1987) which require symbolic representations of the objects before the clustering can be performed. Unlike these systems, the clusters which are formed by CECoS are described in a suitable abstract representation language which is provided by a domain expert during the application of CECoS.

Figure 6.3 presents an overview of the construction and integration phases in which abstract problem descriptions are formed by CECoS. In phases I and II, a set of prototypical cases which delineates the desired competence of the knowledge base is selected and the judgements of a domain expert about their relatedness are used to form a problem class hierarchy by a hierarchical cluster analysis. This clustering relies upon the expert's judgement about deep relationships rather than on the surface form of the case descriptions. The formation of the abstraction hierarchy is thus independent of any incidental selection of a specific representation language but grounded in an expert's understanding of the domain. In phase III, the expert attributes informal abstract features to the different problem classes and assigns these features to the different views, which are determined by the model of skeletal plan refinement. After these construction phases, CECoS determines an agenda for consistency and redundancy checks yielding an early validation of the acquired knowledge. These checks have to be executed by the expert. In phase V a stepwise formalization is performed in

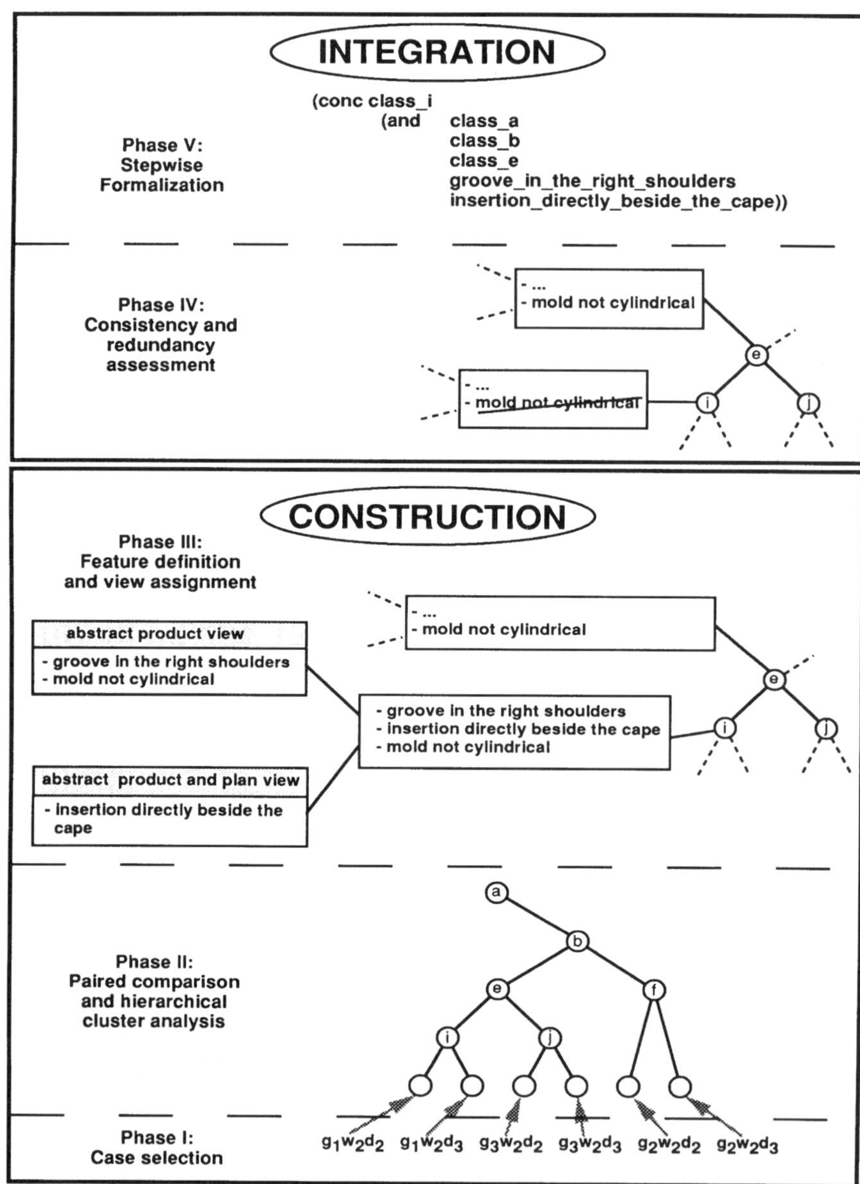

Figure 6.3 With the Case-Experience Combination System (CECoS), the construction and integration processes of knowledge formation are performed in five phases (adapted from Reinartz and Schmalhofer, 1994)

cooperation between expert and system: several templates are used to establish an adequate and more fine-grained semantic structure of the various features. The templates are filled by the expert and were constructed so that they can be independently translated into the terminological language TAXON (Hanschke *et al.*, 1991). With the inference services of the terminological representation language the abstraction hierarchy is verified and new problems can be classified. In a similar vein, an abstraction hierarchy is established for various operators which occur in the different production plans. The generation of the abstract operator descriptions is thereby supported by COKAM+.

6.3.3 Skeletal plan generation with SP-GEN

SP-GEN is an autonomous ML tool which constructs skeletal plans, i.e. generalizations of concrete production plans. SP-GEN is based on the idea of explanation-based learning (Mitchell *et al.*, 1986), which is a form of analytic learning. Explanation-based learning (EBL) is a method where generalizations are formed from a single case by employing a body of background knowledge, a target concept and a desired description level, which is defined by so-called operationality criteria. EBL explains or proves that the case (training example) satisfies the requirements of the target concept (goal concept) using the background knowledge as the domain theory. In other words it is deduced from the domain theory that the training example is an instance of the goal concept. The deduced proof is generalized to a more usable concept definition in terms of the desired description level (operationality criteria). This generalization is guided by the background knowledge rather than by some unknown inductive bias and brings the relevant features of the case in focus while irrelevant features are ignored.

A characterization of SP-GEN as an EBL-method is presented in Table 6.1. The domain theory provides significantly more structure than the domain theories of similar systems (DeJong and Mooney, 1986; Minton *et al.*, 1987; Mitchell *et al.*, 1986). Unlike DeJong and Mooney's GENESIS that uses a goal state as the target concept, a generic problem and solution description is used. A specific manufacturing problem and its solution serves as training example. The operationality criteria are based on the problem class definitions which have been acquired with CECoS. The learning result of SP-GEN is a blueprint (i.e. a skeletal plan) that can be reused for manufacturing similar workpieces.

A skeletal plan is constructed in four phases (Schmalhofer *et al.*, 1991). In the first phase, the execution of the source plan is simulated and explanations for the effects of the individual operations are constructed. In the second phase the generalization of these explanations is performed with respect to a criterion of operationality, that specifies the vocabulary for defining general operators for the skeletal plan. In the third phase, a dependency analysis of the resulting operator effects unveils the substantial interactions of the plan at the more general level of the skeletal plan. And finally in the fourth phase the concept descriptions for the

Table 6.1 Characterization of SP-GEN as an EBL-method

Domain theory	Hierarchically structured knowledge base in terms of state and operator definitions, problem classes, abstraction and refinement rules.
Target concept	Generic problem and solution approach (non-operational).
Training example	Success case: initial and goal states, sequence of concrete operations (e.g. a production plan that has been successfully used in the real world).
Operationality criteria	Terms used by domain experts to describe states and operators (acquired with CECoS and COKAM+).
Learning result	A skeletal plan as a blueprint for solving future problems (i.e. a well structured specification of a problem description and its solution in operational terms).

generalized operators of the skeletal plan are formed by collecting and normalizing the important constraints for each operation that were indicated by the dependencies.

SP-GEN has been successfully applied in the mechanical engineering domain for generating skeletal plans from concrete production plans. Thus, skeletal plans could be provided for all terminal classes of CECoS problem class hierarchy. However, when we tried to apply SP-GEN to non-terminal problem classes, it became clear that explanation-based generalization is not sufficient for these classes. Whereas SP-GEN can form generalizations from cases for quite specific problem classes, true abstractions would be required to generate procedure schemata for the more abstract problem classes. Michalski and Kodratoff (1990) have recently pointed out that generalization needs to be distinguished more clearly from abstraction. While generalization normally uses the same representation language, abstraction involves a change in the representation space to transform the representation language into a simpler language than the original. The problem class descriptions provided by a domain expert in CECoS were at such an abstract description level.

In order to generate a procedure schema for these classes, one must combine different numbers and different sequences of operators. But SP-GEN offers no support to generalize over the given operator sequence. Although the dependency analysis of SP-GEN finds interdependencies between single operations, it cannot construct a uniform procedure schema that subsumes substantially different operator sequences and plans with different numbers of operators. The construction of such procedure schemata requires the formation of true abstractions, which led us to develop the explanation-based abstraction method and the PABS procedure which will be described in the following section.

6.3.4 Explanation-based abstraction with PABS

PABS constructs abstract procedure schemata from a concrete problem description and the associated concrete plan. PABS is guided by the abstract descriptions which were previously established with CECoS and COKAM+. It relies upon the hierarchy of abstract problem classes and the hierarchy of abstract operators that are constructed with CECoS and additional background knowledge that is elicited with the knowledge acquisition tool COKAM+. Whenever possible, the intermediate states which result from the execution of the concrete plan are described by the abstract description language. Concrete states are thus mapped into abstract states. Only the essential concrete states, which have a corresponding abstract state, are thus denoted by the abstract language. A reduction in the number of states as well as a more coarse-grained description of the selected states results directly from the fact that the abstract language is less expressive. Thereby unimportant or irrelevant information is filtered out. After applicable abstract operators have been constructed between the abstract states, the final procedure schema is obtained. In this way PABS forms procedure schemata for all terminal classes of the problem hierarchy which can be used as a supplement or substitute to SP-GEN's skeletal plans. Schemata for superordinate classes are constructed by combining the schemata of their direct subclasses.

Explanation-based abstraction is defined by two mappings. State abstraction mappings transform concrete into abstract state descriptions. The sequence abstraction mapping relates an abstract to a concrete state sequence so that (a) the initial and goal states at the abstract and concrete level correspond to each other and (b) the sequence of the selected concrete states is maintained by the respective abstract state sequence. This relation between the concrete and the abstract representations has been more formally described by Bergmann (1992b) and Schmalhofer *et al.* (1993).

Figure 6.4 presents the construction and integration phases which form an abstract procedure schema from a concrete case. In phase I the concrete state sequence is computed from the corresponding plan and its initial state. After associating abstract to concrete states in phase II, all applicable abstract operators between abstract states are identified in phase III. A sequence of abstract operators, which establishes a consistent path of operators from the initial to the goal state (i.e. an abstract plan) is then selected. The user is asked to provide the lacking knowledge if the domain knowledge is incomplete, i.e. abstract operators are missing or abstract states are not sufficiently described. Finally, the procedure schema is obtained by generalizing the operators of the abstract plan and constructing a respective directed graph in phase V. This procedure is applied to each of the concrete cases which were already used in CECoS. The resulting procedure schemata are associated to the corresponding terminal nodes of the problem class hierarchy. These schemata are the input for a graph union algorithm which constructs the procedure schemata of the superordinate classes.

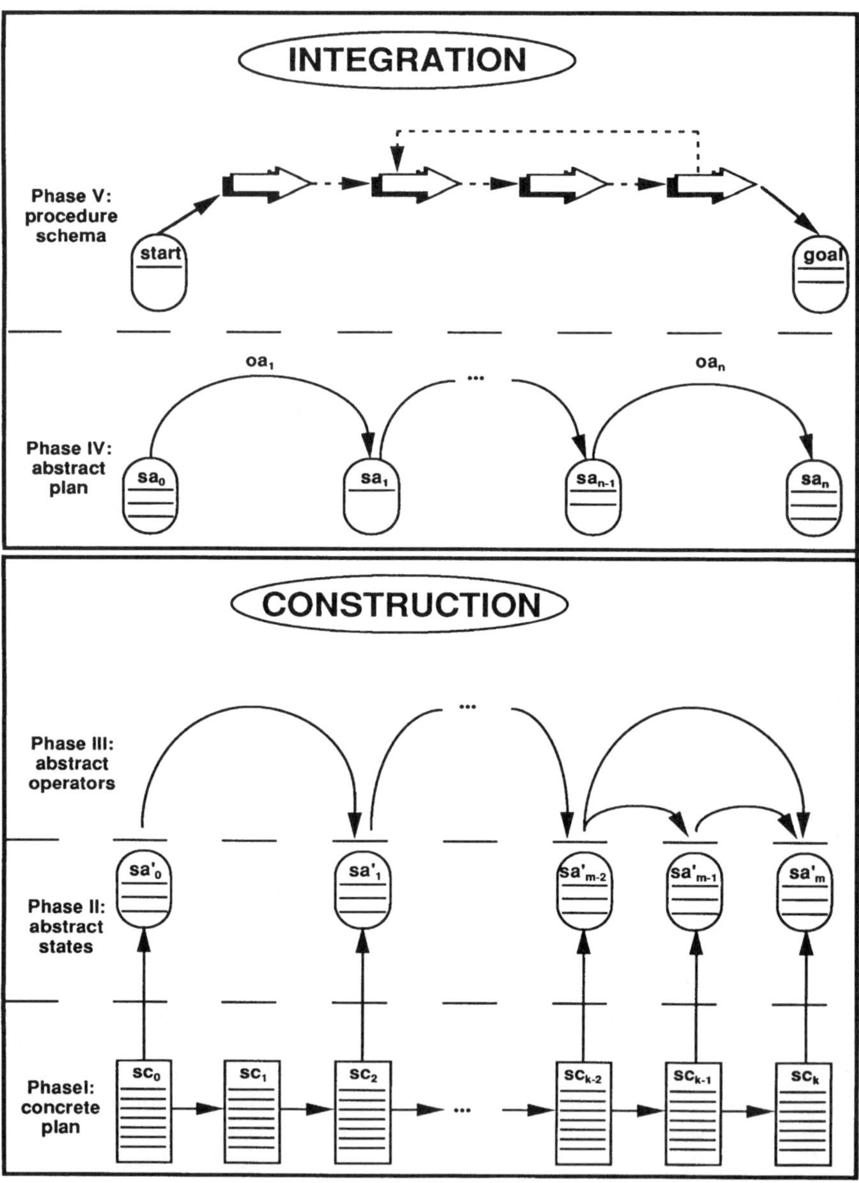

Figure 6.4 With the Plan ABStraction procedure (PABS), the construction and integration phases for forming an abstract procedure schema are performed in five phases (from Schmalhofer *et al.*, 1995)

As mentioned before, the user guidance in CECoS yields the right level of abstraction for a description language to overcome the complexity of real-world problems. Thereby an appropriate domain ontology is obtained to construct useful procedure schemata from concrete plans.

Although PABS forms explanation-based abstractions rather than generalizations, it nevertheless stands in the tradition of the EBL paradigm. A body of background knowledge consisting of a concrete and an abstract language for denoting states and operators as well as the abstraction rules provides the pertinent domain theory. The abstract problem description of transforming an initial state into a goal state would be equivalent to the target concept. A concrete plan consisting of a sequence of operators corresponds to the training example in standard EBL. The operationality criterion of PABS requires that a sequence of abstract operators and a respective transition network are constructed that are sufficient for transforming the abstract initial state into the abstract goal state. Thus, PABS can be understood as an EBL procedure.

6.4 Cooperative problem solving and learning: growth of knowledge, use and update of the KBS

6.4.1 Clinical testing of new drugs

Traditionally, KBS have mostly been employed as intelligent assistant systems or autonomous problem solvers in rather narrow domains. Knowledge sharing and reuse efforts and the integration of KBS in larger environments and broader contexts have been disregarded to a large degree. In our view of a KBS as an intelligent documentation and communication tool these aspects have to be thoroughly considered. We will show the application phase of such a KBS in the medical domain of clinical studies and describe this system as a communication medium and a partner for discussion and learning.

In the pharmaceutical industry, each new drug is tested in clinical studies before it is released on the market. These studies aim to ensure drug efficacy and drug safety with respect to potential side-effects and interactions with other substances (Aschenbrenner *et al.*, 1993). In the course of such a study, a variety of adverse events[1] may occur which must be classified and explained to determine whether they are caused by the drug under investigation. This decision is made by clinical project managers based on respective data delivered by the investigator from the hospital. Therefore information and knowledge from numerous heterogeneous sources is employed. The experts must process all relevant information in order to generate a causal model as an explanation for the event. Several judgements are derived from the causal model and finally the resulting explanation is documented. In particular, in the explanation of adverse events strict time

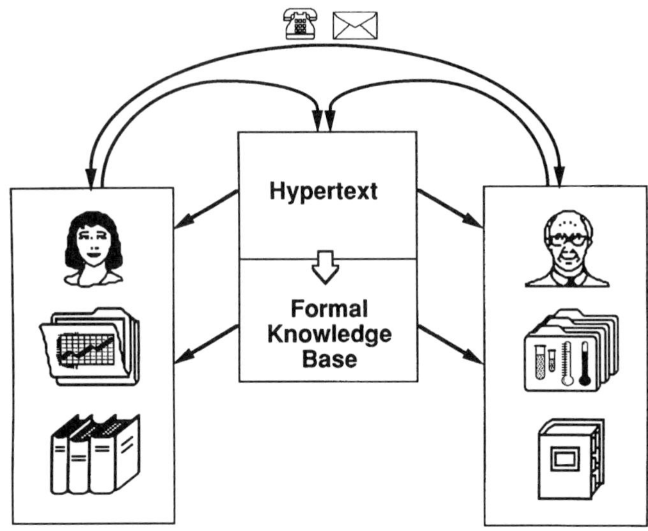

Figure 6.5 Traditional communication paths are supplemented by the KBS

restrictions must be considered. Consequently, communication between clinical project manager and investigator becomes a major bottleneck in this process.[2]

6.4.2 KBS as communication medium

Usually, the communication between investigators in the hospital and clinical project managers is supported only by passive media, such as telephone, mail, or fax (Figure 6.5). At work, both experts rely on data from their specific information sources, such as literature and representation of cases. Often, this information is not shared between them. This scenario is now extended by the KBS which serves as an active communication medium between the experts. Information from both sides is (informally and/or formally) represented as a structured hypertext in the system. Information flows from the system to the experts (system as discussion partner) and vice versa (system as learning partner). Thereby, an indirect communication through the KBS can take place in addition to traditional communication paths. Knowledge from different information sources can be shared among several experts and the communication is temporally and logically decoupled. The temporal decoupling yields a more or less static storage of single entities and may also be realized via standard communication media like mail or fax. However, through logical decoupling the information is not only passively stored, but prepared and well structured for further use. The KBS may answer queries of an expert by applying knowledge provided by other experts. Thus, the KBS serves as an active agent supplementing the communication among several experts.

Beyond the indirect communication support, a KBS could further facilitate the direct communication between experts through newest advances in technology. Videophone (and videoconferencing) via computers will be well established soon. Experts at different sites will be able to discuss an actual case which could be presented on the screen in addition to the video window. A highly interactive working environment could further provide means to manipulate the case (i.e. its presentation on the screen) textually or graphically.

To employ a KBS as a communication medium between experts several preliminaries must be fulfilled concerning the use and update of such a system. In the following we will show which facilities are required to employ the KBS as a partner for discussion (use) and learning (update) in the domain of clinical studies.

6.4.3 KBS as discussion partner

The seeding phase provides a KBS which supports decision making during the explanation of adverse events in the following way. A new adverse case report is classified into the hierarchy of problem classes which has been acquired with CECoS. An associated explanation schema which has been constructed by an explanation-based abstraction procedure (an adapted version of PABS) can now be employed to explain the adverse event: the expert refines the chosen schema according to the actual case data. Although we regard this way of problem solving as widely applicable and useful, the human problem solver should by no means be forced to follow this procedure. The KBS should additionally provide the expert with all information (data and knowledge) which is usually employed during problem solving. Moreover, knowledge-based inference services (functionalities) should be offered which are beneficially applicable in the specific application domain. This enables the expert to determine the procedure of problem solving according to his or her specific needs. The expert is free to ask for an explanation schema as a hypothesis, to draw his or her own conclusions from the available case data, or to explore available information sources either dependent or independent of specific case data.

Consequently, the KBS must allow an intelligent information retrieval from a variety of heterogeneous sources, e.g. from the adverse case report, from medical information sources and from previous cases. Therefore, suitable interfaces to existing databases must be built.

The principle of task sharing guides the selection of suitable application-oriented inference services. The KBS should be employed when it is more powerful to solve the current task than human experts. However, human experts should perform challenging tasks whenever their expertise is essentially necessary. Thus, system and user supplement each other and build the system–user tandem which has been illustrated by the metaphor in Section 6.2 (Figure 6.1). By appropriately sharing the tasks between system and user considerable expert time can be saved.

In order to enable access to all these facilities, the KBS must provide a highly interactive working environment. The user can easily access all relevant data and functions. The information provided by the system must be easy to perceive and handle. An information presentation strategy should help to inform the users about the various building blocks of the interface. Figure 6.6 shows a part of the hypermedia user interface of the IDEAS[3] system (Birk *et al.*, 1995). Adverse event reports are prepared so that all items with further links in the KBS are mouse-sensitive and thus directly accessible by the user.

The system keeps track of the user's work, i.e. any processing or evaluation of selected items is recorded. Furthermore, the problem solving progress is documented graphically. The investigation state of (selected) items is visualized by different colours. Depending on the investigation results the items change their colour. However, the system should not only passively listen to the user. Moreover, the system should intervene when it can provide significant suggestions. For example, consider the investigation of a drug for a causal relationship to an adverse event. A known side-effect of the drug registered in a database seems to be a plausible explanation for the event. Based on data of the adverse case report, the temporal reasoner of the KBS concludes that there is no temporal relation between the administration of the drug and the onset of the adverse event. This inconsistency is documented in the investigation report and directly presented to the user. Thus, the system can give crucial hints to the user providing the right information at the right time.

6.4.4 KBS as learning partner

According to the previously mentioned levels of formalization the KBS can acquire informal, as well as formal, knowledge during its use (growth). These updates are provided by the expert. Nevertheless, their acquisition is supported by a documentation component and the tools CECoS and PABS. The acquisition of informal and formal knowledge during the application of the KBS will be illustrated by two examples from our medical domain.

Example 1: Elicitation of informal knowledge

The clinical project manager investigates a case, where a patient suffered from diabetes mellitus. In order to reveal symptoms of this disease to explain the adverse event he or she selects the respective text item in the adverse case report. The KBS presents a dialogue explaining that no information is currently stored. The dialogue provides access to the documentation component of the system. The expert documents the lack of data, entering that the relevant information can be found in a specific textbook. This input is included into the

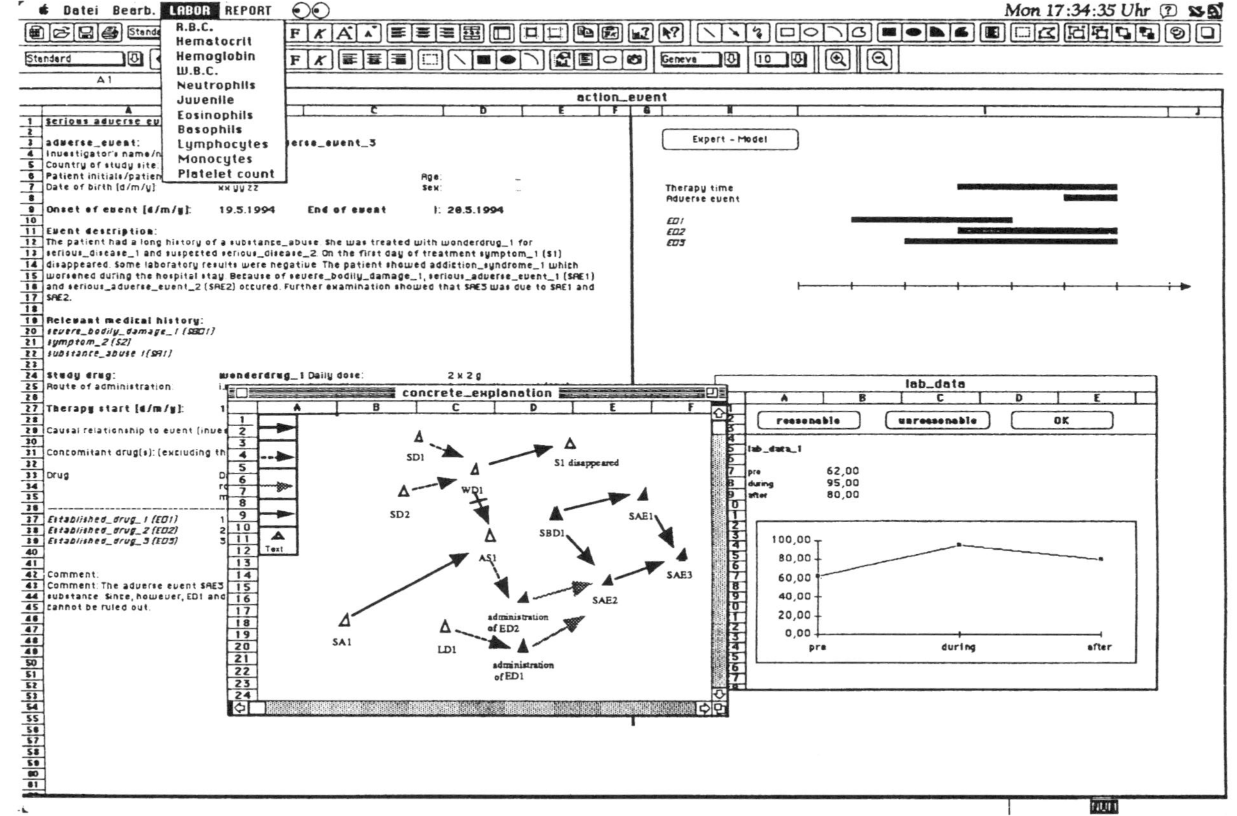

Figure 6.6 Snapshot of a system–user interaction for constructing a so-called action event model

hypertext at the location where the relevant information has been missing. When diabetes mellitus is accessed in further applications of the system the stored reference is presented.

Example 2: Acquisition of formal knowledge with KA and ML tools

The clinical project manager has explained a case outside the current competence of the KBS. Since no appropriate procedure schema has been provided by the classification in the problem class hierarchy, keeping this case may improve the system. Thus, the expert decides to keep this case in the record of adverse case reports. Therefore, he or she reinvokes the knowledge acquisition tool CECoS, extending the problem class hierarchy by inserting the case as a terminal node. Then the expert defines the class providing the characteristic features. The user is free to employ further phases of CECoS or to stop at this informal level. If a class description is completely formalized (the adapted version of) PABS can be reinvoked. An explanation schema for the new class is constructed and the schemata of superordinate classes are appropriately updated. Within further applications of the KBS these schemata can be employed for explanation of adverse events.

When a considerable number of updates has been provided during the use of the KBS a reorganization of the system must be performed (reseeding phase) to guarantee efficiency and reliability of the system. This is done in cooperation of expert, knowledge engineer and system and will be discussed in the following section.

6.5 Reseeding: generational changes of the KBS

In order to guarantee an efficient and reliable use of the KBS the updates performed during application, as well as newly available data and knowledge, have to be considered in the reseeding phase. Domain experts and knowledge engineers confirm and further elaborate all updates in cooperation with the KBS. The system kept track of all updates and makes them easily accessible for the users. Hypertext nodes which have been included into the system via the documentation component can be replaced by respective documents or can be linked to such documents. For example, the Hypertext node with the reference to "diabetes mellitus" would be linked to the respective chapter in a book on internal medicine which is electronically stored on an external database. For new classes of the problem class hierarchy which have not been formalized during the application of the KBS, CECoS could be applied to proceed with the formalization. The whole problem class hierarchy could be restructured by inserting reasonable non-terminal classes which subsume several new or combinations of new and old cases with support from CECoS. In addition, PABS would be reapplied to respective classes.

6.6 Conclusions

In this chapter we reviewed some of the research in knowledge acquisition and machine learning that was conducted over the last five years at the German Research Center for Artificial Intelligence in Kaiserslautern. This work was driven by the requirements of complex real-world domains rather than by classical AI paradigms, like search, deduction, or terminological logics. Nevertheless, some of the results from these paradigms were shown to be quite useful for developing knowledge-based systems for industrial use. Considering the life cycle of knowledge-based systems and apprenticeship learning, we described cooperative knowledge evolution as a framework that emerged from our specific experiences with practitioners from different fields (i.e. mechanical engineering, material sciences, laboratory medicine, clinical studies). The proposed framework of cooperative knowledge evolution fits quite well with the design environments proposed by Fischer and his collaborators (Fischer *et al.*, 1994) on the one hand, and apprenticeship learning on the other hand. Cooperative knowledge evolution is in a much closer agreement with the expectations and needs of the users in the studied domains (see Kühn and Höfling, 1994; Birk *et al.*, 1995) than earlier approaches to machine learning and knowledge acquisition.

Acknowledgements

This work was supported by grants ITW 8902 C4 and 413-5839-ITW9304/3 from the BMFT and by grant SCHM 648/1 from the DFG. Further financial support was provided by the Hoechst AG/Frankfurt and by the Institut Dr. Viollier AG/ Zürich. We would like to thank all previous and current colleagues in the ARC-TEC, KIWi and VEGA projects who contributed to this research in various ways, as well as the practitioners from the different companies, who shared some of their domain knowledge with us.

Notes

1. An adverse event is defined as any undesirable sign, symptom or other finding occurring in subjects or patients exposed to a drug.
2. Consider the following situation. The clinical project manager needs additional information from the investigator about the patient who suffered from the adverse event and calls him in the hospital. Since the investigator is not

within reach at that moment he requests ring back. When the investigator calls back the clinical project manager is not within reach a.s.o.
3. IDEAS stands for "Intelligent Documentation for the Explanation of Adverse events in clinical Studies".

References

Aitken, S., Kühn, O., Shadbolt N. and Schmalhofer, F. (1993). A conceptual model of hierarchical skeletal planning and its formalization. *Proc. 3rd KADS User Meeting*, March 8–9, Munich, Germany, pp. 229–247.

Aschenbrenner, K. M., Gertzen, H., Kühn, O., Schmalhofer, F. and Schmidt, J. (1993). *IDEAS: Unterstützung der Arzneimittelsicherheit durch eine umfassende Wissensnutzung mittels neuer Informationstechnologien.* Projektbeschreibung. Hoechst AG, Frankfurt and Deutsches Forschungszentrum für Künstliche Intelligenz, Kaiserslautern, Deutschland.

Bergmann, R. (1992a). Knowledge acquisition by generating skeletal plans from real world cases. In Schmalhofer, F., Strube. G. and Wetter. Th. (editors), *Contemporary Knowledge Engineering and Cognition*, pp. 125–133. Springer, Berlin.

Bergmann, R. (1992b). Learning Plan Abstractions. *Proceedings of the 16th German Workshop on Artificial Intelligence (GWAI '92)*, August 31–September 3, Bonn, Germany, pp. 187–198.

Birk, A., Tschaitschian, B., Schmalhofer, F., Thüring, M. and Gertzen, H. (1995). Architecture and User-Interface of the IDEAS Intelligent Documentation System. In Schuler, W. and Hannemann, J. (editors), *Methodological Issues on the Design of Hypertext-based User Interfaces* pp. 79–94. Springer-Verlag, Berlin.

Boose, J. H. and Gaines, B. R. (1989). Knowledge acquisition of knowledge-based systems: notes on the state-of-the-art. *Machine Learning*, 4: 377–394.

Breuker, J. and Wielinga, B. (1989). Models of expertise in knowledge acquisition. In Guida, G. and Tasso, C. (editors), *Topics in Expert System Design, Methodologies and Tools*, pp. 265–295. North-Holland, Amsterdam.

Buchanan, B. G. (1989). Can machine learning offer anything to expert systems? *Machine Learning*, 4: 251–254.

DeJong, G. and Mooney, R. (1986). Explanation-based learning: an alternative view. *Machine Learning*, 1: 145–176.

Ellman, T. (1989). Explanation-based learning: A survey of programs and perspectives. *ACM Computing Surveys*, 21: 163–222.

Fischer, G., McGall, R., Ostwald, J., Reeves, B. and Shipman, F. (1994). Seeding, evolutionary growth and reseeding: supporting the incremental development of design environments. *CHI '94 Conference Proceedings*, April 24–28, Boston, MA.

Fisher, D. H. (1987). Knowledge acquisition via incremental conceptual clustering. *Machine Learning*, 2: 139–172.

Friedland, P. E. and Iwasaki, Y. (1985). The concept and implementation of skeletal plans. *Journal of Automated Reasoning*, 1: 161–208.

Hanschke, P., Abecker, A. and Drollinger, D. (1991). TAXON: A concept language with concrete domains. *Proceedings of the International Workshop on Processing Declarative Knowledge (PDK '91)*, July 1–3, Kaiserslautern, Germany, pp. 411–413.

Knoblock, C. A. (1990). Learning abstraction hierarchies for problem solving. *Proceedings of the Eighth National Conference on Artificial Intelligence*, July 29–August 3, Boston, MA, pp. 923–928.

Kühn, O. and Höfling, B. (1994). Conserving corporate knowledge for crankshaft design. *Proceedings of the Seventh International Conference on Industrial & Engineering Applications of Artificial Intelligence and Expert Systems*, May 31–June 4, Austin, Texas.

Kühn, O. and Schmalhofer, F. (1992). Hierarchical skeletal plan refinement task and inference structures. *Proc. 2nd KADS User Meeting*, February 17–18, Munich, Germany.

Lebowitz, M. (1987). Experiments with incremental concept formation: UNIMEM. *Machine Learning*, 2: 103–138.

Michalski, R. S. and Kodratoff, Y. (1990). Research in machine learning: recent progress, classification of methods and future directions. In Kodratoff, Y. and Michalski, R. S. (editors), *Machine Learning: An Artificial Intelligence Approach Volume 3*, pp. 3–30. Morgan Kaufmann, San Mateo, CA.

Minton, S., Carbonell, J. G., Etzioni, O., Knoblock, C. A. and Kuokka, D. R. (1987). Acquiring effective search control rules: explanation-based learning in the PRODIGY system. *Proceedings of the Fourth International Workshop on Machine Learning*, pp. 122–133. Morgan Kaufmann, Irvine, CA.

Mitchell, T. M., Keller, R. M. and Kedar-Cabelli, S. T. (1986). Explanation-based generalization: a unifying view. *Machine Learning*, 1: 47–80.

Reinartz, Th. and Schmalhofer, F. (1994). An integration of knowledge acquisition techniques and EBL for real-world production planning. *Knowledge Acquisition*, 6: 115–136.

Schmalhofer, F., Bergmann, R., Boschert, S. and Thoben, J. (1993). Learning program abstractions: model and empirical validation. In Strube, G. and Wender, K. F. (editors) *The Cognitive Psychology of Knowledge*, pp. 203–231. Elsevier, Amsterdam.

Schmalhofer, F., Bergmann, R., Kühn, O. and Schmidt, G. (1991). Using an integrated knowledge acquisition method to prepare sophisticated expert plans for the reuse in novel situations. *Proceedings of the 15th German Workshop on Artificial Intelligence*, September 16–20, Bonn, Germany, pp. 62–71.

Schmalhofer, F., Kühn, O. and Schmidt, G. (1991). Integrated knowledge acquisition from text, previously solved cases, and expert memories. *Applied Artificial Intelligence*, 5: 311–337.

Schmalhofer, F., Reinartz, Th. and Tschaitschian, B. (1992). Intelligent documentation as a catalyst for developing cooperative knowledge-based systems. In Wetter, Th., Althoff, K. D., Boose, J., Gaines, B. R., Linster, M. and Schmalhofer, F. (editors),

Current developments in knowledge acquisition – EKAW '92, pp. 406–424. Springer, Berlin.

Schmalhofer, F., Reinartz, Th. and Tschaitschian, B. (1995). A unified approach to learning for complex real world domains. *Applied Artificial Intelligence*, 9.

Schmalhofer, F. and Thoben, J. (1992). The model-based construction of a case-oriented expert system. *AI Communications*, March, 3–18.

Schmalhofer, F. and Tschaitschian, B. (1993). The acquisition of a procedure schema from text and experiences. *Proceedings of the 15th Annual Conference of the Cognitive Science Society*, June 18–21, Boulder, CO, pp. 883–888.

Schmidt, G. (1992). Knowledge acquisition from text in a complex domain. *Proceedings of the Fifth International Conference on Industrial & Engineering Applications of Artificial Intelligence and Expert Systems*, June 9–12, University of Paderborn, Germany, pp. 529–538.

Shipman, F. M. and McCall, R. (1994). Supporting knowledge-base evolution with incremental formalization. *CHI '94 Conference Proceedings*, April, 24–28, Boston, MA.

Tecuci, G. and Kodratoff, Y. (1990). Apprenticeship learning in imperfect domain theories. In Kodratoff, Y. and Michalski, R. S. (editors), *Machine Learning: An Artificial Intelligence Approach, Volume III*, pp. 514–552. Morgan Kaufmann, San Mateo, CA.

CHAPTER 7

A machine learning approach to knowledge-based software engineering

Christopher A. Miller and Keith R. Levi

Abstract

We developed a knowledge acquisition system that uses an explanation-based learning (EBL) domain theory as a *knowledge repository* from which general knowledge structures can be compiled and then translated by *smart translators* into the various specialized representations required for the separate expert system modules of a distributed pilot aiding system. We call this two-stage, learning-plus-translation, process *linked learning*. This architecture addresses learning for multiple modules with different knowledge representations and performance goals, which must all perform together in an integrated fashion. It also addresses learning for an intelligent agent which must perform in a real-world, dynamically-changing environment with multiple sources of uncertainty. Finally, it serves as a case study offering insights into the integration of machine learning into the software engineering process for a large knowledge-based system development effort.

7.1 Introduction

As intelligent, knowledge-based systems become more prevalent and complex in real-world domains, the task of acquiring, representing and later updating and revising those systems becomes more difficult. We have developed a knowledge acquisition system which uses explanation-based, machine learning techniques to aid human knowledge engineers in addressing these problems for a coordinated suite of large expert systems whose task is aiding the pilot of an advanced fighter aircraft.

Knowledge engineering involves several major stages, including elicitation, representation and implementation. Our focus involves the use of machine

Machine Learning and Knowledge Acquisition
ISBN 0–12–685120–4

learning techniques to automate large portions of the representation and implementation stages. These techniques help to resolve the knowledge acquisition bottleneck in that they provide a bridge between representations that are favorable for knowledge elicitation and representations that are favorable for implementation.

In machine learning applications, it is common to distinguish between the *learning system* and the *performance system*. The goal of the learning system is to acquire new knowledge, or to refine existing knowledge, for use by the performance system. The goal of the performance system is to perform some activity within a domain. In our application, the performance system is a set of coordinated, knowledge-based systems which may be used to assist advanced fighter pilots, while the learning system we constructed is designed to assist in acquiring and representing the knowledge required for the knowledge bases of the performance system.

The input to our learning system is a specific learning instance, e.g. an example of an aircraft maneuver flown on a flight simulator. The output of our system is software for an expert performance system which could be used to aid the pilot in a next-generation fighter aircraft. This software is implemented in a specialized and efficient representation for performance in the aircraft environment. For example, the software might be composed of a set of special purpose Ada (or perhaps C) functions rather than some general purpose artificial intelligence (AI) architecture such as a production system.

The architecture of our learning system is a two-stage process which we have labelled *linked learning*. The first step in our linked-learning procedure is to use Explanation-Based Learning (EBL) (DeJong and Mooney, 1986; Mitchell *et al.*, 1986), to learn a new tactical plan from a single instance of pilot behavior. Our EBL process first explains how the observed and recorded behavior of the pilot and the world combined to achieve a known goal. This explanation is then generalized so that it can be reused to achieve the goal in similar, future instances. The second step in our linked-learning process is to translate this generalized representation into the specialized implementation used by the performance system. Thus, our emphasis is on using machine learning (first step) and knowledge-based techniques (second step) to automate part of the software engineering process in a knowledge-based system.

Our approach contrasts with more traditional uses of machine learning such as discovery learning and speed-up learning. For example, in discovery learning one might use machine learning to try to discover novel maneuvers or tactics (Lewis, 1986; Erickson and Zytkow, 1988; Gordon and Greffenstette, 1990). In contrast we start with a maneuver already well-known by human experts and provide an automated method to efficiently represent and implement this maneuver in a target expert system.

Our work also contrasts with a large class of applications of machine learning referred to as "speed-up learning". Speed-up learning has been the typical paradigm for applications of EBL (Minton, 1990). Speed-up learning assumes that the target performance system will be some general-purpose AI architecture such as a production system or AI planning architecture. Speed-up learners typically use EBL to abstract out intermediate reasoning steps and thereby improve the speed of a performance system. In many real-world systems, however, this is not sufficient. In very demanding applications, performance systems cannot use unification, interpreters and other general-purpose AI computing techniques. Rather, they must be coded for maximum efficiency using special-purpose functions and languages such as C. Thus, speed-up learning applications of EBL might be thought of as an optimization process that stays within a given representation. Our use of explanation-based learning is more like compiling one representation into another representation, or compiling one language into a second, more efficient, language. As such, it has much in common with what Goel (1991) and others have called "knowledge compilation".

In the remainder of this chapter, we first describe the performance system which benefited from our learning system, with emphasis on the knowledge acquisition and knowledge engineering problems posed by this performance system. Then we will describe the learning system we developed in detail and describe its integration into the knowledge acquisition and knowledge engineering process. Finally, we discuss how our learning system addresses many of the problems posed by the performance system and we offer suggestions and lessons learned for the use of this approach in future, large knowledge engineering projects.

7.2 The performance system: the Pilot's Associate

The application domain of our knowledge acquisition system is the US Air Force's Pilot's Associate (PA) system (Banks and Lizza, 1991). Future aircraft will have tremendous sensor, control and information resources which will greatly extend the pilot's capabilities, but will carry increased workload demands if they are not managed in an intelligent way. The goal of PA is to offer proper, effective assistance to the pilot when necessary in order to improve the overall performance of the man–machine system. In order to accomplish this, PA performs a number of disparate functions simultaneously throughout the mission:

- Interpreting external sensor data to assess the current state of the world.
- Interpreting internal sensor data to assess the state of the aircraft.
- Using this data to monitor mission status.
- Monitoring and interpreting pilot actions, in combination with current world, aircraft and mission status, to infer pilot goals and detect pilot errors.
- Recommending plans to further known goals.
- Configuring displays to improve pilot situation awareness and decision making.
- Subsuming tasks (if previously authorized) when the pilot is too busy to perform them.

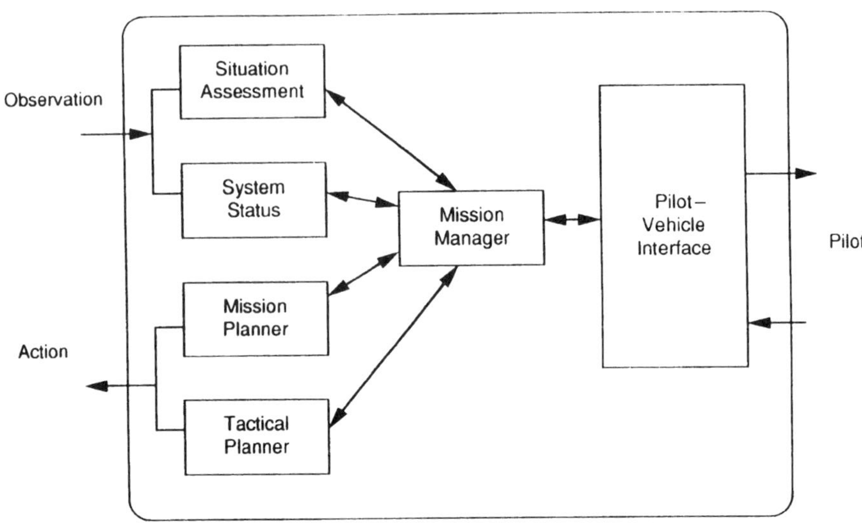

Figure 7.1 Subsystems of the Pilot's Associate

To accomplish these functions, PA relies on a distributed architecture consisting of five expert system modules which communicate via a sixth, blackboard-like "Mission Manager" subsystem. This architecture is displayed in Figure 7.1. Each of the five modules is knowledge-based to a greater or lesser degree. The five subsystems and their functions are:

- The System Status module assesses the internal state of the aircraft.
- The Situation Assessment module assesses the state of the world external to the aircraft.
- The Mission Planner performs route planning and assesses the impact of world states on the long-term objectives of the mission.
- The Tactics Planner creates tactical plans for short-term actions and maneuvers.
- The Pilot–Vehicle Interface interprets pilot intentions and provides for transfer of information between the other modules and the pilot via display configurations.

There are several aspects of the PA task domain and architecture which contribute to the size and complexity of the knowledge engineering task. We will discuss each of these below. These features of the PA have served as motivators for the development of our knowledge acquisition tool, but none of these problems is unique to PA and most of them will be shared by any large, modular knowledge-based system.

7.2.1 Problem 1: Multiple knowledge representations

Each PA module (see Figure 7.1) requires a large knowledge base to attain expert performance in its task. Each module requires both specialized knowledge and a specialized knowledge representation in order to perform appropriately. For example, both the Tactics Planner and the Pilot–Vehicle Interface reason about pilot plans, but their representations of these plans are substantially different. The Tactics Planner reasons about world-states and represents plans as sets of such states, but the Pilot–Vehicle Interface must infer when the pilot wants to perform a particular plan. Thus, the Pilot–Vehicle Interface represents plans in terms of pilot actions. These actions achieve the world-states which the Tactics Planner reasons about, but the link between pilot action and Tactics Planner world-states is never made explicit in the PA knowledge bases.

7.2.2 Problem 2: Coordinated knowledge representations

In spite of the need for multiple knowledge representations, the knowledge in each PA module must be "coordinated" with all the others. The various modules must work together so that the emergent behavior of the whole system is adequate to the PA tasks; mismatches between the modules will mean suboptimal performance, as illustrated below.

To accomplish this coordination, the various modules must share a "vocabulary" of concepts. If the Tactics Planner's conception of the appropriate circumstances for a plan differs from the other modules', the result could be a significant mismatch in the emergent PA behavior. If, for example, the Tactics Planner assumes it is appropriate to do a certain maneuver against *all* types of surface-to-air missile (SAM) sites, while the Pilot–Vehicle Interface assumes the maneuver is only effective against a certain subclass of SAMs, the result might be that the SAMs shown on displays selected by the Pilot–Vehicle Interface would not include those against which the Tactics Planner recommended the maneuver.

During PA development, this coordination was facilitated by the use of an explicit, global data structure known as the *plan–goal graph* (Leavitt and Smith, 1989). Although not initially implemented in the PA software, this data structure was used during PA planning sessions to organize the thinking of the various design teams and to provide them with a common perspective on the world. The plan–goal graph is a hierarchical "and/or" tree of goals and plans to achieve them. Each plan or goal in the tree represents a *global* behavior for the overall man–machine system, but each separate design team was charged with interpreting and implementing the relevant portions of that behavior in their module. That is, the plan–goal graph might include, as one of its nodes, a specific plan for evading enemy radar but, in practice, each PA module would implement only those portions of the plan relevant to its performance (e.g. sensor control actions for the Situation Assessment module, display reconfiguration commands for the Pilot–Vehicle Interface, etc.).

7.2.3 Problem 3: Real-time performance

PA must operate in the highly time-constrained environment of the fighter pilot. Thus, PA software has been heavily optimized for speed. One key way for PA to achieve fast knowledge-base performance is to compile out intermediate reasoning steps and retain only the final decisions or actions associated with an initial state. Most PA knowledge bases rely on highly compiled or "implicit" procedural rules which reflect this omission of rationale information. The Tactics Planner selects skeletal plans on the basis of world-states via an "if–then", rule-like formalism. Similarly, the Pilot–Vehicle Interface contains compiled lists of "information requirements" to be met whenever a given plan is activated, rather than a detailed logic which would enable the system to deduce information requirements based on aspects of current plans. In each case, the use of compiled procedural architectures improves PA speed, but only at the cost of reducing the traceability and explicitness of the knowledge structures carried by the PA.

7.2.4 Problem 4: Multiple designers

Implicit, compiled knowledge representations become especially problematic when they must be used by multiple knowledge engineers over time. The various PA modules were developed at multiple sites over eight years, employing more than 30 different knowledge engineers as individuals joined and left the project. Further, knowledge had to be acquired from a multitude of subject matter experts (e.g. pilots, tacticians, diagnosticians, avionics engineers, display designers, etc.). The system was simply too large to be the product of any small and coherent group of developers.

The integration of knowledge across time and individuals would be facilitated by the use of a single, perspicuous knowledge representation, yet this is at odds with the need for multiple, specialized and highly compiled knowledge representations as described above. The result is an escalating learning curve for each new knowledge engineer brought into the project.

7.2.5 Problem 5: Dynamic knowledge

A final problem which complicates knowledge engineering for PA is the fact that PA domain knowledge is not static. Aircraft tactics change, new tactics are discovered, operational procedures change, and aircraft equipment (and, thus, capabilities) changes over time. If the PA is to remain useful, it too must change. Yet propagating a change through the multiple, coordinated, and highly-compiled knowledge bases of the PA is a non-trivial task.

The operational environment of the PA requires that its knowledge bases be revisable in a matter of hours. Such speed, while maintaining accuracy and coordination among the knowledge bases, was thought to be essentially impossible using traditional knowledge acquisition and knowledge engineering techniques.

7.2.6 Addressing the problems

In an effort to address these problems, we investigated the application of machine learning techniques to knowledge acquisition and knowledge engineering for the PA program. We completed a prototype system which illustrates the use of explanation-based learning in a knowledge compilation tool which partially automates the acquisition and incorporation of new knowledge structures into two of the five PA modules. This partial automation results in faster, more accurate and more complete knowledge acquisition and knowledge engineering than when humans alone perform the same tasks. Our prototype is known as the Learning System for Pilot Aiding (LSPA). In what follows, we will describe the LSPA system in detail and then discuss why we believe this approach eliminates or reduces many of the PA problems.

7.3 The Learning System

The general architecture of the LSPA system (Shalin *et al.*, 1988; Levi *et al.*, 1990, 1992; Miller *et al.*, 1992b) is presented in Figure 7.2. LSPA employed an explanation-based learning approach to learn general, plan-like data structures and then used a set of "smart translators" to transform them into the specific knowledge representations required by two PA modules. This two-stage process was called *linked learning*. Each stage will be described below.

7.3.1 Explanation-based learning in LSPA

An initial study (Levi *et al.*, 1987) of machine learning techniques recommended explanation-based learning as having the highest expected payoff for the two PA modules with the greatest knowledge acquisition needs – the Tactics Planner and the Pilot–Vehicle Interface. There were two primary reasons for this recommendation. First, explanation-based learning can learn new data structures given a single learning instance. Since PA expertise is costly, limited and rare (e.g. most US Air Force pilots have never engaged in real combat or missile evasion) it would be difficult or impossible to acquire large quantities of realistic examples of aircraft tactics. Second, explanation-based learning uses an explicit, detailed *domain theory* to perform its learning. This factor offered the best opportunity to capture, represent and revise knowledge necessary to perform activities in the PA. Explicit representation of knowledge makes it easier to understand why learned

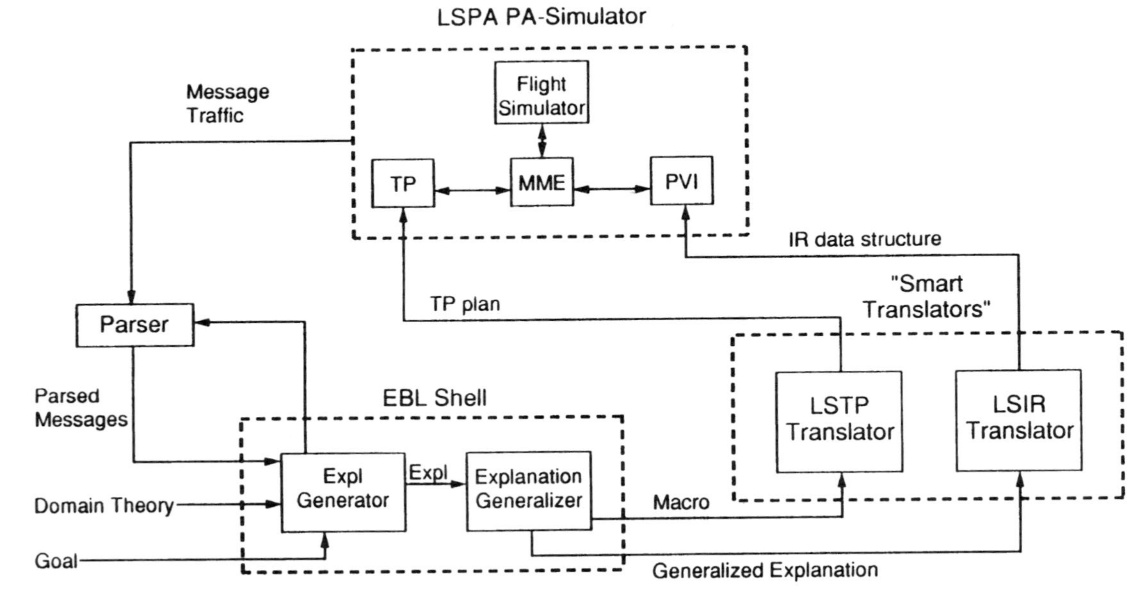

Figure 7.2 The high-level architecture of the LSPA system

plans work and, therefore, to ascertain whether the newly learned plans are accurate and complete. Also, explicit knowledge representation provides better traceability for knowledge in the domain, which facilitates its use by multiple, disparate knowledge engineers.

Our implementation of explanation-based learning, following DeJong and Mooney (1986), requires four components: a *learning instance* in which a known *goal* was achieved, a *domain theory* of facts about the target domain which can explain how the goal was achieved, and a set of *operationality criteria* which determine the "depth" at which the explanation will be usable by a performance system in future instances.

Figure 7.2 illustrates our use of these components in LSPA. Throughout this section, we will describe the functioning of LSPA by presenting a sample plan learned by the system. This is a plan for a "Doppler Notch" maneuver – a specific tactical maneuver which a pilot may use to avoid being targeted by the radar of some types of SAM sites. Essentially, this maneuver involves flying in a circular path around the site. Some types of SAMs use doppler radars, which operate by detecting changes in the range of an object to the radar. Since flying in a circle around the SAM means flying at a constant distance, this maneuver provides no signal to those SAM sites, which means the aircraft can evade their targeting radars.

LSPA's *learning instances* come from records of actual pilot behavior in a flight simulator. Before using LSPA, the pilot or knowledge engineer must identify a need for learning – e.g. a desirable plan that is missing from PA. There are a number of ways in which the need for new or revised plans might be detected. Pilots could identify cases where PA failed to recommend a desired plan or to understand and assist pilot performance of a tactic. PA itself could identify some such instances by noting cases where known pilot goals are achieved but no known plan was used (as determined by the plan tracking and inferencing capabilities of the Pilot–Vehicle Interface). Also, changes or revisions to Air Force tactical doctrine could signal the need for plans to be added or revised in PA. In fact, PA was at a stage in its development where a large number of plans and tactics had been identified (via traditional knowledge acquisition techniques involving pilot experts) and had been represented by place holders in the plan–goal graph (see Section 7.2.2 above), but had not yet been implemented in PA knowledge bases. For the LSPA project, we simply chose a particular branch of the plan–goal graph to flesh out – that associated with missile evasion.

Next, a scenario that exemplifies the plan is scripted and the pilot flies the scenario in a flight simulator. In a real, fielded aircraft, this step could potentially involve the capture of actual flight data from a mission computer. The simulator maintains a time-stamped record of all simulator state changes in the form of message packets which include the pilot's control actions, the position, velocity, azimuth, etc. of his or her ship, enemy aircraft, enemy missiles, and ground threats such as SAM sites. The packet traffic is parsed syntactically to filter out irrelevant packets and to perform simple temporal aggregation prior to use.

The record of state changes in the aircraft and the world during which the pilot performed the desired tactic (as well as a host of largely irrelevant actions) then becomes the learning instance from which LSPA will acquire the tactic as a new PA plan. In order to learn the Doppler Notch tactic, we scripted a scenario involving the detection of the SAM site, a notification that the site had achieved a radar lock on the aircraft, followed by pilot actions to steer the aircraft into a circular path around the SAM, and the SAM's losing its radar lock on the aircraft. This scenario took 1–3 minutes to fly in real time on the average, and yielded 2000–8000 simulator state message packets.

The second learning input is the pilot's *goal* in the learning scenario. Goals are frequently predefined by the plan–goal hierarchy of PA. The goal is selected by the pilot and the knowledge engineer. For the Doppler Notch scenario, pilots could easily tell us that the tactic was performed to achieve the goal of being "safe-from-sam-site" which was already present in PA's plan–goal hierarchy (see Section 7.2.2).

The final learning input is a *domain theory* of rules containing simple facts about the capabilities and behaviors of the aircraft and the world which it inhabits, as well as knowledge for integrating these capabilities to achieve aggregate states. A sample of three LSPA rules is presented in Figure 7.3. These can be read as follows:

1. One way to be safe-from-sam-site is by breaking the SAM's track on you.
2. A SAM's track may be broken if the target denies doppler range rate data, given that the SAM is of a certain type, is using doppler radar and is in radar mode TRACK.
3. One way to deny doppler range rate data, if you are within missile range, is to maintain a constant distance from the SAM.

Additional rules in our domain theory provide various ways of maintaining constant distance, of establishing a SAM's missile range, etc.

The LSPA domain theory is generated by the pilot and the knowledge engineer in a traditional knowledge acquisition process. Acquiring domain theory is costly and time consuming, but we believe that it is both easier and more efficient than acquiring individual plans for each PA module directly. We will discuss this issue further in the last section of the chapter.

Explanation-based learning techniques will learn a correct plan from a single learning instance if and only if the domain theory used in learning that plan is correct. It will only learn all possible plans insofar as the domain theory is complete. Developing and maintaining a correct and complete domain theory for a performance system the size of PA is an extraordinarily difficult task – and one which we have not solved on the LSPA project.[1] We believe, however, that it will be easier to validate and maintain the explicit, shared domain theory of a LSPA-like system than to validate and maintain the multiple, individual, compiled knowledge structures of a full PA system. We have considered tools and

```
(c-rule
   :name 'make-safe-from-sam-site
   '((safe-from-sam-site (target ?target) (sam-id ?sam) (interval ?int1))
     (break-track (target ?target) (sam-id ?sam) (interval ?int1))))

(c-rule
   :name 'break-track
   '((break-track (target ?target) (sam-id ?sam) (interval ?int1))
     (and
        (track-class (track-id ?sam) (object-type 1) (interval ?int4))
        (track-status (track-id ?sam) (radar-mode track) (interval ?int5))
        (deny-doppler-range-rate (target ?target) (track-id ?sam) (interval ?int2))
        (using-doppler-radar (track-id ?sam) (interval ?int3))
        #f(intersect ?int2 ?int3 ?int4 ?int1)
        #p(interval-meets ?int5 ?int1 5))))

(c-rule
   :name 'deny-doppler-range-rate
   '((deny-doppler-range-rate (target ?target) (track-id ?sam) (interval?int3))
     (and
        (maintain-constant-distance (agent1 ?target) (agent2 ?sam) (interval ?int1))
        (inside-missile-range (target ownship) (track-id ?sam) (interval ?int2))
        #f(intersect ?int1 ?int2 ?int3))))
```

Figure 7.3 Three rules in the LSPA domain theory

range, and that flying a relative azimuth of ± 90 degrees to a stationary object (a circular path) would result in maintaining a constant distance from it.

Unlike traditional explanation-based learning, we do not place the newly-learned macro back into the domain theory in an effort to speed up a performance system. In LSPA we intentionally separate the domain theory knowledge base from the specialized knowledge bases used by each of the PA modules. Rather than *compiling for speed*, we *compile (or translate) for multiple functionality*. That is, we translate the learned plan from one representation – formed in the declarative vocabulary of the LSPA domain theory – into other representations – those required for the Tactics Planner and the Pilot–Vehicle Interface. We have labelled this two-stage process of learning followed by multiple, specialized translations *linked learning*, though it bears much in common with "task-specific knowledge compilation" (Goel, 1991) and with "knowledge-adding knowledge compilation" (Bylander, 1991) since our translators themselves must contain knowledge about what the newly-learned macro *means* from the perspective of the modules into which it must ultimately be translated.

For this reason, Figure 7.2 shows that the explanation-based learning process and domain theory are separate from the knowledge bases required for the PA subsystems and our learned results are not fed directly back into PA but are first processed through two "smart translator" systems. The translating system for the Tactics Planner representations was known as "Learning System for Tactics Planner" (LSTP) while the translator for the Pilot–Vehicle Interface was known as the "Learning System for Information Requirements" (LSIR). These translators are described in the next section.

7.3.2 Smart translators

Applying explanation-based learning to a general domain theory about piloting produces general plans for accomplishing PA goals. These general plans are at a level similar to the abstract, unified plans in PA's conceptual plan–goal graph described in Section 7.2.2. Our "smart translators" perform the task of the separate design teams who reasoned from the general plan to a specialized plan containing the information appropriate to, and in the knowledge representation of, the different PA modules. This translation process involved syntactic components, but also required the addition of knowledge to the general plan in some instances. The translating steps for both LSTP and LSIR are described separately below.

7.3.2.1 Translating for the Tactics Planner

The purpose of the LSTP translator is to transform an explanation-based learning macro into the representation required by the Tactics Planner. The Tactics Planner was built as a hybrid, hierarchical, planning system adapted to support reactive planning through continuous skeletal plan re-parameterization and applicability evaluation (Edwards and Hoffman, 1987). Tactics Planner plans are continuously visited using a context-dependent tree search algorithm. Each plan has a life cycle that includes the following phases: specialization (instantiation of the skeletal plan with current parameters), selection (if appropriate), execution (if approved), and transition (when the plan succeeds or fails). There are other phases as well, but these were the most appropriate to the leaf-level plans learned in LSPA.

Plans in the Tactics Planner are represented as a collection of rule-structures reflecting these phases. For example, selection rules check for conditions that must be true for a plan to be viable. Execution rules monitor conditions that are manipulated during the life of the plan. Transition rules monitor conditions that indicate plan success or failure. And so on.

The LSTP Translator transforms explanation-based learning macros into Tactics Planner plans in two steps:

1. Partition the clauses of a macro into the plan phase categories required by the Tactics Planner.
2. Then translate each clause into the Tactics Planner syntax.

The most significant and interesting development in our work on the LSTP Translator was the procedure we created for partitioning the clauses of a macro into plan categories. This procedure should be readily generalizable to other domains since it is largely syntactic and algorithmic.

To partition the macro, we defined two ways of categorizing macro clauses. First, we categorize clauses by whether they represent a state that is *easily-pilot-controllable*. For example, turning a sensor on is easily controllable, but locking a sensor onto a target or repairing a malfunctioning sensor is not. This form of categorization is a source of knowledge-added during the translation step and is the one domain-specific portion of the procedure, yet it has proven very simple for human knowledge engineers to perform. Second, we categorize clauses by whether their arguments are constants or variables. Constant arguments are *class defining* because their value must hold for all instances of the plan. Variable arguments which occur in the macro's postcondition are *instance defining* because they do not change during any specific plan instance. Finally, variable arguments which are not bound in the postcondition are *updatable* during the execution of the plan.

Using these categories, we can automatically sort the macro's clauses into the Tactics Planner rule types. Figure 7.5 shows the partitioned Doppler Notch macro. Selection rules come from clauses that are not easily controllable. If these clauses are not satisfied a priori, the plan should not be proposed since it will have preconditions the pilot cannot easily achieve. Similarly, execution rules come from clauses that are easily-controllable and updatable, since conditions

```
SPECIALIZATION:
(track-class (track-id ?track) (object-type 1))
(track-status (track-id ?track) (radar-mode track))
(relative-track-position (track-id ?track) (azimuth ?noa))

SELECTION:
(track-class (track-id ?track) (object-type 1))
(track-status (track-id ?track) (radar-mode track))
(relative-track-position (track-id ?track) (range ?range))
(lisp (greater-than ?range 50))

EXECUTION:
(relative-track-position (track-id ?track) (azimuth ?noa))
(fctn (abs-value ?noa ?abs-noa)
(pred (abs-diff-lt ?abs-noa 90 7.5))

TRANSITION:
absence of one of:
(track-class (track-id ?track) (object-type 1))
(track-status (track-id ?track) (radar-mode track))
(relative-track-position (track-id ?track) (azimuth ?noa))
```

Figure 7.5 Partitioned Doppler Notch macro

which change during a plan via pilot control are precisely what the Tactics Planner represents as execution knowledge. Similar heuristics exist for transition and specialization rules (see Levi and Miller, 1992).

Once the clauses are partitioned, another algorithm rewrites them into the Tactics Planner syntax. This has proven to be mostly a non-theoretic process of syntactic sugaring requiring understanding (and in some cases proposing) consistent coding conventions for the Tactics Planner.

There are some exceptions that require more sophisticated translation methods but, as a practical tool, LSPA is content to produce a *nearly* complete Tactics Planner plan. Our experience has been that it is straightforward for a knowledge engineer to fill in the final non-syntactic details. Further, because the translator automates the writing of Tactics Planner plans, it avoids many common errors encountered by human knowledge engineers, including syntactic programming errors, partitioning errors, and syntactic and semantic style differences between knowledge engineers. Figure 7.6 presents the selection and execution portions of the Tactics Planner code for a "doppler notch plan" which was learned by the LSPA system.

During the LSPA project, we produced domain theory and learning instances sufficient for LSTP to acquire eight novel Tactics Planner plans – all in the area of

```
(DEFRULE NEW-DOPP12-9-SELECTION
  DOC    "SELECTION rule documentation for NEW-DOPP12-9"
  LOCAL  MVAR-57-ID (SECOND (FIRST (FIRST (ASSERTIONS '(MVAR-57 +)))))
         MVAR-57-ID-OBJECT (FIND-OBJECT-FROM-SA-OBJECT-ID MVAR-57-ID)
  TEMPS  (G53 OBJECT-TYPE RADAR-MODE)
  IF     (SETQ RADAR-MODE (PROP 'RADAR-MODE MVAR-57-ID-OBJECT))
         (SETQ OBJECT-TYPE (TYPE-OF MVAR-57-ID-OBJECT))
         (SETQ G53 (PROP 'RANGE-FROM-SELF MVAR-57-ID-OBJECT))
         (< G53 50)
         (EQUAL OBJECT-TYPE 'SAM-SITE)
         (EQUAL RADAR-MODE 'TRACK)
  THEN   (ASSERT (LIST 'INVOCATION-REQUEST (CLASS) %PLAN%) :WHO PARENTS)
  GOAL   ((NEW-DOPP12-9-SELECTION-GOAL))
  THRESH 0.0
  CONF   (1.0 1.0)
  CALC   'INDEPENDENT)

(DEFRULE NEW-DOPP12-9-EXECUTION
  DOC    "EXECUTION rule documentation for NEW-DOPP12-9"
  LOCAL  MVAR-57-ID (SECOND (FIRST (FIRST (ASSERTIONS '(MVAR-57 +)))))
         MVAR-57-ID-OBJECT (FIND-OBJECT-FROM-SA-OBJECT-ID MVAR-57-ID)
  TEMPS  (G49 G48 HEADING)
  IF     (SETQ G48 (NOSE-OFF-ANGLE *LEAD-PLANE* MVAR-57-ID-OBJECT))
         (SETQ G49 (ABS G48))
         (OR (> G49 (+ 90 7.5)) (< G49 (- 90 7.5)))
  THEN   (REMOVE-ASSERT '(PARAMETER HEADING +))
         (SETQ HEADING
               (ROUND
                 (PERPENDICULAR-HEADING *LEAD-PLANE* MVAR-57-ID-OBJECT)))
         (ASSERT (LIST 'PARAMETER 'HEADING HEADING))
         (NEW-SUGGEST)
  GOAL   ((NEW-DOPP12-9-EXECUTION-GOAL))
  THRESH 0.0
  CONF   (1.0 1.0)
  CALC   'INDEPENDENT)
```

Figure 7.6 Tactics Planner code for portions of a Doppler Notch plan generated by LSPA

SAM and missile evasion. This required 53 domain theory rules. Procedures outlined in Miller *et al.* (1992a) have yielded an estimate of 4000–6000 rules required to cover all of the domain theory necessary for a LSPA system to cover the full PA domain. LSTP plans all compiled and ran successfully in the PA Tactics Planner and they were judged to be as accurate and more complete and consistent than similar plans produced by human knowledge engineers. Using a

LSPA-produced partially-complete plan significantly reduced development time – especially for novice knowledge engineers who went from two person-weeks to produce three Tactics Planner plans without LSPA help, to producing a plan per hour with LSPA in a between-subjects comparison (Miller *et al.*, 1992a).

7.3.2.2 Translating for the Pilot–Vehicle Interface

As a result of the explanation-based learning process described above, LSPA was capable of learning new tactical plans, but this was not sufficient for PA. PA was not merely a planner, but also performed many other functions for the pilot, including information management. In order to perform its information management functions, PA must have knowledge about how displays should be configured for each plan it knows about. To provide this information for the newly-learned plans provided by the LSTP Translator, the LSIR Translator reasons about what information the pilot will need in order to perform the new plan, and how he will need it. The result of the LSIR translation process is an *information requirements list* for the new plan. The Pilot–Vehicle Interface module of the PA uses these data structures to determine the configuration of displays dynamically throughout the mission. This information management process is described in more detail in Geddes and Hammer (1991).

The generation of information requirements lists for plans was not a particularly time-consuming problem on the PA program, but it was fraught with errors and inconsistencies. Producing a complete, consistent, accurate and appropriately coordinated information requirements list for each plan proved difficult for human knowledge engineers and pilot experts. LSIR sought to address these problems.

The Information Management functions of the Pilot–Vehicle Interface rely on a plan-based aggregation of information elements. Information elements are abstract classes of information (e.g. heading, airspeed, fuel status, etc.) which may be provided by various displays in the cockpit. Each plan in PA must have associated with it a list of the elements the pilot will need in performing the plan – known as the information requirements list for that plan. When a plan is activated (either by the Tactics Planner or the pilot), its information requirements list is added to the information requirements lists from all other active plans and the Information Management function within the Pilot–Vehicle Interface then selects a configuration of cockpit displays to optimally meet this aggregate list. A partial information requirements list for the Doppler Notch plan is presented in Figure 7.7.

LSIR must derive an information requirements list for each plan learned by explanation-based learning. We, as many others (Greeno, 1983; Geddes, 1989), view information as the arguments to a problem-solving process. Thus, our best guide to the set of information requirements for a novel plan is *the set of tasks that the pilot must perform during the plan.*

Obtaining the list of pilot-level tasks involved in any plan proved to be a

```
(plan
  (name (doppler-notch-maneuver))
  (pilot-info-requirements
    (cd-list
      (info-elt
        (name      (radar-status))
        (importance (1))
        (scope      (5))
        (bandwidth  (5))
        (resolution (5))
        (control    (6)))
      (info-elt
        (name      (sam-sites))
        (importance (10))
        (scope       (8))
        (resolution  (3))
        (bandwidth   (3))
        (control     (0)))
                  etc.
```

Figure 7.7 Partial information requirements list for the Doppler Notch plan

significant problem in LSPA. The LSTP effort led LSIR, both temporally and conceptually, during the LSPA program. As a result, the domain theory used to explain learning instances proved to be better suited to the reasoning and concerns of the Tactics Planner than of the Pilot–Vehicle Interface. The issue was the level of *operationality criteria* of an explanation. While LSTP was content to drive explanations only to the level of "easily-pilot-controllable" world-states, this was where things got interesting for LSIR. LSTP stopped reasoning when a pilot could be assumed capable of achieving a state, but *how* the pilot achieved that state was precisely LSIR's concern. This information was retrievable from the simulator trace and could be explained and generalized via standard explanation-based learning techniques, but there was a practical reason for not pursuing finer-grained, pilot-action-centered explanations in LSPA. Essentially, this was because PA itself gives conceptual priority to the Tactics Planner level of plan aggregation.

Any generalization of a learning instance represents an abstraction away from the specifics of the instance. There are, however, a large number of ways one can abstract. Because the level of pilot-centered actions used by the Pilot–Vehicle Interface is "finer-grained" than that used by the Tactics Planner, there are potentially many more "pilot-action plans" which could be learned than there are Tactics Planner-level "world-state plans". In order to minimize the combinatorial explosion of plans, PA has tended to give pre-eminence to Tactics Planner-level plans, thereby aggregating a potentially large set of "pilot-action plans" under each Tactics Planner plan.

For example, the Doppler Notch plan learned above relates a number of world-states: an aircraft and a SAM site are to maintain a distance and azimuth relationship while the SAM is in a certain radar mode. Nothing is said about how the pilot is to achieve the range and azimuth states or the state of knowing the SAM's radar mode. In fact, there are several methods of accomplishing each state – each with different information requirements implications. When information requirements lists are generated for PA plans by human knowledge engineers, the knowledge engineers must, with pilot help, reason about the set of activities which may be used to accomplish states in the Tactics Planner-level plan. Then they must make hard choices about which of these activities to support via the information requirements list for that plan. In general, the most common method of performing the plan is supported, though significant alternatives may be partially represented as well.

LSIR addressed this problem by closely emulating the human knowledge engineers. LSIR's technical approach (Miller *et al.*, 1992a, b) is presented in Figure 7.8. Note that we begin, as do Pilot–Vehicle Interface knowledge engineers, with a generalized representation of the plan – the abstracted explanation-based learning explanation – to ascertain what states the pilot must achieve. In order to reason about how pilots achieve these states, we defined a set of approximately 100 pilot-level "Events". Events are common combinations of pilot-level activities which share a set of information requirements. Plans may involve various combinations of pilot-level Events. Frequently, Events are the methods by which the pilot performs the plan (e.g. *jammer-use*, *long-range-radar-use*), but Events can also be uncontrolled occurrences about which the pilot will want to be informed (e.g. *enemy-launch*, *engine-failure*). Decomposing full plans into pilot-level events proved very useful for knowledge acquisition, as will be shown below.

Deducing Events implied by a plan description was automated using a series of knowledge-intensive production rules contained in the LSIR translator system. These rules embody the knowledge and heuristics that a Pilot–Vehicle Interface knowledge engineer might use to reason from a plan description to a reasonable picture of pilot activities during the plan. For example, the Doppler Notch explanation stipulates the presence of an object of "type 1" (a SAM site which uses doppler radar) for this plan. This implies that the pilot will need to know about the presence and class of the SAM site. There are various methods for detecting and classifying objects available to a modern fighter, but the combination of the likely distance of the object (as stipulated by other parts of the explanation) and its nature (ground-based and a radio-frequency emitter) all imply that the best or most likely method will be the short-range use of a Radar

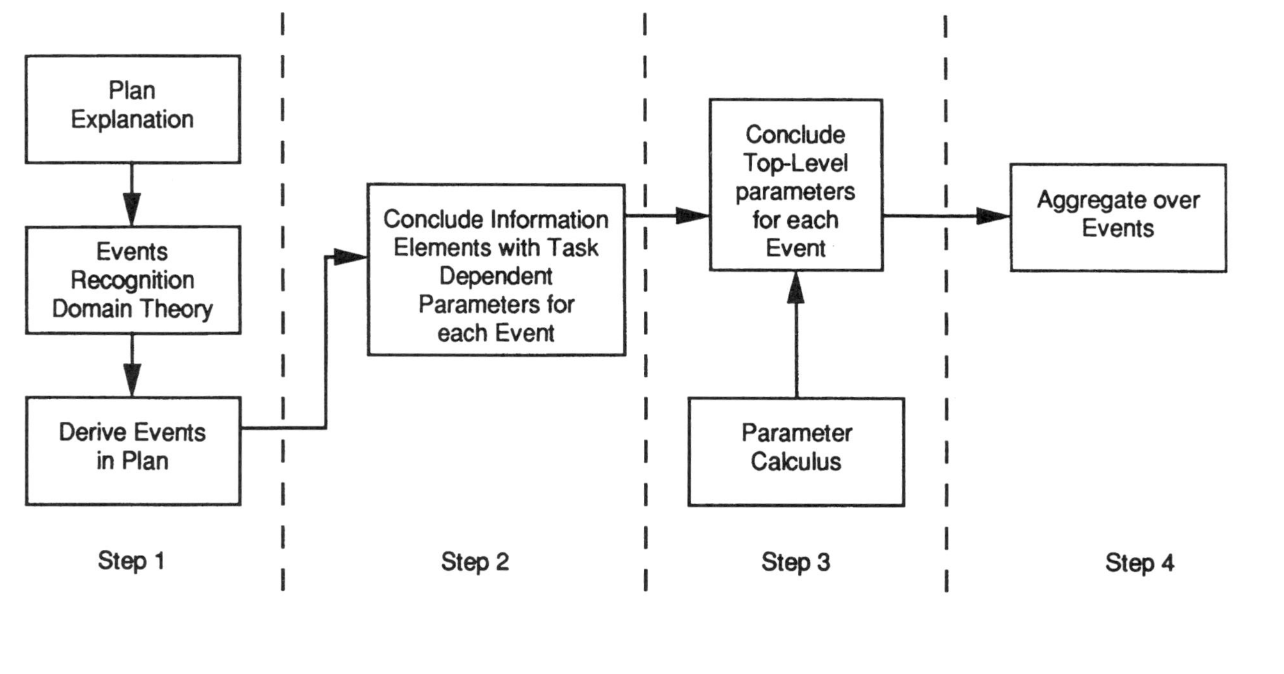

Figure 7.8 The high-level approach taken by the LSIR translator

Warning Receiver. Hence, LSIR deduces the presence of a "Radar Warning Receiver Use, Short Range" Event for the Doppler Notch plan.

Note that our rules are generally insufficient to isolate a single method for each plan state; instead, they supply a set of Events that *might* occur in various instances of the plan. To date, we have reasoned about information requirements for this aggregate set of Events, but a reasonable improvement would be to cull the list on the basis of probability at this point.

Each Event is linked directly to a set of required information elements by an *Event-to-IE rule* or *molecule* – a rule which asserts the list of information elements needed whenever the Event occurs. The reduced level of aggregation in an Event (as opposed to a full plan), made it easier for pilots to provide us with consistent lists of information requirements for Events than they could for full plans. For example, having defined a *Radar Warning Receiver-use, short range* Event as any use of the Radar Warning Receiver to detect a non-cooperative target within 20 nautical miles, the pilot can easily tell us that information about the status and mode of the Radar Warning Receiver will be critical, information about the track's position, range, azimuth, bearing, and closure rate will also be important, and information about the status of ownship's jamming devices will be somewhat useful, since they can interfere with the Radar Warning Receiver.

Another advantage to obtaining information requirements lists at the level of Events rather than plans is that the molecules are intended to be combinable across the construction of all plans. Once defined, a molecule can be reused for many plans – each of which would require separate expert knowledge acquisition and knowledge engineering time under the old approach.

The last steps in the LSIR process involved reasoning about "parameters" associated with each information requirement. For the Pilot–Vehicle Interface, we had to indicate not only what information requirements were needed for each plan, but also how the information was needed. Specifically, the Pilot–Vehicle Interface knowledge representation scored each information element on five parameters as follows:

- *Importance* The relative necessity of this information for plan success.
- *Scope* The proportion of the possible range of element values required during the plan (e.g. should 360º of heading be shown or would a 30º window around the current value be better?).
- *Resolution* The level of detail required for the element (e.g. should heading be shown in 1º or 10º increments?).
- *Bandwidth* The frequency with which the data must be sampled and updated.
- *Control* The need to affect the value of the element (as opposed to simply monitoring it).

The process by which we derived these parameter values involved another knowledge-intensive system known as the *Parameter Calculus*. A full account of the Calculus is beyond the scope of this chapter, but it should be noted that the Calculus provides another example of the power of moving knowledge acquisition closer to the level at which the experts think. The five "high-level" parameters used in the Pilot–Vehicle Interface knowledge representation (Importance, Scope, Resolution, etc.) proved difficult for both pilots and knowledge engineers to reason about. The result was a significant consistency problem in the information requirements lists – one knowledge engineer might give an information requirement an importance value of 10, while another might give it an 8; knowledge engineers might give substantially different parameter values to information requirements in nearly identical plans when the plans were composed at different times, etc.

We simplified this consistency problem in two ways. The first involved reducing the scope of consideration from the full plan to a more specific, pilot-level Event (as described above). The second involved decomposing the "high-level" abstract concepts of scope, resolution, bandwidth, etc. into "low-level" and more concrete concepts such as the *dynamic range* of values which the information element could take during the Event (e.g. if heading information is required, how many degrees is the heading value likely to range over during the Event?), the Event-specific *significant difference* in information element values (e.g. how many degrees of heading change makes a difference for this event?), the Event-specific *rate of change* for element values, etc. Once obtained, these low-level values were computationally transformed, via the Parameter Calculus, into the higher level values of scope, resolution and bandwidth.

In general, it was easier for pilots to provide low-level, concrete parameters for information elements in Events than to provide the aggregated parameters for an element in the whole plan. For example, pilots found it easier to tell us the likely task-rate-of-change of heading values during a precision course maneuver, rather than to give an accurate, consistent value for the bandwidth required for heading over the whole Doppler Notch plan (which involves several conceptually distinct pilot-level maneuvers). Although we can provide only anecdotal evidence of improvements in knowledge acquisition, the LSIR evaluation showed the success of this approach for knowledge engineering. LSIR's information requirements lists were generally judged to be as consistent and accurate as those of human knowledge engineers, and LSIR's parameter values were consistently judged *better* than those produced by human knowledge engineers, in blind tests involving Pilot–Vehicle Interface knowledge base designers as judges.

The final LSIR step is a simple, algebraic aggregation of elements and their parameter values across the Events for the full plan. The result is an information requirements list aggregated for the plan as a whole, and coordinated with the plan as translated for the Tactics Planner.

7.4 Solutions to knowledge acquisition problems

LSPA successfully demonstrated the capability of using explanation-based learning techniques to automate portions of PA knowledge acquisition. We have demonstrated an explanation-based, linked learning system which acquired novel Tactics Planner plans and Pilot–Vehicle Interface information requirements lists faster and more consistently than unaided human knowledge engineers could produce them.

7.4.1 Benefits of LSPA approach

The architecture developed in LSPA provides the basis for addressing many of the PA knowledge acquisition and knowledge engineering problems as described in Section 7.2. Two major aspects of our application of explanation-based learning were the use of a domain theory as a "common knowledge repository" for all of the PA knowledge bases (rather than having separate representations of similar knowledge in each knowledge base), and the separation of the learning system from the PA performance system by the means of smart translators. Each of these attributes of our architecture offered different benefits, as we describe below.

7.4.1.1 Common knowledge repository

LSPA indicated that an explanation-based learning domain theory can serve as a "common knowledge repository" where all expert knowledge is placed and from which a variety of specialized knowledge can be derived to be used by specialized planning, diagnosis and pattern-matching systems – each with its specialized knowledge representation. This finding should have strong implications for the development of distributed and knowledge-based systems:

- The domain theory serves as a set of axioms from which all possible plans are derived, thus placing knowledge in the domain theory should save time in the long run over reimplementing it each time it is called for in a new plan.
- The small, incremental rules of the domain theory are arguably easier for domain experts to supply than the full-fledged "plans" (in their specialized knowledge representations) required by the PA modules. Thus, speed and consistency in knowledge acquisition and knowledge engineering are improved.
- The use of a *common* knowledge repository facilitates coordination among plans and, with automatic compilation techniques, facilitates the ability to modify all affected plans when a fact about the world changes (e.g. new SAM sites have longer missile ranges).
- We suspect that the explicitness and traceability of the explanation-based

learning domain theory and its explanations of plans should improve the ability to reconstruct *why* a data structure is the way it is. This, in turn, should minimize the learning curves for new knowledge engineers and make it easier to revise the knowledge bases with confidence as the system evolves.

7.4.1.2 Separate learning and performance systems

The separation of learning system from performance system, accomplished by our use of "smart translators", offers additional benefits over what could be accomplished with a traditional explanation-based learning system:

- It enables the use of different knowledge representations in each system – an explicit, deductive representation in the learning system to facilitate knowledge engineering and communication and coordination among multiple designers, and implicit, highly specialized representation(s) in the performance system(s) to facilitate speed. It is doubtful that a single learning system could have provided benefit to more than one of the distributed PA modules without this linked learning architecture.
- It enables a reduction in the seriousness of Minton's (1990) *utility problem* (see note 3). Since we have separated the fine-grained rules of the domain theory from the macro operators of the performance system, we have reduced redundant combinations of rules. More importantly, since we are using a human-mediated approach to selecting learning instances based on a perceived gap in plan coverage, we have greatly increased the likelihood that each new plan will offer novel utility to the performance system.
- Changes in the performance system need have little impact on the knowledge acquired. LSPA was developed concurrently with PA and, hence, was not available for use during much of the PA project. In its absence, when PA changed from LISP to C, it was necessary to reimplement the knowledge bases of all PA modules. Other changes during the life of the Tactics Planner caused a complete rewriting of the Tactics Planner knowledge bases four separate times. Some of these costs could have been saved by storing initially acquired knowledge in a common repository, restructuring the translators at each revision, and then recompiling the knowledge bases.

Finally, developing a semi-automated machine learning or knowledge acquisition system *along with* a performance system can have additional benefits for both projects. In the course of developing LSPA, our main contribution to the PA program has been the formalization of many knowledge engineering practices. These practices are developed by various engineers at various times, are generally intuitive and only inconsistently applied, and are rarely shared by the entire group of knowledge engineers. The need to formalize these techniques in a computational learning system or "smart translator" can serve to greatly increase the rigor with which knowledge representation techniques are developed and knowledge bases are constructed.

7.4.2 Improvements to LSPA

LSPA also taught us some lessons about integrating knowledge acquisition and machine learning in a large software engineering project. One such lesson is alluded to above: start early. LSPA was an adjunct project to PA, was begun almost three years after PA started, and finished only as PA was ending. While this sequencing of projects was necessary for an initial development of LSPA-like techniques, future machine learning efforts of this sort should start along with the design of the performance system, should ensure that all knowledge be stored in the explanation-based learning domain theory, and should work with performance system knowledge engineers to develop formal, computational methods for translating this knowledge into all of the performance system modules.

More theoretically interesting findings stem from the nature and use of the LSPA domain theory. These fall into four areas: (1) the nature of LSPA's knowledge representation, (2) the need for knowledge base management tools to support the LSPA domain theory, (3) the integration of knowledge between LSPA's domain theory and its smart translators, and (4) the acquisition of domain theory. We will briefly discuss each of these below.

7.4.2.1 The LSPA knowledge representation

LSPA's explanation-based learning domain theory rules were written as if–then rules in a predicate calculus representation adapted for use in the LISP programming language (see Figure 7.3). Our rules were Horn clauses in the sense that there could be many antecedent conditions but only one consequent condition. Individual conditions generally represented either a relation between several objects or an attribute-value of an object. Each condition also had an associated interval that signified the time during which the condition was true. These time intervals were used in a temporal reasoning component described elsewhere (Levi *et al.*, 1992). Finally, conditions could also be calls to LISP functions which would either return a truth value or would bind a value to some variable in the rule.

While this representation was sufficient for the prototype system, more sophisticated knowledge representations would certainly facilitate scaling up LSPA to serve a full-fledged PA knowledge engineering project. The hierarchical nature of the objects and relationships in the piloting domain, coupled with the fact that these objects tend to behave in regular, reasonably well-defined ways, leads us to suspect that a structured-object knowledge representation might offer the best support for LSPA scale-up.

7.4.2.2 *Knowledge base management tools*

One of the strengths of the LSPA approach, the notion of maintaining a common knowledge repository, might also prove a weakness. Since the LSPA domain theory must store all relevant PA knowledge (including explanatory and causal knowledge which the PA knowledge bases edit out), it will necessarily be larger and more complex than the knowledge base of any one of the PA modules. Further, since the domain theory is intended as a common location for PA knowledge, it will be used by many knowledge engineers simultaneously throughout the project. Such complexity in other large software engineering projects is generally regarded as beyond the ability of human project engineers to manage without assistance. Fortunately, there are a number of tools and techniques either currently in use or under development which should serve to ease this problem. Among these are tools for database construction, manipulation and inspection, tools for truth maintenance in knowledge bases, and tools to support change and configuration management in large software development projects (Brown *et al.*, 1992). We have not investigated the application of these techniques to the LSPA domain theory, but they appear to hold promise.

7.4.2.3 *Domain theory integration*

LSPA's explanation-based learning domain theory did not represent knowledge about pilot-level actions and states used to perform plans. Although we were able to compensate for this by adding knowledge to the LSIR translator, this solution seems less than optimal. Any knowledge which lies outside of the "common knowledge repository" will not be susceptible to access, interpretation and modification along with the rest of PA knowledge. Under our current implementation, if we add a new piece of equipment to the PA aircraft, we must reflect the capabilities and implications of that equipment in two separate locations: in the main explanation-based learning domain theory and in the Event deduction rules of LSIR. Changes in one of these locations must be manifested in the other via a hand-crafting process that hides the relationships between the two types of knowledge.

Ideally, a *common* knowledge base should model all of the knowledge required by the PA modules in a consistent, interdependent fashion. In this way, if we alter a tactic or a piece of aircraft equipment, we should be able to use knowledge base maintenance tools to update the rest of the knowledge base and detect potential conflicts with, for example, human information needs (i.e. information requirements). Such a knowledge representation would have to be very broad and powerful, but our recent research (Levi *et al.*, 1993; Miller *et al.*, 1993) suggests that *Functional Representation* (Vescovi *et al.*, 1993) may be suitable for these needs.

7.4.2.4 Acquiring domain theory

Although LSPA has taken steps to improve the utility of knowledge once acquired, the acquisition of LSPA domain theory remains a daunting task. Our recent research (Levi *et al.*, 1993; Miller *et al.*, 1993) indicates that some of the knowledge required for LSPA domain theory exists within various modeling languages currently being used or developed to design and create aircraft equipment. Chief among these is the VHSIC Hardware Definition Language (VHDL). The US Air Force has recently mandated that all future electronics equipment procurements will be delivered along with VHDL models of their structure and behavior. In our recent research, we have been able to demonstrate the capability of acquiring pertinent information about the performance of an aircraft's display system directly from a VHDL model of the graphics processor for that aircraft. We believe this approach holds promise for reducing the knowledge acquisition load and improving the resolution and accuracy of domain theory knowledge for future LSPA-like systems. Furthermore, ongoing work in Stanford's How Things Work project (Gruber *et al.*, 1992) holds promise for extending this approach to integrated, knowledge-sharing design environments which operate across multiple levels of knowledge-base aggregation.

Acknowledgements

This work was supported by the Learning Systems Pilot Aiding contract from the U.S. Air Force's Wright Laboratories (Contract Number F33615–88–C–1739) – technical monitor, Gurdial Saini. A large number of researchers have played significant roles in the LSPA program. We are indebted to Jerry DeJong, Barry Druhan, Gary Edwards, Dave Fautheree, Norm Geddes, Mark Hoffman, Belinda Hoshstrasser, Dale Moberg, David Perschbacher, Valerie Shalin and David Smith for their efforts in developing LSPA and for their inputs to prior papers.

Notes

1. This is one of the reasons we claim that LSPA is a *semi*-automated, rather than fully automated, knowledge acquisition tool. We expect that it will be impossible and undesirable to eliminate a phase of human evaluation, review and refinement of the plans learned by the LSPA system.
2. Our primary departure from traditional explanation-based learning has been the incorporation of temporal reasoning capabilities into the algorithm. The nature of this modification is discussed in detail elsewhere (Levi and Miller, 1992; Levi *et al.*, 1992; Miller *et al.*, 1992a).

3. As Minton (1990) has pointed out, however, the learning of a new macro operator increases the total number of rules in the performance system and this means that the system will have to take additional time to find the appropriate rule for the situation. This phenomenon is known as the *utility problem*. Unless care is taken to learn only rules which will be used frequently, learning macro operators may actually cause the performance system to run slower, rather than faster.

References

Banks, S. and Lizza, C. (1991). Pilot's Associate: a cooperative knowledge-based system application. *IEEE Expert*, 6(3): 18–29.

Brown, A., Dart, S., Feiler, P. and Wallnau, K. (1992). The state of automated configuration management. In VanScoy, R. L. (editor), *Software Engineering Institute Technical Review*. SEI, Carnegie Mellon University, Pittsburgh, PA.

Bylander, T. (1991). A simple model of knowledge compilation. *IEEE Expert*, 6(2): 73–75.

DeJong, G. and Mooney, R. (1986). Explanation-based learning: an alternative view. *Machine Learning*, 1: 145–176.

Edwards, G. and Hoffman, M. (1987). The KADET planning framework. In *Proceedings of the DARPA Knowledge-based Planning Workshop*, pp. 16–21.

Erickson, M. and Zytkow, J. (1988). Utilizing experience for improving the tactical manager. In Laird, J. (editor), *Proceedings of the Fifth Inernational Conference on Machine Learning*. Morgan Kaufmann, Palo Alto, CA.

Geddes, N. D. (1989). Understanding human operators' intentions in complex systems. *PhD thesis*, Georgia Institute of Technology.

Geddes, N. D. and Hammer, J. M. (1991). Automatic display management using dynamic plans and events. In *6th Aviation Psychology Symposium*, Columbus, OH.

Goel, A. (1991). Knowledge compilation: a symposium. *IEEE Expert*, 6(2): 71–93.

Gordon, D. and Greffenstette, J. (1990). Explanations of empirically derived reactive plans. In Porter, B. and Mooney, R. (editors), *Proceedings of the Seventh International Conference on Machine Learning*, pp. 198–203. Morgan Kaufmann, Palo Alto, CA.

Greeno, J. (1983). Conceptual entities. In Gentner, D. and Stevens, A. (editors), *Mental Models*. Lawrence Erlbaum Associates, Hillsdale, N.J.

Gruber, T., Tenenbaum, J. and Weber, J. (1992). Toward a knowledge medium for collaborative product development. In *Proceedings of the Second International Conference on AI in Design*, pp. 413–432, Kluwer, Pittsburgh, PA.

Leavitt, C. and Smith, D. (1989). Integrated dynamic planning in the Pilot's Associate. In *Proceedings of the AIAA Guidance, Navigation and Control Conference*, volume 1, pp. 327–331. American Institute of Aeronautics and Astronautics, Boston, MA.

Levi, K. and Miller, C. (1992). Automated acquisition of plans and information requirements in an intelligent agent architecture. In *Proceedings of the Workshop on Architectures for Supporting Machine Learning and Knowledge Acquisition, 9th International Machine Learning Conference*, Aberdeen, Scotland.

Levi, K., Moberg, D., Miller, C. and Rose, F. (1993). Multilevel causal-process modeling: bridging the plan, execution and device-implementation gap. In *Proceedings of Applications of AI XI*, pp. 240–250, SPIE, Orlando, FL.

Levi, K., Perschbacher, D., Hoffman, M., Miller, C., Druhan, B. and Shalin, V. (1992). An explanation-based learning approach to knowledge compilation: a Pilot's Associate application. *IEEE Expert*, 7(3): 44–52.

Levi, K., Shalin, V. and Perschbacher, D. (1990). Automating acquisition of plans for an intelligent assistant by observing user behavior. *International Journal of Man–Machine Studies*, 33: 489–503.

Levi, K., Shalin, V., Wisniewski, E. and Scott, P. (1987). An analysis of machine learning applications for pilot-aiding expert systems. Technical Report TR–87–1147, AFAWL.

Lewis, C. (1986). Identification of Rule-Based Models. *PhD thesis*, Georgia Institute of Technology.

Miller, C., Levi, K. and Rose, F. (1993). Learning system for pilot aiding program: follow-on final report. Technical Report WL-TR-93-1102, Wright-Patterson AFB.

Miller, C., Levi, K. and Shalin, V. (1992a). Learning system for pilot aiding: final report. Technical Report WL-TR-92-6002, Wright-Patterson AFB.

Miller, C., Shalin, V., Geddes, N. and Hoshstrasser, B. (1992b). Plan-based information requirements: automated knowledge compilation to support information management in an intelligent pilot–vehicle interface. In *Proceedings of the 11th Digital Avionics Systems Conference*, Seattle, WA. IEEE and AIAAA.

Minton, S. (1990). Quantitative results concerning the utility of explanation-based learning. *Artificial Intelligence*, 42: 363–391.

Mitchell, T., Keller, R. and Kedar-Cabelli, S. (1986). Explanation-based generalization: a unifying view. *Machine Learning*, 1: 47–80.

Mooney, R. and Bennett, S. (1986). A domain independent explanation-based generalizer. In *Proceedings of the Fifth National Conference on Artificial Intelligence*, volume 1, pp. 551–555. Morgan Kauffmann, Philadelphia, PA.

Shalin, V., Wisniewski, E., Levi, K. and Scott, P. (1988). A formal analysis of machine learning for knowledge acquisition. *International Journal of Man–Machine Studies*, 29: 429–446.

Vescovi, M., Iwasaki, Y., Fikes, R. and Chandrasekaran B. (1993). CFRL: A language for specifying the causal functionality of engineered devices. In *Proceedings of the Eleventh National Conference on AI*, pp. 626–633, Washington, DC. AAAI Press/ MIT Press.

CHAPTER 8

Knowledge acquisition and learning by experience – the role of case-specific knowledge

Agnar Aamodt

Abstract

As knowledge-based systems are addressing increasingly complex domains, their roles are shifting from classical expert systems to interactive assistants. To develop and maintain such systems, an integration of thorough knowledge acquisition procedures and sustained learning from experience is called for. A knowledge level modelling perspective has shown to be useful for analysing the various types of knowledge related to a particular domain and set of tasks, and for constructing the models of knowledge contents needed in an intelligent system. To be able to meet the requirements of future systems with respect to robust competence and adaptive learning behavior, particularly in open and weak theory domains, a stronger emphasis should be put on the combined utilization of case-specific and general domain knowledge. In this chapter we present a framework for integrating KA and ML methods within a total knowledge modelling cycle, favoring an iterative rather than a top-down approach to system development. Recent advances in the area of case-based reasoning provide a suitable basis. Focus is put on the knowledge maintenance part, for which a case-based method for learning from experience is described and exemplified by existing systems. Our own approach to integration of case-specific and general domain knowledge (the CREEK system) is briefly sketched, and used as a context for discussing case-based approaches to knowledge modelling in general.

8.1 Introduction

The quality of a knowledge-based system stands and falls with how well relevant parts of the application domain are captured by the system's knowledge. Most knowledge-based systems in use today contain highly domain-specific knowledge,

Machine Learning and Knowledge Acquisition
ISBN 0–12–685120–4

targeted at a particular, narrow application. The knowledge is typically captured in terms of heuristic rules, interconnected in a chained fashion and targeted at a particular, single problem. An advantage of this approach is that knowledge is captured as general experience, based on what humans have found useful for solving problems in the domain. This often leads to a targeted and efficient problem-solving process. Another advantage is that the representation language for that knowledge can be rather simple. The development of such systems is often supported by commercial, user-friendly tools. The knowledge acquisition problem, although responsible for a large part of the development effort needed, is coped with by focusing on one type of knowledge (if–then rules, sometimes augmented with object hierarchies of rule terms) for one application task (e.g. diagnosis of heart failure, assessment of credibility for loan, planning of transportation routes). The widespread commercial use of rule-based expert systems (Harmon, Maus and Morrissey, 1988; Turban, 1992; CACM, 1994) is a solid manifestation of the success of the rule-based, domain-narrow approach.

However, there are also well-known problems related to the rule-based approach. An example is the lack of robustness and flexibility in problem solving due to the narrow and tailored scope of the knowledge. Another example is the difficulties in maintaining and updating a system's knowledge over time, to cope with the normal development of the subject field and changes in the system's operational environment. This has led to a focus on methods that combine heuristics with more principled and deep knowledge (a collection of recent research can be found in David *et al.*, 1993). Hence, *general* domain knowledge can in principle be captured as shallow, heuristic models – e.g. a set of if–then rules – or as models of deeper, more principled knowledge.

Advancements within the machine learning field related to inductive learning in real-world domains have moved machine learning methods from the study of concept formation in general into the development and maintenance of knowledge-based systems. Results from the subarea of multistrategy learning (Michalski and Tecuci, 1990) have particularly contributed to this development. However, the generalization problem, i.e. determining what to generalize from a situation, how far to generalize, what type of generalized descriptions to learn, etc., is still a basic and difficult one. In parallel to the developments in this type of learning, recent research has also studied the direct capturing and utilization of the concrete and *specific* knowledge related to problem-solving experiences. The growth of research and development in the field of *case-based reasoning* has thrown light on the significance of specific problem-solving episodes for the solving of new problems and for learning (Kolodner, 1993; Wess *et al.*, 1994). While traditionally viewed as data or information rather than knowledge, concrete descriptions of past problem-solving episodes become knowledge for case-based reasoning methods, since these methods are able to use cases for drawing inferences, i.e. for reasoning. This has opened up for AI methods based on *memorizing* as a core process of learning, and *reminding* and analogical *reuse* as core methods of reasoning.

There has been a clear development trend over the last years from single-task expert systems to multifunctional knowledge-based systems: a medical knowledge-based system, for example, instead of only suggesting a diagnosis should also be able to support the user in setting up an examination protocol, revising the test scheme according to results, deriving consequences of measurements, criticizing the user's decisions, pointing out missing risk-checks, etc. The history of AI strongly indicates that no single type of knowledge is sufficient to realize this range of functionality, and that combined methods are called for. Knowledge bases are required that can be used for multiple tasks (sometimes referred to as multifunctional knowledge bases), associated with methods that are able to utilize the different types of knowledge in a combined way. There is also a trend towards a merging of knowledge-based and other system types, such as information systems, databases, user-interfaces, hypermedia systems, and decision support systems in general. Knowledge-based systems – or system components – are to an increasing degree viewed as *intelligent decision support* systems, i.e. heavily *user-oriented* systems that cooperate with the human user in the solving of problems,[1] rather than as expert systems in the classical sense (Boy, 1991; Aamodt, 1994). Improving the methods for development and maintenance of this type of knowledge-based systems is what this chapter is about.

The main issue we address is: how can recent advances in knowledge acquisition (KA) and machine learning (ML) be combined, so that the development and continued maintenance of such systems become more feasible? A basic assumption made is that knowledge-based systems need to acquire two types of capabilities. First, they need a certain level of *competence*, i.e. a body of knowledge that is sufficiently deep to cope with the complexity of real-world problems, and sufficiently broad to cope with the variety of tasks in the domain. They should also exhibit a smooth decay for problems outside the core domain. Second, as systems solve problems or assist the user in other ways, they should gradually become more *experienced*. While competence refers to a potential ability based on an established platform of knowledge, experience refers to operational capabilities based on the continually growing number of problems that a system has solved.

As human beings, we are competent and robust problem solvers in our domains of competence since we possess a coherent body of general knowledge, and a huge library of specific past problem-solving cases (see, for example, Schank, 1982). We base our methods on a general understanding of the task environment in which we operate, and we maintain a memory of past problem-solving episodes integrated into this fundamental knowledge structure. Our ability to maintain and coherently utilize a variety of knowledge types has been documented by research in cognitive psychology (Tulving, 1972; Anderson, 1990) and within the interdisciplinary field of cognitive science (Simon and Kaplan, 1989; Strube, 1991). When solving problems or trying to understand situations, we are frequently reminded of similar previous experiences. Using more general knowledge as support, we are able to adapt the solution (or solution path) of a previous case to the solving of a new problem. Through success and failure in achieving our task, we learn to do things better the next time. Although artificial intelligence methods do not necessarily have to duplicate methods of human intelligence, cognitive science has provided highly valuable input to the development of knowledge-based systems in general, and to knowledge acquisition and learning methods in particular (see for example the collection of papers in Van Lehn, 1990). This is particularly relevant for the type of systems discussed here, since cooperative man–machine problem solving should be based on a common "understanding" of domain terms and input data, which in turn is facilitated by some degree of similarity of knowledge organization, interpretation methods, etc. between human and computer agents.

An important challenge for future AI methods will be to combine and synergetically utilize general and case-specific domain knowledge. This is therefore a major issue with respect to the integration of KA and ML methods. The challenges of more complex and user-oriented systems call for a change of view on knowledge acquisition and machine learning. The two main issues motivated and described in this chapter are:

- Knowledge acquisition research has until now mainly focused on the "first round" of system development, i.e. up to the delivery of the system to the end-user. A stronger emphasis on continued everlasting knowledge maintenance (refinement, extension, adaptation) is needed. On this basis, we advocate that systems development in general should be more of an iterative process than a top-down one, and that the integration of KA and ML should be driven by the needs of such iterative approaches.
- Knowledge-based systems has until now mainly focused on utilizing general domain knowledge for solving problems. The difficulty of modelling this type of knowledge, and its insufficiency for a range of problem solving and learning tasks, has led to the increased interest in case-based problem solving and learning methods. On this basis, we advocate that a stronger focus needs be put on the synergetic combination of case-specific and general domain knowledge, with implications for knowledge modelling, problem-solving methods, and learning methods.

The next section introduces the integration issue by describing some commonalities and differences between knowledge acquisition and machine learning methods. This is followed by a general framework for knowledge modelling that identifies basic types of modelling tasks and partial models. The framework provides a discussion ground for KA+ML integration by combining case-specific and general knowledge. In Section 8.4 the case-based reasoning process is elaborated and exemplified by existing methods and systems. A way to integrate KA+ML methods, building upon the assumptions and modelling principles earlier described, is suggested in Section 8.5, followed by a summary of our own integration approach – the CREEK system. In the conclusion section, the results presented are summarized, and consequences for future KA and ML research are discussed.

8.2. Knowledge modelling, knowledge acquisition and learning

8.2.1 General presentation

The process of constructing an appropriate body of knowledge for a system to perform its tasks is here generally referred to as *knowledge modelling*. Along with Clancey (1989) a knowledge-based system can be viewed as a qualitative model of that part of the real world which the system is to reason about. Knowledge modelling is here the whole process that starts with a real-world task environment, and realizes a (partial) model of it in a computer system. It is a general term that covers tasks such as elicitation, analysis, construction, representation, implementation, validation, and maintenance of knowledge, and can be viewed as a synonym to knowledge acquisition in the wide sense. By using this term we want to advocate a strong "modelling" view of knowledge acquisition (Ford *et al.*, 1993), i.e. the view that knowledge acquisition is a constructive modelling process (Morik, 1990), as opposed to the "knowledge extraction" or "knowledge transfer" view assumed by earlier accounts (e.g. Boose, 1986). The knowledge is constructed in a cooperative modelling effort between the domain expert(s) and knowledge engineer(s), and may not have explicitly "existed" anywhere before (Clancey, 1993; Gaines, 1993). Correspondingly, the modelling view also implies that machine learning is regarded as a constructive knowledge modelling process. Any knowledge modelling task may be accomplished by largely manual methods (knowledge acquisition methods), and/or by automatic ones (machine learning methods). We will refer to methods for knowledge analysis and model building that are largely manual, and that assume a cooperation between one or more developers and one or more domain experts (jointly referred to as the "development team"), as *knowledge acquisition*. "Largely manual" also includes computer-assisted methods and the use of automated tools, including inductive learning methods as support for manual conceptualization. We will refer to methods that are largely automatic, and assume that the computer itself is able to generate useful knowledge on the basis of input data, as *machine learning*. "Largely automatic" here also includes manual input and assistance in the learning process.

The problems of increased complexity and extended functionality of systems, as pointed out in the introductory section, are being addressed within the AI community in various ways. An important trend is the emphasis on *knowledge level* analysis now adopted by most KA methodologies (Van de Velde, 1993). Other trends are the integration of knowledge-based components with information system and database parts (Wielinga *et al.*, 1993), and the increased emphasis on modelling for highly user-interactive systems (Clancey, 1993). Examples from machine learning include the growing amount of work on knowledge-intensive learning (Kodratoff and Tecuci, 1987a; Aamodt, 1990b; Leake, 1993), multistrategy learning methods (Michalski and Tecuci, 1990), methods that incorporate the user in the learning loop (Mitchell *et al.*, 1985), and case-based methods for learning by experience (Kolodner, 1993; Aamodt and Plaza, 1994). We will describe some of these approaches in more detail below.

A major requirement for the type of systems we are discussing here is their ability to *adapt*, in some way, to a continually *evolving environment*. It is for practical reasons infeasible to rely solely on manual updating and refinement procedures for maintaining the knowledge over time. If a system is to continually maintain and improve its problem-solving competence, it will therefore need to incorporate methods for automated *learning by experience*. An increasing amount of machine learning research is concentrating on incremental methods that enable learning while solving real problems. This includes approaches for learning of generalized knowledge (e.g. Tecuci, 1988; Van de Velde, 1988) as well as for learning of specialized knowledge (Riesbeck and Schank, 1989; Porter *et al.*, 1990; Aamodt, 1991). These activities have shown promising results that have encouraged more intensive research into sustained learning methods for real-world knowledge-based systems applications. Results achieved within the following three research areas are of particular relevance:

- *Knowledge-intensive learning* Most of the current research on knowledge-intensive learning methods is gathered under the term *explanation-based learning*, of which an early overview was given in DeJong (1988). Knowledge-intensive learning methods differ from approaches based on superficial and syntactic similarity and discrimination criteria. They include deductive methods based on a complete domain theory (EBL/EBG; see Mitchell *et al.*, 1986, and DeJong and Mooney, 1986), methods to generate and use plausible explanations in an incomplete knowledge base (Schank *et al.*, 1986; Lenat and Guha, 1989), knowledge-intensive case-based learning/case-based reasoning (Hammond, 1989; Koton, 1989; Porter *et al.*, 1990) and analogical reasoning and learning methods (Kedar-Cabelli, 1988; Kodratoff, 1990).
- *Apprenticeship learning* The notion of *learning apprentice* systems was introduced in Mitchell *et al.* (1985) as "interactive knowledge-based consultants that directly assimilate new knowledge by observing and analysing the problem solving steps contributed by their users through their normal use of the system". This does not represent a particular learning method or set of methods, but a general approach to sustained learning where new knowledge is continually acquired through observation and analysis. The approach is also well-suited to the application of semi-automatic learning methods, since an

apprentice should be allowed to ask questions in order to increase its understanding (Kodratoff and Tecuci, 1987b; Murray and Porter, 1989).

- *Case-based reasoning* Learning of specific knowledge in terms of past cases represents the major approach to sustained learning in today's machine learning research. The learning becomes a process of extracting relevant information from a problem-solving experience, and indexing this case in the system's knowledge structure in a way that facilitates retrieval when a similar problem is later encountered. The case-based approach to reasoning and machine learning has had a considerable growth during the last few years (Kolodner, 1993; Richter *et al.*, 1993; Aamodt and Plaza, 1994). Earlier research of fundamental importance to this field includes Schank's and Kolodner's work on memory structures for learning and reasoning (Schank, 1982; Kolodner, 1983) and the work on transformational and derivational analogy by Carbonell (Carbonell, 1983, 1986).

A few attempts have been made to develop systems based on an integration of methods from all these three areas. One example is the Protos system (Bareiss, 1989), handling the problem of classifying auditory diseases. Ongoing work at the University of Trondheim also focuses on such an integration (Aamodt, 1994). While Protos emphasizes the apprenticeship approach to case-based learning, our approach is stronger on model-driven, knowledge-intensive support to the CBR processes. Further, and unlike Protos, our approach does not advocate sustained case-based learning as an *alternative* to initial knowledge acquisition and model building, but as *complementary* to it. However, we shall see that by attacking the knowledge maintenance task with a method for sustained learning from experience, the initial knowledge modelling task is also relieved of some of its burdens.

8.2.2 Domain and task characteristics

The type of applications we address here are real-world problem solving and interactive decision support in open and weak theory domains. An *open* problem domain is characterized by incompleteness and frequent changes. Heavy interaction and feedback between a reasoning agent and its external environment is therefore required for successful decision making. A *weak theory* domain is characterized by uncertain relationships between its concepts (Porter *et al.*, 1990). Typical open and weak theory domains are medical diagnosis, geological interpretation, investment planning, and most engineering domains (i.e. domains that involve interaction with the external world). The stronger a theory, the more certain are its relationships. Domains with strong domain theories are, for example, mathematical domains, closed technical domains, and some games, such as checkers and chess. Even some strong theory domains may incorporate problems that turn out to be open when addressed by a problem solver. Chess, for example, has a strongest possible – a complete – domain theory, but solving the problem of chess-playing by an implementation of the theory is violated by its intractability: the concept of a "winning plan" in chess is theoretically deducible, but there is no efficient algorithm to infer it in the general case. Some closed and in principle well-understood technical domains, such as fault-finding in VLSI-circuits, are subject to the same difficulty.

The fact that a domain is open and has a weak theory does not necessarily imply that there is little domain knowledge available. It only implies that the knowledge is theoretically uncertain and incomplete. In order to compensate for the lack of strong knowledge for which deductive, proof-oriented methods would apply, such systems therefore typically need a larger body of knowledge than systems for strong-theory domains. The knowledge should capture the domain and task reality from different perspectives which together constitute a coherent model. Such knowledge is typically used for reasoning based on *abductive* methods, i.e. methods of inference based on hypothesis generation and evaluation by producing the strongest possible explanations for hypothesis support and justification.[2]

A strong emphasis on explanations as an essential part of the reasoning process requires a thorough and deep type of knowledge in order to produce meaningful explanations. There are in general many different perspectives to a body of knowledge, as well as to a single concept. A car, for example, means different things to a car mechanic and to an environmental activist. The meaning of inter-dependencies between concepts, constraints, and other relationships is determined by the concepts' interpretation within a particular context. For a knowledge-intensive approach to problem solving and learning, knowledge has to be interpreted with respect to its purpose and intended use, within particular problem solving and learning contexts (Compton and Jansen, 1989; Chandrasekaran, 1992).

8.3. A framework for knowledge modelling

In this section a generic knowledge modelling cycle is presented. It is based on the combination of a basically top-down driven, constructive modelling approach to initial knowledge acquisition, and the bottom-up modelling view represented by continuous learning through retaining problem-solving cases. Within this context, the more specific issues of acquiring an initial knowledge model, representing knowledge models, and achieving sustained learning are discussed.

8.3.1 General presentation

For the purpose of integrated KA and ML modelling along the lines we have drawn here, it is appropriate to split the overall knowledge modelling process, or cycle, into two top-level, successive tasks: *initial knowledge modelling* and *knowledge maintenance.*

The objective of the *initial knowledge modelling* task is to analyse the domain and task in question, to develop the conceptual, mediating models necessary for communication within the development team, and to design and implement the initial operational and fielded version of the system. Initial knowledge modelling, in this sense, covers all phases up to the realization of a computer system according to specifications. Incomplete as this initial model may be, it constitutes the knowledge environment wherein problem solving initially takes place, and from which experiential learning starts out.

The *knowledge maintenance* task takes over where the initial knowledge modelling ends, and its objective is to ensure the refinement and updating of the knowledge model as the system is being *regularly used.* This includes to correct errors and improve the knowledge quality, to improve performance efficiency, and to adjust system behavior according to changes in the surrounding environment, such as changing the type of users interacting with the system or the type of use made of it. The knowledge maintenance task continues throughout the entire lifetime of the system.

In Figure 8.1 the two outer, large boxes (with rounded corners) illustrate these two top-level tasks of the knowledge modelling cycle. Within each of the two tasks, the major subtasks (round corner rectangles) and models (sharp corner

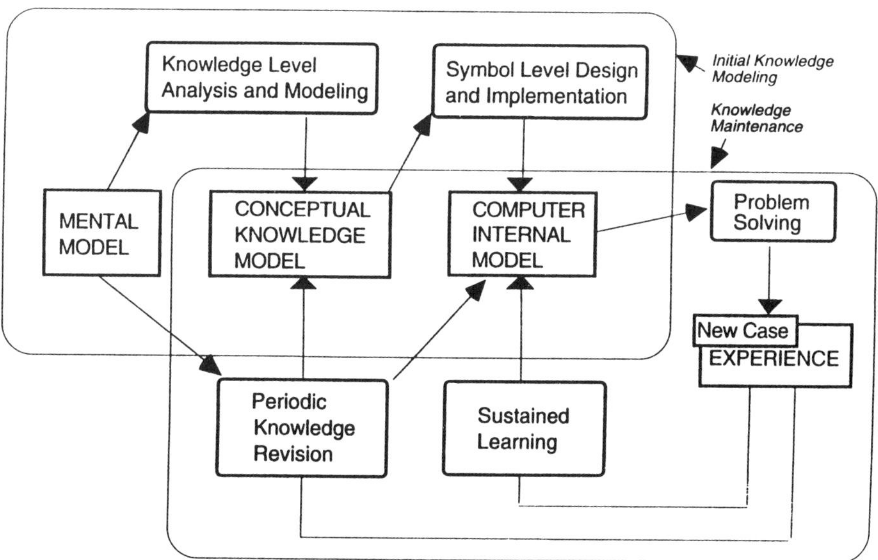

Figure 8.1 The knowledge modelling cycle

rectangles) taken as input and returned as output from these tasks are shown. Arrows indicate the main flow of knowledge and information, and show the most important input/output dependencies between subtasks and models. As shown by the area where the two large boxes overlap, the conceptual knowledge model and the computer internal model are shared by subtasks of both initial knowledge modelling and knowledge maintenance.

A knowledge modelling cycle typically starts with a high level specification (e.g. functional specification) of the target computer system, at some level of detail. As interpreted by the *mental models* possessed by the human beings involved, this forms the basis for analysing the relevant task types, domain models, and problem-solving strategies in question. The resulting submodels are structured into a *conceptual knowledge model*. The purpose of this model is to capture and structure various types of knowledge from the perspective of the application domain and the tasks of the target computer system, without being constrained by implementational limitations. The knowledge is described at what is referred to as the *knowledge level*, where the emphasis is to capture the *goal-directed behavior* of the system, its interaction with the environment, and the real world *content* of the relevant knowledge types. The result of this intermediate stage should be a model of domain knowledge and problem-solving methods suitable for communication among the developers, and for getting a thorough understanding of the application domain and the system's tasks in relation to the external task environment. Computer-assisted analysis and modelling tools, and prototype building in order to get feedback for improving the conceptual model, are typical means of developing this model.

Once the conceptual knowledge model is in an acceptable state, it forms the basis for designing and implementing the *computer internal model*, i.e. the knowledge model of the operating target system. This model is described at a level referred to as the *symbol level*, which deals not only with intentional knowledge content, but with manipulation of *symbols* that *represent* knowledge for the computer. The type of "transfer method" suitable for going from the conceptual model to the computer internal one depends on how close the conceptual model is to an executable one. It may be a rather simple transfer process close to copying or minor refinement, or a full rebuilding using the conceptual model merely as a specification.

The lower, partially overlapping box illustrates the main subtasks of knowledge maintenance. It is important to note that the knowledge maintenance phase starts when a system has been put into regular operation and use. All prototyping, testing and refinement that are parts of the pre-operational development process, including knowledge validation, are covered by the initial knowledge modelling task. The knowledge maintenance task has two optional subtasks as indicated in the figure. The one we focus on here is *sustained learning*, i.e. the direct updating of the computer internal model each time a new problem has been solved. The other subtask involves a periodic and more substantial revision process, i.e. a more thorough analysis, which in this model is assumed to be made after some amount of new experience has been gathered, and not after each problem-solving session. As illustrated, this revision task may lead directly to the modification of the symbol level model (computer internal model), but it may also go through an update of the knowledge level model (conceptual knowledge model) first.[3] The sustained learning task, on the other hand, regards each new problem-solving episode, i.e. each problem just solved, as a source for immediate learning. This implies that the knowledge model (read: the knowledge base) is updated each time a problem is solved. As we shall see, case-based reasoning is a problem-solving and learning approach highly suitable for this type of learning.

A crucial issue for all the modelling tasks is how to represent the knowledge in a way expressive enough to capture all relevant knowledge, efficient enough to make the knowledge available when needed, and close enough to a human interpretable language to facilitate manual inspection and refinement. The representation problem applies to the representation of a conceptual knowledge model as well as of the computer internal model, and in particular to the transfer between the two models. Hence, orthogonal to the two top-level knowledge modelling tasks, we can identify the following three core problems related to each of them:

- The knowledge acquisition problem
- The knowledge representation problem
- The learning problem

In the following three subsections, each of these problems will be elaborated – within the context of combining case-specific and general domain knowledge, and related to the integration of KA and ML methods. Each subsection is introduced by naming a development trend that has had – and still has – important impact on the problem addressed. It is natural to start with the knowledge acquisition problem, since some characteristics of the task and domain should be analysed before the representation problem is addressed. The representation problem, in turn, has to be addressed before the learning problem. Based on recent research, we shall see that a promising way of KA and ML integration is to rely on a tool-assisted knowledge acquisition methodology for the initial knowledge modelling task,[4] and a machine learning method that continually learns case-specific knowledge by experience, for the knowledge maintenance task.

8.3.2 The knowledge acquisition problem

The important development trend here is the increased emphasis on *knowledge level* modelling. The adoption of the knowledge level as the most suitable descriptive level for conceptual knowledge modelling is shared by most knowledge acquisition methodologies recently developed. Well-known examples are the KADS methodology (Wielinga *et al.*, 1992), the Components of Expertise framework (Steels, 1990), the Generic Tasks (Chandrasekaran, 1992) approach, Role Limiting Methods (McDermott, 1988), and the "method-to-task" approaches underlying the PROTEGE systems (Musen, 1989; Puerta *et al.*, 1991). Attempts to unify several existing viewpoints and methodologies within a knowledge-level perspective are also under way, as exemplified by the multiple perspective approach of the KREST methodology (Steels, 1993) – based on the Components of Expertise framework, and by CommonKADS (Wielinga *et al.*, 1993).

In Newell's original paper (Newell, 1982) the knowledge level was proposed as a distinct level of description of computer systems, defined to lie above the level of data structures and programming languages. The latter was referred to as the *symbol level*. The knowledge level has knowledge (goals and means to attain them) as its medium and the principle of rationality as its basic behavioral law.[5] At the symbol level, the medium is symbols (data structures and programs), and the behavioral law is sequential interpretation of procedures. A system is described at the knowledge level as an intelligent agent with its own goals and with knowledge of how to achieve its goals. The principle of rationality states that an agent always will use its knowledge in a way that ensures the achievement of its goals – provided the agent has the knowledge needed.

The ways in which the knowledge level perspective is utilized within a particular knowledge acquisition methodology varies. However, it seems to be a consensus that knowledge can be grouped into three main types, or viewed from three perspectives: tasks, domain knowledge, and problem-solving methods (see Figure 8.2). Tasks are defined by the goals that a system tries to achieve. Problem-solving methods are used to accomplish tasks (i.e. to solve problems). Domain knowledge[6] is needed for methods to accomplish their tasks.

The original knowledge level idea has undergone some modification over the years, from Newell's highly intentional, purpose-oriented way of describing a system, to a somewhat more structured and useful type of description. This transition has also led to modifications of the knowledge level notion itself, associated with terms such as the "knowledge use level" (Steels, 1990), a "knowledge level architecture" (Sticklen, 1989), and the notion of "tractable rationality" (Van de Velde, 1993). The original notion of knowledge level has been extended by introducing high-level structural and methodological constraints. This makes the knowledge level more operational and useful for conceptual knowledge modelling purposes, while retaining its competence-oriented and implementation-independent aspects.

A number of tools have been – and are being – developed to support knowledge-level modelling. They range from relatively general tool boxes, such as the KEW system developed in the Acknowledge project (Jullien *et al.*, 1992), to strongly methodology-driven workbenches, usually including libraries of reusable modelling components. Some of these approaches are aimed at knowledge-level modelling only (e.g. Wielinga *et al.*, 1992), while others attempt to provide a

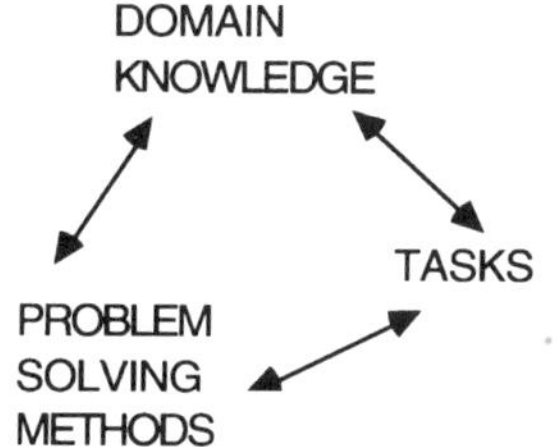

Figure 8.2 Knowledge perspectives

bridge to a symbol-level realization as well (e.g. Klinker *et al.*, 1991; Linster, 1992).

8.3.3 The knowledge representation problem

The important development trend here is the increased focus on capturing *knowledge content* in representation systems, as opposed to a focus on formal neatness and proof-deductive properties. Discussions related to the CYC system (Guha and Lenat, 1990), and the accompanied CYCL language, have posed important questions and provided new insight into core issues of knowledge representation.

The knowledge representation problem applies for knowledge-level as well as symbol-level modelling. Representation languages at the knowledge level, also referred to as conceptual modelling languages, are part of modelling tools such as KREST and the CommonKADS workbench.

Increased understanding of the representation problem at the symbol level, and of the related reasoning issues, has also come out of work on intelligent system architectures (Van Lehn, 1990; Weintraub, 1992), frame-based knowledge representation systems (Van Marcke, 1988; Lenat and Guha, 1989; Mitchell *et al.*, 1990), and systems for integrated problem solving and learning through user-active participation (Tecuci and Kodratoff, 1990; Althoff and Wess, 1991; Bareiss and Slator, 1992; Plaza and Arcos, 1993; Aamodt, 1993). These and related results contribute to the realization of knowledge-based systems that can deal with real-world, open application domains, and problems which are substantially more complex than we could deal with using previous methods. This fact has in turn motivated research on knowledge-level modelling, since the increased complexity and depth of symbol level models has made it more important to make a thorough analysis at the conceptual level.

Given that a knowledge-level model is different in purpose and scope from a symbol-level model, an important question is how to "bridge the gap" between the two models, so that the knowledge-level model can be effectively utilized for developing the symbol level one. We will come back to this question in section 8.5.

8.3.4 The learning problem

The important development trend here is the *case-based* approach to *sustained* learning by experience. The problems of actively maintaining a knowledge-based system have until now received surprisingly little attention in AI. Improving manual maintenance methods is one of the motives behind a structured modelling approach to knowledge acquisition. In manual methods, as well as some earlier automated methods for "knowledge base refinement" (e.g. the SEEK systems; Ginsberg *et al.*, 1985), updating and refining the knowledge is a separate, periodic effort, not a by-process of a normal problem-solving session.

Figure 8.3 shows the basic scheme for *sustained learning*, i.e. learning as a natural subprocess of problem solving. The figure is an expansion of a part of Figure 8.1. The upper right box illustrates the problem-solving steps. First, make an internal description of the problem, i.e. try to understand the problem by integrating it into the system's internal knowledge model. Next, use whatever type of knowledge and reasoning method is appropriate to suggest a solution to the problem. Finally, evaluate the solution by applying it in the real world or by other means. Based on the evaluated solution, learning takes place. The learning task (lower left) retains knowledge learned from a particular experience, by extracting potentially useful information from it, and by integrating it into the

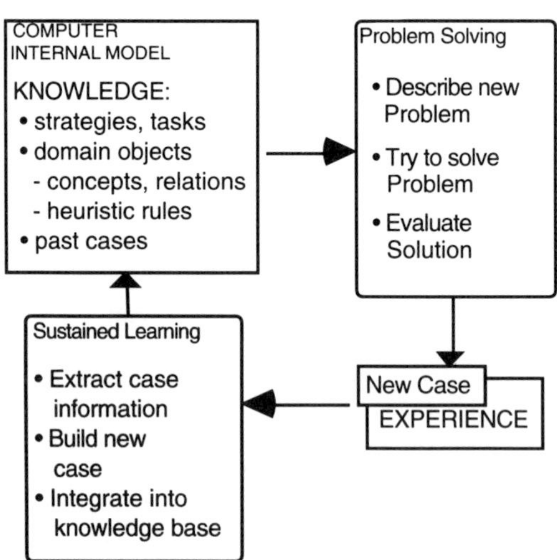

Figure 8.3 Sustained learning through problem-solving experience

knowledge base. The extracted information may be retained as a new case, or used to update the knowledge base by other means. In the next section we elaborate on these steps for a case-based learner.

A fundamental principle for sustained learning is that each problem-solving experience is a powerful source of learning. For this type of learning to be successful, a mistake once made should not be repeated. Sustained learning in this sense is a perspective to learning that has similarities to reinforcement learning (Sutton, 1992), but differs by being a symbolic, knowledge-based learning approach, whereas reinforcement learning normally uses numeric tuning and optimization methods. Further, case-based reasoning usually involves user feedback, while reinforcement learning generally is unsupervised.

In general, experiences may be stored and indexed as single, specific cases, or generalized to experience types. Recent work in machine learning on knowledge revision (including theory revision) addresses the general problem of updating a knowledge base when new information is received which contradicts or is unexplainable by the current knowledge. Although this research typically addresses the incremental learning of concepts as part of the initial knowledge modelling and testing phase (e.g. Craw and Sleeman, 1990; Nedellec and Rouveirol, 1993; Mooney and Ourston, 1994; Matwin and Plante, 1994), these methods should also be possible candidates for sustained learning in the type of domains they address. Normally, however, knowledge revision systems address the problem of identifying and correcting an error when a conflict is detected, and not experiential learning as a continuous process.

Some problems related to sustained learning of generalizations in open domains, and suggestions on how to deal with some of them, were demonstrated by the DISCIPLE (Tecuci, 1988) and CONCLAVE (Van de Velde, 1988) systems. However, as elaborated below, the main advantages of retaining experiences as specific cases, i.e. as instances of problem-solving episodes instead of as generalized rules, is that experiential learning becomes much easier – and particularly in real-world domains that do not have strong domain theories. A system that combines case-based learning with rule generalization, in a closed technical domain, has recently been developed within the MOLTKE workbench (Althoff, 1992).

The learning of generalizations, in some form or another, is what machine learning traditionally has been about. Although there have been significant advancements over recent years, the generalization problem – within a knowledge model or on a data set of some complexity – is still far from solved. Storing experiences as cases relies on methods that are able to utilize this type of knowledge when solving new problems. Such methods are provided by the subfield of *case-based reasoning*. A case-based reasoning method takes a problem description as input, looks for a similar case in the collection of past cases, uses the solution of that case to derive a solution for the new problem, and learns from the problem just solved by adding a new case or in other ways updating the case base. In effect, this is also a generalization process, but an implicit one: when solving a new problem, the matching of the problem to past cases in order to find the most similar one is always a *partial matching*, which can be viewed as a matching at a more general or abstract level. The role of general domain knowledge in this process is to guide the retrieval and matching process by providing a knowledge-rich ground[7] in which supporting explanations or meaningful relationships can be derived.

Some CBR methods also provide means of case generalization, for example generalizing feature values by climbing subclass hierarchies, but this is an extremely "lazy" type of generalization compared to the more eager one performed by inductive machine learning methods. Unlike other ML methods, a case-based system does not have to explicitly generalize its instances in order to learn. A type of generalization which is common in CBR systems, however, is the generalization of case indexes, in order to improve the similarity assessment procedure during case retrieval.[8]

The characteristics of a case-based learning method are therefore that (1) instance generalization is done during problem solving, not during learning, and (2) generalization is implicit in the similarity assessment made during case retrieval. In a learning-and-problem-solving perspective, part of the burden is therefore taken away from the learning part and given to the problem-solving part. In this way, information (knowledge) is not "generalized away" during learning. The learning step therefore does not have to make strong assumptions about what the learned knowledge will be used for, since the generalization is postponed until an actual problem is being solved. Since the generalization process becomes a part of the matching of a given problem to a past case, all the information available about the actual problem can be used in the process. In a multifunctional knowledge base, where the knowledge is assumed to serve different functions, i.e. to be used for various types of tasks, this is clearly advantageous. The disadvantage is that very much relies upon the similarity assessment procedure performed during case retrieval. Hence, the structuring of a case-memory, the indexing of cases, and the problem of similarity assessment are all active research areas of case-based reasoning. However, even if treated differently in CBR learning than in other ML methods, the generalization problem is a major concern of case-based reasoning as well. Ongoing research on integration of case-based and inductive learning – and case-based and generalization-based problem solving – may provide new insights into this problem (e.g. Althoff *et al.*, 1993).

In this section we have described a type of KA+ML integration that addresses a very important problem for future knowledge-based systems: how to develop and continually update a knowledge base by integrating KA and ML methods. We have argued that the main role of KA methods (possibly including inductive ML methods) is in the initial knowledge modelling phase, while the role emphasized for ML methods is in knowledge maintenance. The learning method advocated is the retaining of new experiences as concerete cases by integrating them into the existing knowledge base (containing general domain knowledge as well as a set of past cases). The rest of this chapter is devoted to mechanisms of case-based reasoning (next section), and to a method for combining knowledge acquisition and machine learning within the scope just summarized (Section 8.5).

8.4. Case-based problem solving and learning[9]

8.4.1 General presentation

Problem solving by reusing past cases is a powerful and frequently used reasoning method for humans. This claim is supported by results from cognitive psychological research. Part of the foundation for the case-based approach is its psychological plausibility. Several studies have given empirical evidence for the dominating role of specific, previously experienced situations (what we call cases) in human problem solving (e.g. Ross, 1989). Schank (1982) developed a theory of learning and reminding based on retaining of experience in a dynamic, evolving memory[10] structure. Studies of problem solving by analogy (e.g. Gentner, 1983; Carbonell, 1986) also show the frequent use of past experience in solving new and different problems. Case-based reasoning and analogy are sometimes used as synonyms (e.g. by Carbonell), viewing CBR as *intra-domain analogy*. However, as will be discussed later, the main body of analogical research (Kedar-Cabelli, 1988; Hall, 1989) has a different focus, namely analogies across domains (Burstein, 1989).

8.4.2 Main types of CBR methods

Case-based reasoning is a broad term, covering many particular types of methods. Below is a list of different CBR methods, distinguished by their different solutions to core CBR problems such as case representation, reasoning methods, and learning strategies:

- *Exemplar-based reasoning*
  In the exemplar view, a concept is defined as the contents of its set of exemplars. CBR methods that address the learning of concept definitions for classification tasks are sometimes referred to as exemplar-based (e.g. Kibler and Aha, 1987; Bareiss, 1989). The class of the most similar past case becomes the solution to the classification problem, and there is no adaptation involved.
- *Instance-based reasoning*
  This is a specialization of exemplar-based reasoning into a highly *syntatic* CBR-approach. The lack of guidance from general domain knowledge is compensated for by a large number of instances. This is a non-generalization approach to the concept learning problem addressed by classical, inductive machine learning methods (Aha *et al.*, 1991).

- *Memory-based reasoning*
  Memory organization and access within a *large memory* of cases is the focus of this type of method. The utilization of *parallel processing* techniques is a characteristic, and distinguishes this approach from the others. The access and storage methods may rely on purely syntactic criteria, as in the MBR-Talk system (Stanfill and Waltz, 1988), or they may attempt to utilize general domain knowledge, as the work done in Japan on massive parallel memories (Kitano, 1993).
- *Mainstream case-based reasoning*
  Case-based reasoning is often used as a generic term, but also as a label to CBR methods in a more typical sense than above. For example, a typical case has a certain degree of richness of information, and a certain *complexity* with respect to its internal organization. A feature vector holding some values and an associated class is not a typical case. Further, typical CBR methods are able to *modify*, or adapt, a retrieved solution when applied in a different problem-solving context. They also utilize, in some way or the other, *general domain knowledge* within the CBR processes.
- *Analogy-based reasoning*
  Although sometimes used as a synonym to the typical case-based approach just described (e.g. Veloso and Carbonell, 1993), or as a more general notion (Helman, 1988), it usually characterizes methods that solve new problems based on past cases from a *different domain* (Burstein, 1989). The major focus of study has been on the *reuse* of a past case, what is called the mapping problem, i.e. to map the solution of an identified analogue (called source or base) to the present problem (called target) (Kedar-Cabelli, 1988).

8.4.3 The CBR cycle

At the highest level of generality, the CBR cycle may be described by the four processes:[11]

1. RETRIEVE the most similar case or cases.
2. REUSE the information and knowledge in that case to solve the problem.
3. REVISE the proposed solution.
4. RETAIN the parts of this experience likely to be useful for future problem solving.

A new problem is solved by *retrieving* one or more previously experienced cases, generating a solution by *reusing* the case in one way or another, *revising* the solution by checking its correctness/usefulness – updating the solution if needed – and *retaining* the new experience by incorporating it into the existing knowledge-base (case-base). The four processes each involve a number of more specific steps. In Figure 8.4, this cycle is illustrated.

An initial description of a problem (top of figure) defines a *new case*. This new case is used to RETRIEVE a case from the collection of *previous cases*. The *retrieved case* is combined with the new case – through REUSE – into a *solved case*, i.e. a proposed solution to the initial problem. Through the REVISE process this solution is tested for success, e.g. by being applied to the real world environment or evaluated by a teacher, and repaired if failed. During RETAIN, useful experience is retained for future reuse, and the case base is updated by a new *learned case*, or by modification of some existing cases.

As indicated in the figure, general knowledge usually plays a part in this cycle, by supporting the CBR processes. This support may range from very weak (or none) to very strong, depending on the type of CBR method. As previously pointed out, general knowledge refers to general domain-dependent knowledge, as opposed to the specific knowledge embodied by cases. For example, in diagnosing a patient by retrieving and reusing the case of a previous patient, a model of anatomy together with causal relationships between pathological states may constitute the general knowledge used by a CBR system. A set of rules may have the same role.

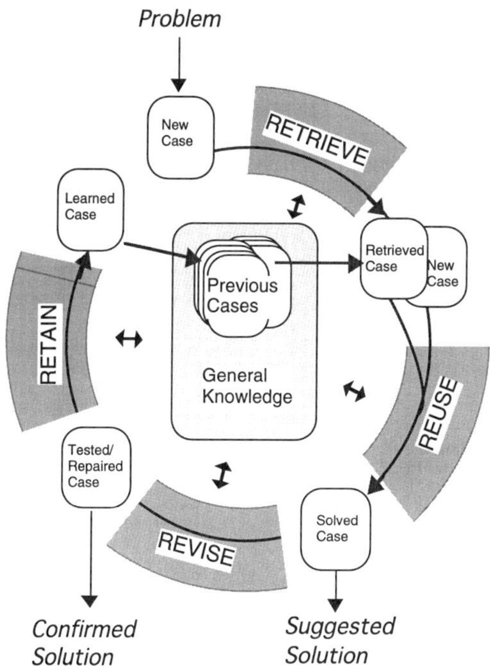

Figure 8.4 The CBR cycle

A core part of case-based reasoning is its "inherent" learning mechanism. The driving force behind case-based methods has to a large extent come from the machine learning community. Learning in CBR occurs as a natural by-product of problem solving. When a problem is successfully solved, the experience is retained in order to solve similar problems in the future. When an attempt to solve a problem fails, the reason for the failure is identified and remembered in order to avoid the same mistake in the future.

Case-based reasoning favors learning by experience, since it is usually easier to learn by retaining a concrete problem-solving experience than to generalize from it (as elaborated at the end of Section 8.3.4). Still, effective learning in CBR requires a well worked out set of methods in order to extract relevant knowledge from the experience, integrate a case into an existing knowledge structure, and index the case for later matching with similar cases.

In the following, the CBR cycle is explained in more detail, focusing on case-based reasoning in the typical, mainstream sense.

8.4.4 Mainstream CBR tasks

The *RETRIEVE* task starts with a (partial) problem description, and ends when a best matching previous case has been found. Usually, an initial identification subtask comes up with a set of relevant problem descriptors, a matching subtask returns a set of cases that are sufficiently similar to the new case – given a similarity threshold of some kind – and a selection subtask then works on this set of cases and chooses the best match (or at least a first case to try out). While some case-based approaches retrieve a previous case largely based on superficial, *syntactical similarities* among problem descriptors (e.g. the CYRUS system (Kolodner, 1983), ARC (Plaza and López de Mántaras, 1990) and PATDEX-1 (Richter and Wess, 1991) systems), some approaches attempt to retrieve cases based on features that have deeper, *semantical similarities* (e.g. the Protos (Bareiss, 1989), CASEY (Koton, 1989), CREEK (Aamodt, 1991) and MMA (Plaza and Arcos, 1993) systems). Syntactic similarity assessment – sometimes referred to as a "knowledge-poor" approach – has its advantage in domains where general domain knowledge is very difficult or impossible to acquire beforehand. Semantically oriented approaches, on the other hand, often referred to as "knowledge-intensive",[12] are able to use the contextual meaning of a problem description in its matching, for domains where general domain knowledge is available.

REUSE of the retrieved case solution in the context of the new case focuses on two aspects: (a) the differences between the past and the current case and (b) what part of a retrieved case can be transferred to the new case. In simple classification tasks the differences are abstracted away and the solution class of the retrieved case is transferred to the new case as its solution class. This is a trivial type of reuse. More typically, systems have to take into account differences in (a) and thus the reused part (b) cannot be directly transferred to the new case but requires an *adaptation* process that takes into account those differences. There are two main ways to reuse past cases:[13] reuse of the past case solution (transformational reuse) and reuse of the past method that constructed the solution (derivational reuse) (Carbonell, 1986).

Case *REVISION* consists of two tasks. Evaluate the case solution generated by reuse – and if successful, learn from the success. Otherwise repair the case solution using domain-specific knowledge. The evaluation task takes the result from applying the solution in the real environment (asking a teacher or performing the task in the real world). This is usually a step outside the CBR system, since it – at least for a system in normal operation – involves the application of a suggested solution to the real problem. The results from applying the solution may take some time to appear, depending on the type of application. In a medical decision support system, the success or failure of a treatment may take from a few hours up to several months. The case may still be learned, and be available in the case base in the intermediate period, but it has to be marked as a non-evaluated case. A solution may also be applied to a simulation program that is able to generate a correct solution. This is done in CHEF (Hammond, 1989), where a solution (i.e. a cooking recipe) is applied to an internal model assumed to be strong enough to give the necessary feedback for solution repair. Case repair involves detecting the errors of the current solution and retrieving or generating explanations for them.

The RETAIN task takes care of the learning step. It incorporates into the existing knowledge what is useful to retain from the new problem-solving episode. Learning from a successful or a failed problem-solving attempt is triggered by the outcome of the revision and possible repair tasks. It involves selecting what information from the experience should be retained, in what form it should be retained, whether a new case should be constructed, how a new case should be indexed for later retrieval, and how it should be integrated in the memory structure and knowledge base in general. A new case may be built, or the old case may be generalized or strengthened to subsume the present case as well. If the problem was solved by other methods, including asking the user, a new case is constructed. The "indexing problem" is a central and much focused problem in case-based reasoning. It amounts to deciding what type of indexes to use for future retrieval, and how to structure the search space of indexes. Through interaction with the user, the general domain knowledge may also be updated – for example when holes or inconsistencies have been discovered during attempts to explain the new case.

8.4.5 Two examples of CBR systems

Below, two example CBR systems are described. They are both well known from the literature, and they represent two different ways of combining knowledge acquisition and machine learning methods.

Protos

Protos is a case-based[14] approach to concept learning and classification problem solving. A system for diagnosing hearing disorders has been developed and evaluated (Bareiss, 1989). A problem presented to Protos is described as a set of features, and the system's task is to retrieve the previous case that best matches the feature set. Cases are indexed by *remindings* from features. The category of a retrieved case is proposed as a solution to the problem, without adaptation. If the proposed solution is rejected by the user, a learning session is initiated. Protos may be asked to look for another solution or to accept a solution from the user. The user is forced to define entered terms that are unknown to Protos, by describing their relations with existing terms. In this way general domain knowledge is gradually built up.

General domain knowledge is represented as a semantic network of categories, features and relations. A category is represented by its set of member cases, and its set of links to other categories. A case is represented by its set of features, and the category to which it belongs. Each feature in a stored case is associated with a numerical importance value. This value expresses how important the feature is for classifying the case as a member of the category. For example, the feature "backrest" is more important than "wheels" for the category "chairs". A comprehensive set of relations are defined (e.g. "part-of", "specialization-of", "causes", "enables", "suggests") where each relation has a number of explanatory strengths associated. An explanation is a chain of relationships between two features or between a feature and a category. An explanation is accepted if its strength – calculated by combining strengths of each relation in the chain – is above some threshold value.

Protos always learns from a problem-solving case: if a problem is successfully solved in the first attempt, no new case is constructed, but the remindings from relevant features to the case are strengthened. If a problem is successfully solved in second or later attempts, Protos tries to find the cause of the initial failure. Protos learns from the failure by weakening remindings from the features to the faulty retrieved case. If Protos is unable to suggest a solution, the case is stored as a new case. Remindings to the case, and difference links to similar cases, are installed. During the learning process, the user is asked to confirm or change suggested modifications to the case structure, and to revise explanations if needed.

Protos is a learning apprentice that relies heavily on its user. This is both a strength and a weakness. A positive effect is a quick adaptation to the real-world problem environment; the system will always be up to date with knowledge related to cases it has recently seen. The major weakness is that the knowledge model of the system eventually will represent a resource that is only partially utilized.

Protos has been thoroughly evaluated, by comparing it to senior medical students in the domain of hearing disorders. It performed at least at the level of these students (Bareiss, 1989).

CASEY

CASEY (Koton, 1988) is a system that combines case-based and model-based reasoning. When a problem turns out to be unsolvable by retrieving a past case, a general domain knowledge model is used in a second attempt to solve the problem. The domain model also plays an active part in supporting the case-based reasoning and learning processes. Type of problems addressed are diagnosis of heart diseases. The general knowledge model in CASEY is a pure *causal model*, relating features to their causal states. A problem is solved by retrieving a case, and – unlike Protos – *adapting* the past solution to the new problem. Each case contains a causal explanation that relates its features to the diagnosis. The solution to a new problem is derived by using the knowledge model to modify the explanation of the retrieved case. The reasoning method is a combination of case-based and model-based reasoning. The case-based method is applied first, model-based reasoning within the causal model being performed if the case method fails to find a sufficiently similar past case. In addition to being a separate reasoning method, model-based reasoning also supports the case-based process.

Cases are stored in a dynamic memory structure as described in Schank (1982) and Kolodner (1983). The structure is a discrimination network, where the top node contains common properties of all cases in the structure. Downwards in the memory structure cases are indexed according to their differences with other cases. The cases themselves are leaves in the tangled tree-structure. An intermediate node represents a generalized description of the cases indexed under the particular node. A feature is regarded more general than another if it is contained within more cases than the other. Concerning expressiveness, the only relation for deep modelling is "causes". The only moderator of the causal relation is a numeric probability – or likelihood – measure. This measure does not capture the underlying reasons for one cause being more plausible than another. Expressiveness is also limited by features and states being flat (property-name property-value) pairs, with no structuring of properties.

CASEY always learns from a problem-solving case. If a problem is successfully solved by case-based reasoning, CASEY stores the new case if it has significant features different from the previous case. If the new case is identical to the previous one, information about the importance of a feature is updated. If case-based reasoning fails, and the causal model solves the problem, a new case is created and indexed in the memory structure. The learning in CASEY does not involve user interaction. The system is designed to improve performance efficiency of model-based reasoning within the deep heart failure model. CASEY learns associational, compiled knowledge by extending or modifying[15] its case base.

Unlike Protos, CASEY does not interact with the user in its problem-solving and learning phases. In a sense, it is a counter-example of the type of interactive decision-support system addressed in this chapter. However, CASEY is interesting because of its tight coupling between case-based and generalization-based reasoning, based on its integration of general domain knowledge developed by normal knowledge acquisition means, and specific knowledge learned by the case-based method.

CASEY was evaluated on the basis of improvement of performance speed compared to the problem solving within the causal system itself. Its improvement increases with the number of cases seen, of course, and tests at several states of development all reported highly significant improvements (Koton, 1989).

8.4.6 Fielded CBR applications

Even if still a young field, there are some fielded CBR systems that have been in use long enough to have become evaluated. We briefly summarize two of these systems, to illustrate how CBR methods can successfully realize knowledge-based interactive decision support systems.

The first fielded CBR system was developed at Lockheed, Palo Alto. The problem domain is optimization of autoclave loading for heat treatment of composite materials (Hennessy and Hinkle, 1991). An autoclave is a large convection oven, where airplane parts are treated in order to get the right properties. Different material types need different heating and cooling procedures, and the task is to load the autoclave for optimized throughput, i.e. to select the parts that can be treated together, and distribute them in the oven so that their required heating profiles are taken care of. There are always more parts to be cured than the autoclave can take in one load. The knowledge needed to perform this task reasonably well used to reside in the head of just a few experienced people. There is no theory and very few generally applicable schemes for doing this job, so to build up experience in the form of previously successful and unsuccessful situations is important. The motivation for developing this application was to be able to remember the relevant earlier situations. Further, a decision support system would enable other people than the experts to do the job, and help train new personnel. The development of the system started in 1987, and it has been in regular use since the fall of 1990. The results so far are very positive. The current system handles the configuration of one loading operation in isolation, and an extended system to handle the sequencing of several loads is under test. The development strategy of the application has been to hold a low-risk profile, and to include more advanced functionalities and solutions as experience with the system has been gained over some time.

The second application was developed at General Dynamics, Electric Boat Division (Brown and Lewis, 1991). During construction of ships, a frequently recurring problem is the selection of the most appropriate mechanical equipment, and to fit it to its use. Most of these problems can be handled by fairly standard procedures, but some problems are harder and occur less frequently. These type of problems – referred to as "non-conformances" – also repeat over time, and because regular procedures are missing, they consume a lot of resources to get solved. General Dynamics wanted to see whether a knowledge-based decision support tool could reduce the cost of these problems. The application domain chosen was the selection and adjustment of valves for on-board pipeline systems. The development of the first system started in 1986, using a rule-based systems approach. The testing of the system on real problems initially gave positive results, but problems of brittleness and knowledge maintenance soon became apparent. In 1988 a feasibility study was made of the use of case-based reasoning methods instead of rules, and a prototype CBR system was developed. The tests gave optimistic results, and an operational system was fielded in 1990. The rule-base was taken advantage of in structuring the case knowledge and filling the initial case base. In the fall of 1991 the system was continually used in three out of four departments involved with mechanical construction. A quantitative estimate of cost reductions has been made. The rule-based system took 5 man-years to develop, and the same for the CBR system (2 man-years of studies and experimental development and 3 man-years for the prototype and operational system). This amounts to $750,000 in total costs. In the period December 1990–September 1991 20,000 non-conformances were handled. The reported cost reduction, compared to previous costs of manual procedures, was about 10%, which amounts to a saving of $240,000 in less than one year.

8.5. KA+ML integration in an iterative modelling cycle

8.5.1 General presentation

We have previously described the knowledge level account to modelling as a means to construct a conceptual model of the application domain, its tasks and possible methods. We have further contrasted knowledge level modelling with symbol level model realization, resulting in an implemented and operational system. In order to take advantage of a thoroughly worked out knowledge level model in constructing the model at the symbol level – and to maintain that model over time – there has to be a means for going from one model to the other. This is, generally, far from a straightforward matter, and the bridging of the two description levels is currently a problem of great concern within the knowledge acquisition community (Klinker *et al.*, 1991; Steels, 1993; Duursma and Van de Velde, 1992; Greboval and Kassel, 1992; Linster, 1992). Our thesis is that the gap between the knowledge and symbol levels should be shrunk by adopting a more *iterative*, less top-down driven modelling process. The potential of realizing sustained learning by case-based techniques is our motivation for relaxing the focus on initial knowledge modelling in favor of knowledge maintenance and iterative system development.

Top-down modelling is characterized by being a type of *refinement* process, where important decisions are taken at an early stage, and further specialized, or refined, in course of development. From a general development perspective, this is of course a cyclic, and also iterative process – for example iterating between suggested specializations at the knowledge level, their symbol level implementation, testing, and feedback to the knowledge level model. The term iterative, however, also has a stronger interpretation in the context of system development, which involves a more balanced contribution from bottom-up and top-down modelling methods. This type of iteration typically involves frequent *backtracking* of decisions earlier made, which in principle is different from a (iterative) refinement process.

Ideally, a top-down refinement process is what we would want, and our methods should support the kind of thorough analysis and comprehensive structuring that minimizes backtracking. However, the world is not ideal, and backtracking in model development will always be necessary. This is why it has to be an inherent part of any knowledge acquisition and learning strategy, no matter how good analysis methods and tools we are able to develop. And further, given that there will always be backtracking, it may be worthwhile to pull it into the iterative design process in the first place, to see if it can be turned into a positive contributor to model building, instead of necessarily something to avoid. This is the rationale behind the strongly iterative approach suggested in the following, and also the reason for putting a stronger emphasis on bottom-up learning within what is referred to as the *iterative modelling cycle*.

Figure 8.5 gives a top-level view of the iterative modelling cycle (KL = knowledge level, SL = symbol level). It illustrates iterative modelling composed of modelling at the knowledge and symbol levels. It covers initial conceptual

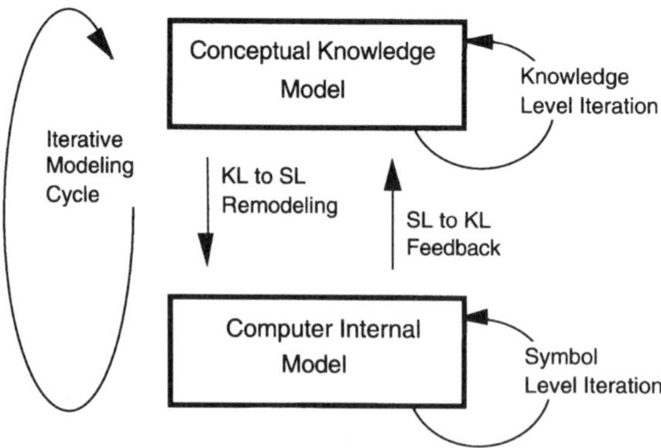

Figure 8.5 Iterative knowledge level and symbol level modelling

modelling at the knowledge level, initial symbol level realization, and intra- and inter-model feedback loops to both of the model types. The arrows represent different types of modellng activities. They may all involve manually driven KA methods as well as ML techniques. It should be noted that the cycle is *not a total system development cycle*. It describes only the part related to *knowledge modelling*. At this level of abstraction, the modelling cycle is, in principle, open to be specialized into almost any knowledge modelling method, and may therefore serve as a basis for discussing different approaches.

8.5.2 Specifying the general framework

The first step toward a specialization of the iterative modelling cycle may be found in the figure's naming of the KL-to-SL arrow. It is important that this process is regarded as a *remodelling* process, to indicate that the transition is more complicated than a mere transformation. This is a central issue in our framework, since the bridging of the KL–SL gap is a major motivation for our research, and since our proposal differs from methodologies that attempt to make this transition an automatic one.

Current approaches to an automatic bridging of this gap may be split into two types: those based on an *automatic operationalization* of knowledge-level models into executable, symbol level ones, and those based on a set of *predefined links* between types of knowledge level constructs and existing symbol level program components. Unfortunately, both methods impose severe constraints on the expressive power and flexibility of modelling choices at one or both of the levels. In the first approach (e.g. Vanwelkenhuysen and Rademakers, 1990; Linster, 1992), where a common representation language is used at both levels, a well worked-out KL model is more or less automatically made operational at the symbol level. The *degree of automated transfer* between the two levels is the major, and significant, difference between this approach and our remodelling approach. This difference reflects different views on the role of top-down vs. bottom-up modelling, since the weakening of a strong, definitional role for top-down modelling necessarily leads to a reduced reliance on the strength and power of the knowledge-level model.

The second approach (e.g. Klinker *et al.*, 1991; Steels, 1993) emphasizes the reuse of symbol-level components, and some of these methods have a less developed notion of the knowledge level. This represents a rather programming-driven approach, leaning toward a software-reuse tool, and hence some distance away from a knowledge modelling approach in the sense we have used the term in this chapter. Further, it assumes a rather well-described domain (since the linking is predefined and rather straightforward), and rather simple, well-known inference and reasoning methods (part of the reusable library). It represents an over-simplification of the tedious and difficult task of developing competent and robust knowledge-based systems tailored to particular problem domains and environments. In a longer time perspective, however, when more experience has been gained in how to develop useful, competent and reliable knowledge-based systems, this approach seems a very promising one.[16]

The first approach is top-down driven, while the second to a large extent is driven by bottom-up programming. By giving a stronger role to iterative modelling through knowledge maintenance, made possible by case-based reasoning methods, a new approach to combined KL and SL modelling can be defined, based on the following characteristics:

- A balanced integration of top-down, knowledge-level driven, and bottom-up, symbol-level driven modelling.
- The development of an initial knowledge level model is always the first modelling step, and here is where KA methods play their major role. Modelling should be based on recent insight into knowledge level modelling, and a systematic knowledge analysis should be made by studying the relationships between goals/tasks, methods to solve tasks, and the domain-specific knowledge and information needed by these methods (Aamodt, 1990a).
- Continuous evolution of models by sustained learning from experience. Given the problems with generalization-based learning methods for real-world domains, case-based reasoning should be the core ML method, at the symbol level. Application problem solving should combine case-based and generalization-based (model-based) reasoning methods.
- Active user involvement in problem solving and learning will identify errors or holes in the general domain knowledge, which should feed into KA methods that update the knowledge-level model (the SL–KL feedback, see Figure 8.5). This may, in turn, lead to a new traverse of the KL–SL link since the integration of new/updated knowledge at the KL in turn is elaborated to produce new knowledge.
- A modelling language is needed, at both levels, which is expressive and flexible, and this should be based on the object-oriented representation paradigm. It may be the same language syntax, at the two levels, but the semantics will have to be different. The semantics at each level should be specified from the needs of modelling at that level. User transparency, as well as a procedural but clearly defined semantics, are important properties of such a language.

The result should be a coherent model of general knowledge (domain models) and situation-specific knowledge (cases) at the two levels, and a system at the symbol level that reasons and learns by combining case-based and generalization-based methods. As an example of a system architecture for realizing systems according to the above characteristics, and which is also motivated by an effective integration of KA and ML methods, the CREEK system is summarized in the following.

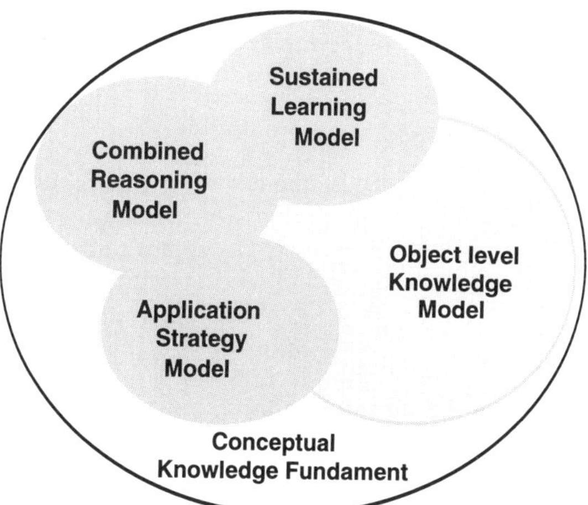

Figure 8.6 The knowledge modules in CREEK

8.5.3 CREEK – iterative modelling through knowledge-intensive case-based reasoning and learning

The CREEK system (Aamodt, 1991, 1994) is an architecture for knowledge-intensive case-based problem solving and learning, with the goal of studying the impact of sustained learning on the overall knowledge modelling cycle.

CREEK contains, at the top level, four modules integrated within a common conceptual basis as illustrated in Figure 8.6.

Each module represents a particular submodel of knowledge. The four modules are an object-level domain knowledge model, a strategy level model (for example a model of diagnostic problem solving), and two internal meta-level models – one for combining case-based and other types of reasoning, and one for sustained learning. CREEK integrates problem solving and learning into one functional architecture. The user is able to – and assumed to – interact with the system in all its phases of problem solving and learning.

Previously experienced cases and general knowledge of domain relationships are held in the object-level knowledge model. The other models contain general knowledge in the form of concept models and/or rules. It is important to note that all the concepts are "glued together" into a single, interconnected knowledge model. Diagnosis task concepts, for example, such as "symptom" and "diagnostic-hypothesis" (part of the application strategy model), and learning task concepts, such as "case-indexing" and "failure-generalization" (part of the sustained learning model), are defined within the same representation structure as general domain concepts like "appendicitis" and "fever", and case-related domains terms as "Patient#123456" and "current-radiation-dosage" (which all are part of the object-level knowledge model).

8.5.3.1 Representation

All types of knowledge and information are captured in a frame-based representation language called CreekL, an extension of SFL (Aakvik *et al.*, 1990, 1991). It is a flexible and extendible language, with a procedural semantics and similarities to FRL (Roberts and Goldstein, 1977) and RLL (Greiner and Lenat, 1980).

A knowledge model represented in CreekL is viewed as a semantic network, where each node and each link in the network is explicitly defined in its own frame. Each node in the network corresponds to a concept in the knowledge model, and each link corresponds to a relation between concepts. A concept may be a general definitional or prototypical concept, a case, or a heuristic rule, and describe knowledge of domain objects as well as problem-solving methods and strategies. A frame represents a node in the network, i.e. a concept in the knowledge model. Each concept is defined by its relations to other concepts, represented by the list of slots in the concept's frame definition. Main characteristics of the representation are:

- Concepts are represented as a network of frames.
- Concepts are either entities or relations.
- Entities are physical or abstract objects of a domain.
- Relations are named associations (links) between concepts.

A CreekL frame is basically a four-level structure of frame, slots, facets and value-expressions, where a value-expression is a list containing the actual value itself and annotations such as the justification for a value, a time stamp, etc. A part of the frame structure in BNF form is:

```
<knowledgebase>      :=  {<frame>}
<frame>              :=  <framename {<slot>}>
<slot>               :=  <slotname {<facet>}>
<facet>              :=  <facetname {<value-expression>}>
<value-expression>   :=  <proper-value
                           value-justification
                           value-source
                           value-time-stamp
                           value- miscellaneous>
```

Next, two example frames are shown; the first is a general domain concept and the second a case:

```
car
  has-subclass            value            family-car sports-car limousine van
  subclass-of             value            vehicle means-of-transportation sporting-gear
  has-part                value            wheel fuel-system engine electrical-system
  has-number-of-wheels    default          4
  has-colour              value-class      colour
  has-fault               value-class      car-fault
  has-age                 value-dimension  years
                          if-needed        (time-difference *current-year*
                                           self.has-production-year)

case#461
  instance-of             solved-case car-starting-case
  of-car                  N-VD-123456
  has-process-status      solution-proposed
  has-input-time          22/07/93 12:10
  has-electrical-status   electrical-system-ok
  has-engine-status       engine-turns engine-does-not fire
  has-ignition-status     spark-plugs-ok distributor-ok
  has-weather-condition   low-temperature moisty normal-air-pressure
  has-location-of-problem inside-garage
  has-driving-history     normal-driving
  has-solution            (water-in-gas-tank)
                                    (0.92
                                       ((engine-does-not-fire caused-by water-in-gas-mixture)
                                        (water-in-gas-mixture caused-by water-in-gas-tank))
                                       (carburettor-fault has-status false)
                                       (((low-temperature combined-with moist) leads-to
                                          condensation-in-gas-tank)
                                       (condensation-in-gas-tank causes water-in-gas-tank)
                                       (water-in-gas-tank does-not-violate
                                       (electrical-system-ok spark-plugs-ok distributor-ok
                                         engine-turns normal-air-pressure))
  same-solution-in        case#06 case#88 case#388 case#401
  difference-case         case#128
```

Facets are shown for the `car` concept, but left out for `case#461` since they are all `value` facets. A case solution (`has-solution` slot of a case) also contains a justification or support for the solution, in the form of an explanation with a computed explanation strength (0.92 in the above case).[17]

Each slot in a CreekL frame corresponds to a relation in the knowledge network, and each symbolic term is represented as a concept. Figure 8.7 illustrates how cases and general knowledge are integrated into the general knowledge structure. The nodes in the network are concepts and the links are relations. For drawing clarity, only a very small knowledge network, and only a very small number of relations to/from each node, is shown. Generic concepts are contained in a fixed part of the knowledge base, and includes top level "world" concepts (e.g. `thing`) as well as representational primitives (e.g. `frame`, `slot`).

To enable a thorough representation of knowledge, CreekL facilitates explicit definitions of relations as well as of symbolic values.[18] For example, if the user

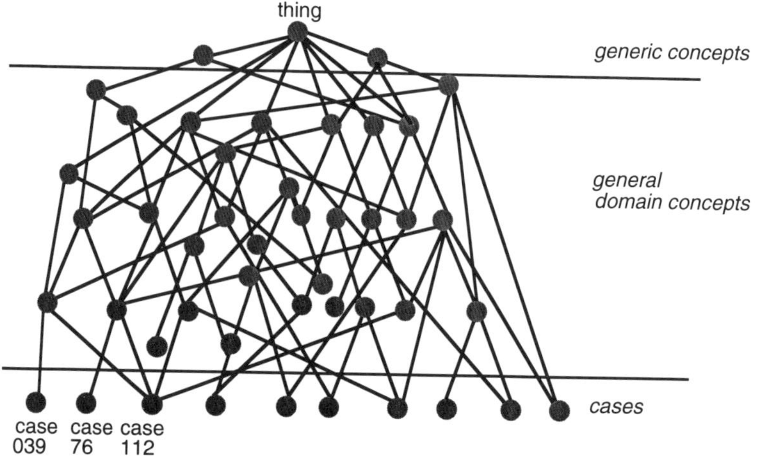

Figure 8.7 Integrating cases and general knowledge

wants to introduce a new slot, called *has-color*, on the frame *car*, the system will automatically create the frame *has-color* and give it a slot called *used-to-describe* with the value *car*. The user may enter additional slots on the *has-color* frame in order to better describe what it means to have color. The system also automatically creates a frame for each symbolic value entered into a slot. The inference methods that operate within this semantic network of frames are typical frame language methods like property inheritance (default and forced inheritance), frame matching (concept recognition), and constraint enforcement (constraint propagation). Access methods exist to retrieve and update any information item at any of the five levels of a frame structure.

Since the language has an operational (procedural) semantics, it enables the expression of informal and vague models (at the knowledge level) as well as specialized and detailed models (at the symbol level). Hence the remodelling involved in moving between the levels may be performed within the same basic object structure, and based upon a common representational syntax.

8.5.3.2 Problem solving

The case-based interpreter in CREEK contains a three-step process of (1) activating relevant parts of the semantic network, (2) generating and explaining derived information within the activated knowledge structure, and (3) focusing towards and selecting a conclusion that conforms with the goal. This *activate-explain-focus* cycle, referred to as an "explanation engine" (Aamodt, 1994), is a general mechanism that has been specialized for each of the four CBR tasks described in Section 8.4 (see Figure 8.8).

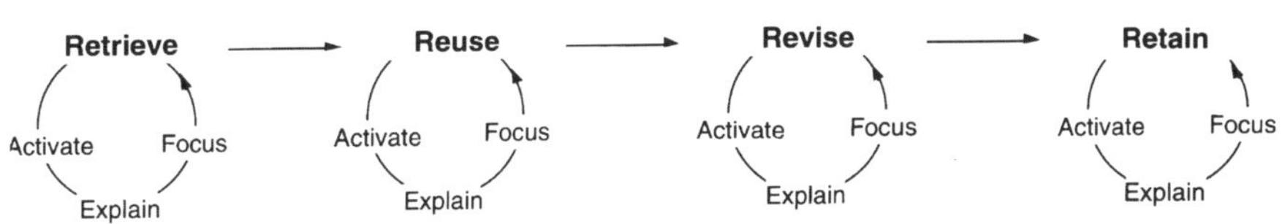

Figure 8.8 The CBR process and the explanation engine

The extensive, explanation-driven way of utilizing general domain knowledge in the CBR subtasks is a feature that distinguishes CREEK from other CBR systems.

The process of remembering (retrieving) and reusing previous cases may be used extensively in all three steps, but a more typical pattern is to use general knowledge in the activation step, cases for generating hypotheses, and a limited number of cases together with general knowledge for the focusing step.

The case-based method of CREEK thus relies heavily on an extensive body of general domain knowledge in its problem understanding, similarity assessment, case adaptation and learning. The general domain knowledge is assumed to be extensive enough to provide a back-up capability of problem solving on its own: if reasoning from case-specific knowledge fails, for example when no similar situation has previously occurred, the system may use its general knowledge to generate a suggested solution. This knowledge is typically built up by rather "deep" relationships – for example a combination of causal, structural and functional relations (depending on what is most appropriate within the application domain). It may also contain more shallow associations, in the form of if–then rules. Figure 8.9 shows the top level combined reasoning algorithm.

The process of selecting the initial reasoning paradigm starts after relevant features have been extracted from the input case, and halts when either a reasoning method has been chosen, or a plausible solution to the problem has been found. If the problem features give a reminding to a previous case that is above a certain threshold, case-based problem solving is tried (Figure 8.9, lines 8–9), otherwise generalization-based reasoning is activated (lines 14–15). Generalization-based reasoning includes rules-based as well as deeper model-based reasoning. The value of the threshold level depends upon the relative size and contents of the case base. It is set manually to begin with, and automatically adjusted over time according to how well the chosen reasoning paradigm performs. If the system is unable to suggest a solution, the user has to solve the problem by other means (lines 17–18).

8.5.3.3 *Sustained learning*

CREEK learns from every problem-solving experience. If a successful solution was directly copied from, or just slightly modified on the basis of, a previous case, the reminding to that case from each relevant feature is strengthened. No new

```
1  Input representational-primitives KB;
2  Input general-domain-knowledge KB;
3  Input case KB;
4  Interconnect all concepts in the three KBs;
       <result is a semantic network of general concepts and cases>
5  While general-domain-knowledge does not need off-line revision
   For each problem do                                        <case-based reasoning>
   Begin
6   Input problem case;
7   Determine relevant features;
8   If strong reminding to a case
9     Retrieve the case most strongly reminded of;            <case retrieval>
10    Assess relevance of retrieved case for current problem case
      and justify the validity of its solution;
11    If solution of retrieved case is acceptable
12      Learn from the experience;                            <to learning>
13    Else
14      If case-based-reasoning failed                        <cbr termination test>
15        Attempt generalization-based-reasoning;
16          Learn from the experience;                        <to learning>
17        If generalization-based-reasoning fails
18          Ask user for solution and justification;
19          Learn from the experience;                        <to learning>
20      Else
21        Attempt to modify solution of retrieved case;       <case adaptation>
22        If case adaptation successful
            Go to 11;
23        If sufficiently strong reminding to another case
            Go to 9;
24        Attempt to update problem case in the light of new
          information;
            Go to 8; ;                                        <final CBR attempt>
25  Else
26    If case-based-reasoning failed                          <cbr termination test>
        Go to 15;
27    Else
        Elaborate to get more information about problem case;
        Go to 7; ;
28 End; ; ;
```

Figure 8.9 Combined reasoning in CREEK

case is stored. If a solution was derived by significantly modifying a previous solution, a new case is stored and difference links between the two cases are established. A new case is also created after a problem has been solved from rules or from the deeper knowledge model alone.

The main target for the learning process in CREEK is thus the case base. But a system may also update its general knowledge through interaction with the user during problem solving. Since heuristic rules are represented within the conceptual model, they are available for the same tasks as the conceptual model in general. A rule is viewed as a shallow type of relation, and may also be used to support case-based problem solving as well as learning. Even if the explanatory strength of a shallow relation in general is low, it may add to other explanations

```
If solution for problem case was derived from case-based-reasoning
  If adaptation of solution from retrieved case was needed
    Construct new case based on retrieved case and justification;
    Weaken remindings to retrieved case;
  Else
    If retrieved case and problem case are mergable
      Modify retrieved case;
      Strengthen remindings to retrieved case;
    Else
      Construct new case based on retrieved case;;
Else
    If solution for problem case derived from
    generalization-based-reasoning
      Construct new case based on solution and justification;
    Else
      Construct new case based on solution and justification
      from user;;
Check new case by re-running the initial problem;
If new case is not retrieved
  Update reminding strengths to new case;
Update case base;
```

Figure 8.10 Learning in CREEK

for the same hypothesis and, thus, contribute to a justification of an hypothesis. Figure 8.10 illustrates the learning algorithm. The user is assumed to actively take part in both the problem-solving and learning processes.

This approach to integrated problem solving and learning also has an impact on the *validation* issue, since what will be validated is not only application problem-solving behavior, but also learning behavior. On the one hand, this increases the complexity and difficulty of validation. On the other, explicit validation in the traditional sense becomes less important, *since the system continually improves through the solving of problems*. The shift from thinking about systems in the traditional sense of development followed by a periodic maintenance scheme, to adaptive and continually evolving systems, is important and has many possible implications.

8.5.3.4 An example of case-based reasoning in CREEK

The example case previously shown, case#461, is a case that has been solved and learned. Below we will briefly describe the main steps from an initial problem description to a solved and learned case, by referring to the four-task reasoning model of Figure 8.8, in which each subtask is described by the Activate-Explain-Focus cycle. For a more extensive description of this example, see Aamodt (1994).

The system assists the diagnosis of car starting problems. Let us assume that the following input case description is given. (All facets are "value" facets, and facet names are dropped for the sake of simplicity):

```
case#0
  instance-of                initial-state-case car-starting-case
  of-car                     N-VD-123456
  has-task                   find-car-starting-fault
  has-electrical-status      electrical-system-ok
  has-engine-status          engine-turns engine-does-not fire
  has-ignition-status        spark-plugs-ok distributor-ok
  has-weather-condition      low-temperature moisty normal-air-pressure
  has-location-of-problem    inside-garage
```

Retrieve starts by activating the problem-solving context. We assume a large, multifunctional knowledge base, in this case of knowledge about cars and other vehicles, and in order to produce focused explanations later on, we want to activate just those parts and perspectives of this knowledge that is potentially relevant for the current task. The context is determined by a method of goal-focused spreading activation that activates all input findings and goal-relevant concepts. In our example the spreading starts out from the top-level application task, i.e. `find-car-starting-fault`, and the input features (`has-electrical-status`, etc.). Spreading-relations include general taxonomic ones (`has-subclass`, `subclass-of`, `has-instance`, `instance-of`), causal relations (`causes`, `caused-by`), associational relations (`occurs-together-with`, `leads-to`), and application-specific relations (`tested-by`, `test-for`). The final jòb of Activate is to use the findings as indexes to the case base and retrieve a set of cases whose matching strength is above a certain threshold. A finding concept has a slot `relevant-finding-in` which holds a list of cases and a computed relevance factor for the finding with respect to each case. For example:

```
spark-plugs-ok
  subclass-of                ignition-system-finding
  relevant-finding-in        (case#19 0.7) (case#85 0.6) (case#366 0.95)
                             (case#123 0.6)
  . . .
```

Combined remindings from the findings to the cases they point to are computed, and a set of matching cases are retrieved. The Explain step then evaluates the match between the problem case and the cases retrieved. This is necessary since the initial case retrieval was based on a rather superficial matching process. The relevance to the problem has to be justified for findings that match well, and mismatched findings have to be explained as not important. The system tries to "explain away" findings that mismatch, and attempts to construct an explanation that shows the similarities of findings with syntactically different values in the two cases. For example, a finding in one of the retrieved cases that is missing in the input case is that the recent driving condition is `hard-driving`. In the knowledge model, hard driving and broken carburettor membrane are connected:

`hard-driving` *`always-leads-to`* `extreme-engine-load` *`may-lead-to`* `abnormally-high-carburettor-pressure` *`causes`* `broken-carburettor-membrane`

Based on this explanation, `has-recent-driving-history` is regarded as an important finding. The system therefore asks the user about the value of this finding in the input case. The user replies that the recent driving has been normal. The degree of match of the case in question is then reduced.

The Focus step of Retrieve makes the final selection of the best case, or rejects all of them. In our example case#123 being returned as the outcome of the Retrieval task:

```
case#123
  instance-of                solved-case car-starting-case
  has-task                   find-car-starting-fault
  of-car                     N-CC-345678
  has-solution               carburettor-valve-stuck
  has-electrical-status      electrical-system-ok
  has-engine-status          engine-turns engine-does-not fire
  has-ignition-status        spark-plugs-ok distributor-ok
  has-weather-condition      high-temperature moisty low-air-pressure
  has-location-of-problem    inside-garage
  . . .
```

Reuse uses the solution of the selected case in solving a new problem, often involving some kind of modification of the past solution. The Activate step starts out from the solution of the best matching case, and spreads activation to concepts representing all expected findings given the solution of the retrieved case. The spreading relations used for this typically include causal and functional relations, as well as direct associations (e.g. `implies` and `co-occurs-with` relations). Values of expected findings that are not known are requested when needed, i.e. during the Explain step.

Explain has two main jobs to do. One is to evaluate the solution proposed by the retrieved case. Expected findings have to be confirmed, or explained as irrelevant for the present problem. An attempt is made to infer expected findings before asking the user. If all relevant expectations are covered for, control is given to the Focus step. If not, the second Explain step, modification of the solution, is triggered. An attempt is made to produce an explanation structure that justifies a replacement or tweaking of the solution. For example: the solution in the retrieved case was stuck carburettor valve. This is suggested to the user, but after inspection the carburettor turns out to be OK. The main explanation path from this solution to the findings is

carburettor-valve-stuck *causes* too-rich-gas-mixture-in-cylinder cxi *causes* no-chamber-ignition *causes* engine-does-not-fire

(see Figure 8.11). Before looking for a better matching case, the system tries to modify its explanation of the findings. By searching backwards along the explanation path (lower part of Figure 8.11) for other explanations of its states, it finds that engine-does-not-fire may also be caused by water-in-gas-mixture, in turn caused by water-in-gas-tank. The fault water-in-gas-tank is also supported by the findings moisty and low-temperature, via their relations to condensation-in-gas-tank (not shown in the figure), and is therefore the solution suggested by Explain.

Focus checks whether the proposed solution confirms with external requirements, and proposes the suggested solution to the user. The condensation-in-gas-tank suggestion is checked and confirmed by the user. Focus also extracts a minimal, sufficient explanation for the case, based on the explanation structures produced by the Explain step. The result of this is given as input to the learning task (i.e. Retain).

Revise evaluates the suggested solution – condensation in gas tank – by applying it to the actual problem. In this example the fault is confirmed, and needs no revision.

Retain is the learning task that captures the experience from the problem just solved. The Activate step here works on the structure returned from Retrieve and extracts potential concepts and structures for learning, i.e. the possible contents of

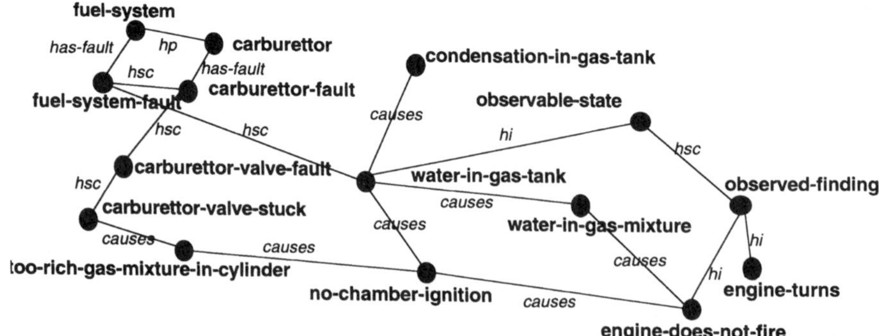

Figure 8.11 Partial knowledge structure in the car domain

a new case, and explanation structures that support the solution. New or modified concepts that may have been introduced by the user are also marked for the learning process.

The Explain step performs three tasks. First, it justifies whether a new case needs to be constructed or not. This is needed if no similar past case was found, if a retrieved solution needed significant modification, or if the set of relevant problem findings are sufficiently different in the two cases. Explanations have to be produced in order to assess the significance of a modification or of feature differences. In our example a new case is added to the case base. The second subtask is to determine what structures to retain from a problem-solving experience. Among these are the relevant findings with respect to the final solution. For each finding currently in the case, its relevance is explained. The strongest explanation from the solution to the findings, i.e. a structure of explanatory relationships, is retained in the learned case. If this does not constitute a sufficiently strong explanation for the solution (threshold value), additional "parallel" explanation paths are added. Learning of generalizations does not play a strong role in our method, but a lazy generalization of values for findings is done if justified by an explanation or by the user. Given that a new case is to be stored, the third subtask is to compute the importance (degree of necessity) and predictive strength (degree of sufficiency) of case findings, in order to determine their relevance factors.

The Focus step puts together the new structures into a case frame, and actually stores the new or modified case and its indexes. This also includes updating the `relevant-finding-in` slot of relevant findings. A finding may be relevant even if it is not an explicit part of an explanation path. The status of the electrical and ignition systems, for example, support the fact that a solution is found within the fuel system. In our example, the explanation structure being stored contains four paths that together explain the relevant findings. This leads to retaining the new case#461, with the content as previously shown.

Following the learning task, a test is run by entering the initial problem once again. It is checked whether the case just learned is retrieved, or – if no new case is learned – whether the problem-solving procedure is otherwise improved.

8.6. Conclusion and future trends

The insight which changed the focus of AI research from general problem solving to explicit knowledge modelling was an important one. During the last ten to fifteen years the notion of an explicit knowledge model has been substantially extended and refined. Starting from a view of explicit knowledge as a collection of if–then rules, it has been realized that the knowledge models which are needed to develop competent and robust real-world systems are substantially more complex. Methods are needed that are able to capture and utilize the various types of knowledge available: heuristic rules as well as deeper, principled domain knowledge, generalized knowledge as well as specialized knowledge related to problem cases, and object-level knowledge as well as knowledge to control the problem-solving and learning processes.

Any attempt to also include learning methods into such a complex environment may seem to reach beyond a realistic level of ambition. We will argue that the contrary is the case, for two reasons.

First, the kind of systems we are aiming at may turn out to be too complex to be fully developed before they are put into operation. Therefore, methods that are able to capture a system's experience as it is used, and improve the system's knowledge and behavior as more problems are being solved, may be what is required in order to facilitate a practical realization of such systems. It is a reasonable assumption that the users of intelligent decision support systems are more likely to accept a system with some weaknesses, as long as the system is able to improve over time. And particularly so, if the system is able to interact with the user in an intelligible way. So, incorporating methods for sustained learning into future knowledge-based systems will help the development and user acceptance of the systems, rather than impair it.

Second, in order to examine the potential of machine learning methods for gradually improving a system's behavior during normal operation, the methods need to address learning in a highly knowledge-intensive environment. Our learning methods should be able to take advantage of the various types of existing knowledge in their learning methods. The development of such systems should be based on a system architecture that enables the expert and knowledge engineer to explicitly express the various types of knowledge relevant for a particular application. This architecture should also contain problem-solving and learning methods which are able to effectively utilize a continually improving body of knowledge.

The integrated approach described here is a step in this direction. A framework for knowledge-intensive learning and problem solving by integration of KA and ML methods has been described, and some existing integration approaches have been discussed within this framework. Further, the CREEK system has been used to illustrate a system design based on the integration framework. CREEK suggests an improved approach to competent knowledge-based systems that continually learn from experience, extending results achieved within knowledge-intensive learning methods, learning apprentice methods, and the case-based reasoning approach to problem solving and learning. At the University of Trondheim we are currently exploring the impact of case-based reasoning on other methods for knowledge acquisition, problem solving and learning. We are working together with the research institute SINTEF to develop industrial applications in this area, currently directed toward a case-based decision support system for drilling operations (Nordbø *et al.*, 1992). We are also moving into medical diagnosis and treatment, another domain ideal for research on methods for open and weak theory domains.

There are many issues we need to address in order to obtain real synergy from KA+ML integration in a total knowledge modelling context. This paper has been an attempt to structure this discussion by raising some important questions, providing a framework for discussion, and suggesting a new direction of focus. There are two main messages from the work reported here. The first is that KA+ML integration should in its current state be conducted within the context of a total, iterative knowledge modelling cycle, rather than at the detailed level of specific algorithms. Otherwise it will be difficult to move machine learning into real-world, user-interactive decision support systems. The second is that, since it is regarded as a must for future knowledge-based systems to be able to learn from their problem-solving experience, we have to focus much more on modelling development through sustained learning, and to weaken our reliance on top-down modelling and on maintenance schemes based on manual, periodic updates.

Notes

1. Note that the term "problem solving" has a very general interpretation in this chapter. Problem solving is not necessarily the finding of a concrete solution to an application problem; it may be any problem put up by an application task. For example, to justify or criticize a solution proposed by the user, to interpret a problem situation, to generate a set of possible solutions, or to generate expectations from observable data are examples or problem solving.
2. Abductive inference is often referred to as "inference to the best explanation" (e.g. Thagard, 1988). While its original meaning, as defined by C.S. Pierce (Ayer, 1968), was as hypothesis formation only, its common interpretation in AI (e.g. Josephson and Josephson, 1994; Leake, 1993) is as a non-deductive alternative to both hypothesis formation and evaluation.
3. Note that the framework is a *descriptive*, not a *prescriptive* one. Hence it does not assume that any particular approach is more preferable than another. We will later use the framework to discuss such issues.
4. This may include inductive learning methods to form concept definitions or classification rules, but that type of KA+ML integration is not the topic of this chapter (our focus being on learning for knowledge maintenance).
5. The medium is what is being processed, and the behavioral law is the basic principle describing how what the medium expresses leads to a system's behavior.
6. Actually, domain knowledge is not a very good term, since task- and method-knowledge often are domain specific as well. It is hard to find a better term to indicate this type of knowledge, however, although "object knowledge", "application knowledge" and just "models" have been proposed. We will stick to domain knowledge, but bear in mind that the other knowledge types are not necessarily domain independent.

7. Sometimes referred to as "background knowledge". This is a suitable term to describe some knowledge support to an algorithmic-driven learning method, but it easily leads to a wrong perspective on knowledge-intensive learning methods, where the emphasis is on learning *within* the existing knowledge, not by using it as a background.
8. A simple inductive learning of case indexes is also incorporated in some commercial CBR shells (Harmon, 1992).
9. This section is based on a compression of parts of Aamodt and Plaza (1994), modified to fit to the context of this chapter.
10. The term "memory" is often used to refer to the storage structure that holds the existing cases, i.e. to the case base. A memory, thus, refers to what is remembered from previous experiences. Correspondingly, a reminding is a pointer structure to some part of memory.
11. As a mnemonic, try "the four REs".
12. Note that syntactic-oriented methods may also contain a lot of general domain knowledge, implicit in their matching methods. The distinction between knowledge-poor and knowledge-intensive is therefore related to *explicitly represented* domain knowledge. Further, it refers to *generalized* domain knowledge, since cases also contain explicit knowledge, but this is *specialized* (specific) domain knowledge.
13. We here adapt the distinction between transformational and derivational analogy, put forth in Carbonell (1986).
14. Actually, Protos is called an *exemplar-based* system, emphasizing that all cases are stored exclusively as concrete, non-generalized exemplars. A concept definition is viewed extensionally, as a category, defined by the collection of cases (exemplars) that belong to the category.
15. Modification of feature importances, measured by the number of times a feature occurs in cases, and the number of times it is used in a causal explanation.
16. Interestingly, this approach has the potential of being the basis for a case-based knowledge modelling tool that learns by retaining its modelling experiences and assists knowledge engineers by reusing these experiences.
17. The most detailed description of CreekL is given in Aamodt (1991). An account of the explanation-driven reasoning and learning processes, including an example that involves the above two frames, is given in Aamodt (1994).
18. A symbolic value is a proper value that is not a number, a text string or a lisp-function.

References

Aakvik, G., Aamodt, A. and Nordbø, I. (1991). A knowledge representation framework supporting knowledge modeling. *Proceedings EKAW-91, Fifth European*

Knowledge Acquisition for Knowledge-based Systems Workshop, Crieff, Scotland, May 1991.

Aakvik, G., Mengshoel, O. J., Nordbø, I. and Vestli, M. (1990). SFL – The Sintef Frame Language. The Acknowledge Project, ACK-STF-T3.1-WP-003-A. Trondheim.

Aamodt, A. (1990a). A computational model of knowledge-intensive problem solving and learning. In Bob Wielinga *et al.* (editors), *Current Trends in Knowledge Acquisition*. IOS Press, Amsterdam.

Aamodt, A. (1990b). Knowledge-intensive case-based reasoning and learning. *Proceedings of ECAI-90*, Ninth European Conference on Artificial Intelligence, Stockholm, August 1990, pp. 1–20.

Aamodt, A. (1991). A knowledge-intensive, integrated approach to problem solving and sustained learning. *Ph.D. Dissertation*, University of Trondheim, Norwegian Institute of Technology, Department of Computer Systems and Telematics. May 1991. Also as University Microfilms International, Dissertation 9208460.

Aamodt, A. (1993). A case-based answer to some problems of knowledge-based systems. To appear in *Proceedings of SCAI, Fourth Scandinavian Conference on Artificial Intelligence*, Stockholm, May 1993. IOS Press, Amsterdam.

Aamodt, A. (1994). Explanation-driven case-based reasoning. In Wess, S., Althoff, K., Richter, M. (editors), *Topics in Case-based Reasoning*, pp. 274–288. Springer-Verlag, Berlin.

Aamodt, A. and Plaza, E. (1994). Case-based reasoning: foundational issues, current state, and future trends. *AI Communications*, 7(1): 39–59.

Aha, D., Kibler, D. and Albert, M. K. (1991). Instance-based learning algorithms. *Machine Learning*, 6(1).

Althoff, K-D. (1992). *Eine fallbasierte Lernkomponente als Bestandteil der MOLTKE-Werkbank zur Diagnose technischer Systeme*. (University of Kaiserslautern, Doctoral dissertation.) Infix Verlag.

Althoff, K-D., Bergmann, R., Maurer, F., Wess, S., Manago, M., Auriol, E., Conruyt, N., Traphoener, R., Braeuer, M. and Dittrich, S. (1993). Integrating inductive and case-based technologies for classification and diagnostic reasoning. In Plaza, E. (editor), *Proc. ECML, Workshop on "Integrated Learning Architectures"*.

Althoff, K-D. and Wess, S. (1991). Case-based knowledge acquisition, learning and problem solving for real world tasks. *Proceedings EKAW-91, European Knowledge Acquisition Workshop*.

Anderson, J. R. (1990). *Cognitive Psychology and Its Implication, 3rd edition*. Freeman, Oxford.

Ayer A. J. (1968). *The Origins of Pragmatism; Studies in the Philosophy of Charles Sanders Pierce and William James: Book I, Charles Sanders Pierce*, Chapter 3, pp. 63–100. Freeman, Cooper & Co., New York.

Bareiss, R. (1989). *Exemplar-based Knowledge Acquisition: A Unified Approach to Concept Representation, Classification, and learning*. Academic Press, London.

Bareiss, R. and Slator, B. M. (1992). *From Protos to ORCA: Reflections on a unified approach to knowledge representation, categorization, and Learning*. Northwestern University, Institute for the Learning Sciences, Technical Report # 20.

Boose, J. (1986). *Expert Transfer for Expert Systems Design*. Elsevier, New York.

Boy, G. (1991). *Intelligent Assistant Systems*. Academic Press, London.

Brown, B. and Lewis, L. (1991). A case-based reasoning solution to the problem of redundant resolutions of non-conformances in large scale manufacturing. In Smith, R. and Scott, C. (editors), *Innovative Applications for Artificial Intelligence 3*. MIT Press.

Burstein, M. H. (1989). Analogy vs. CBR: The purpose of mapping. *Proceedings from the Case-Based Reasoning Workshop, Pensacola Beach, Florida, May–June 1989*, pp. 133–136. Sponsored by DARPA. Morgan Kaufmann, San Mateo, CA.

CACM (1994). *Communication of the ACM*, March 1994, volume 37, no. 3. (Special issue on commercial applications of AI.)

Carbonell, J. (1983). Learning by analogy – formulating and generalizing plans from past experience. In Michalski, R. S., Carbonell, J. G. and Mitchell, T. M. (editors), *Machine Learning – An Artificial Intelligence Approach, Volume 1*, pp. 137–161. Morgan Kaufmann, San Mateo, CA.

Carbonell J. (1986). Derivational analogy. In Michalski, R. S., Carbonell, J. G. Mitchell, T. M. (editors), *Machine Learning – An Artificial Intelligence Approach, volume 2*, pp. 371–392. Morgan Kaufmann, San Mateo, CA.

Chandrasekaran, B. (1992). Task-structure analysis for knowledge modeling. *Communications of the ACM*, 35(9), September (Special issue on modeling), pp. 124–137.

Clancey, W. (1989). Viewing knowledge bases as qualitative models. *IEEE Expert*, 4(2): 9–23.

Clancey, W. (1993). The knowledge level reinterpreted: Modeling socio-technical systems. *International Journal of Intelligent Systems*, 8(1): 33–50.

Compton, P. and Jansen, R. (1989). A philosophical basis for knowledge acquisition. *EKAW 89, Third European Workshop on Knowledge Acquisition for Knowledge-Based Systems*, pp. 75–89 Edited by J. Boose, B. Gaines and J.G. Ganascia. ECCAI/ AFCET/ARC, Paris.

Craw, S. and Sleeman, D. (1990). Automating the refinement of knowledge-based systems. *Proceedings of ECAI-90, Ninth European Conference on Artificial Intelligence*, Stockholm, August, pp. 167–172.

David, J-M., Krivine, J-P. and Simmons, R. (editors) (1993). *Second Generation Expert Systems*. Springer Verlag, Berlin.

DeJong, G. (1988). An introduction to explanation based learning. In *Exploring Artificial Intelligence*; papers from the *6th and 7th National Conferences on Artificial Intelligence*, pp. 45–81. Morgan Kaufmann, San Mateo, CA.

DeJong, G. and Mooney, R. (1986). Explanation based learning – an alternative view. *Machine Learning (journal)*, 1: 145–176.

Duursma, C. and Van de Velde, W. (editors) (1992). *Operationalising Knowledge Models*. KADS-II Project Report KADS-II/T1.2/VUB/RR/004/1.0, Free University of Brussels – VUB, October.

Ford, K., Bradshaw, J., Adams-Webber, J. and Agnew, N. (1993). Knowledge acquisition as a constructive modeling activity. *International Journal of Intelligent Systems*, 8(1): 9–31.

Gaines, B. (1993). Modeling practical reasoning. *International Journal of Intelligent Systems*, 8(1): 51–70.

Gentner, D. (1983). Structure mapping – a theoretical framework for analogy. *Cognitive Science*, 7: 155–170.

Ginsberg, A., Weiss, S. and Politakis P. (1985). SEEK2 – A generalized approach to automatic knowledge base refinement. *Proceedings IJCAI-85*, pp. 367–374. Morgan Kaufmann, San Mateo, CA.

Greboval, C. and Kassel, G. (1992). An approach to operationalize conceptual models: The shell Aide. In Wetter, T., Althoff, K.-D., Boose, J., Gaines, B.R., Linster, M. and Schmalhofer, F. (editors): *Current Developments in Knowledge Acquisition: Proc. of the 6th European Acquisition Workshop EKAW'92*, pp. 37–55. Springer Verlag, Berlin.

Greiner, R. and Lenat, G. (1980). A representation language language. *Proceedings AAAI-80*, pages 165–169. Morgan Kaufmann, San Mateo, CA.

Guha, R. and Lenat, D. (1990). Cyc: A midterm report. *AI Magazine*, Fall, 33–59.

Hall, R. P. (1989). Computational approaches to analogical reasoning; A comparative analysis. *Artificial Intelligence*, 39(1): 39–120.

Hammond, K. (1989). *Case-based Planning*. Academic Press, London.

Harmon, P. (1992). Case-based reasoning III. *Intelligent Software Strategies*, VIII (1).

Harmon, P., Maus, R. and Morrissey, W. (1988). *Expert Systems Tools and Applications*. John Wiley & Sons, Chichester.

Helman, D. H. (editor) (1988). *Analogical Reasoning*, pp. 65–103. Kluwer, Boston.

Hennessy, D. and Hinkle, D. (1992). Applying case-based reasoning to autoclave loading. *IEEE Expert*, 7(5): 21–26.

Josephson, J. and Josephson, S. (1994). *Abductive Inference, Computation, Philosophy, Technology*. Cambridge University Press, Cambridge, UK.

Jullien, C., Shadbolt, N. and Wielinga, B. (editors) (1992). *Acknowledge Project Final Report*. ACK-CSI-WM-DL-007, Cap Gemini Innovation.

Kedar-Cabelli, S. (1988). Analogy – from a unified perspective. In Helman, D.H. (Ed.), *Analogical Reasoning*, pp. 65–103. Kluwer, Boston.

Kibler, D. and Aha, D. (1987). Learning representative exemplars of concepts: An initial study. *Proceedings of the Fourth International Workshop on Machine Learning, UC-Irvine, June*, pp. 24–29.

Kitano, H. (1993). Challenges for massive parallelism. *IJCAI, Proceedings of the Thirteenth International Conference on Artificial Intelligence, Chambery, France*, pp. 813–834. Morgan Kaufmann, San Mateo, CA.

Klinker, G., Bohla, C., Dallemagne, G., Marques, D. and McDermott, J. (1991). Usable and reusable programming constructs. *Knowledge Acquisition*, 3: 117–136.

Kodratoff, Y. (1990). Combining similarity and causality in creative analogy. *Proceedings of ECAI-90, Ninth European Conference on Artificial Intelligence, Stockholm, August*, pp. 398–403.

Kodratoff, Y. and Tecuci, G. (1987a). What is an explanation in DISCIPLE. *Proceed-*

ings of the Fourth International Workshop on Machine Learning, Irvine, California, July, pp. 160–166. Morgan Kaufmann, San Mateo, CA.

Kodratoff, Y. and Tecuci, G. (1987b). Techniques of design and DISCIPLE learning apprentice. *International Journal of Expert Systems*, 1(1): 39–69.

Kolodner, J. (1983). Maintaining organization in a dynamic long-term memory. Reconstructive memory, a computer model. 2 papers in *Cognitive Science*, 7: 243–280 and 7: 281–328.

Kolodner, J. (1993). *Case-based Reasoning*. Morgan Kaufmann, San Mateo, CA.

Koton, P. (1988). Using experience in learning and problem solving. *Ph.D. dissertation*, Massachusetts Institute of Technology, Laboratory of Computer Science. MIT/LCS/TR-441.

Koton, P. (1989). Evaluating case-based problem solving. In *Proceedings from the Case-Based Reasoning Workshop, Pensacola Beach, Flordia, May–June 1989*, pp. 173–175. Sponsored by DARPA. Morgan Kaufmann, San Mateo, CA.

Leake, D. (1993). Focusing construction and selection of abductive hypotheses. In *IJCAI*, pp. 24–31. Morgan Kaufmann, San Mateo, CA.

Lenat, D. and Guha, R. (1989). *Building Large Knowledge-Based Systems; Representation and Inference in the CYC Project*. Addison-Wesley, Reading, MA.

Linster, M. (1992). Linking models to make sense to modeling to implement systems in an operational modeling environment. In Wetter, T., Althoff, K.-D., Boose, J., Gaines, B. R., Linster, M. and Schmalhofer, F. (editors). *Current Developments in Knowledge Acquisition: Proc. of the 6th European Acquisition Workshop EKAW'92*, pp. 55–74, Springer Verlag, Berlin.

Matwin, M. and Plante, B. (1994). Theory revision by analyzing explanations and prototypes. In Michalski, R. and Tecuci, G. (editors), *Machine Learning, a Multi-Strategy Approach, Volume IV*, pp. 217–238. Morgan Kaufmann, San Mateo, CA.

McDermott, J. (1988). Preliminary steps toward a taxonomy of problem solving methods. In Marcus, S. (editor), *Automating Knowledge Acquisition for Expert Systems*, pp. 226–266. Kluwer.

Michalski, R. and Tecuci, G. (editors) (1990). *Machine Learning: A Multistrategy Approach, Volume IV*. Morgan Kaufmann, San Mateo, CA.

Mitchell, T., Allen, J., Chalasani, P., Cheng, J., Etzoni, O., Ringuette, M. and Schlimmer, J. C. (1990). Theo: A framework for self-improving systems, In VanLehn, K. (editor), *Architectures for Intelligence*, pp. 323–356. Lawrence Erlbaum, Hillsdale.

Mitchell, T., Keller, R. and Kedar-Cabelli, S. (1986). Explanation based generalization – a unifying view. *Machine Learning (journal)*, 1: 47–80.

Mitchell, T., Mahadevan, S. and Steinberg, L. (1985). LEAP: a learning apprentice for VLSI design. *Proceedings of IJCAI-85*, pages 573–580. Morgan Kaufmann, San Mateo, CA.

Mooney, R. and Ourston, D. (1994). A multistrategy approach to theory refinement. In Michalski, R. and Tecuci, G. (editors), *Machine Learning, a Multistrategy Approach, Volume IV*, pp. 141–164. Morgan Kaufmann, San Mateo, CA.

Morik, K. (1990). Integrating manual and automatic knowledge acquisition – BLIP. In

McGraw, K. L. and Westphal, C. R. (editors), *Readings in Knowledge Acquisition*, pp. 213–232. Ellis Horwood, Chichester, UK.

Murray, K. and Porter, B. (1989). Controlling search for the consequences of new information during knowledge integration. In: *Proceedings of the Sixth International Workshop on Machine Learning, Cornell University, June 26–27*, pp. 290–296. Morgan Kaufmann, San Mateo, CA.

Musen, M. A. (1989). Conceptual models of interactive knowledge acquisition tools. *Knowledge Acquisition*, 1(1): 73–88.

Nedellec, C. and Rouveirol, C. (1993). Hypothesis selection biases for incremental learning. *AAAI, Special Workshop on Training Issues in Incremental Learning.*

Newell, A. (1982). The knowledge level, *Artificial Intelligence*, 18: 87–127.

Nordbø, I., Skalle, P., Sveen, J., Aakvik, G. and Aamodt, A. (1992). *Reuse of Experience in Drilling – Phase 1 Report.* SINTEF DELAB and NTH, Div. of Petroleum Engineering. STF 40 RA92050 and IPT 12/92/PS/JS. Trondheim.

Plaza, E. and Arcos, J. (1993). *Reflection, Memory, and Learning.* Institut d'Investigacio en Intelligencia Artificial, CSIC/CEAB, Report de Recerca IIIA 93/2. Also to appear in *Proceedings from MSL, Workshop on Multistrategy Learning.*

Plaza, E. and López de Mántaras, R. (1990). A case-based apprentice that learns from fuzzy examples. *Proceedings, ISMIS, Knoxville, Tennessee*, pp. 420–427.

Porter B., Bareiss R. and Holte R. (1990). Concept learning and heuristic classification in weak theory domains. *Artificial Intelligence*, 45(1–2): 229–263.

Puerta, A., Egar, J., Tu, S. and Musen, M. (1991). A multiple-method knowledge-acquisition shell for the automatic generation of knowledge-acquisition tools. In *KAW-91, Proceedings of the 6th Banff Knowledge Acquisition Workshop.* AAAI/University of Calgary.

Richter, M. and Wess, S. (1991). Similarity, uncertainty and case-based reasoning in PATDEX. In R.S. Boyer (editor): *Automated Reasoning, Essays in Honor of Woody Bledsoe*, pp. 249–265. Kluwer, Boston.

Richter, M., Wess, S., Althoff, K. D. and Maurer, F. (1993). *EWCBR, 1993: First European Workshop on Case-Based Reasoning.* University of Kaiserslautern SEKI Report SR (1993)-12 (SFB 314) Kaiserslautern, Germany, November 1993.

Riesbeck, C. and Schank, R. (1989). *Inside Case-based Reasoning.* Lawrence Erlbaum, Hillsdale.

Roberts, R. and Goldstein, I. (1977). *The FRL Manual.* MIT AI Laboratory Memo 409, Cambridge.

Ross, B. H. (1989). Some psychological results on case-based reasoning. *Case-Based Reasoning Workshop, DARPA 1989. Pensacola Beach*, pp. 144–147. Morgan Kaufmann, San Mateo, CA.

Schank, R. (1982). *Dynamic Memory; a Theory of Reminding and Learning in Computers and People.* Cambridge University Press, Cambridge, UK.

Schank, R., Collins, G. and Hunter, L. (1986). Transcending inductive category formation in learning. *Behavioral and Brain Sciences*, 9: 639–650. Pages 651–686 contain commentaries by several authors.

Simon, H. and Kaplan C.A. (1989). Foundations of cognitive science. In M.I. Posner (editor): *Foundations in Cognitive Science*, pp. 1–47. MIT Press (A Bradford Book).

Stanfill, C. and Waltz, D. (1988), The memory based reasoning paradigm. In: *Case Based Reasoning. Proceedings from a Workshop, Clearwater Beach, Florida, May 1988*, pp. 414–424. Morgan Kaufmann, San Mateo, CA.

Steels, L. (1990). Components of expertise. *AI Magazine*, 11(2): 29–49.

Steels, L. (1993). The componential framework and its role in reusability, In David, J.-M., Krivine, J.-P. and Simmons, R. (editors), *Second Generation Expert Systems*, pp. 273–298. Springer Verlag, Berlin.

Sticklen, J. (1989). Problem solving architecture at the knowledge level. *Journal of Experimental and Theoretical Artificial Intelligence*, 1(4): 233–271.

Strube, G. (1991). The role of cognitive science in knowledge engineering. In: Schmalhofer, F. and Strube, G. (editors), *Contemporary Knowledge Engineering and Cognition: First Joint Workshop, Proceedings*, pp. 161–174. Springer Verlag, Berlin.

Sutton, R. S. (editor) (1992). *Machine Learning*, 8(3–4). Special issue on reinforcement learning.

Tecuci, G. (1988). DISCIPLE: a theory, methodology and system for learning expert knowledge. University de Paris-Sud, Centre d'Orsay. These presente pour obyenir le titre de Docteur en Science.

Tecuci, G. and Kodratoff, Y. (1990). Apprenticeship learning in imperfect domain theories. In Kodratoff and Michalski: *Machine Learning: An Artificial Intelligence Approach, Volume III*, pp. 514–551. Morgan Kaufmann, San Mateo, CA.

Thagard, P. (1988). *Computational Philosophy of Science*. MIT Press/Bradford Books.

Tulving, E. (1972). Episodic and semantic memory. In E. Tulving and W. Donaldson: *Organization of Memory*, pp. 381–403. Academic Press, London.

Turban, E. (1992). *Expert Systems and Artificial Intelligence*. Macmillan, London.

Van de Velde W. (1988). Learning from experience. *Ph.D. Dissertation*, Free University of Brussels – VUB.

Van de Velde, W. (1993). Issues in knowledge level modeling. In David, J.-M., Krivine, J.-P. and Simmons, R. (editors), *Second Generation Expert Systems*, pp. 211–231. Springer Verlag, Berlin.

Van Lehn, K. (editor) (1990). *Architectures for Intelligence*. Lawrence Erlbaum, Hillsdale.

Van Marcke, K. (1988). The use and implementation of the representation language KRS. *Ph.D. Dissertation*, Free University of Brussels – VUB. VUB AI Lab Technical Report 88 2.

Vanwelkenhuysen, J. and Rademakers, P. (1990). Mapping a knowledge level analysis onto a computational framework. *Proceedings of ECAI-90, Ninth European Conference on Artificial Intelligence, Stockholm, August*, pp. 661–666.

Veloso, M. M. and Carbonell, J. (1993). Derivational analogy in PRODIGY. In *Machine Learning* 10(3): 249–278.

Weintraub, M. (editor) (1992). *Proceedings of the ML92 Workshop on Computational*

Architectures for Machine Learning and Knowledge Acquisition, Aberdeen, Scotland.

Wess, S., Althoff, K-D. and Richter, M. M. (editors) (1994). *Topics in Case-Based Reasoning: Selected Papers from the First European Workshop on Case-Based Reasoning – EWCBR, 1993.* Springer Verlag, Berlin.

Wielinga, B. J., Schreiber, A. Th. and Breuker, J. A. (1992). KADS: A modeling approach to knowledge engineering. *Knowledge Acquisition*, 4(1).

Wielinga, B., Van de Velde, W., Screiber, G. and Akkermans, H. (1993). Towards a unification of knowledge modeling approaches. In David, J.-M., Krivine, J.-P. and Simmons, R. (editors), *Second Generation Expert Systems*, pp. 299–335. Springer Verlag, Berlin.

CHAPTER 9

Learning control knowledge through case-based acquisition of user optimization preferences in ill-structured domains

Katia Sycara and Kazuo Miyashita

Abstract

We have developed a framework of iterative revision integrated with knowledge acquisition and learning to capture context-dependent user preferences and use them for solution optimization in ill-structured domains. The ill-structuredness of both the solution space and the desired objectives make many optimization problems difficult to formalize and costly to solve. In such domains, neither the system nor the human expert possess causal domain knowledge that can be used to guide solution optimization. Current optimization technology requires explicit formulation of a single global optimization criterion to control heuristic search for the optimal solution. Often, however, a user's optimization criteria are subjective, situation dependent, and cannot be expressed in terms of a single global optimization function. We developed the CABINS system, which captures situation-dependent user's preferences in cases along with contextual information. This knowledge is then reused by the system to guide solution revision. During iterative revision of a solution, cases are exploited for multiple purposes, such as revision action selection, revision result evaluation and recovery from revision failures. Our approach was tested in the domain of job shop scheduling. Extensive experimentation on a benchmark suite of job shop scheduling problems has shown that CABINS (1) is capable of acquiring user optimization preferences and trade-offs, (2) can improve its own competence through knowledge refinement, (3) is a flexible schedule optimization methodology that produces high quality schedules,

Machine Learning and Knowledge Acquisition
ISBN 0-12-685120-4

and (4) is robust in that it improves schedule quality irrespective of the method of initial schedule generation.

9.1. Introduction

Many practical problems, such as scheduling and design, belong to ill-structured domains, where optimization is computationally intractable and optimization criteria often involve context- and user-dependent tradeoffs which are impossible to realistically consolidate in a cost function (Simon, 1973). We present a problem-solving computer program called CABINS (CAse-Based INteractive Scheduler), which demonstrates the capability of acquiring user context-dependent optimization preferences and reusing them to guide iterative solution improvement for those problems. This capability is very important for two main reasons:

- Traditional search methods, both OR-based and AI-based, that are used in combinatorial optimization, need explicit representation of objectives in terms of a cost function to be optimized (Reeves, 1993).
- Expert system approaches, while having the potential to capture context-dependent tradeoffs of optimization criteria in the form of rules, require considerable knowledge acquisition effort (Prerau, 1990).

Our approach uses case-based reasoning (CBR) which has the potential for dealing with noisy data (Ruby and Kibler, 1992; Aha *et al.*, 1991), acquiring user knowledge in complex domains (Chaturvedi, 1993; Mckay *et al.*, 1988), and expending less effort in knowledge acquisition compared with knowledge acquisition for rule-based systems (Simoudis and Miller, 1991; Lewis *et al.*, 1991). The optimization method utilized in CABINS is iterative revision of a complete but suboptimal solution. Revision actions are applied to the current solution and the result is evaluated according to user preferences.

9.1.1 Case-based reasoning

Case-based reasoning (CBR) is the problem-solving paradigm where previous experiences are used to guide problem solving (Kolodner *et al.*, 1985; Hammond, 1989; Sycara, 1987). Cases similar to the current problem are retrieved from memory according to a similarity metric, the best case is selected from those retrieved and compared to the current problem. If needed, the precedent case is adapted to fit the current situation based on identified differences between the precedent and the current cases. Successful cases are stored in the case base so that they can be retrieved and reused in the future. Failed cases are also stored so that they can warn the problem solver of potential difficulties and help recover from failures. If a current case has features similar to a past failure, then the problem solver is warned not to attempt the past solution. Instead, if there is a repair for the past failure already stored in memory, the problem solver can try that successful repair. After a problem is solved, the case base is updated with the new experience. Thus, *learning is an integral part of case-based problem solving.*

Knowledge acquisition is different for CBR than for rule-based systems since the knowledge a CBR system operates on is in the form of cases rather than rules. In comparison to other knowledge acquisition and learning paradigms, CBR has a number of practically desirable features which encourage CBR applications in many domains. Acquiring knowledge from experts in the form of rules is a notoriously difficult and lengthy process (Buchanan and Wilkins, 1993). On the other hand, because cases express particular experiences, they are a better "cognitive match" for the expert in the sense that it is easier for experts to solve the problem case (drawing from their experience with other similar cases) rather than try to abstract the particulars of one or more problem cases in order to formulate a rule. Hence, CBR has been considered as a more natural and less time-consuming method of knowledge acquisition (Lewis *et al.*, 1991). Since both successes and failures are recorded in the case base, each additional case helps refine and reformulate the knowledge in the case base. This is done without additional computational overhead, such as duplication/contradiction checks required for rule additions, since each case is a "package of knowledge" that is independent of the other cases in the case base. On the other hand, while the refined or reformulated knowledge is explicitly captured in rule-based systems, in CBR the refined knowledge is implicit and is extensionally stored in the case base.

One of the most important differences of CBR as compared with rule-based knowledge acquisition and system operation is that, since a rule-based system will usually give meaningful performance only after a sufficient amount of the relevant rules are collected, the lengthy process of knowledge acquisition has to precede the practical system operation. In traditional rule-based knowledge acquisition, the user has to invest time to provide the knowledge to the rule-based system without getting useful problem-solving advice from it. Since *during routine system operation* CBR acquires knowledge incrementally by collecting the cases and can give a user some support even with a very limited number of cases, case-based knowledge acquisition can save the user significant overhead.

It should be noted, however, that CBR is not a panacea that obviates any overhead associated with knowledge acquisition. It defines new types of knowledge acquisition tasks, i.e., definition of appropriate indices and a similarity metric for case retrieval. Most often, however, the acquisition of these types of knowledge is simpler than acquiring rules. We believe this to be true for the following reasons. First, a rule effects a mapping from features of a situation to an outcome action whereas case indexing and similarity pertains only to situations. Second, superfluous features, albeit taking up storage space, do not affect the accuracy of the system's performance. They can be weeded out, if desired, as the system operation is monitored. In other words, CBR is a more forgiving knowledge acquisition method tolerating noisy data quite well. In terms of practical issues, because of its capability for partial matching, a CBR system can give potentially useful advice even if it has only an initial small set of cases in the case base. In this way, knowledge acquisition and reuse of the learned knowledge is effected smoothly and non-intrusively.

9.1.2 General characterization of the CABINS system

CABINS acquires, stores and reuses two categories of concepts that reflect user preferences: (1) what heuristic local optimization action to choose in a particular context, and (2) what combinations of effects of application of a particular local optimization action constitute an acceptable or unacceptable outcome. These concepts are recorded in the case base and are used by CABINS to guide iterative optimization and infer from the case base optimization tradeoffs in evaluating the current solution. In this way, the acquired knowledge is exploited to enhance the incomplete domain model in CABINS and improve efficiency of problem solving and quality of resulting solutions according to user preferences. The optimization criteria are not explicitly represented as case features or in terms of a cost function but are implicitly and extensionally represented in the case base.

In contrast to case-based knowledge acquisition systems, such as PROTOS (Bareiss, 1989), where the program requires causal explanations from an expert teacher to acquire domain knowledge, in our approach neither the user nor the program are assumed to possess causal domain knowledge. The user cannot give a solid explanation as to his or her selection of a revision action, because of not being able to predict the effects of the selected action on the solution. In other words, the user does not have *control knowledge* to guide a solution repair process. The user's expertise lies in his or her ability to perform consistent evaluation of the results of problem solving and impart to the program cases of problem-solving experiences and histories of evaluation tradeoffs.

CABINS has been evaluated in the domain of iterative optimization of job shop schedules (Miyashita and Sycara, 1994). In contrast to approaches that utilize a single repair heuristic (Minton *et al.*, 1990) or use a statically predetermined model for selection of repair actions (Ow *et al.*, 1988) in scheduling, our approach utilizes a repair model that is incrementally learned and encoded in the case base. Learning allows dynamic switching of repair heuristics depending on the repair context. In Zweben *et al.* (1992) plausible explanation-based learning has been successfully used to learn schedule repair control rules for system speed-up. Experimental results reported in Miyashita and Sycara (1993) show that keeping the case base rather than inducing rules from it and then utilizing these rules for problem solving results in superior performance.

In this chapter, we present initial experimental results to test the following hypotheses. First, our CBR-based incremental revision methodology shows good potential for capturing user optimization preferences in ill-structured domains, such as job shop scheduling, and reusing them to guide optimization. Second, the method is robust in the sense that it improves schedule quality independent of the method of initial schedule generation. Third, CABINS can learn control knowledge and improve its own competence through knowledge refinement. Fourth, CABINS produces schedules of high quality as compared with other schedule optimization techniques. To test the last hypothesis, we compared the schedules produced by CABINS with explicit optimization criteria, with schedules produced by Simulated Annealing (SA), a well known iterative optimization technique, for the same criteria. The experimental results, shown in this chapter, confirmed these hypotheses.

The rest of the chapter is organized as follows. Section 9.2 presents characteristics and challenges of the job shop scheduling domain. Section 9.3 presents the anatomy of the CABINS approach. Section 9.4 describes the experimentation method and presents results. Section 9.5 presents additional experimental results to address the issue of what is an effective case size. Section 9.6 presents concluding remarks.

9.2. The problem domain

Scheduling assigns a set of tasks over time to a set of resources with finite capacity. One of the most difficult scheduling problem classes is job shop scheduling. In job shop scheduling, each task (from now on to be called a job or an order) consists of a set of activities to be scheduled in a partial activity ordering that must be determined by the scheduling system so that the problem constraints are not violated. The dominant constraints in job shop scheduling are: temporal precedence constraints that specify the relative sequencing of activities within a job over time and resource capacity constraints that restrict the number of activities that can be assigned to a resource during overlapping time intervals.

The activity temporal precedence constraints along with a job's release date and due date restrict the set of acceptable start times for each activity. The capacity constraints restrict the number of activities that can use a resource at any particular point in time and create conflicts among activities that are competing for the use of the same resource at overlapping time intervals. The goal of a scheduling system is to produce schedules that respect temporal precedence and resource capacity constraints, and optimize a set of objectives, such as minimize tardiness, maximize resource utilization, etc.

Job shop schedule optimization has been very difficult to automate for a variety of reasons as follows:

- It is one of the most difficult NP-hard combinatorial optimization problems (French, 1982).
- The evaluation itself of what is a "high quality" schedule is difficult because of the need to balance conflicting objectives and tradeoffs among them. For example, work-in-process inventory (WIP) and weighted tardiness, two of the

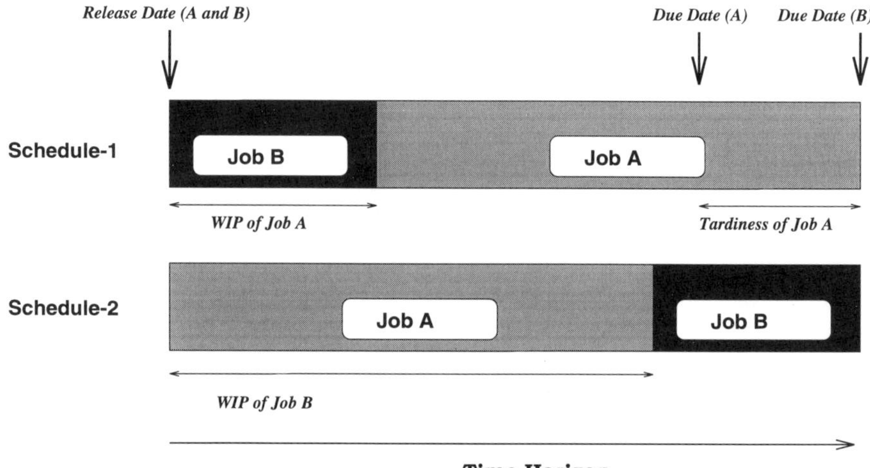

Figure 9.1 Example of conflicting objectives

most common optimization objectives, are not always compatible with each other. WIP is a function of the time an activity waits in the factory before it is processed. In order to reduce the cost of keeping such inventories, WIP needs to be minimized. Weighted tardiness is the tardiness of a job weighted according to the job's priority. To avoid penalties from the clients of the job, weighed tardiness must also be minimized. But, as shown in Figure 9.1, there are situations where a repair action has the effect of reducing weighted tardiness, but increasing WIP. Therefore, whether Schedule-1 or Schedule-2 in Figure 9.1 is of higher quality depends on the user's preferred tradeoff between WIP and weighted tardiness.

- Due to the tight interactions among scheduling constraints and the often conflicting nature of optimization criteria, it is impossible to assess with any precision the extent of schedule revision or the impact of a scheduling decision on the global satisfaction of optimization criteria. For example, suppose in Figure 9.2 ORDER3 is tardy. To repair the tardiness, a human scheduler may move forward the last activity of ORDER3 to make the order finish earlier. Then, since the slack in Machine1 is smaller than the duration of the moved activity, the move causes a capacity constraint violation on Machine1. Because of tight constraint interaction among activities and resources, this constraint violation is propagated downward the schedule to create downstream cascading constraint violations as is shown in the figure. Thus, any small action in a schedule may change the entire schedule drastically. Therefore, the only way for a user or a system to evaluate the desirability of a scheduling action and assess its effects on his/her/its optimization preferences is to apply the action to

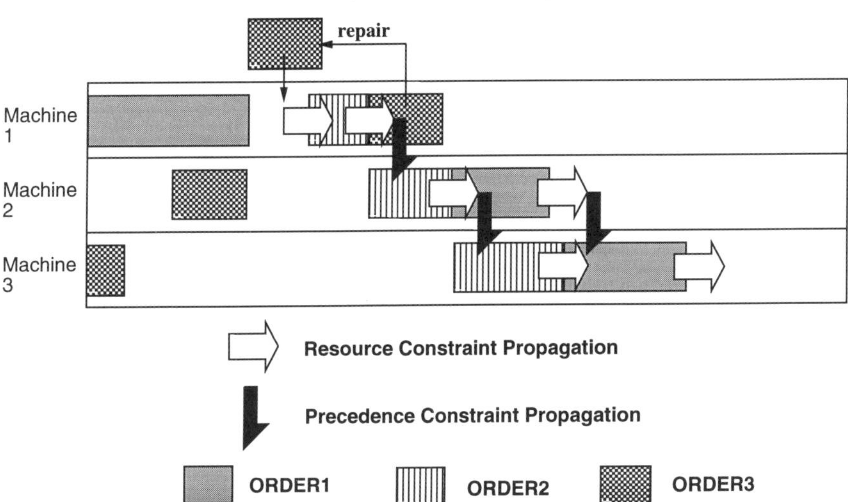

Figure 9.2 Example of tight constraint interactions

the problem, see the resulting schedule and evaluate it in light of the evaluation preferences.

- Scheduling cannot be realistically treated as a static optimization problem of generating a predictive schedule that is assumed to be executed without any deviations. In practice, due to the presence of uncertainty in the execution environment unexpected events, both serendipitous, such as activities finishing earlier than predicted, and harmful, such as loss of available resource capacity and activity delays, necessitate solution change. CABINS utilizes the same methodology to acquire user optimization preferences for both quality improvement of a predictive schedule and also for reactive schedule repair. We have reported results on reactive schedule repair in Sycara and Miyashita (1994).

A crucial point for schedule optimization in practice is that user preferences could be implicit and context-dependent (e.g., may depend on the state of the scheduling environment at a particular time). Also, interactions among preferences and effective tradeoffs very often depend on the particular schedule produced. This means that generally a user of the scheduling system cannot fully specify his or her preferences a priori before getting the scheduling results from the system. By looking over the obtained schedule results, the user often thinks of additional preferences. Consider, for example, a situation where a human scheduler does not like to use MACHINE-A which is substitutable for MACHINE-B but is of lower quality than MACHINE-B for processing ORDER-X. The reason high quality results are desired is that ORDER-X belongs to a very important client. Suppose, however, that the schedule indicates that ORDER-X is tardy by an amount above an acceptable tardiness threshold due to demands on MACHINE-B (by orders more important than ORDER-X). Then the human scheduler may decide to use the less preferable machine, MACHINE-A. If the tardiness was below the threshold, he or she may prefer to allow a tardy order. It is very difficult to elicit this type of preference and preference thresholds from the human scheduler in the absence of a particular scheduling context. A case-based, interactive knowledge acquisition methodology is well suited for eliciting such context-dependent user preferences.

Moreover, it is impossible for any given knowledge-based scheduling model to include all the constraints that may be relevant. Current advanced scheduling systems can exploit very complicated models to represent the factory, jobs and user's preferences. But no matter how richly the model is constructed, there are always additional factors which may influence the schedule but had not been represented in the model. For example, for a certain foundry it may be good to decrease usage of a sand casting machine during the summer, because the combination of heat and humidity of the weather may make it slower than usual. But how should the model of the scheduling system represent the season, weather or humidity? And isn't it necessary for the model to represent time of the day, strength of wind or health of a machine operator and so on (Mckay *et al.*, 1988)? Nevertheless these factors, that an experienced human scheduler learns to take into consideration, could have a big influence on schedule quality but it is very difficult to represent in a principled manner so they can be used by an automated scheduling system.

The above characteristics of the job shop schedule optimization task, and the demands of the knowledge acquisition task in that domain, make it clear that (a) an iterative schedule revision optimization technique would be most suitable, and (b) recording the user's judgements in a case-base is an effective and flexible way of eliciting user optimization preferences.

CABINS *incrementally revises a complete but sub-optimal schedule* to improve its quality. Revision-based approaches to scheduling have also been investigated by Minton *et al.* (1990), Zweben *et al.* (1990), Biefeld and Cooper (1991) and Laarhoven *et al.* (1992). In those systems, the initial schedule is repaired by several techniques, such as the min-conflict heuristic or simulated annealing, to minimize the number of constraint violations or optimize a simple cost function (e.g. make-span) of the schedule. The value of incorporating context-dependent user preferences in operational scheduling environments is becoming increasingly recognized (e.g. Mckay *et al.*, 1988) but adequate techniques are lacking.

In this chapter we experimentally demonstrate that in a domain where neither the human expert nor the program possess domain causal knowledge, such as job shop scheduling, control knowledge can be acquired through past cases to improve the efficiency of rather costly iterative optimization process while preserving the quality of results.

9.3 CABINS overview

CABINS is a unified framework for knowledge acquisition of user optimization preferences that can be learned and used as control knowledge to guide scheduling decisions during predictive schedule generation and reactive schedule management in response to unpredictable execution events. CABINS can be used in the following modes:

- **Knowledge acquisition interactive** mode to acquire user preferences and generate the case base.
- **Decision-support interactive** mode where the previously acquired case base that incorporates user preferences suggests revision actions and evaluation outcomes to the user who can accept a suggestion or override it with a new suggestion.
- **Automatic** mode where previously acquired user preferences are reused to guide scheduling decisions without any interaction with the user.

9.3.1 Architecture

Figure 9.3 depicts the overall architecture of CABINS. CABINS is composed of three modules: (1) an initial schedule builder, (2) an interactive schedule repair (case acquisition) module and (3) an automated schedule repair (case reuse) module.

To generate an initial schedule, CABINS can use one of several scheduling methods including traditional dispatching rules (Morton and Pentico, 1993) and constraint-based search (Fox *et al.*, 1989). CABINS starts with an empty case base and through interaction with a user, it gathers the following relevant information in the form of cases:

- A suggestion of which repair heuristic to apply: a user's decision on what repair heuristic to be applied to a given schedule for quality improvement.
- An evaluation of a repair result: a user's overall evaluation of a modification result.
- An explanation of an evaluation: when a user evaluates the modification result as unacceptable, he or she indicates the set of undesirable effects that have been produced. The explanation given to CABINS consists of the numerical rating of each identified effect.

Our basic assumption on knowledge acquisition through CBR is that, in spite of ill-structuredness of the problem, the following three types of domain knowledge are available and constitute useful case features:

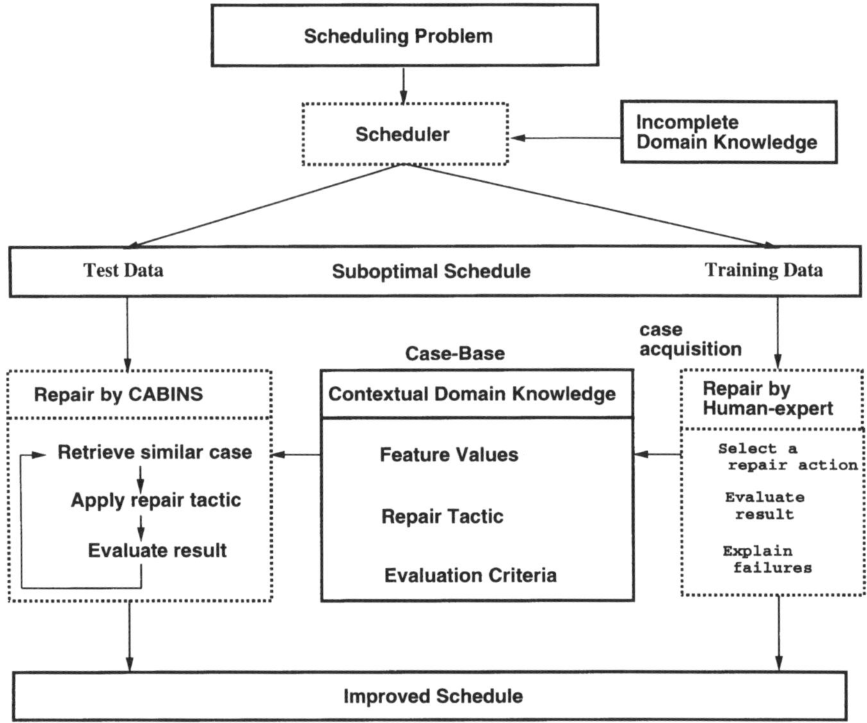

Figure 9.3 CABINS architecture

- Repair tactics: a set of local patching heuristics that can be applied to a schedule.
- Descriptive features: attributes of a schedule that describe a particular scheduling situation and might be useful in estimating the effects of applying repair heuristics to the schedule. These features will be described in detail in Section 9.3.2.
- Evaluation criteria: quantification of different aspects of the effects of applying repair heuristics to the schedule. The degree of importance of these criteria is in general user- and state-dependent.

9.3.2 Case representation

In each repair iteration, CABINS focuses randomly on one activity at a time, the *focal_activity*, and tries to repair it. *A case in CABINS describes the application of a particular modification to a focal_activity.* Figure 9.4 shows the information

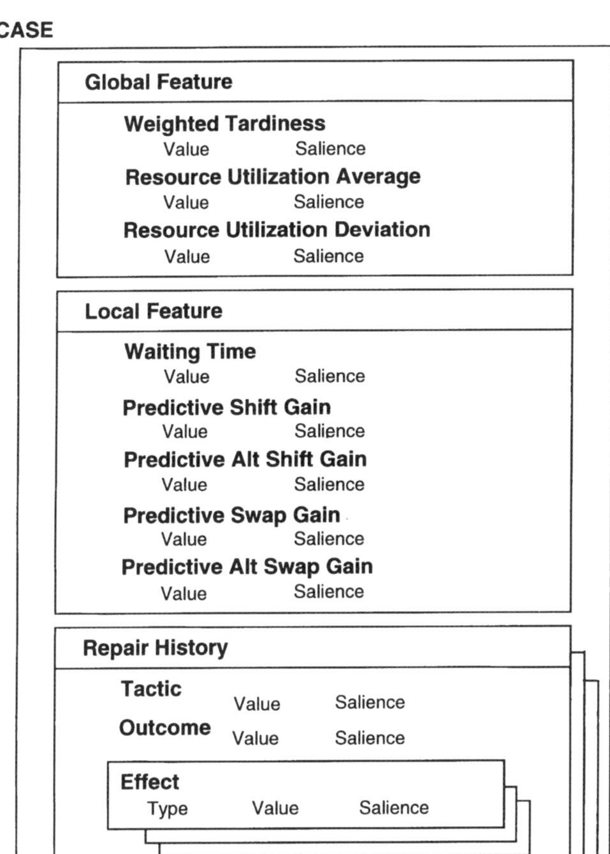

Figure 9.4 CABINS case representation

content of a case. The global features reflect an abstract characterization of potential repair flexibility for the whole schedule. High "Resource Utilization Average", for example, often indicates a tight schedule without much repair flexibility.

Associated with a focal_activity are local features that we have identified and which potentially are predictive of the effectiveness of applying a particular repair tactic. These features are local because they pertain, not to the schedule as a whole but to the application of one revision tactic to one activity within a neighborhood of the activity under repair. This locality is called the *repair time horizon*. In the current implementation, the repair time horizon of a focal_activity

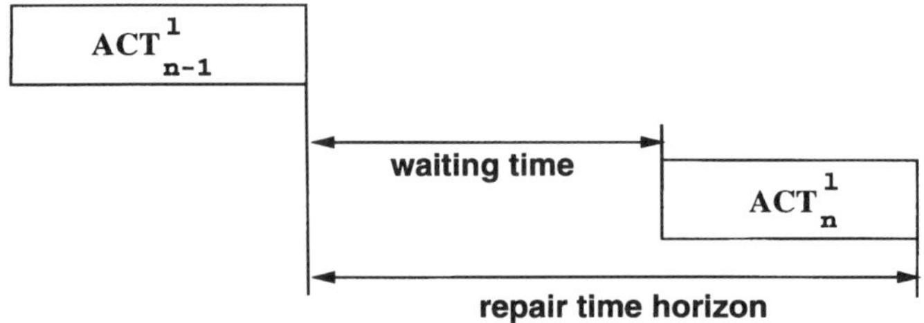

Figure 9.5 Repair time horizon of focal-activity (ACT^1_n)

is the time interval between the end of the activity preceding the focal_activity in the same focal_job and the end of the focal_activity (see Figure 9.5). The *waiting time* of a focal_activity is the time interval between the end of the activity that precedes the focal_activity in the same job and the start-time of the focal_activity. *Predictive shift gain* predicts how much overall gain will be achieved by moving the current focal_activity earlier on its time horizon. In particular it predicts the likely reduction of the focal_activity's waiting time when moved to the left on the same resource within the repair time horizon. *Predictive alt shift gain* predicts the likely reduction of the focal_activity's waiting time when moved to the left on a substitutable resource within the repair time horizon. *Predictive swap gain* predicts the amount of likely difference between the reduction of the focal_activity's waiting time and the increase of a swapped activity's waiting time when the focal_activity is swapped within the repair time horizon on the focal_activity's resource. *Predictive alt swap gain* predicts the corresponding likely difference when the focal_activity is swapped within the repair time horizon on the focal_activity's substitutable resources. Because of the ill-structuredness of job shop scheduling, local and global features are heuristic approximations that reflect problem space characteristics.

Currently CABINS has 11 revision tactics, including:

- left_shift: try to move the focal_activity on the same resource as much to the left on the timeline as possible within the repair time horizon, so as to minimize the amount of capacity overallocation created by the move.
- left_shift_into_alt: try to move the focal_activity on a substitutable resource as much to the left on the timeline as possible within the repair time horizon, so as to minimize the amount of capacity overallocation created by the move.
- swap: swap the focal_activity with the activity on the same resource within the repair time horizon which causes the least amount of precedence constraint violations.
- swap_into_alt: swap the focal_activity with the activity of a substitutable resource as much to the right on the timeline as possible within the repair time horizon, while preserving the sequence of all activities.
- give_up: give up further repair for the current focal_activity.

CABINS has an interface that allows definition of additional revision tactics. Application of a repair action may cause constraint violations. These are identified by CABINS, their effects are propagated and any resulting constraint violations are resolved by constraint satisfaction (Sadeh and Fox, 1990).

The repair history records the sequence of applications of successive repair actions, the repair outcome and the effects. Repair effect values describe the impact of the application of a repair action on scheduling objectives (e.g., weighted tardiness, WIP). A repair outcome is the evaluation assigned by a user to the set of effects of a repair action and takes values in the set ["acceptable", "unacceptable"]. An outcome is "acceptable" if the user accepts the tradeoffs involved in the set of effects for the current application of a repair action. Otherwise, it is "unacceptable". The effect salience (Figure 9.4) is assigned when the outcome is "unacceptable", and indicates the significance of the effect to the repair outcome. This value is decided by a domain expert subjectively and interactively. The user's judgement as to balancing favorable and unfavorable effects related to a particular objective constitute the explanations of the repair outcome.

9.3.3 Case acquisition

To gather enough cases, sample scheduling problems are solved by a scheduler. CABINS identifies jobs that must be repaired in the initial sub-optimal schedule. The user selects a repair tactic to be applied. Tactic application consists of two parts: (a) identify the activities, resources and time intervals that will be involved in the repair, and (b) execute the repair by applying constraint-based scheduling to reschedule the activities identified in (a).

After tactic selection and application, the repair effects are calculated and shown to the user who is asked to evaluate the outcome of the repair. For example, repair of the current focal_activity may decrease WIP by 200 units and decrease weighted tardiness of the focal-order by 180 units while at the same time increasing weighted tardiness of another order by 130 units and increasing WIP by 300 units. If the user evaluates the repair outcome as "acceptable", CABINS proceeds to repair another focal_activity and the process is repeated. If the user evaluates the repair outcome as "unacceptable", he or she is asked to supply an explanation in terms of rating the salience/importance of each of the effects. The repair is undone and the user is asked to select another repair tactic for the same focal_activity. The process continues until an acceptable outcome for the current focal_activity is reached, or the repair is given up. Repair is given up when there are no more tactics to be applied to the current focal_activity. When repair of the current focal_activity is given up, CABINS carries on repair of another activity. The sequence of applications of successive repair actions, the effects, the repair outcome, and the user's explanation for failed application to

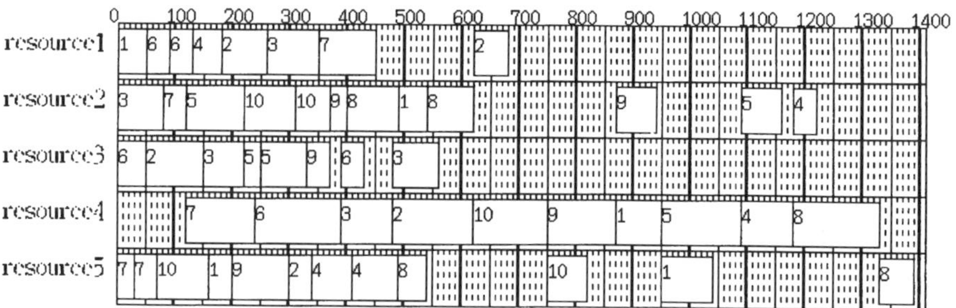

Figure 9.6 Original schedule results

repair one focal_activity are recorded in the repair history of a single case. In this way, a number of cases are accumulated in the case base.

9.3.4 Case retrieval and reuse

Once enough cases have been gathered, CABINS repairs sub-optimal schedules without user interaction. CABINS repairs the schedules by (1) focusing randomly on a focal_activity to be repaired in each repair cycle, (2) invoking CBR with global and local features as indices to decide the most appropriate repair tactic to be used for each focal_activity, (3) applying the selected repair tactic, (4) invoking CBR using the repair effect features (type, value and salience) as indices to evaluate the repair result, and (5) when the repair result seems unacceptable, deciding whether to give up or which repair tactic to use next. Experiments of using different indexing schema in case of failure are described in the following section.

In CABINS concepts are defined extensionally by a collection of cases. Due to characteristic of the current implementation as a research prototype, case memory structure in CABINS is a linear list, which is less efficient in case retrieval than other more sophisticated organizational structures such as a discrimination network. The similarity between the ith case and the current problem is calculated as follows:

$$\exp\left(-\sqrt{\sum_{j=1}^{N}\left(SL_j^i \times \frac{CF_j^i - PF_j}{E\_D_j}\right)^2}\right)$$

where SL_j^i is the salience of the jth feature of the ith case in the case base, and its value has been heuristically defined by the user. CF_j^i is the value of the jth feature of the ith case, PF_j is the value of the jth feature in the current problem, E_D_j is the standard deviation of the jth feature value of all cases in the case-base. Feature values are normalized by division by a standard deviation of the feature value so that features of equal salience have equal weight in the similarity function.

9.3.5 An example of CABINS repair process

We briefly illustrate the repair process with a very simple example schedule to be repaired shown in Figure 9.6. The example has ten jobs ($J_1, \ldots, J_{10}$) and each job has five activities with linear precedence constraints (e.g. O_1^n BEFORE $O_2^n, \ldots,$ O_4^n BEFORE O_5^n). Resources R_1 and R_2, R_3 and R_5 are substitutable; resource R_4 is a bottleneck. Suppose that the job under repair is J_8. This job has a weight of 2, a due date of 1250 and the scheduled end-time of its last activity is 1390. Hence it has a weighted tardiness of $2 \times (1390 - 1250) = 280$. Suppose the current focal_activity is O_4^8. CBR is invoked with global features ("Weighted Tardiness" = 280, "Resource Utilization Average" = 0.544, "Resource Utilization Deviation" = 0.032) plus the set of local features as indices and selects swap as a repair tactic. One can see from the figure that this is a good choice since the focal_activity is scheduled on machine R_4, which does not have any substitutable machine and any idle time in the repair time horizon (time between the end of O_3^8 and the end of O_4^8).

The swap repair tactic roughly calculates the effects of swapping the current focal_activity with each activity within the current focal_activity's time horizon and selects the activity that gives the biggest net gain (note that swapping an activity that is scheduled earlier with one that is scheduled later will now delay the earlier activity). In the example, suppose that activity O_4^4 is selected as the activity to be swapped with the current focal_activity O_4^8. The effect of applying the swap tactic is that O_4^8 and O_4^4 are unscheduled on R_4 and O_4^8 is rescheduled to start at time 1090 (the start time of activity O_4^4 prior to the swap) and O_4^4 is moved to start at time 1180 (the start time of activity O_4^8 prior to the swap). Because the new assignments of two activities overlap each other, constraint propagation is invoked and the assignment of O_4^4 is further delayed. Due to the delay of activity O_4^4, now there is the ripple effect of a precedence constraint violation between activity O_4^4 and its successor activity O_5^4 on resource R_2 (in general, many activities could be affected and must be rescheduled). Constraint propagation discovers this constraint conflict and shifts activity O_5^4 further to the right on resource R_2. Since Job J_4 has weight 3, its weighted tardiness is now $3 \times (1370 - 1320) = 150$. The repaired schedule result is shown in Figure 9.7.

CABINS calculates both local effects (i.e., effects on the repair target, J_8) and global effects (i.e., effects on the whole schedule) for result evaluation. In this example, "local_weighted_tardiness" is estimated as +180 time units and "local_inprocess_inventory" is estimated as +200 units, both being improved by the change of O_4^8. And "global_weighted_tardiness" is +30 units (i.e., $180 - 150$) and "global_inprocess_inventory" is -750 units (as the waiting time in J_4 increases by 950 units). CBR is invoked using these effect values as indices to

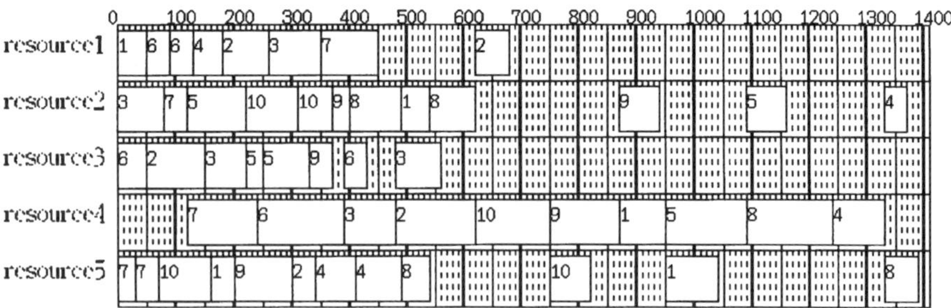

Figure 9.7 Schedule results after the repair on A_4^8

determine whether this repair outcome is acceptable or not. If there are more significant "acceptable" cases than "unacceptable" cases in the retrieved *k*-nearest neighbors, the repair is considered reflecting the tradeoffs of user's preference (in this example, little weight on "global_inprocess_inventory") and the outcome is considered as acceptable. Otherwise, the outcome is considered as unacceptable, thus showing that loss in "global_inprocess_inventory" is more critical than possible gain in weighted tardiness according to the user's preferences.

9.4. Evaluation of different facets of CABINS

In the following subsections we will describe some of our studies that were conducted to evaluate different dimensions of the CABINS approach. In particular, in this chapter, we report experimental results to evaluate CABINS as a method for: (a) acquiring user optimization preferences and reusing them to guide schedule optimization, (b) learning and refining control knowledge, (c) producing schedules that have high quality, and (d) producing schedules that are robust, in the sense that CABINS improves schedule quality irrespective of the method used for the initial schedule generation. These capabilities are difficult to test since, due to the subjective and ill-defined nature of user preferences, it is not obvious how to correlate scheduling results with the captured preferences or how to define quality of a schedule whose evaluation is subjective.

9.4.1 Experimental design

To address these issues, we had to devise a method to test the hypotheses in a consistent manner. To do that, it is necessary to know the optimization criterion that would be implicit in the case base, so that the experimental results can be evaluated. In the experiments reported here, we used different explicit criteria, i.e., "weighted tardiness" and "WIP+weighted tardiness", to reflect the user's optimization criterion and built a rule-based reasoner (RBR) that goes through a trial-and-error repair process to optimize a schedule. Since the RBR was constructed not to select the same tactic after a tactic's repair of an activity was calculated as unacceptable, it could go through all the tactics before giving up repairing an activity. For each repair, RBR calculated the repair effects and, on this basis, since RBR had a predefined evaluation objective, it could evaluate the repair outcome in a consistent manner. Since RBR knows the exact objective function for evaluation, it can work as an emulator of a human scheduler, who cannot repair a schedule in the most efficient way, but can make consistent evaluations of repair results. Therefore, we used RBR not only for generating the case base for CABINS but also for making a comparison baseline for the CABINS experiments. Thus, RBR was used to generate a case base with 1000 cases for each of the explicit optimization objectives. Naturally, the objective, though known to RBR, is not known to CABINS and is only implicitly and indirectly reflected in an extensional way in each case base. By designing an objective into the RBR so it could be reflected in the case base we obtained an experimental baseline against which to evaluate the schedules generated by CABINS.

We evaluated the approach on a benchmark suite of 60 job shop scheduling problems where parameters, such as number of bottlenecks, range of due dates and activity durations, were varied to cover a range of job shop scheduling problem instances with the following structure. Each problem class has 10 jobs of 5 operations each and 5 machines. Two parameters were used to cover different scheduling conditions: a range parameter controlled the distribution of job due dates and release dates, and a bottleneck parameter controlled the number of bottleneck resources. Six groups of 10 problems each were randomly generated by considering three different values of the range parameter, and two values of the bottleneck configuration (1 and 2 bottleneck problems). Although the problems are relatively small in scale compared with realistic problems in manufacturing, traditional OR approaches such as branch-and-bound method cannot find "optimal" solutions for these problems with given criteria in reasonable time. These problems are variations of the problems originally reported in Sadeh (1991). Our problem sets are, however, different in two respects: (a) we allow substitutable resources for non-bottleneck resources whereas the original problems did not, and (b) the due dates of jobs in our problems are tighter by 20 per cent than in the original problems. To test scalability, we also tested the approach on another set of 60 problems of 20 orders and 5 resources with similar results. For details, see Miyashita and Sycara (to appear).

A cross-validation method was used for evaluating CABINS learning capability. Each problem set in each class was divided in half. The training sample was repaired by RBR to gather cases. These cases were then used for case-based repair of the validation problems. We repeated the above process by interchanging the training and test sets. Reported results are for the validation problem sets.

9.4.2 Evaluation of the ability of CABINS to acquire user optimization preferences

We conducted a set of experiments on the benchmark suite of 60 scheduling problems to test the hypothesis that our CBR-based incremental modification and reuse methodology could be effective in acquiring user schedule optimization preferences and reuse them to control schedule optimization. To test this hypothesis, we used RBR with two different rule bases, one to reflect preference for repairs that minimize weighted tardiness and the second to reflect the more complex criterion of minimizing the combination of weighted tardiness plus WIP. We used these two rule bases to correspondingly acquire two case bases, one to reflect weighted tardiness and the other to reflect WIP+weighted tardiness.

Figure 9.8 shows the performance of CABINS using "weighted tardiness" case base (labelled in the figures as CABINS(WT)) vs. performance of CABINS using the "weighted tardiness and WIP" case base (labelled in the figures as CABINS (WT+WIP)). The cases constituted the only source of knowledge for CABINS. In other words, there was no objective given to CABINS explicitly. The case bases were used both as a source of suitable repairs, and also as a source of advice regarding repair evaluation. From the results we observe that CABINS(WT) generated higher quality schedules with respect to minimizing weighted tardiness than CABINS(WT+WIP). Conversely, CABINS(WT+WIP) generated higher quality schedules with respect to WIP, and weighted tardiness plus WIP than CABINS(WT). These results indicate that CABINS can acquire different and subjective user preferences.

9.4.3 Evaluation of the capability of CABINS to learn and refine control knowledge

In job shop schedule revision, we do not know how many different features are necessary to precisely predict the most successful tactic to be applied. But, since scheduling constraints are tightly interconnected, the necessary number of features for fully representing a problem must be very large. Therefore, the number of features in the current case representation could be insufficient. But we should keep the number of features moderate, because if a case has a large number of features, the number of cases required for training increases drastically (i.e., dimensionality problem). Therefore, with a moderate number of features and training cases, the system cannot avoid making some wrong predictions. To compensate for the lack of a large number of case descriptive features, failure experiences can be used to derive useful information to improve predictive accuracy.

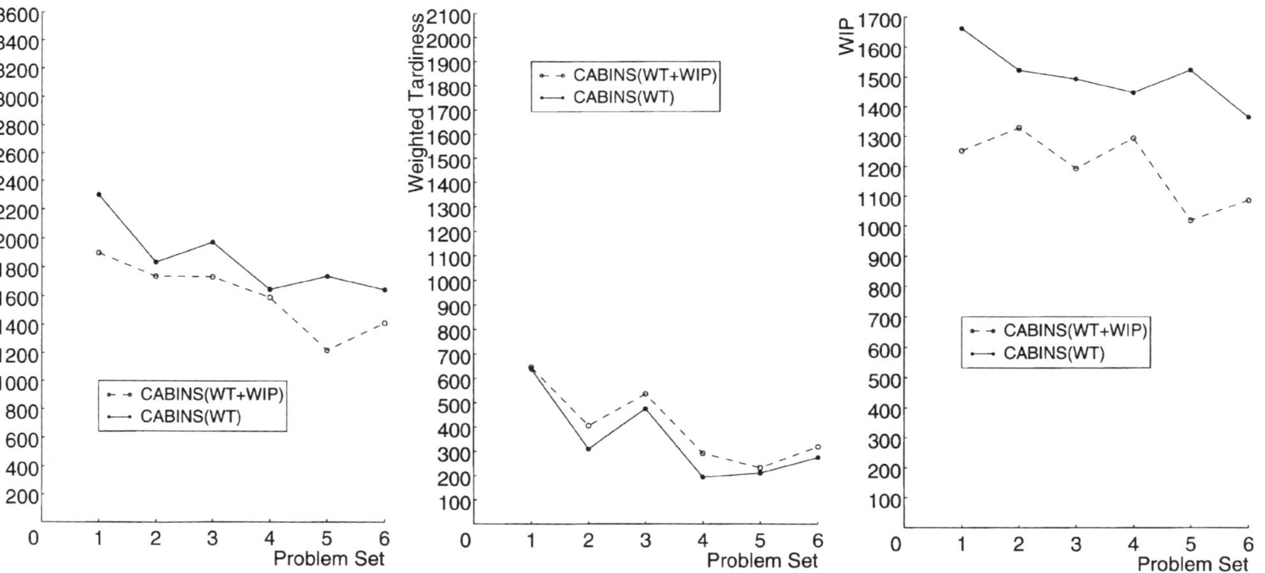

Figure 9.8 Scheduling results with different case bases

Our hypothesis is that CBR enables CABINS to (1) learn a control model of repair action selection from cases that are created from superficial rules and (2) refine its learned knowledge and thus improve its competence both in repair quality and efficiency by utilizing failure information recorded in the cases. To analyse the correctness of our hypothesis, we divided cases into three categories: *immediate success* cases where the first application of a repair tactic was evaluated as success, *eventual success* cases where a focal_activity was repaired after several failed tactic applications, and *failure* cases where a focal_activity could not be repaired. We experimentally implemented the following three repair strategies: *one-shot repair*, *exhaustive repair* and *limited exhaustive repair*.

In one-shot repair, CABINS selects a repair tactic by retrieving the most similar immediate success cases, applies it to a focal_activity and proceeds to repair the next focal_activity regardless of repair outcome.

In exhaustive repair, CABINS selects a repair tactic and applies it to repair a focal_activity. If the repair outcome is deemed either unacceptable or infeasible, another tactic is selected from eventual success cases to repair the same focal_activity, using as indices global and local case features, the failed tactic, and the indication of the failed outcome. This process is continued until successful repair is achieved or no other repair tactics remain untried. This CBR invocation retrieves similar past failures of the tactic that were eventually successfully repaired and the tactic that was eventually successful in fixing the past failure. For example, when a repair result is judged as unacceptable after application of the left_shift tactic, another case that has the most similar global and local features is retrieved from eventual success cases where left_shift has failed. The tactic that finally succeeded in repairing the selected case is retrieved and used to repair the current activity. The intuition here is that a similar outcome for the same tactic implies similarity of causal structure between the past and current case. Therefore, the eventually successful tactic of a similar failure can potentially be successful in the current problem.

In limited exhaustive repair, CABINS gives up further repair when it determines that it would be a waste of time. To decide whether to give up further repair, failure cases are utilized in conjunction with immediate success cases and eventual success cases to determine case similarity. If the most similar case is a failure, CABINS gives up repair of the current focal_activity, and switches its attention to another focal_activity. Since, in difficult problems, such as schedule repair, failures usually outnumber successes, if both case types are weighted equally, overly pessimistic results could be produced (i.e., CBR suggests giving up too often). To avoid this, we bias (negatively) the use of failure cases by placing a threshold[1] on the similarity value. Failure experiences whose similarity to the current problem is below this threshold are ignored in similarity calculations. Since the similarity metric selects the tactic which maximizes the sum of

[1] Currently its values is heuristically fixed as 0.75.

the most similar k (in current implementation $k = 5$) cases, this biases tactic selection in favor of success cases which are moderately similar to the current problem.

The graphs in Figure 9.9 show comparative results with respect to schedule quality improvement (weighted tardiness) and repair efficiency (in CPU secs) among limited exhaustive repair, exhaustive repair, one-shot repair and rule-based repair, which is an emulation of repair by a human scheduler. The results show that one-shot repair is the worst in quality (even compared with rule-based repair) but best in efficiency. Exhaustive repair outperformed one-shot repair and rule-based repair in quality. But, the efficiency of exhaustive repair was worse than that of one-shot repair or rule-based repair. We attribute the increase in CPU time for exhaustive repair to two reasons: (1) greediness – exhaustive repair applies the tactic from the most similar success cases no matter how small their similarity is, and (2) stubbornness – exhaustive repair continues to repair the current focal_activity without giving up when the problem seems difficult.

The quality of repairs by limited exhaustive repair is only slightly worse than that by exhaustive repair, but is still comparable to that of rule-based repair. The efficiency of limited exhaustive repair is much higher than both rule-based repair and exhaustive repair. Although the efficiency of limited exhaustive repair is comparable to that of one-shot repair, the quality of repairs by limited exhaustive repair is much better than that of one-shot repair. One potential reason for these results is that, as described in Section 9.2, the effects of schedule repair are pretty unpredictable and there is a good chance that another application of repair tactic may make the problem, which once seemed difficult, easier by changing the existing schedule fundamentally so that we can go back to the problem afterwards and repair it without wasting much effort. With respect to repair quality, we can observe the following: (1) immediate success cases alone do not have enough information to induce a complicated causal model of schedule repair process, and (2) prediction accuracy of repair tactic selection can be improved by using information about failed application of a repair tactic as additional index feature.

9.4.4 Evaluation of CABINS as a revision-based schedule optimization method

In this set of experiments we tested the hypotheses that (1) the approach is robust in that the schedules produced by CABINS consistently improve a schedule independent of the method used for initial schedule generation and (2) as an iterative optimization method, the approach produces schedules of high quality.

In order to test the hypothesis that CABINS consistently improves schedule quality independent of the method of initial schedule generation, we generated initial schedules for the benchmark suite of problems using three different dispatch scheduling heuristics – EDD (Earliest Due Date), WSPT (Weighted

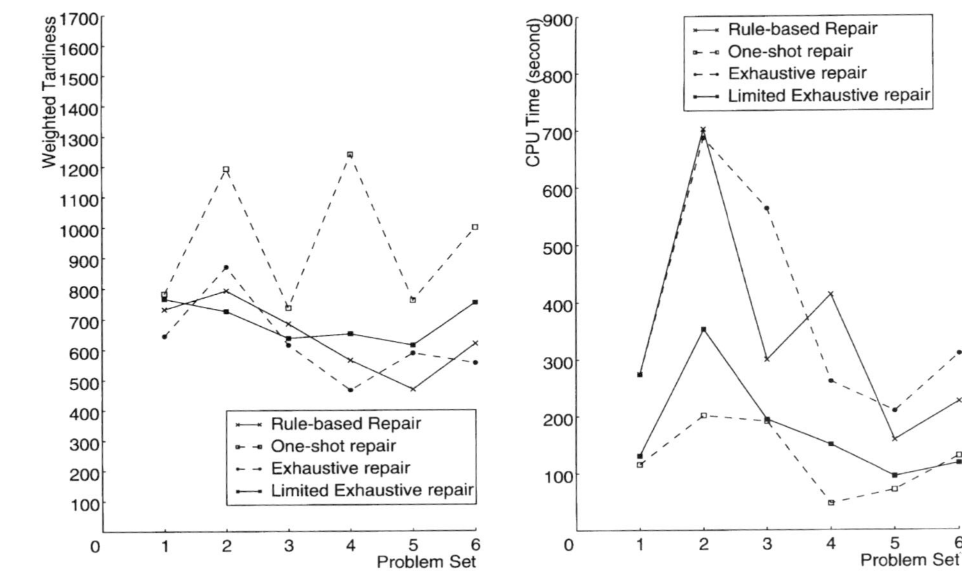

Figure 9.9 Effect of repair strategies in quality and efficiency

Table 9.1 Repair by CABINS and Simulated Annealing (SA) based on different methods of initial schedule generation

	Wei.Tar.	*WIP*	*Total*	*CPU sec.*
Schedule by EDD	956.0	1284.6	2240.6	0.1
Repair by CABINS	349.5	1311.2	1660.7	73.5
Repair by SA	340.5	1333.4	1673.9	388.2
Schedule by WSPT	584.0	1241.0	1825.0	0.1
Repair by CABINS	321.0	1254.9	1575.9	72.1
Repair by SA	328.5	1320.4	1648.9	398.3
Schedule by R&M	556.0	1242.0	1798.0	0.1
Repair by CABINS	305.3	1264.9	1570.2	84.9
Repair by SA	330.1	1290.8	1620.9	450.5
Schedule by CBS	1173.0	1481.0	2654.0	17.4
Repair by CABINS	405.3	1195.0	1600.3	296.5
Repair by SA	395.5	1220.0	1615.5	1380.0

Shortest Processing Time), R&M (WSPT with order time urgency factor (Morton and Pentico, 1993)) – and a constraint-based scheduler (CBS) based upon constraint-based search (Sadeh and Fox, 1990). The optimization objective was WT+WIP. Table 9.1 presents the average of all 60 problems in the benchmark and shows that CABINS improved schedule quality independent of method to create the initial schedule. To test the hypothesis that CABINS generates schedules of high quality, we compared the schedules generated by CABINS with the explicit objective of WT+WIP against schedules generated by Simulated Annealing (SA), a well known iterative optimization scheme (Johnson *et al.*, 1989, 1991; Zweben *et al.*, 1990; Laarhoven *et al.*, 1992). Table 9.1 shows that CABINS generated schedules of comparable quality but was on the average 4–5 times more efficient than simulated annealing.

9.5. How many cases are "enough"?

The graphs in Figure 9.10 show the comparison of CABINS' performance with different sized case bases. The results were obtained based on CABINS with WT+WIP type of case bases. The initial schedule generation method is CBS. From the viewpoint of knowledge acquisition, an interesting question is when knowledge acquisition can be terminated because sufficient knowledge has been acquired to enable high quality performance of a knowledge-based system. For case-based knowledge acquisition, this question becomes how many cases would

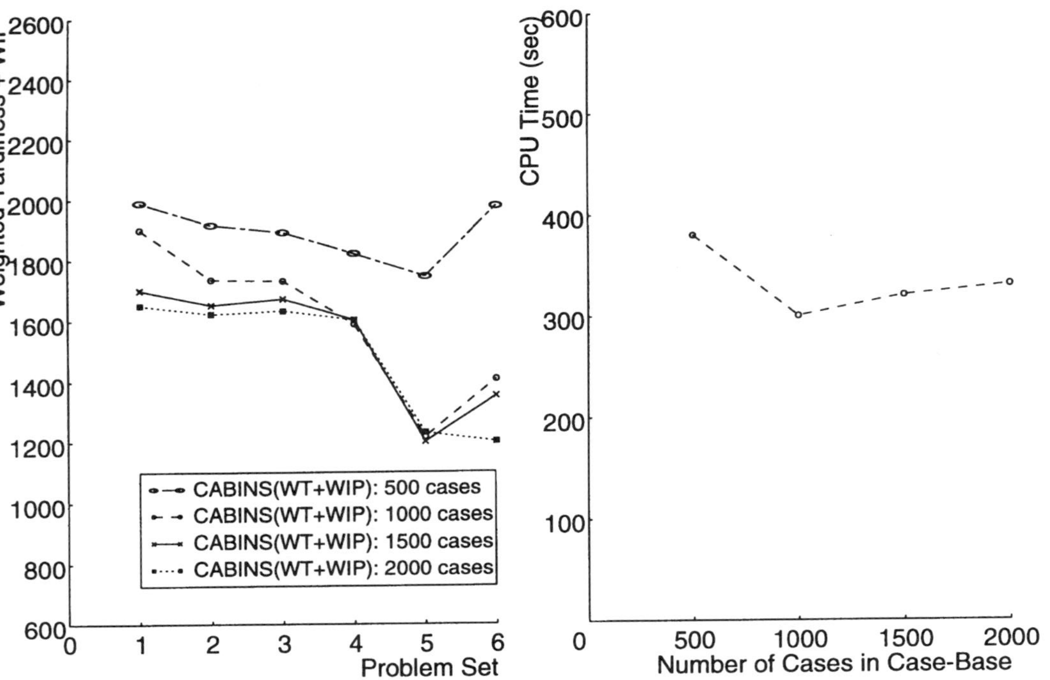

Figure 9.10 Effect of case-base sizes in quality and efficiency

be enough for knowledge capture and reuse and for guaranteeing overall satisfactory performance. Unfortunately, it is very difficult to answer this question in general due to the ill-structuredness of the scheduling problem and the approximate nature of CBR (since no causal model is available). We believe, however, that there exists some appropriate size of the case base which will give us relatively satisfactory results in terms of schedule quality without excessive overhead for case acquisition or case retrieval from the case base. Our experimental results (Figure 9.10) support this hypothesis as follows.

1. The larger the number of cases, the better the schedule quality. However, the marginal payoff from the increase in case-base size decreases. This can be explained partially by the fact that some number of cases (say, 1000 cases) captures well characteristics of the problem space, and an additional 1000 new cases may give much redundant information. When the size of the case base is relatively small, every time new cases are acquired, we may get information about a different part of the problem space which results in higher quality improvement.
2. In terms of efficiency of the system, we observe from the graphs that the case base with 1000 cases might be the optimal choice. Actually, both in terms of CPU time and quality improvement, the case base with 1000 cases obviously outperforms the case base with 500 cases. Moreover, case bases with more cases than 1000 do not seem to provide a payoff proportional to the case base size increase.

In Veloso and Carbonell (1993) the issue of the tradeoff between optimal case retrieval time interval and search efficiency is discussed in the planning domain. However, the assumptions on which their theoretical analysis was based seem not to hold in an ill-structured domain, such as scheduling. How to theoretically predict the optimal size of case base is still an open research problem and we are currently investigating it.

9.6. Conclusions

We have presented a case-based approach to acquiring user optimization preferences and reuse them to guide iterative solution optimization in ill-structured domains. We experimentally demonstrated the effectiveness of the approach in capturing user preferences and creating efficiently high quality solutions on job shop scheduling problems. More importantly, CABINS can acquire those cases from user's interaction during the process of solution improvement, thus imposing low additional effort on the user but enhancing solution quality.

In addition, we examined various ways of exploiting past repair experiences in an ill-structured domain. Our experimental results show that our methodology can learn and refine revision control knowledge thus improving its own performance by: (1) using a failure experience as a contextual index of the problem, and (2) trading off the use of success and failure cases depending on the context in which a repair tactic is applied. This use of CBR in the space of failures is a domain-independent method of acquiring and refining control knowledge that allows the problem solver to improve its efficiency while preserving solution quality in domains without strong domain knowledge. We believe the CABINS approach can be effectively applied to a wide range of problems, such as layout design and personal calendar management (Dent *et al.*, 1992).

As an extension of the current research, we have performed initial experiments that demonstrated the ability of CABINS to acquire and reuse user preferences that change dynamically (Sycara *et al.*, 1995). We are now pursuing integration of knowledge acquisition techniques such as knowledge-level modelling and ontologies (Chandrasekaran *et al.*, 1992; Mizoguchi, 1993) and case-based learning in the framework of the CABINS system (Miyashita *et al.*, 1994). We believe this line of research is most promising for further reducing the burdens of constructing and improving knowledge-based systems.

Acknowledgements

This research was partially supported by the Defense Advance Research Projects Agency under contract #F30602-91-C-0016. Most of the work was performed when the second author was a visiting scientist at the Robotics Institute at Carnegie Mellon University under the support of Matsushita Electric Industrial Co. We are indebted to Mr. Dajun Zeng for help with the experimentation and insightful discussions.

References

Aha, D. W., Kibler, D. and Albert, M. K. (1991). Instance-based learning algorithms. *Machine Learning*, 6: 37–66.

Bareiss, R. (1989). *Exemplar-Based Knowledge Acquisition: A Unified Approach to Concept Representation, Classification, and Learning*. Academic Press, New York, NY.

Biefeld, E., and Cooper, L. (1991). Bottleneck identification using process chronologies. In *Proceedings of the Twelfth International Joint Conference on Artificial Intelligence*, pp. 218–224. IJCAI, Sydney, Australia.

Buchanan, B. G. and Wilkins, D. C. (editors) (1993). *Readings in Knowledge Acquisition and Learning: Automating Construction and Improvement of Expert Systems*. Morgan Kaufmann, San Mateo, CA.

Chandrasekaran, B., Johnson, T. R. and Smith, J. W. (1992). Task-structure analysis for knowledge modeling. *Communications of ACM*, 35(9): 124–137.

Chaturvedi, A. R. (1993). Acquiring implicit knowledge in a complex domain. *Expert Systems With Applications*, 6(1): 23–35.

Dent, L., Boticario, J., McDermott, J., Mitchell, T. and Zabowski, D. (1992). A personal learning apprentice. In *Proceedings of the Tenth National Conference on Artificial Intelligence*. AAAI.

Fox, M. S., Sadeh, N. and Baykan, C. (1989). Constrained heuristic search. In *Proceedings of the Eleventh International Joint Conference on Artificial Intelligence*, pp. 309–315. IJCAI.

French, S. (1982). *Sequencing and Scheduling: An Introduction to the Mathematics of the Job-Shop*. Ellis Horwood, Chichester.

Hammond, K. J. (1989). *Case-Based Planning: Viewing Planning as a Memory Task. Academic Press,* New York, NY.

Johnson, D. S., Aragon, C. R., McGeoch, L. A. and Schevon, C. (1989). Optimization by simulated annealing: An experimental evaluation, part I (graph partioning). *Operations Research* 37(6): 865–892.

Johnson, D. S., Aragon, C. R., McGeoch, L. A. and Schevon, C. (1991). Optimization by simulated annealing: An experimental evaluation, part II (graph coloring and number partitioning). *Operations Research* 39(3): 378–406.

Kolodner, J., Simpson, R. and Sycara, K. (1985). A process of case-based reasoning in problem solving. In *Proceedings of the Ninth International Joint Conference on Artificial Intelligence*, pp. 284–290. Los Angeles, CA: IJCAI.

Laarhoven, P. J. M. V., Aarts, E. H. L. and Lenstra, J. K. (1992). Job shop scheduling by simulated annealing. *Operations Research* 40(1): 113–125.

Lewis, L., Minior, D. and Brown, S. (1991). A case-based reasoning solution to the problem of redundant engineering in large scale manufacturing. *International Journal of Expert Systems* 4(2): 189–201.

Mckay, K., Buzacott, J. and Safayeni, F. (1988). The scheduler's knowledge of uncertainty: the missing link. In *Proceedings of IFIP Working Conference on Knowledge Based Production Management Systems*. IFIP, Galway, Ireland.

Minton, S., Johnston, M. D., Philips, A. B. and Laird, P. (1990). Solving large-scale constraint satisfaction and scheduling problems using a heuristic repair method. In *Proceedings of the Eighth National Conference on Artificial Intelligence*, pp. 17–24. AAAI, Boston, MA.

Miyashita, K. and Sycara, K. (1993). Improving schedule quality through case-based reasoning. In *Proceedings of AAAI-93 Workshop on Case-Bsed Reasoning*, pp. 101–110. AAAI, Washington, DC.

Miyashita, K. and Sycara, K. (1994). Adaptive case-based control of schedule revision. In Zweben, M. and Fox, M. (editors), *Intelligent Scheduling*. Morgan Kaufmann, San Mateo, CA.

Miyashita, K. and Sycara, K. (to appear). Cabins: A framework of knowledge acquisition and iterative revision for schedule improvement and reactive repair. *Artificial Intelligence*.

Miyashita, K., Sycara, K. and Mizoguchi, R. (1994). Case-based knowledge modeling for ill-structured optimization problems. In *Proceedings of the Third Japanese Knowledge Acquisition for Knowledge-Based Systems Workshop, JKAW'94*, pp. 213–227.

Mizoguchi, R. (1993). Knowledge acquisition and ontology. In *Proceedings of the International Conference on Building and Sharing of Very Large-Scale Knowledge Bases '93*, pp. 121–128. Japan Information Processing Development Center, Tokyo, Japan.

Morton, T. E. and Pentico, D. W. (1993). *Heuristic Scheduling Systems: With Application to Production Systems and Product Management.* Wiley, New York, NY.

Ow, P. S., Smith, S. F. and Thiriez, A. (1988). Reactive plan revision. In *Proceedings of the Seventh National Conference on Artificial Intelligence*, pp. 77–82. AAAI, St-Paul, MN.

Prerau, D. S. (1990). *Developing and Managing Expert Systems: Proven Techniques for Business and Industry.* Addison-Wesley, Reading, MA.

Reeves, C., (editor) (1993). *Modern Heuristic Techniques for Combinatorial Problems.* Halsted Press, New York, NY.

Ruby, D. and Kibler, D. (1992). Learning episodes for optimization. In *Machine Learning: Proceedings of the Ninth International Workshop (ML92)*, pp. 379–384.

Sadeh, N. (1991). Look-ahead techniques for micro opportunistic job shop sScheduling. *Ph.D. Dissertation*, School of Computer Science, Carnegie Mellon University.

Sadeh, N. and Fox, M. S. (1990). Variable and value ordering heuristics for activity-based job-shop scheduling. In *Proceedings of the Fourth International Conference on Expert Systems in Production and Operations Management*, pp. 134–144.

Simon, H. A. (1973). The structure of ill structured problems. *Artificial Intelligence* 4: 181–201.

Simoudis, E. and Miller, J. (1991). The application of CBR to help desk applications. In *Proceedings of the Case-Based Reasoning Workshop*, pp. 25–36. DARPA.

Sycara, K. (1987). Resolving adversarial conflicts: an approach integrating case-based and analytic methods. *Ph.D. Dissertation*, School of Information and Computer Science, Georgia Institute of Technology, GA.

Sycara, K. and Miyashita, K. (1994). Adaptive schedule repair. In Szelke, E. and Kerr, R., (editors), *Knowledge Based Reactive Scheduling*, pp. 107–124. North Holland, Amsterdam, Holland.

Sycara, K., Zeng, D. and Miyashita K. (1995). Using case-based reasoning to acquire user scheduling preferences that change over time. In *The Eleventh IEEE Conference on Artificial Intelligence Applications.* IEEE.

Veloso, M. M. and Carbonell, J. G. (1993). Toward scaling up machine learning: A case study with derivational analogy in PRODIGY. In Minton, S. (editor), *Machine Learning Methods for Planning.* Morgan Kaufmann, San Mateo, CA.

Zweben, M., Davis, E., Brian, D., Drascher, E., Deale, M. and Eskey, M. (1992).

Learning to improve constraint-based scheduling. *Artificial Intelligence*, 58(1–3): 271–296.

Zweben, M., Deale, M. and Gargan, M. (1990). Anytime rescheduling. In *Proceedings of the Workshop on Innovative Approaches to Planning, Scheduling and Control*, pp. 251–259. DARPA, San Diego, CA.

CHAPTER 10

Industrial applications of machine learning: illustrations for the knowledge acquisition–machine learning dilemma and for situated case-based reasoning

Yves Kodratoff and Hervé Mignot

Abstract

This chapter presents several industrial applications of machine learning in the context of their effort to solve the "knowledge acquisition–machine learning problem", i.e. the problem of merging knowledge acquisition and machine learning techniques. Case-based reasoning is a possible alternative to the problem of acquiring highly compiled expert knowledge, but it raises also many new problems that must be solved, not the least of them being that case-based reasoning needs to be situated (or at least context-dependent) to be efficient.

10.1 Introduction

There are many sides to the description of what an industrial application is. In a recent paper (Kodratoff *et al.*, 1994) we summarized some of the experience gained during the CEC project MLT in counselling a user on which of the many types of machine learning (ML) to use for his special application. In this presentation, we shall consider two of the main subfields of the ones that need

Machine Learning and Knowledge Acquisition
ISBN 0–12–685120–4

merging for an industrial application, seemingly the richest in generating future research problems: validation of knowledge-based systems (KBS), and merging of ML into a knowledge acquisition (KA) method. The first one is almost untouched by specialists in ML, while the second one led to much work, some of which will be reported in the rest of the chapter.

As mentioned, real-world applications require validation of the programs used. We shall now define briefly validation in our context, and what ML can have to do with it.

It seems that "validation" takes three different meanings in the context of KBS. All different types of knowledge originate from the expert's knowledge which is not directly accessible, thus the KA system helps the expert to gather his knowledge in the KA system knowledge level. In KADS' knowledge level (Wielinga *et al.*, 1992), one finds the models, such as the model of tasks, the model of expertise, etc. In the model of expertise, one finds knowledge about the strategies, the tasks, the inference, and the domain. All these kinds of knowledge are usually considered validated because they issue "directly" from the expert. This gives us a first kind of validation, by which an expert reconsiders his or her own knowledge at the knowledge level, and checks its validity. This is not enough in reality since experts do make mistakes from time to time, and even when they agree on the actions to take, they also often disagree on the reasons (that is, what knowledge to use) why these actions are to be taken. It is always good to compare such validated knowledge to the real world. The knowledge must thus be translated to the symbol level, i.e. a language into which programs can be written, to be checked against real applications. During this process, many mistakes are possible, and we have here need for a second kind of validation, the classical one in software engineering, that the knowledge level (the "specification") matches correctly the symbol level (the "algorithm"). During the verification process, the expert will find misbehaviors of the system, that will require some changes. This is also known as the classical "trial and error" validation technique. Notice however the complication arising because transformations can be performed either at the symbol, or at the knowledge, level.

Validation can make use of ML techniques, for both incompleteness and incorrectness. The knowledge to be considered is threefold: the rules of expertise, a deeper kind of knowledge given by a semantic-net and a set of integrity constraints, and a set of examples. When anomalies are detected, the correction is performed according to sets of positive and negative examples of the concept to revise (Lounis, 1993, 1994). Let us underline that very little, besides the cited work of Lounis, has been done in this direction. One can, however, consider that Morik *et al.* (1994) have used MOBAL as a validation system in a medical application. They make use of the deductive abilities of MOBAL in order to find contradictions among the rules learned so far, and then solve by induction these contradictions. MOBAL is not a validation system but it presents so many functionalities that it can be also used in that way, and for this particular medical application, it seems it has been a very efficient way to use it.

During the last year, there have been a good many workshops on industrial applications of ML, and on the merging of ML into a KA method. We will give a few examples of these applications in the following. What must be kept in mind, though, is that all "real" real-world applications met very nicely the requirements of the KA+ML workshops, because they had to solve this problem in the first place. What is the essential difference between an academic and an industrial work? The academic chooses the data from a repertoire of such available data, while the industrial receives data from the users, often demanding ones. These repertoires, at least in ML, tend to contain quite a variety of data of various levels of difficulty, but for all of them the KA phase has been completed beforehand. Thus, the industrial is not only under pressure of the users, but he or she has also to count on them to perform the KA phase, which is a crucial one as we all know. In the following, we will refer to this problem as to the KAML problem, with this mild joke that we indeed need camels to help us cross the desert that expands between the fertile plains of industrial applications and the nice oases of academic research.

As a coarse view, one can say that with respect to KAML, academics have produced one very interesting approach, known as knowledge refinement. On another hand, we personally dug five different ways of integrating ML and KA out of the solutions of the people that tackled real-world applications of ML. This chapter is mainly devoted to the description of solutions to the KAML problem, together with the industrial applications that led to these solutions. We shall successively describe the following: the knowledge refinement approach, how existing ML techniques must be adapted to meet real-life requirements, what kind of knowledge can be acquired from a human expert in order to obtain good ML results, why KA needs ML to enhance the rate of the acquisition, the problem of finding new representation schemes to meet experts' requirements, how to acquire compiled knowledge, and finally the promises and challenges of the CBR approach.

10.2 Knowledge refinement

Knowledge refinement is linked to validation, since a base that would need no refinement can obviously be considered as being validated. We shall not give here any detailed description of the different revision techniques since they have already received considerable acknowledgment in the academic community. We shall, however, give in Section 10.2.3 a brief account of recent research on the topic, and recall some of the earlier work that we did on knowledge refinement roughly around 1985, for an application to air-traffic control, and on DISCIPLE.

From the KAML point of view, we used Morik's sloppy modelling (Morik, 1988, 1989) in which a first "sloppy" approximation of the domain knowledge is required from the expert, to be further corrected and validated through subsequent refinement cycles.

10.2.1 Air traffic control

Our work on air traffic control was published first in 1988 (Cannat and Vrain, 1988), and more recently in a more detailed form (Kodratoff and Vrain, 1993). Very simply put, we used a refinement cycle which makes explicit the role of the user, as indicated in Figure 10.1. It includes the steps necessary to transform the knowledge given by the expert and the learned knowledge. The examples and the knowledge base given by the expert must be translated into a representation

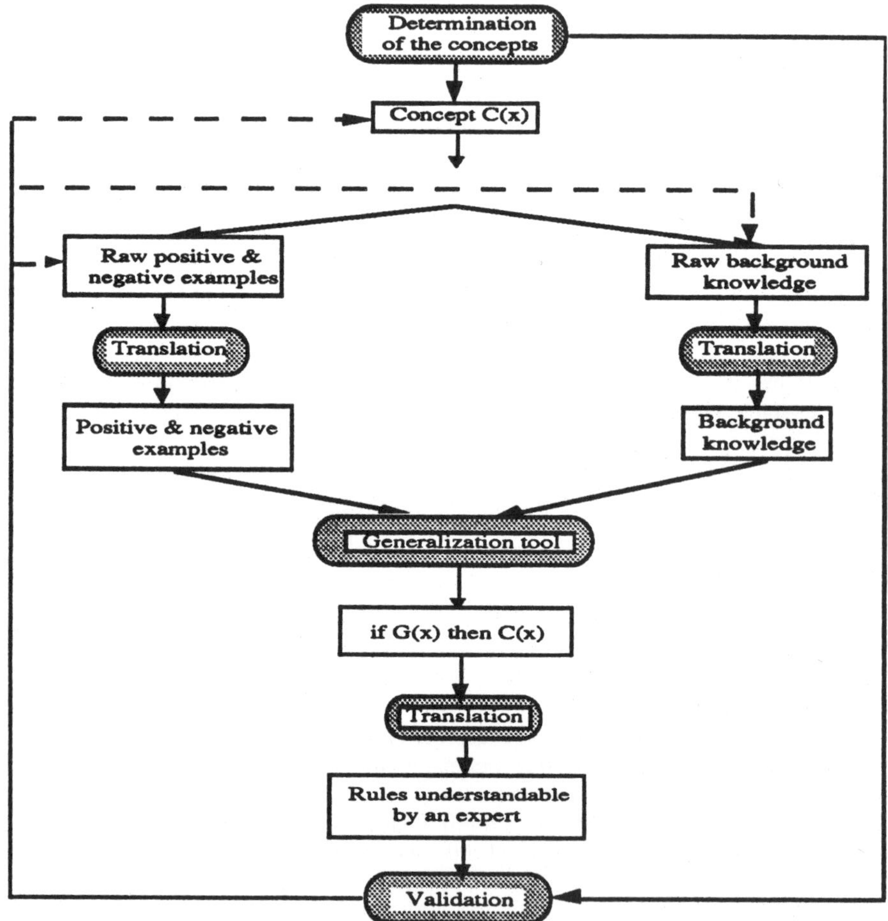

Figure 10.1 The acquisition cycle (Cannat and Vrain, 1988; Kodatoff and Vrain, 1993)

adapted to the generalization tool. In order to make the validation step easier, the learned knowledge must be translated back into a representation understandable by the expert. The importance and difficulty of these translation stages are generally underrated by academics, while they are the very condition at which an application can take place. In principle, the main difficulty comes from the fact that humans do not understand easily relations in first order logic, even when their knowledge, being strongly relational, makes non-stop use of it (Kodratoff and Vrain, 1993; see also Chapter 5 of this volume). This cycle is very similar to the sloppy modelling approach in Morik *et al.* (1993).

10.2.2 DISCIPLE

The main idea behind DISCIPLE (Kodratoff and Tecuci, 1987a, b; Tecuci, 1988; Tecuci and Kodratoff, 1990), and behind more recent versions, APT (Nédellec, 1992; Nédellec and Causse, 1992) and NeoDISCIPLE (Tecuci, 1991, 1992a, b; Tecuci and Hieb, 1994) is exactly the one of user-driven revision, with the idea that experts are better at checking solutions than building theories. DISCIPLE thus proposes a solution to a problem that will become a positive example if the user agrees with the solution, and a negative example if he or she disagrees. The user then chooses among possible causes for this agreement or disagreement, and these causes are used to refine logically the existing rules, by adapting (i.e. generalizing or particularizing depending on the cases) the conditions of the rules to the positive and negative examples. This has been used in a bank application in order to help elicit the knowledge of experts (Nédellec *et al.*, 1994), but it also requests a patient user that is prepared to "play" with the system in order to build the initial data base that can be quite extensive.

10.2.3 Some recent results and problems

The above text contains the implicit assumption that the initial domain theory provided by the user, and possibly completed by the ML system, tends to be incomplete and incorrect. Furthermore, ML systems may add incorrect concept definitions they have learned from incorrect example descriptions or insufficient domain theory. This explains the increasing interest in automatically revising incorrect and incomplete domain theories. Some of the propositional systems are described in Ginsberg (1989), Ourston and Mooney (1990), Craw and Sleeman (1990), Cain (1991), Towell *et al.* (1990) and Wilkins (1990), and some of the first order revision systems are found in Shapiro (1983), Sammut and Banerji (1986), Pazzani (1989), Muggleton and Buntine (1988), Bergadano and Giordana (1989), Duval (1991), Wogulis (1991), Richards and Mooney (1991), Rouveirol (1992), De Raedt (1992), Nédellec (1992), Nédellec and Causse (1992), Esposito *et al.* (1993), Morik *et al.* (1993) and Feldman and Nédellec (1994).

The revision problem can be described as containing two problems, two phases, and two strategies.

The two problems are:

1. *The completeness problem* Given a theory T, and an example E of the concept C, such that T does not recognize the positive example E of C as an example of C, build a theory T' that recognizes E.
2. *The correctness problem* Given a theory T and a negative example NE of the concept C, such that T recognizes the negative example E of C as an example of C, build a theory T' such that T' does not recognize NE.

The two phases are the localization of the culprit clause and the refinement itself.

The two strategies are the monotonic and the non-monotonic one. In the monotonic approach, the version space is reduced by eliminating inconsistent hypotheses for ever, while non-monotonic algorithms may reconsider pruned hypotheses. One can find several examples of these two strategies in Nédellec and Rouveirol (1993).

10.3 Adapting ML to meet real-life requirements

In a series of papers, Schmalhofer and Tschaltschian (1993) and Schmalhofer *et al.* (1995) (see also Chapter 6 of this volume) report a very thorough experience on solving the KAML problem for specific industrial needs. These authors report finding it necessary to adapt both conceptual clustering and explanation-based learning, by integrating expert consultation inside the ML algorithms.

Also typical of this approach is Esposito *et al.* (1993, 1994) which describes an application to document layout recognition in the context of a software environment for office automation distributed by Olivetti. These authors extended a star algorithm (Michalski, 1983) by a flexible matching algorithm, and used a data analysis discriminant system to speed up the star algorithm.

There is, however, no general law relative to the complexity needed for useful application. On the one hand, the two examples just reported illustrate applications that already worked quite well by using statistical methods, but that can still be enhanced when some more symbolic treatment is also performed, in a multistrategic approach. On the other hand, there are also several examples in which a robust ID3, or even exhaustive search, have been the most useful tools.

10.3.1 ML algorithm must be improved

Example 1 Industrial diagnosis (Bergadano et al.*, 1988; Botta* et al.*, 1992; Giordana* et al.*, 1993)*

This interesting application has been motivated by the retirement of an expert and the need to collect his knowledge. A large body of different types of pumps (and other rotating machines) has to be taken care of in case of anomalous behavior. Due to the interactions among components, the formal mechanical models are not enough to detect the kind of anomaly, and where it takes place. This is a typical case where first order logic representations are necessary to represent these interactions. Besides, the complexity of the knowledge made it necessary to build special representations to encode the relations among diagnoses (some may occur only after some others, for instance), giving a special taxonomic representation for the learned rules. By this feature, this application belongs also to Section 10.6. The system built for this application, ENIGMA, is a knowledge-intensive multistrategy system, learning diagnostic rules from descriptions of past cases. ENIGMA's background knowledge consists of the description of the contexts in which features become significant, and of the definition of intermediate concepts to be used in the fault descriptions generated. Since the number of available examples is not very large, ENIGMA uses deductive techniques in order to transform the low-level features into operational ones, understandable to the expert. The system thus inductively learns rules, and transforms them into an understandable form in a deductive way, using the available background knowledge.

Example 2 "Machine learning goes to the bank" (Nédellec et al.*, 1994)*

As in several other cases, ML has been used on the top of an existing expert system, considered not efficient enough. In this case, the user was ready to make the effort to "rethink" his domain theory; this explains why a complex apprentice system such as APT could be used. For this bank application, the original version of APT showed two deficiencies. The first one was that it could not deal with numbers and intervals. The second one was a tendency to overgeneralize so much as to puzzle the users who were unable to recover from the overgeneralizations. These two defects have been corrected. The second one asked for an elaborated generalization in which the smallest possible steps are performed at each generalization, together with an ability to recover from overgeneralizations contradicted by new examples.

Example 3 "Machine learning in the automobile market" (Nakhaeizadeh and Reuter, 1993)

The problem at Daimler-Benz was to predict the needs of the consumers on several markets. Classical ID3 is done for "interpolation" since one learns inside the learning set. In order to perform extrapolations, as statistical regression techniques do, the authors had to adapt the structure of ID3 to their needs, in order to be able to build "regression trees".

10.3.2 ML solves KA problems

ML can be used to solve KA problems in which the representation of knowledge is so complex that traditional KA becomes unbearable.

Example 4 Fault detection in helicopter blades

This application asked the authors (El Attar and Hamery, 1994) to deal with two different problems. First, detection and repair of faults of a helicopter blade is not only a technical process, but also a kind of judicial one, since the repairing person is responsible in case of an accident. The system must thus also give the best possible "argument" to explain why a given repair is suitable. The data being of a symbolic/numeric nature, the authors had to produce the rules that would combine these two natures in the way best suited to the existing validation procedures. Secondly, one of the most important features to determine is a set of intervals into which detection and repair of faults takes place. These intervals were not immediately available from experts. They had to be directly learned from the examples, in such a way that the results were still understandable by (and agreeable to) the experts.

Example 5 Learning on the French justice system

The problem met here is the classical one of the missing values, in its very special version where there are many "don't care" values that are not significant to the solution, as, for instance, the values of the attribute "color of the feathers" for a mammal. One usually simply tries to cut the problem in pieces that avoid such kinds of problems, but it appears that the existing (French) judicial knowledge is in such a form at present that one has to deal explicitly with this problem. Tree-generating procedures cannot deal very well with this kind of problem, which is why Venturini (1994) adapted a genetic algorithms technique to rule generation.

Example 6 Refining rules for a production system in the steel industry (Terano and Muro, 1994)

Once rules have been learned in a classical way, it is always possible to consider that one can improve them by searching in the space of all possible rules, in the vicinity of the existing rules. Genetic algorithms are obviously well-adapted to solve this kind of search problem since strong parents are already available.

10.4 Helping ML by some additional knowledge

10.4.1 Biasing the ML mechanism with acquired knowledge

Biases make explicit which information is essential to decrease the combinatorics of ML, and acquires this knowledge by elicitation.

Example 7 Learning to design VLSI

Learning the most specific generalization from a set of examples is a basic problem of ML since it is one of the best ways to reduce the complexity of the set of examples while keeping their common properties. At zeroth order, this problem is relatively trivial since it amounts to Michalski's "dropping rule" (Michalski, 1983), together with some of his "climbing hierarchies" rule when the dropping is done cleverly. In first order representations (actually, we consider here relational representations making use of universally quantified variables), however, this problem quickly becomes very difficult (Kodratoff and Ganascia, 1986) because each subpart of an object can be bound to any other subpart of another object, thus leading to a combinatorial explosion. Some work has been done to deal with this complexity, as by using Bisson's distance measure, for instance (Kodratoff and Bisson, 1992). Application to VLSI design requires a relational representation (Herrmann and Beckmann, 1994) since it must represent the bindings of the different parts of the circuit. These authors present an original solution making use of the user's knowledge of what parts can be possibly bound to other parts. This is a knowledge which is well-known by the experts, but which is not acquired classically in KA systems because they perform no learning and do not need this information. In other words, it is very clear here that a new kind of knowledge has to be acquired because of the learning component.

10.4.2 The ML mechanism is impossible without manually acquired knowledge

ML requirements make it necessary to ask more information, or a new kind of information to the expert.

Example 8 Prediction of cylinder banding

In the printing industry, banding is a well-known nuisance. In his ICML presentation, Bob Evans (Evans and Fisher, 1993) signalled that the usual approach, to understand the causes of banding, had failed. In that sense, usual causal KA has been failing to solve this problem. Driven by the requirements of his induction algorithm, Evans promoted a new approach, a more pragmatic one, by which he proposes to find only conditions at which banding will appear. He reported having many difficulties having the specialists answering his "trivial" questions, until unexpected features appeared in the prediction for banding, and were confirmed by experience. Since the system outperformed a human expert, it shows the importance of using ML techniques with an open mind regarding what are the important features.

Example 9 Pilots' promotion

The pilots of the Dutch company KLM have the right to bid for a better position at regular times. If this position is free, the company must promote the pilot, even if it is very costly to fill the position he leaves vacant. Since unoccupied planes and pilots are very expensive, it is important for the company to predict accurately the future bids of the pilots. As opposed to classical statistical techniques, Adriaans (1993) solved this problem by including personal information relative to individual pilots in the examples to learn from. This was looked upon as a major departure from the usual acquired knowledge that was of a more statistical nature in the preceding (and less efficient) systems.

10.5 Adapting KA to meet real-life requirements

Example 10 Explanation-based learning (EBL) (Mitchell et al.*, 1986; DeJong and Mooney, 1986) of operational rules in the Pilot Associate*

Honeywell has developed a pilot's associate that contains as much as possible of the knowledge relative to military piloting skills. This system contains six interconnected large expert systems. Each of them needs continuous maintenance since the methods for fight and counter-fight are constantly evolving,

Nevertheless, this rule must be restricted by the condition that if the recommended speed becomes higher than that which any kind of material can stand then this base case must be ruled out, no matter how high the similarity might be.

All these rules are difficult to build, and they are necessary each time causality is not implicitly taken into account in the shallow representation.

10.8.6 A conclusion about using CBR

It is quite usual to consider that the predictive power of science comes from the building of causal theory allowing the explanation of successions of events. Thus many non-causal facts looked upon as suprious are discarded. In some cases, as for example bases of air-traffic incidents, this leads to the forgetting of circumstances linked to the "story" of the events as they have been lived by the expert. Retrieval of past cases becomes tedious for the expert. More generally, we would like to point at the new attitude of relying in some conditions on shallow, non-causal knowledge, either because it is important, or because causal knowledge seems to evade the scientist's efforts. In other words, the link between predictability and causality is no longer deemed compulsory, but simply desirable. Predictability itself is achieved through the recognition of a conjunction of values of shallow features. As seen above, this feature is also one of the features of situated CBR.

CBR involves such non-causal knowledge acquisition. The price to pay for this is obvious. It may well happen that cases superficially very near to each other are actually very different. There are two solutions to this problem. The most obvious one is to use hybrid systems that stick to a causal model as far as possible, and switch to CBR when failing on a problem (or the reverse: do CBR, and check if the causal model validates the findings of CBR). One should notice, however, that this is not suitable when the shallow knowledge is really needed. This is why we would like to explore here the second solution which is to stay in the CBR framework, but to improve it so as to take into account, in a new way, the deep knowledge:

- Define domains of significant features in order to know in which context which features should be used to compute the similarity.
- Define domains of similarity measures in order to know in which context which similarity measure should be used.
- Use classical CBR to select a few cases that might be useful, and select among them those that are really to be used by:
  - ruling out those that violate known integrity constraints
  - ruling out those cases that are not confirmed by given rules that might have a form other than integrity constraints
  - checking the consequences of the choice of a case, i.e. select according to the applicability of the cases.
- Refine the application of the case.

To conclude, it will be often the case that CBR is more efficient than a causal model, especially when the formalization of the field is still incomplete. In order to increase its efficiency, it may be necessary to collect supplementary knowledge which is very different from the one normally considered as causal by scientists.

Our symbolic approximation to situated CBR involves different choices of knowledge acquisition than when dealing directly with symbolic CBR.

10.9 Final conclusion

As a first conclusion, we would like to stress that our experience tells us that machine learning is not an easy solution for knowledge acquisition, but that the solution of the knowledge acquisition–machine learning problem goes through improvement of both knowledge acquisition and machine learning and thus it still needs much research work. Industrial applications are pointing academic research to problems that are somewhat underestimated nowadays.

We presented here examples of seven solutions to the problems of integrating machine learning and knowledge acquisition, although there might be more problems and more solutions that we have not yet met.

A last point we would like to underline is the following. All creators of the systems described above insisted on the need for a good comprehensibility of the results obtained by the knowledge acquisition–machine learning system. Some are even embarrassed to be forced by their experience with users to speak of such an ill-defined concept as comprehensibility. It seems that industrial applications of machine learning call the academics' attention on the importance of the definition of a more precise and measurable definition of comprehensibility.

Acknowledgements

The ESPRIT contract MLT has been the first to show how many applications of many different kinds can use ML. The help of the CEC is thus gratefully acknowledged. This chapter is based on the workshops on industrial applications of ML we organized with Pat Langley at EMLC'93 and IMLC'93, the workshop on KA+ML we organized with Gheorghe Tecuci and Smadar Kedar at IJCAI'93, and finally on a "Special Interest Group" on CBR taking place at the human Machine Interactions and Artificial Intelligence in Avionics and Space congress held in Toulouse, 28–30 September 1993. During this last workshop, we received much interesting information from Michele Visciola from ALENIA, Richard Kraft from NASA Ames, François Allard kindly shared his ESA experience, and we had a long discussion on flight incidents and CBR with Jean Claude Wanner in preparation of the group.